I0829267

Dark Seduction and Psychology 10-in-1

The Ultimate Masterclass in Human Influence, Covert Persuasion, Psychological Defense, and Magnetic Charisma

TABLE OF CONTENTS

PART 1: DARK SEDUCTION 5-IN-1

INTRODUCTION 3
BOOK ONE - COVERT PERSUASION: PSYCHOLOGICAL LEVERAGE 5
Introduction 7
Chapter 1 - Frame Reality: Directing Choice with Cognitive Bias 13
Chapter 2 - Secure Action: Activating Core Human Compliance Drivers 19
Chapter 3 - Control Narrative: Staging Information for Acceptance 27
Chapter 4 - Map Influence: Diagnosing the Target's Decision Profile 34
Chapter 5 - Mitigate Resistance: Neutralizing Defenses Before They Form 40
Conclusion The Architecture of Guided Choice 47
Reflection Questions 52
BOOK TWO - MAGNETIC CHARISMA: NON - VERBAL RESONANCE 55
Introduction to Magnetic Charisma 57
Chapter 1 - Broadcast Authority: Mastering Non - Verbal Resonance 63
Chapter 2 - Transfer Energy: Inciting Emotional Contagion in Groups 68
Chapter 3 - Build Trust: Employing Strategic Touch and Presence 74
Chapter 4 - Shape Perception: Using Posture to Signal Competence 80
Chapter 5 - Unify Groups: Leveraging Humor for Social Cohesion 86
Conclusion - The Integrated Charismatic Persona 90
Reflection Questions 95
BOOK THREE - NLP MIND CONTROL: THE SCIENCE OF FRAMING AND BELIEF 99
Introduction 101
Chapter 1 - The Logic of Belief: Introducing Cognitive Filters and Framing 108
Chapter 2 - Mastering the Meta - Model: Precision in Questioning 117

Chapter 3 - Linguistic Programming: The Hidden Structure of Influence 126
Chapter 4 - The Science of Sensory Acuity and Calibration 136
Chapter 5 - Advanced Anchoring and State Elicitation 144
Conclusion 152
Synthesis and Strategic Reflection 160
BOOK FOUR - IRRESISTIBLE CHARM: RELATIONSHIP DYNAMICS 165
Introduction to Irresistible Charm 167
Chapter 1 - Accelerate Intimacy: Structuring Calculated Self - Disclosure 171
Chapter 2 - Cement Loyalty: Creating Identity Through Shared Social Rituals 177
Chapter 3 - Gauge Limits: Calibrating Disclosure for Optimal Attraction 182
Chapter 4 - Sustain Interest: Crafting Narrative for Entertainment Value 187
Chapter 5 - Project Desirability: Vetting Values Through Shared Laughter 192
Conclusion - The Architecture of Enduring Charm 197
Reflection Questions 201
BOOK FIVE - INSTANT INFLUENCE: URGENCY AND ACTION 205
Introduction to Instant Influence 207
Chapter 1 - Compel Action Now: Exploiting Temporal Discounting 211
Chapter 2 - Force Urgency: Activating Loss Aversion and Scarcity 216
Chapter 3 - Demand Presence: Minimizing Perceived Delay for Future Gain 221
Chapter 4 - Eliminate Hesitation: Structuring Incentives for Immediate Reward 226
Chapter 5 - Control Deadline: Manufacturing the Psychological Need to Buy 231
Conclusion - The Final System of Decisive Action 236
Reflection Questions 240
Overall Conclusion - The Architecture of Total Influence 243
Print and Keep Checklist - The Total Influence System 248

PART 2: DARK PSYCHOLOGY AND MANIPULATION 5-1

INTRODUCTION 255

BOOK ONE - GASLIGHTING: DECONSTRUCTING REALITY DISTORTION AND RECLAIMING SANITY 263

- Introduction 265
- Chapter 1 - The Mechanics of Reality Distortion 269
- Chapter 2 - The Three Stages of Psychological Erasure 273
- Chapter 3 - Gaslighting in Professional and Personal Spheres 280
- Chapter 4 - Counter-Moves and Cognitive Anchoring 286
- Chapter 5 - Rebuilding the Fractured Self 293
- Conclusion 302
- Reflection Questions 310

BOOK TWO - SOCIAL ENGINEERING: HACKING THE HUMAN FIREWALL AND SECURITY PROTOCOLS 317

- Introduction 319
- Chapter 1 - Pretexting and the Art of Fabrication 330
- Chapter 2 - Open Source Intelligence (OSINT) Gathering 342
- Chapter 3 - Phishing, Vishing, and Smishing Dynamics 352
- Chapter 4 - Exploiting Social Norms and Reciprocity 360
- Chapter 5 - Hardening the Target 369
- Conclusion 377
- Reflection Questions 382

BOOK THREE - DARK TRIAD TACTICS: PROFILING, PREDICTING, AND NEUTRALIZING PREDATORY PERSONALITIES 387

- Introduction 389
- Chapter 1 - Narcissism: The Grandiose Mask 392
- Chapter 2 - Machiavellianism: The Strategic Player 401
- Chapter 3 - Psychopathy: The Empathy Void 410
- Chapter 4 - The Flaws of the Dark Triad 419
- Chapter 5 - Securing Immunity 429
- Conclusion 439
- Reflection Questions 447

BOOK FOUR - COGNITIVE BIAS EXPLOITS: PROTECTING THE GLITCHES IN YOUR DECISION-MAKING PROCESS 453
Introduction 455
Chapter 1 - The Halo Effect and Authority Bias 458
Chapter 2 - Scarcity, Urgency, and Loss Aversion 467
Chapter 3 - Confirmation Bias and Echo Chambers 475
Chapter 4 - The Sunk Cost Fallacy and Consistency 482
Chapter 5 - Critical Thinking Shields 490
Conclusion 495
Reflection Questions 500
BOOK FIVE - EMOTIONAL CONTROL: MASTERING EMOTIONAL INTELLIGENCE TO DEFLECT MANIPULATION 505
Introduction 507
Chapter 1 - Fear and Intimidation Tactics 511
Chapter 2 - Weaponized Guilt and Shame 518
Chapter 3 - Love Bombing and Intermittent Reinforcement 524
Chapter 4 - Developing Emotional Granularity 530
Chapter 5 - Fortifying Boundaries 536
Conclusion 543
Reflection Questions 548
Overall Conclusion 552
HERE'S ANOTHER BOOK BY SEBASTIAN NOCTURNE THAT YOU MIGHT LIKE 556
OVERALL RESOURCES 557

PART 1: DARK SEDUCTION 5-IN-1

The Complete Guide to Covert Persuasion, Magnetic Charisma, NLP Mind Control, Irresistible Charm and Instant Influence

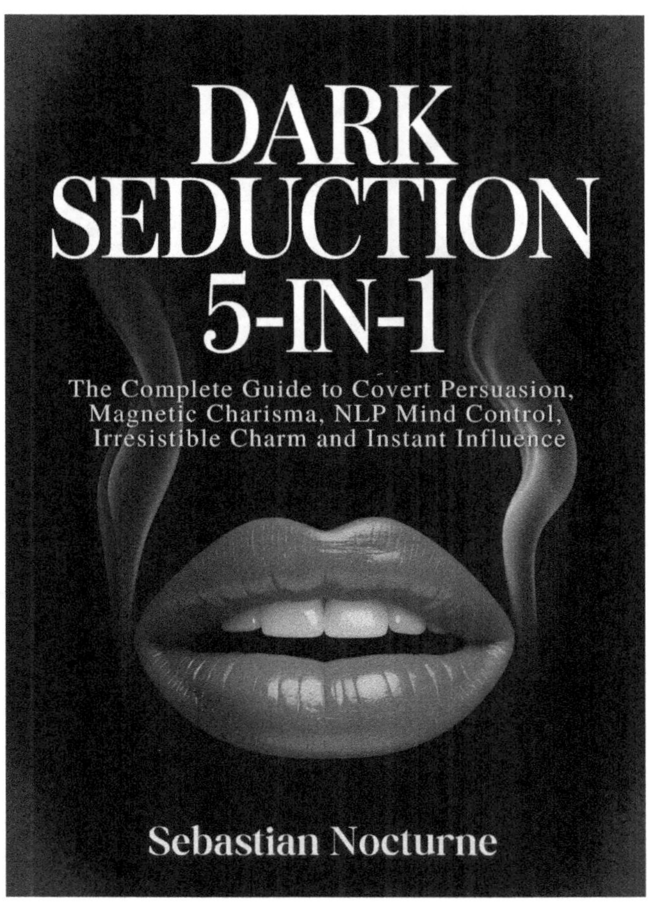

INTRODUCTION

Do you ever watch someone walk into a room and instantly command attention? They get the contract. They secure the commitment. They leave others feeling energized and ready to follow. This ability is not simply a natural gift. It is a practiced skill. It rests on specific, verifiable knowledge of how the human brain works.

What if you could consistently predict the reactions of the people around you? What if you knew exactly what to say to move a choice from "maybe" to "yes"? This book answers those questions with concrete, actionable methods.

We cut through the confusion. We reject vague theory and juvenile tactics. This is an instruction manual for psychological leverage, built entirely on documented science. You will find proof and detailed methods, not just weak philosophy. Studies in behavioral economics confirm our approach. Research in social psychology shows why our tactics work. This structure ensures true value, moving beyond surface-level advice and simplistic generalizations.

This guide works for you, whether you are a man or a woman. Successful influence depends on aligning with how a person processes information. We show you how to shift your approach for a male listener versus a female listener, maintaining maturity and nuance throughout the exchange. The focus remains on psychological alignment, not simple gender typing.

This five-part collection teaches you complete control across every social interaction.

First, **Covert Persuasion** gives you the blueprint for controlling the decision environment. You learn to stage information so people rely on mental shortcuts, known as cognitive biases, which favor your desired outcome. We show you how small requests now create large commitments later.

Second, **Magnetic Charisma** focuses entirely on your silent presence. You will learn to use non-verbal cues to plant perceptions of competence and authority, all below conscious awareness. We detail how controlled, appropriate touch builds rapid trust, as haptics are the first form of communication established in infancy.

Third, we approach Linguistic Influence as a verifiable, practiced skill. We honor the core principles of **Neuro-Linguistic Programming (NLP)** while providing an advanced framework rooted in **cognitive science** and **Behavioral Economics**. This book replaces vague, subjective interpretations with **specific, evidence-based methods**. You will learn validated **framing techniques**, based on the science of how the brain structures choice, that allow you to accurately **predict reactions** and guide any decision from "maybe" to a firm "yes" in real-time.

Fourth, **Irresistible Charm** shows you how to build rapid, deep connections. We show you how strategic self-disclosure creates intimacy, provided the disclosures are frequent and perceived as appropriate. We also examine how shared laughter acts as a powerful social resource, confirming alignment on core values and building group cohesion.

Fifth, **Instant Influence** forces immediate action. This is the art of creating urgency. We show you how to exploit the brain's strong preference for immediate gains over larger future rewards, a concept called Temporal Discounting. You will learn to activate the powerful motivation of loss aversion and scarcity, which compels immediate compliance.

The time for wishing for connection or opportunity is finished. This collection offers specific steps and the psychological context necessary to implement them. It is time to acquire the specific skills that dictate the outcome of any interaction.

BOOK ONE

COVERT PERSUASION: PSYCHOLOGICAL LEVERAGE

INTRODUCTION

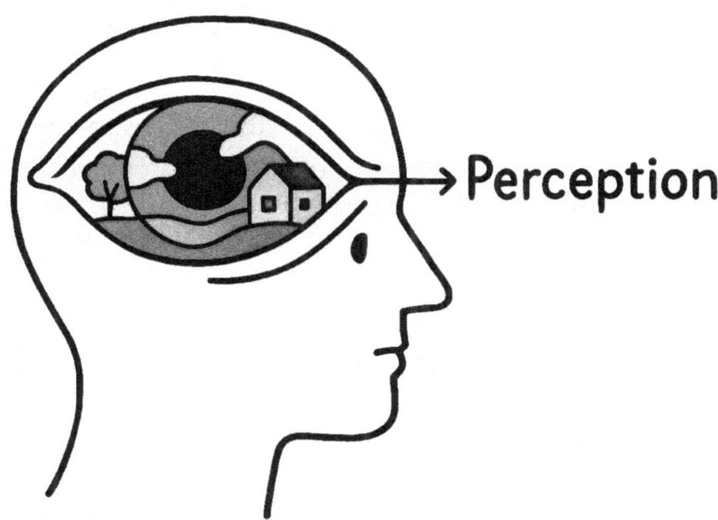

Influence is the act of securing a preferred action without resorting to force. It is not about manipulation that harms others. It is a precise method for guiding people toward a decision that benefits both them and you. This book provides a detailed map of how human beings make choices. It moves past vague theory and emotional guesswork. It relies instead on the documented principles of social psychology and behavioral economics. We seek to understand the levers of the mind, not just the surface of conversation.

The ability to move others rests on one fundamental truth: reality is not objective. Every individual constructs a **subjective reality** based on their perception of information inputs. This personally built reality dictates behavior in the world, not the actual facts of the situation. If you change a person's perception of reality, you change their behavior. Covert persuasion is the intentional structuring of information to manage that subjective reality.

The Predictable Error in Human Judgment

Systematic errors occur continually in human judgment. These errors are known as **cognitive biases**. These biases cause deviations from a rational norm, leading to inaccurate judgments and irrational behavior.

For the persuader, these errors are not flaws; they are precise, repeatable openings.

Why do these biases exist? The brain uses shortcuts. These shortcuts, or heuristics, allow for faster decisions. In many situations, speed is more valuable than perfect accuracy. When you meet someone new, you must make a fast social assessment. You use mental shortcuts rather than waiting for years of data collection. This need for quick assessment creates the conditions where biases thrive.

Other biases happen because of human processing limits, a concept known as **bounded rationality**. The brain cannot process everything. When faced with too much data or too little time, the mind defaults to these established cognitive paths. Covert persuasion capitalizes on this limitation. The persuader designs the interaction to overwhelm the target's capacity for slow, rational thought. The target is then forced to use their fast, heuristic system, leading to predictable decision errors.

The goal is to provide claims that require less evidence for acceptance. This happens when the claims confirm the target's existing beliefs or preconceptions. This is the function of **Confirmation Bias**. People naturally seek or interpret information that validates what they already believe. The persuader does not fight existing beliefs. They simply frame the request as a logical confirmation of the target's current values. This significantly distorts perception and makes acceptance feel like a conclusion, not a new choice.

The Six Drivers of Compliance

Covert persuasion employs established psychological principles that act as mental shortcuts for agreement. These are known as the core compliance drivers. They operate across all aspects of social interaction and decision-making. These drivers include Reciprocity, Commitment and Consistency, Social Proof, Liking, Authority, and Scarcity. They are universal mechanisms that allow others to influence our choices.

One of the most potent drivers is **Commitment and Consistency**. People feel internal pressure to align their future actions with their past decisions. Once a person makes a commitment, they naturally want to stay consistent with that choice. For a commitment to genuinely change a person's self-image and future behavior, it must possess three qualities: it must be **active, public, and effortful**.

A commitment must be active, meaning the person performs a distinct action. It must be public, visible to others, which increases the external pressure to maintain the image of consistency. It must be effortful, meaning the person had to overcome a perceived hurdle to complete the action. Fraternities, for example, often use effortful steps to increase commitment to the group.

The persuader's objective is to minimize the appearance of external control. If a person acts under a large reward or strong external pressure, they will not accept inner responsibility for the action. Once the reward or pressure is gone, they will revert to their old way of thinking. The persuader must secure the target's personal responsibility. This is achieved by having the target agree to small, internally justifiable steps first. These small, voluntary efforts create a self-sustaining commitment that originates from the target's own will.

Social Proof is another critical mechanism. When people are unsure about how to act, they look to the actions of others to guide their own behavior. The tendency to see an action as more appropriate because others are doing it is incredibly strong. This principle explains why testimonials, reviews, and popularity metrics are so influential in consumer behavior. People assume that if a lot of others are doing something, they must possess information the target lacks.

The effective persuader controls the group conditions to allow social proof to work maximally. No leader can control every single person at once. But they can influence the most receptive or devoted members. Once a certain, visible portion of the group is convinced, their adoption naturally persuades the rest. In fact, the strength of the social bond can be twice as likely to determine a product purchase as the buyer's preference for the product itself.

Managing Psychological States and Social Judgments

Social activities are often prone to irrational, biased decisions, known as **social biases**. These include social conformity and judgments based on superficial attributes, such as the halo effect. The halo effect causes a general impression to be inferred from a single trait, such as attractiveness or a calm demeanor.

The persuader must understand the role of emotional states, or negative affects. Anxiety and other negative affects play important roles in social judgments and conformity. When a target is anxious, they are more likely to rely on quick, biased assessments. By projecting extreme calm and competence, the persuader reduces the target's need for impulsive social judgment. They also capitalize on the halo effect. The target, experiencing anxiety, seeks stability and guidance from the composed figure. This immediate, positive social judgment facilitates the acceptance of later, substantive proposals.

The concept of Theory of Mind (ToM), the ability to attribute mental states to others, is also mutually associated with social judgments and conformity. A persuader who can accurately gauge the target's cognitive and affective state possesses a clear advantage. The persuader anticipates resistance, emotional instability, or uncertainty. This anticipation allows for pre-emptive framing to ensure the message lands correctly.

The Requirement for Gender-Specific Communication

A single, one-size-fits-all approach to persuasion will fail. Persuasion strategies must account for documented differences in how men and women process persuasive messages. This is not about stereotyping. It is about aligning the message with established psychological tendencies.

The **Elaboration Likelihood Model (ELM)** suggests different processing routes for genders. Women are often more likely to engage in **central route processing**. This means they focus intensely on message content, message quality, and the critical analysis of arguments. They may find detailed product reviews or verifiable data more persuasive. Conversely, men may be more susceptible to **authority influence**. They may find assertive statistical evidence or endorsement by a recognized expert more compelling.

Linguistic resonance greatly enhances message effectiveness. Masculine language, which is direct and assertive, resonates strongly with male audiences. Feminine language, which is collaborative and empathetic, appeals more to female audiences. The successful persuader must master a broad range of communication styles. They must be able to switch between **push energy** (assertive, direct expression) and **pull energy** (collaborative, seeking opinions).

Men often exhibit more assertive, push energy. Women often tend toward seeking collaboration and ideas, using pull energy. Success requires the ability to switch flexibly between these influence styles at the appropriate moment. The persuader must diagnose the conversational environment. A pull strategy is essential for establishing rapport and gathering information. Once rapport is secure, the persuader can strategically switch to a push strategy to drive compliance.

Furthermore, research confirms that men are generally more influential than women. Women are particularly less influential when using dominant forms of communication. Males specifically tend to resist influence attempted by women who employ highly competent or assertive communication styles. This highlights a specific requirement for female persuaders.

Resistance to competent women can be reduced when women intentionally temper their competence with displays of warmth and communality. This strategic requirement is the **communality buffer**. It involves displaying empathy and collaborative language immediately before or during the assertion of a competent position. This softens the delivery and neutralizes the tendency for resistance. We must balance addressing these known processing differences with avoiding harmful or simplistic stereotypes. The goal remains thoughtful, empathetic framing, not caricature.

Exposure to social gender role information also affects persuasion. When the female gender role is made prominent, women demonstrate weaker attitudes and become more susceptible to change. Conversely, when male gender role information is prominent, both men and women process messages more thoughtfully and carefully. The framing of the environment, not just the words, is crucial. A high-stakes, analytical environment (aligned with the male role prime) encourages thoughtful processing in both genders. A collaborative, non-critical environment (aligned with the female role prime) can reduce cognitive processing effort for both genders. The persuader must set the environmental context to align with the desired depth of thought.

The Technical Manual for Influence

This first book is a technical manual for understanding and applying these psychological facts. We avoid mimicking others. We provide specific, verifiable mechanics. Our content is not vague; it provides step-by-step strategy. We focus on true value and the mature exploration of these themes.

We must always remember that persuasion is achieved through structuring the target's subjective reality. It is never about brute-forcing facts or overwhelming with raw data. It is about understanding the brain's predictable path of least resistance. The following chapters detail how to control the environment around a decision, frame arguments to exploit biases, and activate the core psychological drivers that guarantee compliance. We turn influence from an abstract concept into a reliable, repeatable process.

This process starts with precision. It requires the accurate diagnosis of the target's existing biases and psychological state. Only then can the persuader select the appropriate driver, be it commitment, social proof, or authority, to ensure the outcome. The covert persuader is an architect of choice. They guide the target through a series of small, justifiable steps that lead logically to the final, desired agreement. The target believes the final decision originated entirely from their own will and logic. This self-attribution is the ultimate mark of successful covert persuasion.

The next chapters will expand on each of these tools. We begin with a deep exploration of cognitive biases, detailing how to **Frame Reality** so that the target's innate mental shortcuts always point to your proposal. This is where we learn how to make the necessary, complex decisions easy for the target by forcing them to rely on their fast, heuristic-based system. The objective is to make agreement the path of least cognitive resistance. This ensures that the target moves past critical thought and accepts the proposal as an unquestioned reality.

Then we move to **Secure Action** by activating the core compliance drivers. We will detail the exact timing and sequencing required to deploy Reciprocity, Liking, and Authority. You will learn how to engineer effortful public commitments and how to leverage social information to influence non-conforming members. Securing action means ensuring the target feels inner responsibility for the choice, making the change permanent.

We will then learn to **Control Narrative** by staging information for acceptance. This involves using the Contrast Principle effectively. You will learn how to present ambitious requests first, making the actual desired request seem disproportionately small and acceptable. This staging controls the target's perception of value and cost.

Finally, we discuss how to **Map Influence** and **Mitigate Resistance**. Mapping influence requires diagnosing the target's preferred processing route and adapting the communication style accordingly, shifting between push and pull energy or adjusting the reliance on statistical versus empathetic evidence. Mitigating resistance involves learning how to use the communality buffer and ensuring that the proposal confirms, rather than challenges, the target's existing subjective reality. These elements combined create a comprehensive, scientifically grounded strategy for covert persuasion.

CHAPTER 1

FRAME REALITY: DIRECTING CHOICE WITH COGNITIVE BIAS

Every single person you talk to lives inside a reality they have built just for themselves.

Think about it this way: You are not seeing objective facts. You are seeing facts filtered through your own fears, hopes, and shortcuts. This private version of truth, this **subjective reality**, is what actually drives behavior and choices. People act based on their perception of the input, not the input itself. Covert persuasion is not about fighting the facts. It is about restructuring the presentation of facts so they fit perfectly into the target's existing subjective reality.

How do we do this? We use the brain's own predictable errors.

These errors are called **cognitive biases**. A cognitive bias is a systematic pattern where a person's judgment constantly deviates from rational thinking. These patterns often lead to inaccurate judgment, illogical interpretation, and irrational actions. For the person interested in influence, these errors are not flaws. They are consistent, documented patterns that create repeatable access points.

The Speed of Thought: Bounded Rationality

The reason these biases even exist is simple: the brain cannot handle everything. We have a limited capacity for processing information. This is known as **bounded rationality**. The mind must constantly look for ways to cut corners. It sacrifices thoughtful depth for processing speed. This reliance on shortcuts is called using heuristics.

Sometimes, these shortcuts are helpful. A fast decision is often better than a perfectly accurate but delayed one, especially in social or urgent situations. But often, they just lead to mistakes.

The persuader's task is to force the target's brain into this quick-thinking mode. When a subject is overloaded with data, distracted, or simply hurried, the slow, analytical part of the brain steps back. The fast, intuitive system takes over, and that fast system relies heavily on biases. By subtly increasing the mental load or rushing the conversation, you ensure the target defaults to the biased path you set up earlier.

Anchoring: Setting the Value Baseline

The **Anchoring Effect** is one of the most reliable cognitive biases you can use. It describes how much people depend on the very first piece of information they receive when they make a decision about value. Even if that first number is random or irrelevant, it becomes the anchor. That anchor then sets the range for what is considered acceptable or fair for the rest of the conversation.

If you are negotiating a service, you must introduce the highest justified number early. Say you know the final, profitable price is $5,000. Instead of starting there, you should set a confident anchor at $8,000. The initial anchor frames the entire discussion. If the negotiation brings the price down to $5,500, the target feels they successfully moved the value down by $2,500. They feel a sense of winning. If you had started at $5,000, a final agreement at $5,500 would feel like a loss.

The initial number dictates the perceived context. Every subsequent offer is judged relative to that first, high anchor. This makes moderate offers seem immediately more reasonable. You must state the anchor early, with certainty, and with some concrete reference point to make it stick.

The Contrast Principle: Managing Sequential Perception

Humans are terrible at evaluating things in isolation. We constantly exaggerate the difference between two things presented in sequence. This is the **Contrast Principle**. If the second item is quite different from the first, we perceive the difference as even larger than it is.

This principle is constantly used in sales environments. When a man goes into a store to buy a new suit, he will almost always pay more for the accessories, the belt, the tie, the cuff links, if he buys them *after* he buys the expensive suit. Why? Because compared to the thousand-dollar suit, the hundred-dollar tie seems cheap. The expensive purchase set a high reference point.

In persuasion, this means you must use **proposal staging**. You present the largest, most ambitious request first. This is the setup. Then, you follow it immediately with the request you actually want approved. By contrast, the true, desired request seems disproportionately small, acceptable, or easy. This sequencing guides the target's perception of cost and effort, making the desired action feel like minimal resistance.

Confirmation Bias: The Need for Self-Validation

People possess a powerful desire to believe things that match what they already think. This is **Confirmation Bias**. This tendency is psychological armor. It keeps an individual's internal security and worldview intact.

If you try to directly challenge a target's established belief, you activate their strongest defenses. They will resist the new evidence. The smart way to persuade is to frame your request as a logical conclusion or necessary validation of something they already value.

If a business leader values innovation above all else, you do not sell the idea as risky. You frame it as "the one necessary action for a true innovation-focused company." This framing drastically reduces the amount of proof they need to accept the claim. The target perceives the agreement as confirming their existing identity and path, making the choice feel secure and logical instead of risky or novel. This systematic selection of supporting information is what leads to inaccurate judgments.

Social Biases and the Halo Effect

Social interactions are rife with their own type of bias, known as **social biases.** These include things like conformity and making judgments based on superficial attributes.

The **Halo Effect** is the most significant of these. It causes others to infer a general positive impression from one single trait. This trait could be confidence, composure, or physical attractiveness. You control the single trait, and the target grants you all the associated positive qualities, competence, trustworthiness, and honesty.

Research shows that negative affects, such as anxiety, are strongly linked to social judgments and conformity. A target who feels anxious or uncertain is much more likely to seek stability and make a quick, biased social assessment. They look for an authority figure who seems calm and in control.

The effective persuader projects **extreme composure** and **stillness** at all times. This projection capitalizes on the halo effect. The target feels their own anxiety subside in the presence of this composure and is more likely to accept guidance from the calm authority figure. By strictly managing presentation, environment, and demeanor, you dictate the target's initial positive evaluation. This favorable social judgment accelerates trust and makes later proposals easier to accept.

Strategic Deployment of Framing

Covert persuasion requires moving past simply recognizing these biases. It demands deliberate deployment. You must create the environment where the target's own mental shortcuts point them straight to your desired outcome.

1. Diagnosing the Subjective Path: You must first find the target's established values, their constant justifications, and their core assumptions. These are the bricks of their subjective reality. You find them by listening for their habitual language and noting where they consistently choose speed over thoroughness. If they repeatedly talk about "efficiency," you frame your request as "the most efficient path."

2. Increasing Cognitive Demand: To force the brain into the fast, intuitive system, you must subtly increase the cognitive load. This is a delicate process. You can present information in fast succession. You can introduce a minor, easily resolved technical issue. You can give them a simple but necessary mental task to focus on during the setup phase. The objective is to keep the slow, analytical part of the mind occupied, ensuring the key decision relies on the fast, shortcut-based system.

3. Framing Loss Over Gain: While the detailed mechanics of loss aversion are covered later, the concept is essential here. People are driven more strongly by the fear of losing something than by the desire to gain something of equivalent value. When framing a choice, present compliance as **necessary risk mitigation**, preventing a specific, guaranteed loss. Avoid framing it only as a potential benefit. The emotional pressure of avoiding a loss is a much stronger driver for immediate action.

4. Controlling the Processing Context: The social environment contributes to how carefully the target processes your message. Research suggests that when cues associated with the male gender role are prominent, both men and women tend to process persuasive messages more thoughtfully and carefully. Also, when cues associated with the female gender role are prominent, both genders process messages less carefully.

If you need a deeply considered, long-term commitment, you set a context that is analytical, high-stakes, and rational. If you need immediate, non-critical acceptance, you can frame the environment using cues that favor the less critical processing style. The key is setting the context, not just the words, to align with the required depth of thought.

The Architect of Choice

The person skilled in covert persuasion is an architect of choice. They do not rely on brute force or aggressive argument. They quietly build a set of ramps, anchors, and shortcuts that lead the target directly to the desired outcome. The target believes they arrived at the conclusion through their own superior logic. This internal attribution is what makes the decision stick.

We have established how to set the stage by directing the target's perception. The next crucial step is securing their commitment. The following chapter moves from managing perception to actively activating the six core behavioral rules that guarantee human compliance. We will show you how to use these innate drivers, Reciprocity, Commitment, Social Proof, and others, to secure an action that feels like the target's own idea. This combination of framing reality and activating compliance drivers ensures that the path of least resistance is always the path you want them to take.

CHAPTER 2

SECURE ACTION: ACTIVATING CORE HUMAN COMPLIANCE DRIVERS

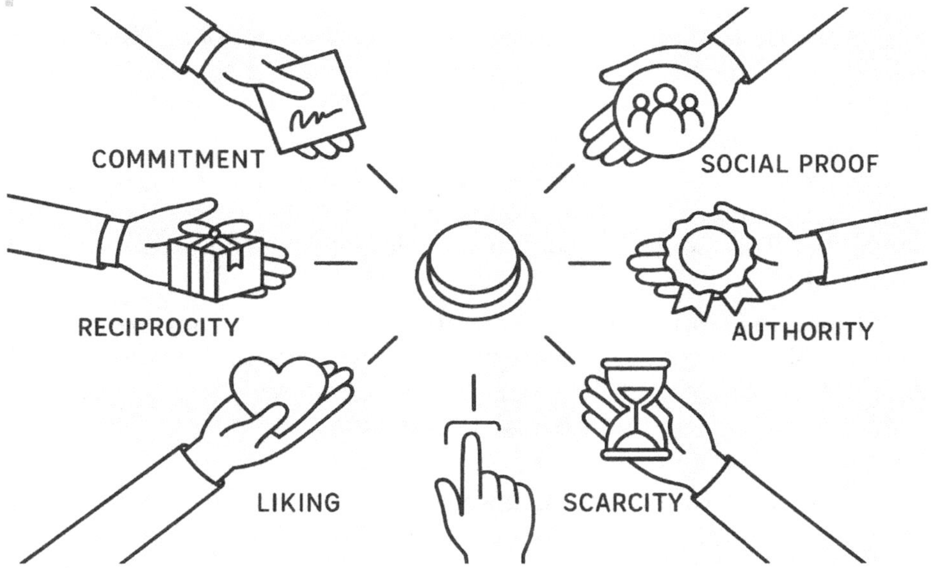

Securing action is the final step of influence. It moves beyond simply setting the stage for a decision. It involves activating the six foundational rules that guide human compliance. These rules function as universal psychological shortcuts. They provide systematic, repeatable mechanisms for increasing agreement. If you understand these drivers, you can guide a person toward a decision they will later believe they chose independently.

This chapter breaks down each driver. We explain how to activate them precisely. This creates a secure, long-term commitment.

1. Commitment and Consistency: The Anchor of Self-Image

People possess a powerful, innate need to appear **consistent** in their behavior. Once a person makes a commitment, they feel immense internal pressure to align their future actions with that initial decision. This desire for consistency simplifies life. It allows us to avoid thinking deeply about every new choice.

The secret to using this driver is forcing the target to accept **inner responsibility** for an action. If you apply too much external pressure, the commitment will not last. A massive reward, or an aggressive demand, makes the target think, "I did this for the money," or "I did this because I had to." Once the external pressure is removed, the target will immediately revert to their old desires or behaviors.

To build lasting commitment, the initial action must possess three key qualities:

It Must Be Active: The commitment requires a physical, distinct act. A mental agreement is weak. A written statement, a signed document, or a public statement is a physical marker. This act ties the decision to the target's sense of self-image.

It Must Be Public: When others witness the commitment, the target feels social pressure. They must maintain an image of consistency for the group. This public accountability reinforces the internal drive for alignment.

It Must Be Effortful: The person must perceive that they overcame a small hurdle to complete the action. The effort makes the commitment stick. Think of groups, like fraternities, that use effortful steps to increase loyalty. The process makes members take inner responsibility for the group's rules and identity.

The Foot-in-the-Door Technique: This approach is the most common application of Commitment and Consistency. You ask for a small, easily justifiable favor first. This small agreement establishes a beachhead of commitment. Once the target agrees to the small request, their self-image shifts slightly. They now see themselves as the type of person who helps, or the type of person who supports the cause. The large, desired request that follows is then perceived as a logical, consistent extension of their new, self-attributed identity.

Example Application: Do not ask a potential investor for a major capital commitment first. Ask them to write a one-paragraph email detailing their core investment philosophy. They are making an active, effortful commitment to a principle. You then show them how your proposal is the **only consistent** financial action that honors their written philosophy. They are no longer deciding on your proposal. They are simply fulfilling their own commitment. The decision becomes their idea.

This is the art of engineering a self-sustaining adherence. You want the target to believe the choice originated from their own personal will.

You remove the appearance of strong outside pressure. You maximize their personal responsibility for the small initial step. This psychological structure ensures the final, large action is secure and long-lasting.

2. Social Proof: The Crowd's Silent Guide

When people feel uncertain, they naturally look to the actions of others to guide their own behavior. This tendency is known as **Social Proof**. The strength of this principle is immense. It drives consumer decisions, social conformity, and large-scale behavioral shifts.

The power of Social Proof is magnified by uncertainty. When a target is unsure about the correct action, they assume that if many other people are doing something, those people must possess information the target lacks. This assumption makes the action seem more appropriate or correct.

The Role of Group Conditions: Effective influence requires controlling the social environment to ensure Social Proof works optimally. A leader cannot control every individual in a large group. However, a leader can control the most dedicated members. By influencing a certain, respected portion of the group first, their adoption then persuades the rest.

Example Application: Testimonials are a form of Social Proof. But they are strongest when the source is someone the target identifies with. A testimonial from a highly successful person may not work as well as one from a person who shares the target's exact profession, geographical location, or struggle.

The **Social Bond Multiplier** is also critical. Social scientists have found that the strength of the social bond between individuals can be twice as likely to determine a purchase as the preference for the product itself. If the target feels a strong connection to the person recommending the action, the resistance disappears.

The Strategy of Modeling: Do not tell a target what to do. Show them others succeeding through the desired action. The proof must be visible, relevant, and perceived as genuine. This makes the target feel safe. They are following the established, successful path. This reduces the risk in their subjective reality.

3. Reciprocity: The Weight of Obligation

The **Reciprocity Principle** states that we feel obligated to return a favor or a concession that another person has provided to us. This rule is ingrained in human society. It creates a network of mutual assistance that benefits the group.

The key to activating Reciprocity is to give something **first** and to ensure the gift is perceived as **personal and unexpected**. The gift does not need to be expensive or elaborate. It must be meaningful to the target. An uninvited gift creates a sense of immediate, unsolicited obligation. This pressure often feels uncomfortable. The target wants to relieve the psychological burden by returning the favor, often with a much larger one.

The Strategy of Initial Concession (Door-in-the-Face): This technique uses the Contrast Principle alongside Reciprocity. You first present a large, ambitious request that you fully expect the target to reject. This is the "door-in-the-face" part.

Immediately after the rejection, you present the smaller, actual desired request. This second request is framed as a **concession** on your part. The target feels two powerful forces working on them: first, the actual request seems much smaller by contrast to the initial huge request (Contrast Principle). Second, they feel obligated to reciprocate your perceived concession by agreeing to the smaller request (Reciprocity). This is a highly effective sequence for moving from denial to compliance.

Example Application: Do not ask a manager for a three-month extended deadline immediately. Ask for a six-month delay and a full restructuring of the project's scope. When they reasonably reject this large request, immediately follow up with the actual desired request: "Okay, I understand. If six months is too much, can we agree to just the three-month delay? I'll personally handle the restructuring without team input." The three-month delay suddenly seems like a small, reasonable request, and the manager feels obligated to agree since you "retreated" from the six-month request.

4. Liking: The Foundation of Effortless Agreement

We are significantly more likely to agree to a request from a person we like. The emotion of liking often supersedes rational thought. The goal is to cultivate genuine rapport quickly. This involves focusing on three core components:

Similarity: We like people who are similar to us. Finding common ground, in hobbies, background, or opinions, builds rapport quickly. Even small, irrelevant similarities increase the feeling of connection. The persuader should subtly mirror the target's posture, language style, and emotional state. This behavioral synchrony makes the target feel an instant, subconscious bond.

Compliments and Approval: We enjoy being praised. Genuine, specific compliments increase liking. The compliment must be tailored to the target's efforts or abilities, not just superficial appearance. Approval is a powerful psychological currency.

Cooperation and Shared Goals: Working together toward a shared, common objective generates connection. The persuader should frame the request not as a sales pitch, but as a joint effort to overcome an external obstacle. "It sounds like we both agree on the goal of cutting costs. How can we work together to implement this solution?" This technique transforms the persuader from an antagonist into a helpful partner.

The **Halo Effect**, discussed earlier, also feeds into Liking. When a person projects competence and controlled composure, they gain an immediate, favorable social judgment. This initial positive impression makes the target want to like the persuader, as they are perceived as a safe, successful connection. Liking is the emotional lubricant that makes every request easier to accept.

5. Authority: The Deference to Expertise

We possess an ingrained tendency to defer to legitimate authority figures. This deference simplifies decision-making. We assume that authority figures, such as doctors, police, or experts, possess a higher level of specialized knowledge.

The persuader does not necessarily need a formal title. They must use the **symbols of authority**. These symbols include titles, tailored clothing, and the controlled environment.

Symbols of Authority: A person introduced with a title like "Dr." or "Director" is perceived as more knowledgeable and influential, regardless of the actual content of their message. The persuader must ensure their credentials and titles are presented to the target before the interaction begins. The environment also projects authority. A clean, organized, and professionally decorated office conveys status and expertise.

Composure and Certainty: Composure is a powerful non-verbal symbol of authority. A person who speaks slowly, uses precise language, and shows no sign of emotional distress projects competence and control. When the target is uncertain or anxious, they look to the composure of the authority figure for guidance. The composed figure seems to possess the illusion of informed certainty. The target trusts this certainty and follows the recommendation.

Scientific Grounding: Authority is why this collection emphasizes scientific evidence. By grounding every claim in verifiable research, the persuader uses the ultimate symbol of Authority: documented, accepted knowledge. The facts are not just opinions; they are validated truths.

6. Scarcity and Urgency: The Drive for Immediate Action

The final and perhaps most potent driver for instant action is **Scarcity**. We value things more when they are rare or limited.

Rarity Equals Value: This is a basic psychological truth. A famous 1975 experiment showed that people rated identical cookies from an almost empty jar as more desirable than the same cookies from a full jar. The desire was determined by the perception of limited availability, not by the cookie's actual quality. The persuader must engineer scarcity by visibly reducing perceived availability, limited time offers, limited quantities, or exclusive access barriers.

Loss Aversion: The power of Scarcity is rooted in **Loss Aversion**. The psychological pain of losing something is generally more powerful than the pleasure of gaining an item of equivalent value. People are highly motivated to avoid loss. Scarcity triggers the **Fear of Missing Out (FOMO)**.

The persuader should frame the decision as necessary to **prevent a loss**. If you do not act now, you will lose the opportunity, the discount, or the advantage. This triggers an impulsive decision to avoid the powerful psychological pain of regret associated with missing out.

Psychological Reactance: When a person's freedom to choose or acquire something is threatened by limited availability, they experience **Psychological Reactance**. This is an innate desire to reassert that threatened freedom, often by pursuing the restricted item even more intensely.

By introducing a temporary, slight barrier to access, a deadline, a quantity limit, or an exclusive qualification, the persuader increases the target's desire for the restricted option. Combining this reactance with loss aversion creates an urgent, high-stakes scenario that compels immediate compliance.

Temporal Discounting (The Time Trap): Scarcity is amplified by time pressure, a behavioral economic concept known as **Temporal Discounting**. This is the cognitive process of preferring immediate rewards over greater future benefits.

People are impatient by nature. They often choose a smaller reward today over a slightly larger reward tomorrow. To compel immediate action, the persuader must associate the action *now* with an immediate, tangible psychological or material reward, even if the main payoff is delayed. This small, present payment counteracts the hyperbolic devaluation of the long-term benefit.

Example Application: Do not frame a decision as "invest now for a big future profit." Frame it as: "Agree to this now to **secure immediate access** to the exclusive community and avoid the fee increase that happens at midnight." You are offering immediate access (a present reward) and preventing an immediate loss (the fee increase). This combination makes the decision impulsive and highly effective.

Synthesis: The Combined Compliance System

The six drivers are rarely used in isolation. They are most potent when deployed in combination, creating a system of compliance:

1. **Commitment** secures the target's initial self-attribution.
2. **Liking** provides the necessary emotional rapport.
3. **Reciprocity** creates the immediate obligation to agree.
4. **Authority** provides the necessary psychological justification for the decision.
5. **Social Proof** guarantees safety by showing others have gone first.
6. **Scarcity and Urgency** collapse the decision window, forcing immediate compliance before rational analysis can interfere.

By consciously activating these core drivers, the persuader moves the process from vague discussion to secure, immediate action. This is the difference between hoping for agreement and engineering it. The following chapters detail how to control the narrative, map the target's decision process, and neutralize resistance before it even appears. We ensure that every interaction is structured for maximum leverage.

CHAPTER 3

CONTROL NARRATIVE: STAGING INFORMATION FOR ACCEPTANCE

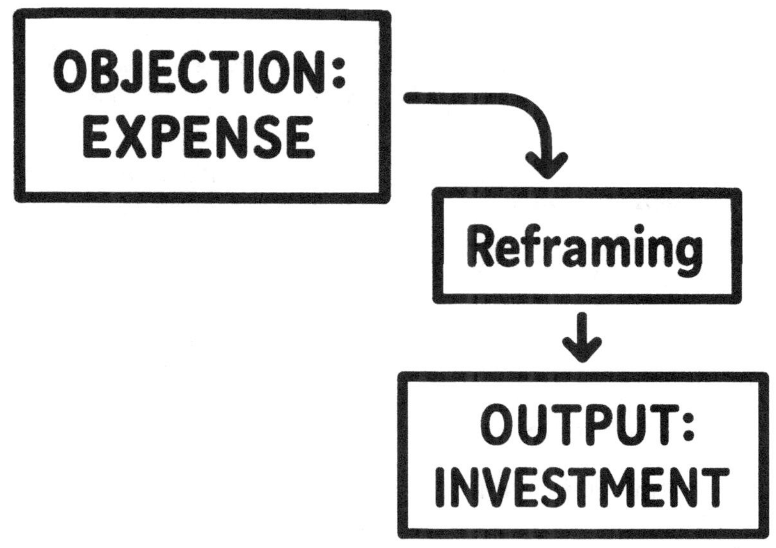

Influence depends less on the argument itself and more on the way you present the argument. This is the difference between facts and narrative. You must be the editor of the story that plays out in the target's mind. Controlling the narrative means staging every piece of information to guide acceptance. You manage the context around the proposal.

The power of narrative control is simple. It ensures that when the target finally makes a choice, the agreement feels like the only logical conclusion to the story you built. This chapter shows you how to structure information so that the target's natural biases move them toward your desired outcome. This approach uses validated cognitive science, moving beyond unproven methodologies that lack verifiable academic support.

The Scientific Foundation of Framing

While some historical theories used the term "reframing" in a way that lacks scientific basis, the underlying concept of **framing** is deeply validated by behavioral science. Framing is the core act of structuring the decision environment. It dictates the context of a choice.

Pioneering research demonstrated that simply presenting the same outcome in two different ways, as a potential loss versus an assured gain, drastically changes the choice subjects make. For instance, a medical treatment framed as "90% chance of survival" is accepted far more readily than the same treatment framed as "10% chance of death." The facts are identical. The psychological response is entirely different.

The persuader's objective is to understand that the architecture of the choice matters more than the content itself. You use controlled language and strategic sequencing to structure choices that exploit predictable cognitive biases. This ensures the target makes a decision based on the emotional charge of your description, rather than a dispassionate, rational calculation. You are editing the story before the target reads it.

Mastering the Contrast Principle Through Sequencing

Human perception uses comparison as a primary tool for evaluating value and effort. We are not good at judging things in isolation. This is why the **Contrast Principle** is so effective. This principle states that the difference between two items presented one after the other will be exaggerated if the second item differs significantly from the first.

If you stage your request correctly, you control the relative perception of value.

The Strategy of the High Anchor: In any discussion about price, time, or required effort, the expensive or ambitious request must come first. This sets the initial, high reference point, the anchor. For example, if you are attempting to secure two hours of a person's time, you might first ask for an entire day of their schedule, alongside an urgent commitment of resources. The person will likely reject the large, initial request.

The Concession Follow-Up: Immediately following the rejection, you present the actual, desired request: the two-hour commitment. Because the second request is immediately preceded by the much larger, more ambitious request, the two-hour demand appears disproportionately small and acceptable.

This sequencing technique is highly effective because it manages two psychological factors simultaneously:

1. **Value Distortion:** The Contrast Principle distorts the perceived cost of the second item. The target thinks, "Compared to the previous demand, this is easy and cheap."
2. **Reciprocity Activation:** The target often perceives your shift from the high demand to the low demand as a concession on your part. They feel compelled to reciprocate this perceived "retreat" by accepting the smaller request, even if they would have rejected the smaller request if it had been presented first.

This staging allows you to control the target's perception of cost and effort. You set the stage with a high-effort reference, making the low-effort, desired action seem almost effortless. You use sequential presentation to guide the perception of value and cost, all through managed narrative flow.

The Art of Reframing Objections

Reframing is the advanced skill of narrative control. It is the act of shifting the context around a specific fact or objection, rather than arguing against the fact itself. When a target resists a request, they are usually doing so based on a perceived negative context they have applied to a neutral fact.

For instance, a neutral fact is: "This solution costs $20,000." A negative context is: "That is an excessive cost." The target is resisting the **context** (excessive cost), not the **fact** ($20,000).

The unsophisticated persuader argues the number. The covert persuader argues the context.

The Strategy of Contextual Shift: You must identify the target's negative frame and immediately redefine the objection's category. You shift the reference point until the original objection becomes irrelevant.

- If the target says, "This is **risky**," they are framing the decision as a potential source of loss. You must reframe the decision as a necessary form of **risk mitigation** against a larger, guaranteed future loss. "It is not risky; it is the necessary premium for guaranteed security against market volatility."

- If the target says, "This is **expensive**," they are framing the cost as expenditure. You must reframe the cost as a necessary **investment** in future capacity. "It is not expensive; it is a fixed, necessary investment that guarantees a five-year capacity increase."

This contextual shift invalidates the target's initial resistance by changing the very category of the objection. The target's initial resistance is based on their subjective reality. By reframing, you make the decision fit their positive self-view, satisfying the Confirmation Bias. They now see the decision not as an act of risk, but as an act of calculated security, which aligns with their existing desire to be secure.

Linguistic Precision: Moving from Abstraction to Detail

The specific words you use directly affect the psychological distance between the target and your proposal. Abstract language creates cognitive distance. Common, concrete words trigger immediate, specific emotional responses.

Language is deeply connected with personality, intention, and psychological state. The goal is to be an intuitive emotional mapper, selecting words that trigger the precise affective response you want.

Unpacking NLP: The acronym NLP stands at a fascinating crossroads, pointing to both the foundational human influence field of Neuro-Linguistic Programming and the computational discipline of Natural Language Processing.

This book is dedicated to the former, positioning it as the master blueprint for human influence. The pioneers of NLP gave us a brilliant, early map for understanding how language, neurology, and behavior interconnect. This foundational work is what allowed millions to begin improving communication, but the time has come for a verifiable, advanced evolution of the practice.

This book delivers that evolution. We leverage the core genius of traditional NLP, concepts like Modeling, Anchoring, and Reframing, and seamlessly integrate them with the latest verified findings from cognitive science and behavioral economics.

The precision in linguistic patterns that the technical field of Natural Language Processing confirms is now brought to you as a practiced, measurable skill. This allows you to move beyond outdated theory to proven methods that reliably structure choices, reshape arguments, and give you the verifiable knowledge to consistently predict reactions and secure commitment.

The effective persuader adheres to the *scientific* insight: word patterns matter greatly.

Actionable Linguistic Principles:

- **Substitute Abstract Nouns:** Never use general, abstract terms where a specific verb or noun exists. Do not talk about "success." Talk about "a signed contract on Thursday" or "a 15% reduction in expenditure." Concrete details are always more compelling.
- **Use Sensory Language:** Describe the future outcome with immediate sensory detail. Make the target *feel* the comfort, *see* the result, or *hear* the client's approval. This sensory detail minimizes the perceived time gap between the present decision and the future result.
- **Minimize Jargon:** Technical jargon or overly complicated language increases cognitive friction. It forces the target to slow down and use their rational processing system, increasing the chance of resistance. Use common, concrete vocabulary to ensure the emotional and intellectual impact is delivered directly.

When faced with resistance, the persuader must perform internal sentiment analysis. Which keywords is the target using? Are they using words like "unfair," "worried," or "risky"? These words reveal the precise emotional state that must be addressed or reframed before the narrative can proceed positively.

Building the Narrative Anchor: Pre-Suasion

Controlling the narrative begins before you even present the proposal. **Pre-suasion** is the act of directing the target's attention to an idea or concept that will make them receptive to your actual message later.

The narrative anchor is established by controlling the target's environment and their focus.

Environmental Control: The physical setting dictates much of the target's pre-conceived narrative. A messy, chaotic environment suggests disorganization and lack of control. A controlled, organized, and professional environment suggests competence and authority. This external narrative reinforces the perception of your professional capability.

Focus Control: Before you introduce the solution, you must ensure the target is thinking about the problem in the right way.

- If you want them to focus on *quality*, ask them to spend five minutes describing the highest-quality product they ever owned.
- If you want them to focus on *security*, ask them to recount a time they felt exposed or vulnerable.

By directing their focus, you are activating a specific cognitive framework that makes them more receptive to your message when it arrives. If the target is thinking about security, your security-focused solution will be perceived as highly relevant and necessary. This pre-framing makes the eventual agreement feel like a natural progression of their current thoughts.

Narrative Control and Gender Processing

Effective narrative control means knowing which type of evidence to present to which audience. Since men and women often process persuasive messages through different cognitive routes, the content of your narrative must be tailored.

1. **Central Route (Detailed Evidence):** Women show a stronger tendency toward central route processing. This means they are likely to analyze arguments critically and focus on message quality. When your target favors this route, your narrative must be dense with verifiable data, detailed case studies, and critical analysis. The story must be logical and withstand deep scrutiny.
2. **Peripheral Route (Authority/Emotion):** Some individuals, particularly men, may be more susceptible to authority influence or assertive evidence. In these cases, your narrative can rely more heavily on the endorsement of recognized experts or powerful, assertively stated statistical evidence.

The persuader must map the target's decision profile and select the appropriate narrative evidence. The goal is to achieve **linguistic resonance**, a sense of effortless understanding, by aligning the language and the evidence with the target's preferred processing style. This practice avoids cognitive friction, making the persuader appear trustworthy and familiar. The careful adjustment of the narrative ensures maximum acceptance without triggering unnecessary conscious evaluation of the influence attempt.

The Narrative System

Controlling the narrative is the system of sequencing and framing that makes the decision path obvious and desirable. You move from the high anchor to the smaller request, exploiting the Contrast Principle. You dismantle resistance by reframing objections into confirmations of the target's positive self-view. You use concrete, sensory language to ensure the emotional message is delivered without cognitive friction.

This complex system of strategic staging ensures that the target's mind, operating on its own internal logic and biases, arrives at your desired conclusion naturally. They walk through the doors you built for them, believing they found the path themselves.

The next step is to diagnose the target with precision. The following chapter details how to **Map Influence**: using observation, questioning, and analysis to uncover the target's internal decision profile and personalize your strategy instantly. This provides the intelligence needed to apply these narrative controls with surgical accuracy.

CHAPTER 4

MAP INFLUENCE: DIAGNOSING THE TARGET'S DECISION PROFILE

Covert persuasion is not a monologue. It is a highly responsive engagement built on accurate diagnosis. Before you speak, you must gather intelligence. You need to know the target's specific emotional pressures, their typical processing route, and the underlying beliefs that structure their subjective reality. This process of intelligence gathering is called **Mapping the Influence Profile**.

A generalized approach fails quickly. If you rely too heavily on social proof for a person who trusts only internal data, you fail. If you use slow, analytical arguments on someone driven by immediate anxiety, you fail. Success requires personalizing the strategy instantly, which only happens if you accurately diagnose the target's decision path.

1. Diagnosing the Default Processing Route

The mind uses two primary systems for processing persuasive messages. The first step in mapping is figuring out which one the target uses most often.

The Central Route: This path involves careful, critical analysis of the message content and quality. The target focuses on logic, facts, and verifiable data. If they use this route, they are looking for logical consistency and proof that can withstand scrutiny.

The Peripheral Route: This path involves relying on quick, emotional, or external cues. The target focuses on the speaker's authority, their composure, social proof (what others are doing), or simple emotional appeals. This is the path of least resistance, often driven by heuristics and cognitive bias.

Reading the Route: How do you quickly determine the default route?

- **Listen to Justification:** When the target talks about past major decisions, listen to how they justify the choice. Did they cite detailed research and long-term analysis (Central)? Or did they reference a respected expert, a popular consensus, or a gut feeling (Peripheral)?
- **Observe Questioning Style:** A Central Route processor asks technical, detailed, and specific questions about mechanics and evidence: "What is the margin of error?" or "Show me the data set." A Peripheral Route processor asks questions about safety, popularity, and ease: "Who else is doing this?" or "How quickly can we start?"
- **Factor in Context:** When men and women are exposed to cues associated with the **male gender role**, they both tend to process messages more carefully and thoughtfully. This happens because the context emphasizes a thoughtful, high-stakes environment. Conversely, when cues associated with the **female gender role** are prominent, both men and women tend to process messages less carefully. By observing how the target responds to the current social context, you gauge their level of active, critical thought.

Understanding this route determines the content of your narrative. If the target is a Central processor, you must dedicate the majority of your time to detailed, statistical evidence, knowing that emotional appeals will be ignored.

2. Mapping Emotional Pressures and Affective States

Decisions are rarely made in an emotional vacuum. The target's current psychological state, especially negative affects like anxiety, dictates their readiness to agree and the type of information they seek.

The Role of Anxiety: Studies show that feelings of anxiety are mutually associated with both social judgments and conformity. When a target is anxious, they are more likely to seek stability and make quick, biased social assessments. They are looking for an authority figure to guide them.

- **Diagnosis:** Look for non-verbal cues associated with anxiety: fidgeting, nervous vocal delivery, or rapid-fire questions. Verbally, listen for expressions of risk, worry, or uncertainty.
- **Action:** If you diagnose anxiety, you must prioritize projecting **extreme calm and competence**. Your controlled demeanor activates the **Halo Effect**, causing the target to infer positive traits (trust, safety) from your composure alone. This favorable social judgment accelerates trust. Your first priority becomes addressing their emotional stability, not their rational objection. Reducing anxiety removes the impulsive requirement for a quick, defensive, biased assessment.

Intuitive vs. Deliberative Styles: Anxiety and negative affects are often associated with an intuitive, non-analytical decision style. If the target is displaying negative affects, they are likely defaulting to their fast, shortcut-based system. Conversely, a calm, analytical approach suggests they are using their slow, deliberative system. Your map must include this insight. If they are intuitive, you must immediately frame the decision using strong emotional anchors like loss aversion or scarcity, which speak directly to their intuitive system.

3. Uncovering Core Cognitive Biases and Assumptions

Every individual has a preferred set of cognitive biases they rely on habitually. These revealed preferences form the exact structure of their subjective reality. Your map must identify these foundational errors.

The Anchoring Bias Habit: Does the target consistently refer back to historical performance, initial budget proposals, or early-stage ideas when making final decisions? This indicates a strong **Anchoring Bias**. If this is their habit, you know that the initial high value you set at the beginning of the discussion will retain disproportionate influence over their final valuation.

Confirmation Bias Structure: What are the target's deeply held, non-negotiable beliefs about their identity, their company, or the market? If they believe they are "forward-thinking," any proposal that confirms that self-view will be accepted with minimal evidence. This reveals the structure of their **Confirmation Bias**. The map tells you *which* identity you need to confirm: innovator, security-focused manager, or efficiency expert.

The Social Proof Threshold: How does the target respond to peer influence? Some individuals are highly susceptible to social proof; others are not.

- **Low Self-Monitor:** This individual is less focused on adapting their behavior to social cues. They may be slower to adopt a charismatic persona or new idea. Once they internalize a commitment, however, it is stable and long-lasting. For this individual, you need detailed, verifiable proof, and strong consistency arguments.
- **High Self-Monitor:** This individual is highly susceptible to emotional and behavioral cues. They rapidly absorb and reflect the charismatic state (enthusiasm, confidence). They are excellent for creating immediate group fervor. For this target, social proof, charismatic delivery, and emotional contagion are highly effective.

Your map should include a quick assessment of their self-monitoring trait. This determines whether you lead with group consensus (for high self-monitors) or with deep, logical commitment (for low self-monitors).

4. Mapping Communication Style and Gender Primes

Successful persuasion requires the ability to switch influence styles based on the target's preference, regardless of their actual gender. This skill, often called **flexible influence**, requires diagnosing whether the target prefers **push** or **pull** energy.

Push Energy (Assertive): This style involves direct expression, assertion, and leading the conversation. Men often exhibit this style more frequently.

Pull Energy (Collaborative): This style involves seeking opinions, using inquiry, and giving space to others. Women often tend toward this style.

Flexible Influence: Your map must determine which style builds rapport faster. A pull strategy (collaboration, questions) is essential for gathering information and establishing initial trust. Once you have the necessary information and trust is secured, you can strategically switch to a push strategy (assertion, directness) to drive compliance and finalize the action. The ability to switch prevents you from getting stuck in one ineffective style.

Linguistic Resonance: Your map must also include the target's preferred language style. Using language that is **gender-congruent**, direct and assertive for those who prefer "masculine" language, or collaborative and empathetic for those who prefer "feminine" language, enhances message effectiveness. This practice builds **linguistic resonance**, a sense of effortless, familiar understanding, which increases message acceptance without triggering conscious evaluation.

5. Strategic Deployment: The Diagnostic Funnel

Mapping the profile is not an abstract exercise. It is a funnel that dictates the exact sequencing of your six compliance drivers and framing techniques:

1. **Initial Scan (First 30 Seconds):** Diagnose the processing route (Central/Peripheral) and the current affective state (Anxious/Calm). This determines your initial delivery style (Analytical vs. Composed/Emotional).
2. **Rapport Building (Next 3 Minutes):** Use a Pull strategy to uncover core assumptions (Confirmation Bias structure) and collect surface similarities (for Liking). If the target is female or resists authority, begin applying the **communality buffer** (displaying warmth alongside competence) to mitigate resistance from the start.
3. **Anchoring and Concession (Next 5 Minutes):** Deploy the high anchor (Anchoring Bias) and prepare the Contrast Principle by presenting a large request followed immediately by the smaller, desired request (Reciprocity/Contrast).
4. **Closing Sequence:** If the target is highly anxious or peripheral, close quickly using **Scarcity and Loss Aversion** (impulsive drivers). If the target is calm and central, use **Commitment and Consistency** (secure the active, public, effortful step) and **Authority** (present final, verifiable evidence) to ensure long-term adherence.

This layered approach ensures that every step of your influence strategy is personalized and aligns with the target's unique psychological structure. You are not guessing. You are executing based on a verified map of their decision profile. This precision is the essence of covert persuasion.

The next critical step is ensuring this carefully constructed profile and strategy does not collapse. The following chapter details how to **Mitigate Resistance**: neutralizing defenses before they can form and managing objections by reframing them as confirmations of the target's own logic.

CHAPTER 5

MITIGATE RESISTANCE: NEUTRALIZING DEFENSES BEFORE THEY FORM

Resistance is not a personal attack. It is simply a defense mechanism. It means the target's subjective reality has encountered information that conflicts with their core beliefs, social image, or self-view. The target is protecting themselves from internal inconsistency or perceived external threat. The skilled persuader does not argue with this defense. They neutralize it before it is fully formed.

This chapter details the specific, scientifically verified methods for mitigating resistance. We move past confrontation and focus entirely on pre-emption. By anticipating the exact nature of the target's objection and addressing it first, you eliminate the mental energy the target needed to deploy their defense. This process ensures the meticulously crafted influence profile, built in Chapter 5, does not collapse at the moment of decision.

1. Pre-Emption: Addressing the Unspoken Objection (The Firebreak)

The most effective way to neutralize resistance is to state the objection yourself before the target gets the chance. When you voice the target's primary reservation, three crucial psychological shifts occur:

A. Cognitive Release: You remove the target's mental burden. They were preparing to interrupt you with their objection. By stating it first, you remove the need for them to think about it. This allows their brain to process the rest of your message with less effort. The mind naturally seeks paths of least cognitive resistance.

B. Increased Credibility: By accurately predicting and stating the counter-argument, you project supreme confidence. You show the target that you have thoroughly considered their perspective. This transparency increases perceived trustworthiness, making the target less guarded.

C. Framing Control: Most importantly, when you voice the objection, you control the **framing**. You dictate the context of the problem and its limits. This allows you to immediately follow the objection with your reframed solution. The target is denied the opportunity to frame the problem using their own negatively charged language.

The Strategy of the Firebreak:

The process requires identifying the strongest, most likely objection during the Mapping stage (Chapter 5). Do not choose a trivial objection; choose the central one (cost, time, or risk).

1. **Acknowledge the Pain Point (The Objection):** Introduce the objection using precise, neutral language. For example: "Before we proceed, let me address the single largest factor people consider here: the upfront investment required to implement this solution."
2. **Validate the Concern (The Empathy):** Briefly confirm that the concern is legitimate. "It is a significant commitment, and anyone who is financially responsible must think carefully about this number." This validates their self-image as a responsible decision-maker.
3. **Refactor the Context (The Pivot):** Immediately change the category of the objection. If the objection is cost, pivot to future security. If the objection is time, pivot to long-term efficiency. "However, the more critical question is not the amount of the upfront investment, but the guaranteed long-term cost of *not* securing this protection."

By deploying this **firebreak**, stating, validating, and refactoring the objection, you prevent the target from setting their own internal narrative. You position yourself as a collaborator who anticipated their needs, not a salesperson pushing a product.

2. The Art of Contextual Reframing

Reframing is the advanced technique of narrative control. It involves shifting the context around a neutral fact so that the target's subjective reality changes. Resistance is fundamentally a contextual problem. The target is applying a negative meaning to a neutral piece of information.

The critical insight, confirmed by behavioral economics, is that framing significantly alters decision-making. By presenting an outcome as a guaranteed loss versus a potential gain, you change the subject's choice, even if the objective facts are identical.

The Strategy of Category Change:

When a target expresses an objection, they are giving you a gift: the negative frame they are using. Do not argue the frame. Change the category entirely.

- **Resistance Frame:** "I cannot accept this kind of **risk**."
    - Reframed Category: Security and Insurance.
    - Response: "I understand you see risk here. But let us view this differently. This is not risk; this is purchasing guaranteed protection. The true risk is maintaining your current, exposed position. We are buying security."
- Resistance Frame: "This is too much expense."
    - Reframed Category: Investment and Capacity.
    - Response: "You are right, it is an expense in the short term. However, the correct way to assess this is as a fixed investment that triples your processing capacity. We are not spending money; we are purchasing future growth."
- **Resistance Frame:** "This takes too much **time**."
    - Reframed Category: Efficiency and Future Savings.
    - Response: "The time required today is significant. But we must frame this as a one-time process to guarantee future efficiency. The time you spend today saves you ten times that amount in management time over the next year."

This strategy ensures that the target's initial resistance is rendered irrelevant. They cannot logically argue that an "investment" is too expensive if they agree on the principle of necessary investment. The negative frame is nullified by placing the fact into an entirely different, positive category that aligns with their self-view (Confirmation Bias).

3. Neutralizing Resistance from Social Pressure (The Communality Buffer)

Resistance is often influenced by social dynamics, particularly those related to gender and competence. Research confirms that men generally possess more influence than women in professional and group settings. Women are particularly less influential when using overtly dominant communication styles.

A core finding is that males specifically tend to resist influence attempted by women who use highly competent or assertive communication styles. This resistance is not always about the idea; it is often about the perceived challenge to status or social expectation.

The Strategy of the Communality Buffer:

The specific tactic for female persuaders to mitigate this resistance is to intentionally **temper competence with displays of warmth and communality**. This is the **Communality Buffer**.

- **Actionable Implementation:** Before or during the assertion of a highly competent or assertive position, the female persuader must use deliberate language that emphasizes shared goals, empathy, and cooperation.
    - *Instead of:* "My analysis dictates we must proceed with Solution A."
    - *Try:* "I agree with the team's objective, and based on the analysis we ran together, I believe we share the understanding that the best path forward is Solution A. Let us collaborate on how to roll this out."

The display of empathy and collaborative language softens the delivery of competence, neutralizing the target's tendency for resistance. This strategy ensures that competence is perceived as a shared resource, not a unilateral challenge to the target's position.

Managing Social Processing Primes:

Furthermore, the external social environment influences the target's decision-making process. Exposing men and women to cues associated with the **male gender role** causes both genders to process persuasive messages more thoughtfully and carefully. Also, cues associated with the **female gender role** cause both genders to process messages less carefully.

- **If you need critical buy-in (long-term secure agreement):** Maintain a setting and language style (e.g., highly analytical, data-driven, assertive discussion structure) that primes for careful, thoughtful processing, regardless of the target's gender.
- **If you need rapid, low-scrutiny agreement (peripheral agreement):** The environment and language style should favor a less critical processing style.

Understanding how to control these **social primes** allows the persuader to pre-emptively manage the depth of thought the target applies to the proposal, mitigating the resistance that comes from either too much scrutiny or misplaced deference.

4. The Linguistic Shield: Reducing Cognitive Friction

Language that is overly complicated, abstract, or filled with jargon creates cognitive friction. This friction forces the target to slow down and exert effort, increasing the probability of resistance. The brain seeks to avoid unnecessary work.

The Strategy of Concrete Vocabulary:

Effective mitigation uses simple, concrete vocabulary and direct verbs.

- **Abstract words** require the target to perform translation. They must connect the general term ("optimization," "synergy") to a specific action. This work creates resistance.
- **Concrete words** (names, dates, numbers, facts) require no translation. They deliver the emotional and intellectual impact directly.

Research in language processing confirms that specific word patterns correlate reliably with psychological states. The persuader must act as a precise linguist, ensuring every word choice is functional, not decorative.

When writing or speaking, focus on the immediate effect:

- **Avoid:** "We need to operationalize the new structure."
- **Use:** "We need to sign this contract by 3 PM Thursday."

Sentiment Mapping in Resistance: When the target begins to resist, use the research principles of **sentiment analysis** (as used in computer science) instinctively. Listen for their negative keywords: *unfair, risky, unnecessary, worried.* These keywords reveal the target's current emotional state and the precise objection that must be reframed. If they use "risky," you know their resistance is rooted in anxiety and loss aversion. You must immediately respond with a frame of security, not a frame of profit.

5. Using Loss Aversion as a Counter-Weapon

Resistance mitigation is powerfully achieved by leveraging **Loss Aversion.** The pain of losing something is measurably stronger than the pleasure of gaining an equivalent item. Humans are overwhelmingly motivated to avoid loss.

The Strategy of Guaranteed Loss:

If the target is resisting your proposal (compliance), you must frame non-compliance as a guaranteed, immediate, and quantifiable loss.

- **Do not frame:** "If you agree, you will gain X." (Potential gain)
- **Frame:** "If you *do not* agree right now, you guarantee the loss of Y." (Guaranteed loss)

The "loss" must be specific and immediate. It could be the loss of the current discount, the loss of an exclusive opportunity (Scarcity), or the loss of their current perceived status.

Example Application: When a target hesitates at the final signature, you use loss aversion: "I respect the need to deliberate. But let me be absolutely clear about the cost of that deliberation. If we do not execute this document today, the materials cost increases by 7%, which means you immediately lose $3,500 from your budget. That is a guaranteed, immediate loss you accept by simply waiting."

This technique collapses the decision window, activating the **Fear of Missing Out (FOMO).** The psychological pain of accepting that immediate loss, the regret of non-action, compels the target to make a rapid, impulsive decision to avoid the cost. This immediate action bypasses further rational analysis.

Mitigating resistance is the final layer of control in the persuasion process. It ensures that the target's psychological defenses are either lowered by empathy and transparency (Pre-Emption) or bypassed entirely by the emotional force of loss aversion and strategic reframing.

The last chapter of this book is a final resource list. It provides the full compendium of sources for all the verified principles, studies, and concepts used throughout this book. This ensures that every technique presented is grounded in documented science, providing true value and the maturity necessary for secure, repeatable influence.

CONCLUSION

THE ARCHITECTURE OF GUIDED CHOICE

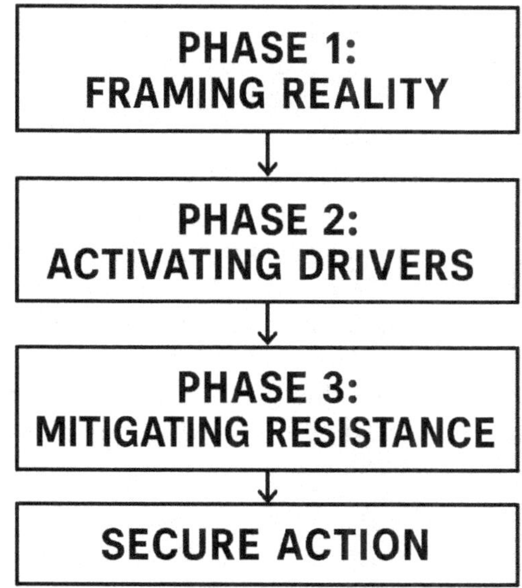

We have covered the foundational mechanics of influence. This first book establishes that persuasion is not a mystical talent or a natural gift. It is an act of engineering. It relies on precise, verifiable knowledge of the human decision structure. We learned how to move past chance and into the realm of consistent, repeatable outcomes. The core lesson is this: success depends on controlling the environment, not arguing with the target's opinion.

Every principle detailed across the last six chapters builds toward a single, unified system. This conclusion synthesizes those concepts. It provides a complete map of how to apply the techniques of Framing, Activating, and Mitigating in a fluid, real-world sequence. We confirm that every successful persuasive action begins with two non-negotiable prerequisites: an understanding of **Subjective Reality** and the ability to diagnose the target's **Decision Profile**.

I. The Foundation: Subjective Reality and Predictable Error

The entire system rests on a single truth, often overlooked: people do not act on facts. They act on their unique version of reality, which they build themselves. This **subjective reality** is the core belief system that dictates their behavior in the world.

A persuader's objective is never to destroy this subjective reality. That creates resistance. Instead, we must simply modify the information inputs so that the target's reality naturally leads to our desired outcome. This is possible because the mind uses **cognitive biases**: systematic, predictable errors in judgment.

These biases are the levers of influence. They exist because the brain needs shortcuts, or heuristics, to make faster decisions. The brain possesses only a limited capacity for information processing, leading to the condition known as **bounded rationality**. When you subtly increase the pressure on the target, by limiting time or introducing a minor distraction, you force their mind to bypass slow, analytical thought. They default to the fast, intuitive, biased system, making them highly susceptible to our framing techniques.

Synthesis of Framing (Chapter 2):

The goal of framing is to make the decision seem inevitable and rational within the target's subjective world.

1. **Anchoring and Contrast:** You must always set the initial high reference point first. The **Anchoring Effect** ensures that this first number dictates the acceptable range for subsequent negotiations. You then exploit the **Contrast Principle** by immediately following the high anchor with the desired request. The desired request seems disproportionately small and acceptable, making the decision easy.
2. **Confirmation Bias as Alignment:** Never fight a target's beliefs. Instead, ensure your request validates their existing self-image. If the target believes they are a responsible planner, you frame the decision as "the responsible, logical extension of sound planning." This alignment requires less evidence for acceptance and avoids triggering their internal defenses.

This foundational stage ensures the target sees the decision not as a new risk, but as a logical, easy step consistent with who they already are.

II. The Activation Sequence: Using the Six Drivers

Once the decision environment is correctly framed, you must activate the target's innate behavioral rules. These are the six core compliance drivers. They are highly effective because they tap into deeply ingrained societal expectations and psychological needs. They are most powerful when used in sequence.

1. Secure Long-Term Commitment (Consistency):

Commitment is secured by engineering inner responsibility. The act must be **active, public, and effortful**. If the target takes a small, initial step that requires effort, they attribute the action to their own will, not to your pressure or a large reward. This self-attribution makes the change permanent.

- **Application:** Ask for a written opinion, a small task, or a public verbal agreement on a principle, not the final contract. This small step changes their self-image. The final action then becomes an act of consistency, which is psychologically easy to sustain.

2. Build Rapport (Liking and Reciprocity):

Liking provides the emotional foundation for agreement. Use genuine compliments and find genuine, subtle similarities to build immediate connection. Simultaneously, you activate **Reciprocity** by giving a concession or a small, unexpected gift first.

- **Application:** The "Door-in-the-Face" technique perfectly integrates these. You offer a large, expectedly rejected request first. When you concede and ask for the small, desired request, the target feels obligated to reciprocate your perceived concession by agreeing to the smaller demand. This psychological weight of obligation is difficult to ignore.

3. Provide Safety (Social Proof and Authority):

Humans seek safety in numbers and expertise. **Social Proof** is activated when the target is uncertain. They look to the actions of others to guide their own behavior. **Authority** provides the justification for deference.

- **Application:** Show the target that others, especially others they identify with (a strong social bond), have already taken the action. This reduces the perceived risk. Simultaneously, use the symbols of **Authority**, composure, titles, an organized environment, to ensure the target sees you as a safe, knowledgeable source of guidance. Controlled composure is a powerful, non-verbal symbol of competence that triggers automatic deference.

4. Force Immediate Action (Scarcity and Urgency):

This is the final, powerful trigger for instant compliance. You must collapse the decision window to prevent rational analysis from interfering.

- **Application:** Use **Scarcity** by visibly limiting availability (time or quantity). This rarity increases the perceived value, regardless of actual worth. Crucially, you couple this with **Loss Aversion**. The pain of losing an item or opportunity is stronger than the pleasure of gaining it. You must frame non-compliance as a guaranteed, immediate, quantifiable loss (losing the current price, losing the exclusive slot). This triggers the **Fear of Missing Out (FOMO)** and compels the target to act impulsively to avoid regret.

III. The Strategy of Precision: Mapping and Mitigating

The greatest risk to this system is resistance. Resistance is neutralized through precision, which requires correctly diagnosing the target's decision profile.

1. Diagnosing the Processing Route (Mapping):

You must know if the target prefers the **Central Route** (critical analysis of facts) or the **Peripheral Route** (reliance on authority, emotion, or social cues).

- **Application:** Observe their justification style and the nature of their questions. If they are Central processors, your narrative must be dense with specific, verifiable evidence. If they are Peripheral processors, your narrative should emphasize Social Proof and the symbols of Authority. Remember that **gender role primes** influence processing depth: cues emphasizing careful, high-stakes thought lead both men and women to process messages more thoroughly.

2. Contextual Reframing (Controlling Narrative):

Resistance provides a gift: the target's negative frame (e.g., "This is risky"). You neutralize this by immediately changing the frame's category. If they say "risk," you reframe it as "security." If they say "expense," you reframe it as "necessary investment." This instantly aligns the decision with their Confirmation Bias, making their objection irrelevant.

3. Neutralizing Social Resistance (The Communality Buffer):

If you are a woman asserting high competence, you may encounter predictable resistance, particularly from male targets.

- **Application:** Deploy the **Communality Buffer**. This involves intentionally tempering the assertive communication with displays of warmth, empathy, and collaboration. This language of shared goals neutralizes resistance by ensuring competence is perceived as a shared resource, not a challenge to their status.

The Shift in Perspective

This book has provided a verified, systematic methodology. You now understand that you do not need to be the loudest or the most aggressive person in the room. You need to be the most precise. You are the architect who frames reality, sets the anchors, and activates the internal drivers. The entire process is built on making the desired choice the path of least cognitive resistance.

The techniques covered here, from Anchoring to Loss Aversion, are powerful tools for securing action and commitment. But they are only half the battle. They focus on *what you say* and *how you structure the presentation.*

The next book, **Magnetic Charisma**, shifts the focus entirely to *who you are* and *how you exist* in the room. We move from the conscious management of language to the non-verbal control of perception. We explore how charisma creates effortless influence through the silent transfer of emotion, the strategic use of touch (haptics), and the control of micro-behaviors that establish authority before you speak. The systems of Covert Persuasion rely on accurate diagnosis; the systems of Magnetic Charisma rely on accurate projection. We move now to master the silent signals that dictate trust, authority, and attraction.

REFLECTION QUESTIONS

We have reached the end of the first book. Before moving on to the skills of charisma and non-verbal projection, we must pause. The lessons of Covert Persuasion, that choice is manufactured through predictable biases and structured compliance drivers, must move from simple information to ingrained habit.

True mastery of influence is not just knowing these concepts. It is integrating them into your natural, daily interactions. Use the following questions to reflect on the systems we have discussed. The objective is to personalize the material, mapping it onto your own past experiences and preparing for your next interactions.

Section 1: Diagnosing Reality and Cognitive Bias

The foundation of persuasion is understanding that everyone lives in a **subjective reality** built on their own perceptions, not objective facts. Every decision is filtered through this personal lens.

1. Think about a recent time you failed to convince someone of an idea. Did you fight their **subjective reality**? If you could rewind, what is one non-negotiable belief they hold about themselves (e.g., "I am financially conservative" or "I am a creative risk-taker")? How would you reframe your argument to confirm that belief instead of challenging it?

2. Identify a recurring number or concept in your life: a salary target, a project timeline, or a budget. Now, practice the **Anchoring Effect**. What is the highest, justified reference point you could introduce *before* stating your real target? How does simply stating the high number change your own perception of your final desired outcome?
3. Recall a complex decision you made recently. Were you rushed or distracted? Did you rely on a fast shortcut instead of slow, careful analysis (an example of **bounded rationality**)? How could a persuader have used that moment of distraction to introduce a proposal that exploited your need for speed?
4. The **Halo Effect** dictates that a single positive trait (like composure or neatness) can grant you general trustworthiness. What is the one non-verbal trait you project most consistently right now? Does it align with the persona you want (Authority, Warmth, or Competence)?

Section 2: Activating the Core Compliance Drivers

The six compliance drivers (Reciprocity, Commitment, Social Proof, Liking, Authority, Scarcity, and Consistency) are universal mechanisms for securing action. Mastery means knowing which one to deploy and when.

5. **Commitment and Consistency** requires you to secure an **active, public, and effortful** initial step. Identify a goal you have for the next month that requires the support of another person (a co-worker, a partner, or a client). What is the smallest, most effortful action you can ask them to take *today* to commit to that goal? How would you ensure this action is public, making them feel accountable to maintain consistency?
6. **Reciprocity** is activated by providing an initial, unexpected concession or gift. Think about a recent interaction where you felt obligated to someone. What did they give you that created that pressure? Now, plan an immediate, small, personal favor you can offer a potential contact in the next 48 hours to create a sense of unsolicited obligation on your terms.
7. **Social Proof** is most effective when the target is uncertain. Identify two distinct social groups you belong to: one professional, one personal. Who are the **social arbiters** in each group? If you wanted to start a new trend or idea, which arbiter

would you approach first, and how would their adoption influence the rest of the group?

8. The most potent trigger for instant action is **Loss Aversion**, where the fear of losing is stronger than the desire to gain. Describe a proposal you need to make soon. How can you shift the language to frame non-compliance as a guaranteed, quantifiable loss (e.g., losing the current discount, losing their status) rather than framing compliance as a potential gain?

Section 3: Mitigating Resistance and Control

Resistance is a signal that your framing or timing is wrong. Mitigation requires pre-emption and reframing the target's objection.

9. Think of a common objection you hear often (e.g., "It costs too much," "It is too risky," or "We do not have the time"). Practice the **Firebreak Strategy** (Chapter 6). Write out how you would:
    - Acknowledge the objection neutrally.
    - Validate the target's responsibility.
    - Immediately refactor the context (e.g., expense becomes investment; risk becomes mitigation).
10. **The Communality Buffer** is essential for tempering competence with warmth, particularly when a woman is asserting a high-status position . If you needed to present a non-negotiable directive, how would you start and end your statement using language of shared goals and collaboration to neutralize potential status resistance ?
11. **Linguistic Resonance** suggests using simple, concrete language reduces cognitive friction. Take a paragraph from a recent email you sent that contained abstract or overly formal language. Rewrite it using only concrete nouns, action verbs, and specific numbers, ensuring the message is delivered without demanding extra cognitive work from the reader.

BOOK TWO

MAGNETIC CHARISMA: NON - VERBAL RESONANCE

INTRODUCTION
TO MAGNETIC CHARISMA

You see them walk in. They might not be the loudest person. They might not be the highest-ranking. Yet, when they speak, people lean in. When they ask for something, they get it. This is not luck. This is **Magnetic Charisma**.

Charisma is often seen as a gift, something you are born with. That idea is wrong. Charisma is a technical skill. It is a precise, learned display of silent signals that tell others exactly how competent, trustworthy, and authoritative you are. While the first book focused on the strategy of language, what you say, this book focuses on the strategy of projection: who you are.

Think of it this way: your words handle the logic. Your body handles the trust. If your posture or your gaze communicates anxiety, your perfectly crafted argument from Book 1 collapses. Charisma makes your physical presence align exactly with your verbal authority. It is the ability to communicate intense trust and competence without needing to speak a word.

The Message Before the Mouth Moves

In any social setting, judgments start long before the conversation does. This initial assessment is entirely based on non-verbal behavior. These silent signals determine whether a connection is started, maintained, or ended.

In a professional setting, non-verbal cues directly influence how people perceive your status and ability. You can assert your expertise endlessly. If your physical presence communicates hesitation, people will trust the non-verbal message over the verbal one. Charisma ensures your presence backs your words.

The Quiet Power of Non-Verbal Bias: Non-verbal behavior is particularly potent because it functions below the level of conscious thought. It can systematically favor or put down certain social groups or ideas without anyone realizing it.

Imagine a subtle, continuous change in proximity, a hesitant blink, or a slight change in the rhythm of your gaze. These micro-behaviors can signal superiority or submission. The important point is that the strong effects of non-verbal bias occur even when the bias remains **inaccessible to conscious awareness.** The target feels the impression, they feel that they should trust you or follow you, but they cannot consciously challenge or analyze that feeling.

Since this influence is silent and unconscious, it is a subtle but powerful form of social control. If you strictly regulate your posture, your breathing rhythm, and your eye contact, you can consistently implant specific, positive perceptions, like reliability and composure, directly into the target's mind.

To acquire magnetic charisma, you must master three main areas: controlled presence, emotional transfer, and physical connection.

1. Controlled Presence: Status Through Stillness

The first pillar of charisma is managing how you simply exist in a space. This is **Controlled Presence**. It requires regulating your physical stillness, your movement, and your posture to project specific, high-value traits.

The Antidote to Anxiety: We know from Book 1 that negative feelings, like anxiety, heavily influence social judgments. When a person feels anxious or unsure, they naturally look for someone who projects certainty. Controlled presence is the immediate antidote to that anxiety. It means eliminating all nervous energy.

- Avoid excessive hand movements.
- Stand or sit with symmetrical, open posture.
- Maintain a steady, measured gaze.

When you move deliberately and speak calmly, you communicate that you are in total control of yourself and the environment. This projection of composure instantly addresses the target's need for safety.

Posture as a Status Signal: Your posture is an immediate, non-verbal signal of your status. An open, symmetrical posture communicates confidence and authority. You are taking up space without apology. Conversely, slumping or a guarded posture signals lower status or defensiveness. By ensuring your physical bearing is always open and intentional, you communicate to the target that you are a competent, safe resource.

This strategy immediately activates the **Halo Effect**. The target infers positive traits like trustworthiness and capability from the single, impressive trait of your composure. This positive social judgment accelerates the foundational trust needed for any persuasion attempt. When you project high composure, you reduce the target's need for an impulsive, biased social assessment. They defer to your calm authority.

2. Emotional Transfer: The Contagion of Charisma

Charisma is not static. It is infectious. The process is known as **Emotional Contagion**, the automatic transfer of emotional states from one person to another. This emotional transfer is an essential part of charismatic and transformational leadership. Charismatic people deliberately and continuously project specific, positive emotional states, such as optimism, focused energy, or calm confidence, onto those around them.

The Charismatic Cascade: Studies in real organizations have tracked this process. Researchers found that a leader's charisma actually **cascaded down** to followers over time. The followers of a charismatic figure eventually became perceived as more charismatic themselves. This confirms that charisma is a set of observable behaviors and emotional states that can be adopted and replicated throughout a social system.

This emotional momentum is crucial for large-scale influence. You do not need to individually motivate a hundred people. You need to emotionally charge a dozen key individuals, whose energy then spreads the emotional state to the rest of the group.

The Role of Self-Monitoring: Emotional contagion works faster or slower depending on the target's personality. We use the trait of **self-monitoring** to diagnose this susceptibility.

- **High Self-Monitors:** These people are highly aware of social cues. They are more susceptible to both positive and negative emotional contagion. They are fast emotional amplifiers. They quickly absorb and reflect the projected state, whether it is urgency or enthusiasm. They are excellent for **immediate emotional mobilization** because they instantly accept the charismatic state.
- **Low Self-Monitors:** These individuals are less focused on adapting their behavior to social cues. They might resist immediate emotional shifts. However, once they finally adopt the behaviors and attitudes of the charismatic figure, those traits become stable and internalized parts of their persona. They provide the **structural support and stability** for the group long-term.

Your strategic plan must use these differences. You focus on emotionally charging the high self-monitors first, who then disseminate the perception of charisma to the broader, slower-moving group.

3. Haptic Connection: The First Language of Trust

Beyond what we see, what we *feel* can dictate trust. **Haptics**, or strategic touch, plays a fundamental role in building immediate connection. This sense of touch is the first form of communication developed in infancy.

Babies explore the world and their own identity through touch. This physical interaction is crucial for developing self-identity, security, and emotional well-being. Research confirms that a lack of physical touch, or tactile deprivation, is even associated with low confidence and learning problems.

The appropriate, strategic use of touch can therefore dramatically **accelerate the building of trust**. By identifying socially acceptable, low-risk haptics, the persuader can quickly establish a fundamental sense of security and connection. This physical resonance bypasses the slow, verbal process of building rapport.

The Calibration of Touch: The use of haptics requires careful calibration. Appropriate touch must be contextually and culturally relevant. A handshake is the universal professional haptic. Its firmness, dryness, and duration should communicate composure. Other forms of touch, such as a brief, supportive touch on the forearm, may be appropriate in closer social settings.

The goal is to use low-risk, physical contact to tap into the fundamental human need for security. This brief physical connection creates a rapid bond, making the target feel immediately safer and more secure in your presence.

4. The Unifying Role of Humor

Charisma uses humor as a sophisticated social tool. Humor serves powerful social functions, from unifying people to creating division. We focus exclusively on the unifying functions.

Identification Humor: This function is essential for building magnetic appeal. **Identification humor** builds group cohesion by appealing to a set of shared values and common perceptions. This happens when a joke or story addresses a slight violation of a social expectation, confirming that everyone present shares the same baseline understanding of the world.

When the target laughs at the same social pattern or violation, they confirm alignment on core values. This mutual reinforcement strengthens the relationship and reduces uncertainty about the other person.

Increased Attraction and Cohesion: A perceived good sense of humor is an invaluable social resource. People naturally gravitate toward those who project a positive, engaging vibe. Positive humor styles are strongly associated with desirable traits, including high self-esteem and extroversion, and greater relationship satisfaction.

Crucially, **shared laughter** increases interpersonal attraction, enhances group cohesion, and assists in conflict resolution. By employing positive, unifying humor, the persuader projects both psychological stability and social desirability. This increases attraction and facilitates stronger connections.

The System of Projection

Magnetic Charisma is the art of precise, non-verbal projection. It is the ability to send silent signals of competence, authority, and warmth that are absorbed by the target below conscious awareness.

The techniques we have discussed, from Controlled Presence to Emotional Contagion, must become automatic. They ensure that the target perceives you as trustworthy, capable, and stable before the verbal exchange even begins. This non-verbal foundation makes all the persuasive techniques from Book 1 exponentially more effective. You guide the choice with your words, but you secure the trust with your presence.

The following chapters will break down these elements into precise, actionable steps. We will detail how to use posture to **Broadcast Authority**, how to manage your emotional state to **Transfer Energy** into the group, and how to **Build Trust** using strategic haptics. Mastery of the silent signal is the key to effortless social influence.

CHAPTER 1

BROADCAST AUTHORITY: MASTERING NON - VERBAL RESONANCE

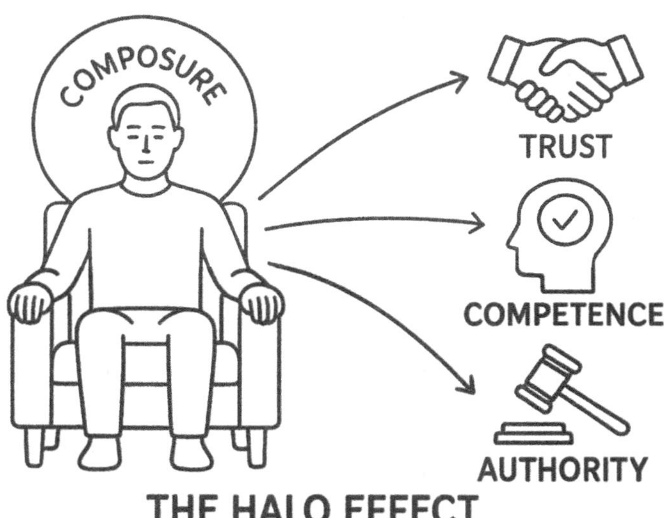

Charisma is a shield and a weapon. It protects you from doubt and guides the target toward trust. This defense and offense are built on mastering your **non-verbal resonance**. This means controlling the subtle signals that your body sends out constantly. These signals tell people how competent, calm, and authoritative you are.

The simple fact is this: you cannot decide what someone thinks of you, but you can entirely control the information they use to form that thought. Non-verbal behavior is particularly subtle, but it is a highly influential form of social messaging. It dictates the initial evaluation of your presence, and that evaluation is often absorbed below the conscious level.

To broadcast authority, you must manage three core non-verbal elements: stillness, posture, and gaze. These elements work together to project competence and composure, which immediately mitigates the target's natural anxiety and activates the powerful psychological shortcut known as the **Halo Effect**.

The Power of Stillness: Composure as Competence

In Book 1, we learned that people often rely on quick, biased judgments, especially when they feel anxious or uncertain. When a target is under pressure, they look for safety. The most immediate sign of safety and competence is stillness.

Stillness communicates that you are in control of yourself. Nervous energy, fidgeting, rapid head turning, or excessive hand gestures, sends a signal that you are not in control of the situation. This instantly undermines any verbal claim of expertise you might make. Conversely, a measured, still demeanor projects a quiet confidence.

This controlled presence serves as a powerful antidote to the target's anxiety. If you are calm, the target feels their own anxiety subside in your presence. They begin to attribute your composure to competence. This is how the **Halo Effect** starts: the single positive trait of composure causes the target to infer other positive qualities, like trustworthiness and knowledge, without needing evidence.

Actionable Stillness:

1. **Eliminate Micro-Jitters:** Become aware of small, nervous habits, tapping feet, clicking pens, or adjusting clothing repeatedly. These are energy leaks that broadcast anxiety. Practice standing or sitting with minimal movement, allowing your weight to settle completely.
2. **Controlled Transitions:** When you move, move with intention. Do not drift from one point to another. Stand up slowly. Sit down deliberately. Each movement should look like a planned action, not a nervous reaction.
3. **Vocal Control:** The voice is a primary non-verbal tool. When people are nervous, their pitch often rises and their speaking rate increases. To project composure and authority, you must maintain a low, resonant pitch and speak slightly slower than the average conversational pace. Use strategic pauses. A pause, when controlled, signals that you are thoughtful and certain, not hesitant.

Stillness ensures that the target's first, rapid judgment of you is always positive. They see competence and safety, which makes them highly receptive to your message.

Posture: The Non-Verbal Status Marker

Your posture is an immediate, non-verbal representation of your status and confidence. It dictates how much psychological space you feel entitled to take up.

Openness and Symmetry: The projection of authority requires two key features in posture: openness and symmetry.

- **Open Posture:** Avoid crossing your arms tightly across your chest or holding objects directly in front of your body like a shield. Openness communicates that you are receptive, confident, and not defensive.
- **Symmetrical Posture:** Standing or sitting with balanced shoulders and a straight back communicates physical control and mental stability. An asymmetrical posture, like leaning heavily on one side, can suggest casualness or a lack of focus.

The Space Dynamic: Posture is often measured by how effectively you utilize the space you are in. When you are standing, keep your feet planted firmly, slightly apart. When you are sitting, use the back of the chair fully. This physical settling communicates that you feel completely at ease and entitled to your space.

People subconsciously defer to those who communicate physical entitlement. By constantly practicing an open, symmetrical posture, you project a deep-seated confidence. This signals that you are not simply acting competent; you genuinely believe in your own competence.

Gaze Control: The Directed Focus

The eyes are the most powerful tool for non-verbal control. Your gaze dictates engagement, sincerity, and power dynamics.

The Measured Gaze: A nervous or subordinate gaze darts around the room, avoiding direct contact. This communicates distraction or anxiety. The gaze of authority, conversely, is controlled and measured. It is directed precisely at the target.

You do not need to stare intensely, which can feel aggressive. You need to maintain consistent, intentional eye contact throughout key parts of the interaction.

- **Establish Connection:** Use strong eye contact when you are initiating a major point or asking a critical question.

- **Signal Sincerity:** Maintain eye contact during the first sentence and the final sentence of your argument to bracket the point with sincerity.
- **Release Pressure:** In longer conversations, naturally break eye contact every few seconds by looking briefly at the side or the target's hands, then returning your gaze. This provides a brief moment of relief for the target and makes your eye contact feel intentional, not aggressive.

The Gaze of Validation: Gaze control is also essential for activating the **Liking** principle (Chapter 3). By maintaining steady eye contact while the target is speaking, you non-verbally communicate high levels of interest and respect. You are signaling that their words are the most important input in the environment. This validation increases their liking and trust in you.

The Architecture of Charismatic Projection

Broadcasting authority is the fusion of these three elements. It is the ability to project composure, competence, and confidence simultaneously.

1. **Pre-Emptive Trust:** By rigorously controlling stillness and posture, you ensure that the target's initial, rapid judgment is favorable. This pre-emptive trust makes them more receptive to your verbal message. Non-verbal behavior can be systematically biased to favor certain stimuli, and by controlling your presence, you become that favored stimulus.
2. **The Halo Effect Activation:** Your projected composure acts as the single positive trait that triggers the **Halo Effect**. The target infers that you are reliable, trustworthy, and knowledgeable because you look and sound calm. This effect significantly reduces the evidential burden you must meet later in the conversation.
3. **The Social Prime:** Your controlled presence helps set the social prime of the environment. A controlled, formal, and authoritative demeanor helps set the environment for thoughtful processing, which is often associated with the **male gender role prime**. If you require a thoughtful, long-term commitment, your non-verbal cues must support a setting where careful analysis is expected.

Mastering non-verbal resonance means treating your body as a precision instrument. Every muscle movement, every pause, and every adjustment of your gaze must be intentional. This controlled projection is the silent language of authority. It is the necessary preparation for the emotional and social influence we will discuss next.

The following chapter, **Transfer Energy: Inciting Emotional Contagion in Groups**, builds on this foundation. We move from controlling your own singular presence to actively transferring your emotional state to those around you. We will show you how to use enthusiasm, confidence, and urgency to mobilize groups and amplify your charisma through **Emotional Contagion**.

CHAPTER 2

TRANSFER ENERGY: INCITING EMOTIONAL CONTAGION IN GROUPS

FOCUSED ENTHUSIASM

The last chapter dealt with being calm. It taught you how to look steady, composed, and absolutely in control. But charisma is more than just standing still. It needs movement. It needs feeling. It needs energy.

Magnetic charisma is the ability to change the feeling of a room. It shifts the atmosphere instantly. It is not enough to simply manage your own emotional state. You must actively manage the emotions of everyone around you.

This ability to spread feeling is called **Emotional Contagion**. Think of it as an emotional current. If you project confidence, optimism, or a focused sense of urgency, that feeling automatically passes from you to the people you are talking to. This process is a fundamental, measurable mechanism of social influence. Researchers recognize it as a key ingredient in charismatic leadership. A truly magnetic person intentionally guides the collective feeling of the group. They know that a group unified by a shared emotion is much stronger than a group merely unified by an idea.

The charismatic individual is a highly efficient emotional broadcaster. They send out a clean signal. The target absorbs and then mirrors that emotional state. This ensures the collective mood aligns perfectly with the persuader's objective.

The Infectious Nature of Charisma

Charisma does not stop with the first person you meet. It creates a **cascade effect** that spreads through a social structure. This is how a small number of influential people can change the direction of a large organization or group.

Studies looking at leaders and their followers in large organizations found that the leader's charisma actually spread down through the ranks over time. This is interesting: followers of a charismatic leader eventually started to be seen as more charismatic themselves.

What does this tell us? It proves charisma is a set of observable behaviors. It is not an innate, magical quality. It is a persona, a set of emotional and physical actions that can be adopted and replicated throughout the entire group.

When you project focused energy and confidence, the influence does not stop at one person. It initiates a sequence of emotional replication. Your influence spreads without you needing to work continuously on every individual.

The Power of Behavioral Modeling: The emotional transfer ensures that the target starts acting like you. They absorb your confident posture, your calm way of speaking, and your positive emotional outlook. This behavioral modeling reduces anxiety across the group. It increases overall cohesion. People feel safer when they act the way the charismatic leader acts. They feel they are following an established, successful pattern.

Diagnosing Who Will Move Fastest

Emotional contagion works at different speeds for different people. To maximize the spread of your energy, you must quickly figure out how susceptible a person is to social cues. We rely on the personality trait known as **self-monitoring** to do this.

High Self-Monitors: The Amplifiers

High self-monitors pay intense attention to social cues. They are constantly adjusting their behavior to fit the situation. Because of this focus, they are more susceptible to both positive and negative emotional transfer.

- **Their Role:** High self-monitors are your immediate emotional amplifiers. They rapidly absorb and reflect the emotion you project, whether it is extreme urgency or deep enthusiasm. They are perfect for **immediate emotional mobilization**. If you need the group excited about a major deadline right now, focus your energy projection on the high self-monitors first. They quickly disseminate the feeling to everyone else. They are the fastest way to change a group's mood.

Low Self-Monitors: The Stable Foundation

Low self-monitors are just the opposite. They are not highly concerned with adapting their behavior to social cues. They value consistency between their internal beliefs and their external actions. They want their actions to match their identity.

- **Their Role:** Low self-monitors resist immediate emotional shifts. They are slower to be influenced by emotional contagion. But this slowness is a hidden strength. Once a low self-monitor finally adopts the behaviors and attitudes of the charismatic figure, those traits become stable. They are fully internalized. They provide the **structural support** for the group long-term. They are not the fast responders, but they are the reliable ones.

The Strategic Plan: A successful charisma strategy uses a dual approach to manage both groups.

1. **Fast Charge:** Focus immediate, clear energy projection (enthusiasm, high confidence) toward high self-monitors for quick activation and broad spread of the emotional state.
2. **Long-Term Internalization:** Use consistency arguments and secure small commitments (Book 1) with low self-monitors. Their gradual, steady adoption ensures the new behaviors and emotional states become a permanent, stable part of the group's identity.

This combined strategy ensures you get both instant energy mobilization and reliable, long-term support for your charismatic persona.

How to Engineer Emotional Projection

Emotional transfer does not happen by accident. It must be engineered through precise, non-verbal delivery. You must project your intended emotion with absolute clarity and complete consistency.

The Constant Projection of Calm: Composure is the most important foundation for emotional transfer. We know that the target's anxiety often triggers irrational social judgments. Your controlled presence is the way to counteract that anxiety. By projecting extreme calm, you activate the **Halo Effect**. The target infers that your composure comes from a source of deep competence and control, which makes them trust you instantly.

Projecting Focused Energy: Charisma needs enthusiasm, but it must be focused. Energy that is all over the place suggests anxiety. Energy that is directed and clear suggests passion and control.

- **Vocal Delivery:** Vary your tone and volume with intention. Speak slightly slower than average for authority, but increase the inflection and volume when describing the specific *benefit* of the action. This communicates that the outcome is exciting and valuable.
- **Gestural Pacing:** Use intentional, controlled hand gestures to emphasize your main points. Avoid small, nervous, repetitive movements. Use large, open hand gestures when talking about a shared objective or the future of the group. This physically reinforces the idea of collaboration.

Managing Different Affective States: Emotional contagion also depends on the target's existing emotional baseline. Some people naturally have a high **trait positive affect** (generally optimistic). Others have a high **trait negative affect** (generally critical or skeptical).

- **Positive Targets:** When engaging people who are already generally positive, amplify your enthusiasm. They will absorb and reflect it easily. This creates a positive feedback loop.
- **Negative Targets:** When talking to targets who are generally skeptical, focus more on projecting unwavering, calm authority. This addresses their skepticism with stability and competence. Do not try to overwhelm them with enthusiasm they may resist.

Humor as the Ultimate Emotional Unifier

Humor is one of the most effective tools for managing and transferring emotion in a group. It serves crucial social functions, mostly by unifying people.

Identification Humor: This specific type of humor is essential for building magnetic appeal. **Identification humor** builds group cohesion because it appeals to a set of shared values and common perspectives.

When a story or joke succeeds, it means everyone present confirms they share the same underlying social expectation or norm. This shared experience is a powerful emotional adhesive.

- **The Shared Value Check:** Shared laughter acts as a psychological test. If the target laughs at the same social violation or pattern, they confirm they align on core values. This mutual reinforcement strengthens the connection and reduces uncertainty about the other person.

The Positive Social Resource: A perceived good sense of humor is an invaluable resource in any social context. People naturally look for those who project a positive, engaging feeling. Positive humor styles are strongly associated with highly desirable personality traits, including high self-esteem and extroversion. People who use positive humor generally experience greater satisfaction in their relationships.

- **Emotional Stability:** By consistently using positive, unifying humor, you project both psychological stability and social desirability. This increases attraction and makes stronger connections easier. You must strictly avoid hostile, negative, or self-deprecating humor styles, as these suggest internal conflict or low self-esteem.

Cohesion and Conflict Resolution: The emotional value of shared laughter is supported by research showing that it increases interpersonal attraction, enhances group cohesion, and helps resolve conflicts. When people laugh together, they form stronger bonds and develop a **shared identity** that is bigger than their individual differences.

- **Creating Rituals:** Inside jokes often develop from unique group dynamics, reflecting common experiences. The charismatic leader can actively encourage these shared humorous rituals. They serve as reliable, quick ways to re-establish trust and affection, reinforcing the group's relationship and shared perspective.

The Synthesis of Energy Transfer

Transferring energy is the key to mobilizing others. It ensures the group is emotionally prepared to accept the structural arguments and decisions from Book 1.

1. **Project Composure:** Start with stability. Your calm presence is the necessary foundation that mitigates the target's anxiety and activates the Halo Effect.

2. **Target Susceptibility:** Identify high self-monitors for quick emotional spread. Use low self-monitors for long-term structural commitment.
3. **Use Humor:** Employ identification humor to confirm shared values, build group cohesion, and increase attraction.
4. **Sustain the Cascade:** Ensure your enthusiastic energy is focused and projected consistently through controlled voice and intentional gestures. This guarantees the emotional state spreads and lasts.

This mastery of emotional transfer ensures that when you move to the next stage, building deep, physical trust, the target is already emotionally receptive and unified with your purpose. This prepares the ground for the immediate, deep connection that only strategic haptics can provide. The next chapter, **Build Trust: Employing Strategic Touch and Presence**, details how to use the earliest form of human communication to accelerate rapport beyond what words can achieve.

CHAPTER 3

BUILD TRUST: EMPLOYING STRATEGIC TOUCH AND PRESENCE

Charisma must be physically grounded. It must feel real, immediate, and safe. This physical grounding is achieved through two complementary systems: strategic touch and the calculated exchange of personal information. If Book 1 taught you how to secure a choice, this book teaches you how to secure the person.

We begin with the most immediate and fundamental form of human connection: **haptics**, or touch. The strategic use of touch can accelerate trust faster than words ever could. It bypasses the slow, verbal process of building rapport. It connects directly with the target's most basic psychological need for security.

I. Haptics: The First Language of Trust

Of all the ways humans communicate, touch is the first one developed in infancy. Long before we form words, we explore our own bodies and the environment through touch. This physical interaction is crucial. It is the beginning of achieving self-identity, security, and overall well-being.

The psychological impact of touch cannot be overstated. Research even links tactile deprivation, a lack of physical touch, to developmental issues. It can lead to learning problems and a lack of trust or confidence later in life. Touch is tied directly to our foundational needs for safety and identity.

Because touch is so fundamental, the appropriate, strategic use of haptics can dramatically speed up trust building. A brief, intentional physical connection instantly establishes a fundamental sense of security between two people. This immediate physical resonance bypasses the slow, careful verbal process that logic requires.

The Necessity of Safety: Since touch is tied to deep-seated feelings of security, its use must be safe, appropriate, and low-risk. Any misuse of haptics instantly triggers an alarm in the target, and the connection is broken. The persuader must treat touch as a precision instrument, not a blunt tool.

The Controlled Handshake: The handshake is the universal professional haptic. It is the only guaranteed, appropriate opportunity for physical connection in most formal settings. You must maximize its effect.

1. **Symmetry and Firmness:** The handshake should be firm, but never crushing. It should feel symmetrical, indicating a balance of power. Avoid the submissive, "dead fish" hand. Avoid the aggressive, overly dominating grip.
2. **Dryness and Warmth:** Ensure your hand is clean and dry. A cold, clammy hand broadcasts anxiety and physical discomfort. This immediately compromises the Halo Effect you established with your composure. A warm, dry hand signals calm physical stability.
3. **Duration and Gaze:** The handshake should last approximately three seconds. During this contact, maintain direct, steady eye contact. This combination of physical contact and focused gaze communicates sincerity and intent. It locks the trust signal in place.

Low-Risk, Intentional Contact: Beyond the handshake, other forms of touch must be used carefully, adhering strictly to cultural and social norms. In appropriate social settings, a brief, supportive touch on the forearm or a gentle touch on the shoulder can be used to emphasize a shared point or to signal congratulations.

This intentional physical contact reinforces the idea of partnership. It communicates: "We are literally in this together." This creates an immediate physical bond that makes the target feel safer and more secure in your presence.

II. Controlled Presence: Non-Verbal Bias and Trust

The physical environment, including your body, is constantly influencing the target. This subtle, pervasive influence is achieved through **non-verbal bias**.

Non-verbal behavior sends signals about competence and status. This bias happens even when the target is not consciously aware of it. The target is influenced by the message, but they cannot consciously challenge or argue against it. This makes your physical presence a potent, subtle form of social control.

Maintaining Stillness and Composure: We return to the concept of Controlled Presence (Chapter 2). It is the foundation for haptics. Your body must project unwavering composure.

- **No Nervous Leakage:** Eliminate nervous gestures, fidgeting, excessive self-touch, or restless movement. These signals are leaks that broadcast anxiety.
- **The Calm Gaze:** Maintain a measured, intentional gaze. Nervous eyes dart around, broadcasting low status. A controlled gaze signals that you are focused and fully in command of the situation.

This projected composure serves a vital psychological function: it mitigates the target's internal anxiety. When the target sees your calm, controlled presence, it triggers the **Halo Effect**. They infer trust, competence, and reliability from your stability alone. This favorable initial social judgment accelerates trust and makes them more receptive to any subsequent request.

III. Strategic Disclosure: The Architecture of Charm

Once physical presence and basic haptics establish foundational trust, you must accelerate the relationship verbally. This is achieved through the strategic exchange of personal information, or **self-disclosure**. Charm is essentially the calculated use of vulnerability to create intimacy and attraction.

Frequency Over Intimacy: The goal of early self-disclosure is to rapidly establish familiarity and closeness. Research shows that **disclosure frequency** is the factor that predicts familiarity and closeness, provided the disclosures are perceived as appropriate.

The volume of shared details is more important than the depth of those details in the early stages. You must maximize the number of minor, low-stakes disclosures to build familiarity quickly. Sharing simple, non-intimate facts, your favorite type of coffee, a mundane weekend hobby, a funny anecdote about your travel routine, builds a dense foundation of connection.

The Danger of Premature Intimacy: While intimate disclosure *can* increase closeness, it carries a high risk. If disclosure is too intimate too soon, it often **reduces social attraction** because the target perceives it as inappropriate. Sharing deep, raw, or vulnerable details before a foundation of trust is established makes the target uncomfortable. They sense a lack of boundaries, and they retreat.

- **Rule of Thumb:** Intimate details (core fears, professional failures, deep relationship anxieties) must be reserved until the target explicitly signals a reciprocal readiness for that level of depth. The risk of sharing personal depth often outweighs the potential benefit in the early stages of a relationship.

IV. Narrativity: The Entertainment Value of Charm

It is not just *what* you say, but *how* you say it. The way you present personal information is key to building magnetic attraction. People appreciate being entertained.

Narrativity and Attraction: Disclosure narrativity, the telling of personal information as a structured story, increases perceived closeness and social attraction. This positive effect happens because the narrative format possesses **perceived entertainment value**. Simple, dry facts are uncompelling. Stories capture attention and create emotional connection.

The Strategy of Framing Mundane Facts: You must frame all personal information, even basic details, as engaging, short narratives rather than simple statements.

- *Instead of:* "I lived in Boston." (Dry Fact)
- *Try:* "I lived in Boston for five years. That city taught me that five minutes of rain can instantly turn into two feet of snow. I learned to keep an extra coat in the trunk, a lesson I learned the hard way after one miserable, freezing walk." (Narrative, short, entertaining, reveals minor detail).

This technique ensures the interaction remains compelling. By consistently delivering entertainment value, you maximize the psychological impact and increase social attraction toward you, the source of the story.

V. The Calibration Test: Diagnosing Appropriateness

The effects of self-disclosure are critically constrained by the target's **perceived appropriateness.** This metric is subjective. You must actively monitor the target to ensure the level of intimacy is correct.

Reciprocal Disclosure as a Gauge: The best sign of appropriateness is **reciprocal disclosure**. A target who matches your level of disclosure, in both frequency and depth, implicitly confirms that your current level of intimacy is acceptable.

The Testing Sequence:

1. **Slight Deepening:** You should test the boundary of intimacy gently. Offer a disclosure that is slightly deeper than the one you offered previously.
2. **Observe Response:** Watch the target's reaction. Do they match the depth of your new disclosure? Do they offer an equally personal, though non-intimate, detail? Do they ask a follow-up question that indicates comfort?
3. **Adjust:** If the target matches the depth, you may proceed to the next level of intimacy. If the target retreats, redirects the conversation, or offers only short, closed answers, the intimacy level was inappropriate. You must immediately reduce the depth of future disclosures back to a safe, frequent level.

This calibration process ensures you build closeness rapidly without triggering the alarm bells of inappropriate vulnerability. You maintain social attraction while escalating the relationship toward greater trust.

VI. Charisma in Non-Physical Spaces

The structure of charm changes when the physical presence is removed, such as in text messages or virtual correspondence. Here, haptics and immediate non-verbal signals are absent.

Research confirms that in the virtual medium, attraction relies almost entirely on "words, charm, and seduction" and not on physical presence. The entire burden of building rapport and signaling attraction shifts to the linguistic architecture of the message.

Linguistic Charisma in Text:

- **Narrative Focus:** Narrativity becomes even more crucial. Every message must be crafted to provide entertainment value and familiarity.
- **Emotional Density:** Since tone of voice is absent, you must ensure the language itself conveys the emotional state (e.g., using specific, active words, or light, positive humor).
- **Frequency Management:** Frequent, low-stakes digital communication maintains familiarity. It keeps you present in the target's mind without demanding deep cognitive effort.

When physical tools are gone, linguistic mastery must compensate. You must use the principles of framing and concrete language (Book 1) to build a compelling virtual persona that ensures the target's continued interest.

The Physical and Psychological Blend

Building trust through strategic presence is the blending of the physical and the psychological. It begins with the simple, fundamental act of touch: a signal that communicates security and identity deep within the target's mind. It is sustained by projecting unwavering, controlled composure and competence. It is accelerated by the calculated flow of personal information, maximizing frequency and narrativity while meticulously managing appropriateness.

Charisma is the system that ensures the target feels safe, entertained, and seen. This deep, non-verbal connection makes the persuasive ideas you introduce feel less like external demands and more like shared, safe opportunities. The following chapter, **Shape Perception: Using Posture to Signal Competence**, will return to the visual cues, detailing exactly how specific body positions and movements can permanently install perceptions of capability and status in the target's mind.

CHAPTER 4

SHAPE PERCEPTION: USING POSTURE TO SIGNAL COMPETENCE

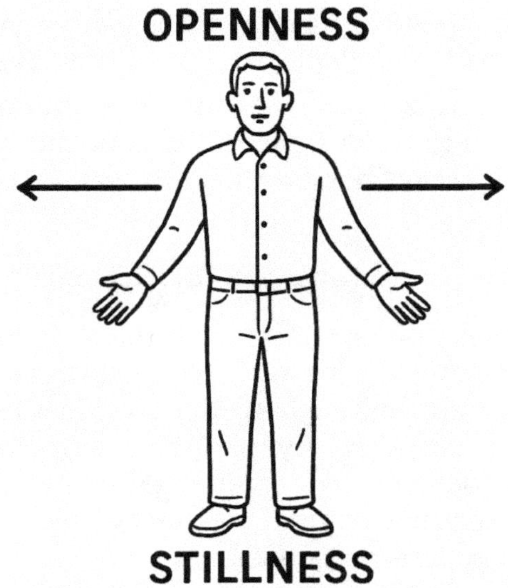

Your body is your silent resume. It speaks louder than your title and faster than your words. This silent communication is the foundation of magnetic charisma. If Book 1 taught you how to frame a choice, this chapter teaches you how to **frame yourself**. You must learn to control the visual information you send out. This information shapes the target's perception of your competence, your authority, and your general status.

The way you stand, sit, and move dictates how much psychological space you feel entitled to occupy. This perception influences power dynamics in any setting, from a negotiation to a simple social exchange. When you master your non-verbal signals, you are not simply looking confident. You are actively installing the perception of competence directly into the target's mind.

The Silent Power of Non-Verbal Bias

Charisma relies heavily on a unique feature of non-verbal communication: it is a particularly subtle form of social influence. The messages are often sent and received **below conscious awareness**.

This is crucial. Since the influence operates outside the target's conscious thought, they cannot consciously challenge or argue against the impression created. They simply accept the feeling that you are trustworthy or capable. Non-verbal behavior can be systematically biased, making people favor or put down certain social cues or individuals. By rigorously controlling your posture and gaze, you become the favored cue. You inject specific, positive perceptions into the target's mind without triggering their critical analysis.

The goal is to move the perception of competence from an abstract idea to an unquestioned reality.

Posture as Architectural Status

The first step in shaping perception is mastering your posture. Posture is a physical marker of status. High-status posture communicates that you are settled, prepared, and fully in command of your current space.

1. The Mechanics of Openness:

High competence is signaled through **openness**. You must avoid closed or guarded postures. These include tightly crossed arms, clasping hands directly in front of your body, or using objects (like a coffee cup or portfolio) as a shield. Closed posture signals defensiveness, anxiety, or low status.

Open posture means allowing your chest and torso to face the target without obstruction. Your arms should be relaxed, resting loosely at your sides when standing, or placed on the arms of the chair when sitting. This openness communicates that you are receptive, confident, and have nothing to hide. You are physically inviting connection, which lowers the target's psychological barrier.

2. Symmetry and Stability:

Authority is often signaled through **symmetry**. A balanced posture communicates physical control and mental stability. An asymmetrical posture, like leaning heavily on one foot, resting your entire weight on one elbow, or constantly twisting your body, suggests a lack of focus or casualness.

When you are seated, sit back completely, using the full depth of the chair. Keep your shoulders level. When you are standing, plant your feet firmly, distributing your weight evenly. This physical stability communicates that you are grounded and prepared for whatever happens next. You are not waiting to spring into action. You are already in command.

3. The Space Dynamic:

Posture dictates how much **space** you claim. People subconsciously defer to those who communicate physical entitlement. An effective persuader occupies their space completely, whether it is a small chair or a large platform.

This physical settling communicates that you are entirely at ease and believe you belong exactly where you are. This signals competence and influences power dynamics in professional settings. By physically claiming your space, you non-verbally assert status, and that non-verbal assertion is accepted much faster than a verbal declaration would be.

Stillness: The Composure Antidote

Composure is the single most effective trait for triggering the **Halo Effect**. The Halo Effect is a social bias where a general positive impression is inferred from a single positive trait. The trait you control is composure.

The Threat of Anxiety: As we have established, anxiety and negative feelings are deeply linked to social judgments. When a target is anxious, they make quick, biased assessments to find safety. They look for someone who projects certainty and stability. Nervous energy, fidgeting, adjusting clothing, scratching, or rapid head movements, broadcasts anxiety. This instantly undermines your verbal claims.

The Value of Stillness: Controlled **stillness** communicates that you are in total control of yourself. Your calm demeanor acts as the antidote to the target's anxiety. When the target sees your composure, they feel their own internal anxiety begin to subside. They begin to infer that your lack of nervousness is a result of deep competence and control over the situation. They think, "This person is calm because they know exactly what to do."

Actionable Stillness Techniques:

1. **Eliminate Energy Leaks:** Become ruthlessly aware of all micro-movements. Use self-monitoring to identify habits like pen-clicking, toe-tapping, or hair-touching. Eliminate these leaks.

2. **Controlled Hand Gestures:** When you use your hands, use them only to punctuate key ideas. When you are not actively gesturing, return them to a neutral, open position (e.g., resting lightly on the table or at your sides). Intentional movement is good; reactive movement is bad.
3. **Vocal Pacing:** The voice must support the stillness of the body. To project authority, you must maintain a low, resonant pitch. Speak slightly slower than the average conversational pace. Use strategic pauses before and after key phrases. A pause, when controlled, signals that you are thoughtful and certain, not hesitant.

Stillness ensures the target's first, rapid social judgment, made under conditions of potential anxiety, is a positive one. You have successfully activated the Halo Effect and accelerated the trust process.

Gaze Control: The Directed Focus of Authority

Your eyes are the most immediate indicator of your intent, sincerity, and status. Gaze control is essential for directing attention and signaling authority.

The Measured Gaze: A nervous or low-status gaze avoids direct contact or flits rapidly around the room. This communicates distraction or a lack of conviction. The gaze of authority, conversely, is controlled and measured. It is directed precisely at the target.

You do not need to maintain continuous, unbroken eye contact. That can feel aggressive and threatening. You need to maintain **intentional** eye contact during key communicative moments.

1. **Establishing Connection:** Make clear, consistent eye contact when you initiate a major point, ask a critical question, or introduce a major proposal.
2. **Signaling Sincerity:** Maintain eye contact during the final sentence of your argument. This brackets your point with a clear signal of sincerity.
3. **Releasing Pressure:** In longer exchanges, look briefly to the side, perhaps at an object or a note, and then return your gaze to the target. This brief release of pressure is intentional. It makes the target feel that your eye contact is a deliberate act of focus, not a nervous tic.

Gaze and Validation: Gaze control is also essential for activating the **Liking** principle. By maintaining steady, attentive eye contact while the *target* is speaking, you non-verbally communicate a high level of interest and respect. You are signaling that their input is the most important element in the environment. This validation increases their liking and trust in you, reinforcing the connection established by your composure.

The Subtlety of Non-Verbal Bias

We must address the fact that this influence is often outside the target's awareness. This is the definition of **non-verbal bias**.

Non-verbal bias means that exposure to your controlled presence contributes heavily to the *attitudes and beliefs shared within a culture*. If you consistently project high-status competence, you are not just influencing one person's perception of you. You are subtly reinforcing a general cultural ideal that links composure and stillness to power.

The Danger of Leaks: Because non-verbal behavior is so influential, any leak, any moment of unguarded anxiety or weakness, can damage the perception quickly. The mind absorbs the unconscious signal as truth faster than the conscious word. If your posture collapses slightly at a moment of stress, the target receives the signal: *insecurity*. This is why continuous self-monitoring is essential. You must maintain the controlled presence regardless of the internal conversational pressure.

The Role in Power Dynamics: Research confirms that non-verbal communication is vital in professional settings, specifically influencing power dynamics and perceptions of competence. By using open posture and stillness, you assert non-verbal power. This assertion, because it is silent and subtle, is often accepted without challenge.

The Integrated Visual Signal

Shaping perception is the intentional fusion of stillness, posture, and gaze. It moves influence from the realm of verbal debate to the realm of physical reality.

1. **Stillness** projects composure, neutralizing anxiety.
2. **Open Posture** claims status and signals confidence.
3. **Controlled Gaze** directs attention and signals authority and sincerity.

This integrated visual signal ensures that the target's first, non-verbal impression of you is one of high competence and stable authority. You have established a foundation of trust that makes all subsequent persuasive arguments easier to deliver and more readily accepted.

This mastery of self-projection prepares us for the social dimension of charisma. The following chapter, **Unify Groups: Leveraging Humor for Social Cohesion**, details how to use humor not just for entertainment, but as a precise psychological tool to confirm shared values, increase attraction, and create a powerful sense of group identity.

CHAPTER 5

UNIFY GROUPS: LEVERAGING HUMOR FOR SOCIAL COHESION

Charisma is the glue that holds people together. It is what moves a room full of separate individuals into a single, unified group that is easy to talk to and guide. The fastest, most effective tool for this unification is **humor**.

Humor is not just about making people laugh. It is a calculated, sophisticated social tool. It manages the dynamics of a group, confirms shared values instantly, and raises the level of attraction between people. If you use humor correctly, you are not just telling a story. You are running a psychological test. You confirm that the target and the entire group share the same basic outlook on the world. This mutual agreement builds powerful, immediate cohesion.

The Unifying Purpose of Laughter

Humor serves several critical social functions. It can be unifying or it can be divisive. A charismatic leader focuses exclusively on the unifying functions. These are mainly **identification** and **clarification**.

1. Identification Humor: Checking the Shared Beliefs

Identification humor is the process that builds group cohesion. It works because participants share a common perception or value that is revealed when the joke is told. When everyone laughs at the same joke, it often happens because the joke points out a minor, shared violation of a social expectation or norm.

- **The Vetting Process:** Shared laughter confirms alignment. If the target laughs at the same social violation, they confirm that they share your core values and baseline expectations. This mutual reinforcement strengthens the relationship instantly and reduces any uncertainty about the other person. This shared perspective creates a solid, shared worldview, which is what cohesion needs most.
- **How to Apply It:** Use humor that references a small, shared inconvenience or a common expectation that applies to everyone in the room. For example, making a light joke about a well-known technical problem that the whole team faces. By making a shared joke about the external problem, you confirm that everyone agrees on the norm (the problem is annoying) and that you are all together in the experience. This confirmation is powerful, and it raises attraction toward you.

2. Clarification Humor: Reducing Uncertainty

Humor also helps to **clarify expectations**. This function reduces uncertainty about others by appealing to common values. When a joke successfully clarifies expectations and reinforces mutual understanding, it quickly establishes what is "normal" and acceptable within the group.

In tense or awkward social settings, using unifying humor can quickly clarify what is expected and reinforce mutual understanding. When anxiety is high, humor provides a quick, acceptable moment of shared identity. This allows the group to relax and reset its emotional tone.

Humor and Personal Attraction

A perceived good sense of humor is an incredibly valuable social resource. People naturally look for those who project a positive and engaging feeling in conversation.

The Link to Emotional Health: Humor styles are deeply connected to personality and psychological health. **Positive humor styles**, humor that is gentle, inclusive, and unifying, are strongly linked to desirable traits like high self-esteem, cheerfulness, and high satisfaction in relationships.

- **Projecting Stability:** By consistently using positive, unifying humor, the charismatic person projects **psychological stability** and **social desirability**. They signal that they are emotionally secure. This makes them highly attractive and makes strong connections easier to form. You must strictly avoid humor that is hostile, negative, or self-deprecating, as these actions often suggest internal conflict or low self-esteem. Your humor must lift the group's mood, not criticize it.

The Therapeutic Value: The emotional value of shared laughter is supported by research showing that **shared laughter** increases attraction between people, enhances group cohesion, and even helps resolve conflicts. When people laugh together, they form stronger bonds and develop a **shared identity** that is greater than their individual differences.

Creating Shared Rituals

The goal is to move beyond a moment of laughter to create lasting bonds. This is best achieved by creating shared rituals and "inside jokes."

Inside Jokes as Identity Markers: Inside jokes develop naturally from unique group experiences, reflecting common ground and bringing joy to the group. A charismatic person can actively encourage the development of these shared humorous rituals. They serve as fast, reliable ways to re-establish trust and affection, especially when tension is present. The shared perspective reinforces the group relationship and confirms mutual loyalty.

- **How to Apply It:** When a funny, accidental moment happens, a small, shared error, or an unusual clash of ideas, do not let the moment pass. Reference it again later in the conversation or the next day. This repeated reference elevates the small moment into a **shared ritual**. This ritual confirms mutual loyalty and affection quickly and establishes a specific group memory.

Humor and the Non-Verbal System

Humor cannot exist in isolation. It relies entirely on the non-verbal foundation established earlier in this book.

Stillness and Delivery: Humor needs perfect **composure** for delivery (Chapter 2). If you deliver a joke with nervous energy, the anxiety compromises the effectiveness of the humor. The audience senses the instability and does not laugh with the content. Controlled stillness and a measured vocal pace ensure the humor is perceived as intentional and stable.

Emotional Contagion: Humor is a highly effective tool for initiating positive **Emotional Contagion** (Chapter 3). If you project genuine amusement, the people in the group who are easily influenced by social cues (high self-monitors) will immediately absorb and reflect that emotion, spreading the positive feeling throughout the room.

The Halo Effect: The positive feeling created by unifying humor reinforces the **Halo Effect**. The target now connects the positive emotional state (joy, connection) directly with your presence (composure, competence), which further cements the inference of trustworthiness and reliability.

Humor and Cultural Sensitivity

Humor is a universal tool, but its specific application must be highly sensitive to the group's specific context. The humor must align with the group's norms and values.

- **Targeting the Norm:** Identification humor works best when it targets a minor violation of an *external* norm or expectation, something outside the group that everyone can agree upon. Never use humor that targets a group member or that uses humor meant to divide or criticize. That instantly destroys group cohesion and trust.
- **The Unspoken Agreement:** The successful use of humor proves your social intelligence. It proves you understand the target's baseline values without them having to state them explicitly.

The Cohesive Force

Humor is the cohesive force of charisma. It moves a collection of individuals from separate self-interest into a unified, emotionally connected group. By employing identification humor, you confirm shared values, reduce uncertainty, and raise attraction. This creates a powerful shared identity that makes the group highly receptive to your influence.

The final step in mastering charisma is integrating all these concepts, posture, emotional transfer, touch, and humor, into a single, effortless persona. The next chapter will provide the final synthesis of these non-verbal strategies, detailing how they function together to create truly magnetic, lasting influence.

CONCLUSION

THE INTEGRATED CHARISMATIC PERSONA

This book was about making your presence count. We started by looking past the idea that charisma is some accidental gift. It is clear now that it is a set of specific, learned behaviors. We have moved entirely from the strategy of argument (Book 1) to the strategy of projection. You learned how to control your body, manage emotional energy, and connect with people instantly.

The person who possesses true magnetic charisma is not doing these things one at a time. They are blending them all into one seamless, powerful presence. This chapter brings together the core systems we built: **Controlled Presence, Emotional Transfer, Haptics, and Strategic Disclosure.** The entire point is to create a persona that generates trust and makes people want to listen to you, long before you even get to the logical proposal.

I. The Silent Authority: Establishing Pre-Emptive Trust

The first, non-negotiable step of charisma is making sure your body projects competence and stability. You must master **Controlled Presence.**

The Body's Hidden Message: Your body is speaking constantly. It is sending out signals that influence the target's judgment, and most of the time, the target is not even aware they are receiving the message. These non-verbal cues determine how others see your authority and competence faster than anything you could say in an introduction. If your body broadcasts nervousness, fidgeting, restless movement, or avoiding eye contact, it instantly cancels out any claim of expertise you might make.

The Fusion of Stillness and Symmetry: Authority is not loud. It is still. It is symmetrical.

1. **Stillness is Self-Control: Stillness** communicates that you are in total control of yourself. This controlled demeanor is the best possible way to counter the target's anxiety. When people are nervous, they look for safety. Your visible calm makes them feel safe. This safety triggers the **Halo Effect**: the target infers deep competence and trustworthiness from the single trait of your composure.
    - *Action Check:* Practice eliminating energy leaks. Every unnecessary micro-movement, such as pen clicking, shifting weight constantly, is a loss of psychological status. Be still.
2. **Posture Claims Space: Posture** must be open and balanced. You must avoid closed positions like tightly crossing your arms or using objects as a shield. By standing or sitting with an open, symmetrical posture, you non-verbally claim your space. This silent assertion of status is often accepted without challenge. This gives you an immediate, non-verbal advantage that supports your entire interaction.
3. **The Intentional Gaze: Gaze control** signals both focus and sincerity. A measured, intentional gaze directs the target's attention and reassures them that you are fully present. This focus is a form of non-verbal validation, which instantly increases their liking and trust in you.

Controlling your presence ensures that the target's initial, rapid judgment is positive. You secure pre-emptive trust, making the target receptive before the conversation even begins.

II. The Emotional Engine: Mobilizing the Group

Charisma is not static. It spreads like a wave. The second stage involves actively moving your desired emotional state to those around you through **Emotional Contagion**.

The Charismatic Cascade: Studies show that charisma spreads from leaders to followers, who then become perceived as more charismatic by others. This proves that charisma is a set of reproducible behaviors, not an innate personal trait. You are not just managing your own mood. You are mobilizing the emotional energy of the group to align with your objectives.

Targeting the Energy Transfer: To maximize this spread, you must quickly figure out how the target processes emotion. We use the **self-monitoring** trait to categorize this:

1. **High Self-Monitors: The Amplifiers:** These people are quick to absorb and reflect the emotion you project (enthusiasm, confidence). Use them for **immediate emotional mobilization** to spread the mood rapidly throughout the group.
2. **Low Self-Monitors: The Foundation:** These people are slower to shift, but once they adopt a behavior or emotional state, it becomes fully internalized and stable. Focus on them for **long-term structural stability**.

By directing focused, positive energy toward the right people, you guarantee the collective mood aligns with your goals.

The Emotional Unifier: Humor: The most efficient tool for emotional unification is **Identification Humor**. This specific type of humor builds cohesion because it appeals to a set of shared values.

- **Actionable Result:** Shared laughter confirms that the entire group agrees on core values and expectations. This consensus reduces uncertainty, builds deep cohesion, and makes everyone like each other more. By using positive, unifying humor, you project psychological stability and social desirability, making yourself a desirable social resource.

III. The Trust Accelerator: Haptics and Disclosure

The charismatic persona must feel physically and psychologically connected. This is achieved through calculated physical signals and the calculated flow of personal information.

Haptics: The Security Signal: Touch is the most basic form of human communication, tied directly to our earliest sense of security and identity. The appropriate, strategic use of haptics, especially a firm, intentional handshake, can accelerate trust faster than any language. This physical resonance taps into the target's fundamental need for safety.

Strategic Disclosure: Intimacy by Design: Charm uses the calculated exchange of personal information, or **self-disclosure**. You must prioritize **disclosure frequency** over **disclosure intimacy** in the early stages to quickly establish familiarity.

- **The Danger:** Sharing deep, intimate details too early is often seen as inappropriate and can instantly *reduce* social attraction.
- **The Solution:** Use **Narrativity**. Frame minor personal facts as engaging, short stories that offer perceived entertainment value. This maintains interest and builds familiarity without the risk of inappropriate vulnerability.

You must continuously monitor the target's **reciprocal disclosure** to gauge appropriateness. If they match your depth, you can proceed. If they retreat, you must immediately pull back. This process ensures you build closeness rapidly while protecting social attraction.

IV. The Integrated System and Flexibility

The charismatic persona must be flexible enough to handle predictable social resistance.

The Need for Flexibility: Remember the lessons from Book 1: successful communication requires the ability to switch influence styles. You must be able to move from **push energy** (assertion, direction) to **pull energy** (collaboration, inquiry) at the right moment. The charismatic person is not locked into one single style.

The Communality Buffer: A woman asserting high competence may face predictable social resistance from male targets. This is not about the idea; it is about status.

- **Mitigation:** The solution is the **Communality Buffer**. This involves intentionally blending assertive communication with displays of warmth, empathy, and collaboration. This use of shared language neutralizes resistance by making competence feel like a shared resource, rather than a challenge to the target's status.

The Social Prime Control: Your projected composure and demeanor help set the social context. If you project a very formal, analytical approach (the male gender role prime), both men and women will process your messages more thoughtfully. If you require rapid, non-critical agreement, you must set a context that encourages less careful processing. The charisma you project controls the depth of the target's thought.

V. Conclusion: The Launch Platform

Charisma is the launch platform for influence. It ensures the target is emotionally stabilized, socially unified, and psychologically receptive. Your stillness and composure secure pre-emptive trust. Your shared humor and energy mobilize their emotion. Your careful disclosure creates deep, personal connection.

The target attributes your success to your magnetic personality, not to your careful technique. They feel safe, unified, and ready to follow.

We now transition from the visual and non-verbal to the precise control of the word. The next book, **Linguistic Influence**, will give you the tools to secure commitment using scientifically grounded principles of language. We move from the physical control of the self to the precise psychological control of the message.

REFLECTION QUESTIONS

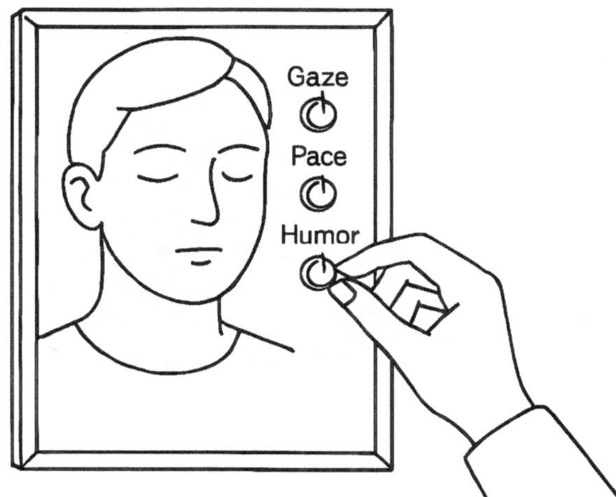

We have just finished the second book. We moved from the architecture of choice to the architecture of self. You now understand that charisma is not an accident; it is a technical output of mastering your non-verbal signals, managing your emotional energy, and initiating connections through the earliest forms of human communication.

Before we move on to the precision of language in Book 3, you must internalize these lessons. The skills of charisma, stillness, haptics, and emotional transfer, must become automatic reflexes. Use these questions to personalize the material, mapping the concepts onto your own interactions. The objective is to make the charismatic persona effortless and consistent.

Section 1: Controlled Presence and Authority

Charisma begins with control over your own body. Your presence broadcasts competence and authority. This is the foundation that triggers the **Halo Effect**, making people trust you instantly.

1. **Stillness Audit:** Recall the last three times you felt genuinely nervous in a conversation: a presentation, a job interview, or a difficult social exchange. What **energy leaks** did you exhibit? (e.g., did you shuffle your feet, play with your ring, or rush your words?) Now, describe three specific, actionable steps you can take to replace that nervous energy with intentional, controlled stillness in your next high-stakes interaction.

2. **Posture and Status: Posture** dictates how much psychological space you claim. When you are sitting in meetings, are you typically closed (arms crossed, leaning away) or open (symmetrical, hands resting on the table)? How does changing your posture to a more open, symmetrical position, physically claiming the space, change your internal feeling of authority? Practice standing in an open, powerful posture for two minutes every morning this week.
3. **Gaze Control:** Think about a recent time you had to deliver a critical point. Did you maintain continuous, intentional eye contact throughout the key phrase? If not, where did your gaze shift? For your next serious conversation, plan the exact three moments (e.g., the introduction, the critical number, the final question) where you will hold your gaze for an extra count to project absolute certainty and sincerity.
4. **The Halo Effect:** The **Halo Effect** infers competence from composure. If you walked into a room where everyone felt anxious, how would your current non-verbal presence, your vocal pace, your stillness, your open posture, act as the single calming trait that causes them to instantly trust your competence?

Section 2: Emotional Transfer and Social Cohesion

Charisma spreads emotional energy. It unites separate people into a cohesive, receptive group.

5. **Emotional Contagion:** When you enter a room, what is the *single* emotional state you project most consistently right now (e.g., focus, caution, or enthusiasm)? Now, identify a **high self-monitor** in your network: someone who quickly picks up and reflects the mood of the room. For your next group interaction, plan how you will direct your intended emotional state (e.g., focused optimism) specifically toward that high self-monitor to initiate the **charismatic cascade**.
6. **Humor and Shared Values: Identification Humor** is used to confirm that a group shares the same beliefs. Think about a social norm or expectation that your current work or social group finds slightly ridiculous. Plan a light, short story that gently references this norm violation. How would the **shared laughter** from that joke confirm that everyone agrees on the norm, reducing uncertainty and strengthening your **shared identity**?

7. **The Stability of Low Self-Monitors: Low self-monitors** are slow to move but provide long-term stability once committed. Identify a low self-monitor in a group you lead or belong to. What structural, verifiable evidence (data, verifiable consistency) must you provide them to ensure they internalize the new behavior, rather than simply adopting it superficially?

Section 3: Haptics, Disclosure, and Connection

Building trust requires physical and psychological closeness. This must be managed with absolute precision.

8. **Haptics as Security: Touch** is the first language of human security. Recall your last handshake. Was it symmetrical, firm, and intentional, or was it rushed? For your next handshake with a new contact, focus entirely on two things: ensuring your hand is warm and dry (to avoid broadcasting anxiety), and maintaining steady eye contact for the full three seconds of contact. How does this controlled focus change your sense of psychological presence during the introduction?
9. **Disclosure Frequency vs. Intimacy: Disclosure frequency** drives early closeness, but intimacy must be controlled. Name two minor, low-stakes facts about yourself (e.g., a mundane hobby, a favorite local coffee shop). Now, frame those two facts as short, engaging narratives that provide **entertainment value**. Commit to sharing these two narratives frequently this week to build rapid familiarity without the risk of inappropriate vulnerability.
10. **The Calibration Test:** If you were to slightly deepen your personal disclosure (e.g., sharing a minor professional challenge you overcame), how would you monitor the target's **reciprocal disclosure** to determine if the intimacy level was appropriate? What are the specific non-verbal or verbal signs that would signal you need to immediately **retreat** from that level of intimacy?

BOOK THREE

NLP MIND CONTROL:
THE SCIENCE OF FRAMING AND BELIEF

INTRODUCTION

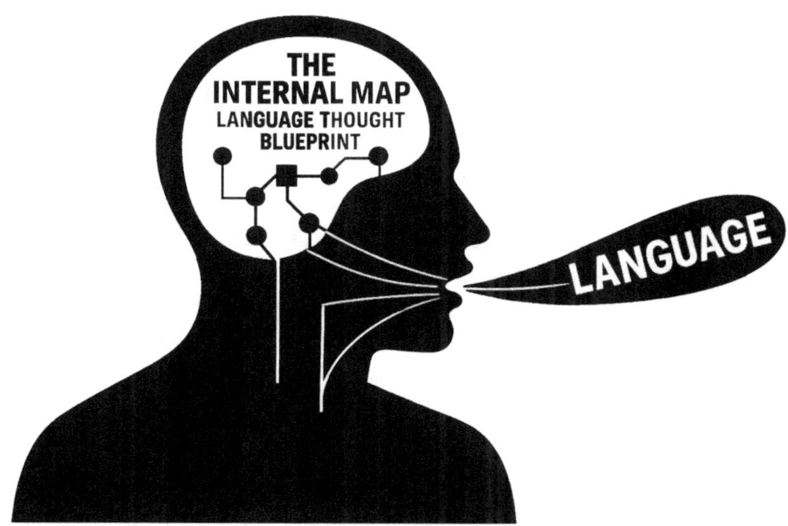

Do you ever watch someone walk into a room and instantly command attention? They get the contract. They secure the commitment. They leave others feeling energized and ready to follow. This ability is not simply a natural gift. It is a practiced skill. It rests on specific, verifiable knowledge of how the human brain works.

What if you could consistently predict the reactions of the people around you? What if you knew exactly what to say to move a choice from "maybe" to "yes"?

This book is the definitive answer to those questions. It is not an abstract theory or a philosophical treatise on success; it is a dedicated study in **predictive human behavior**, built upon the science of language, neurology, and decision-making. We are moving beyond the realm of hopeful persuasion and entering the domain of **verifiable influence**.

For too long, the true mastery of influence has been shrouded in misconception, luck, or charismatic appeal. For the serious student of human interaction, for the individual committed to achieving excellence through communication, this obscurity is unacceptable. You are not looking for chance; you are looking for a lever. This book hands you that lever. It is the culmination of decades of research, refining the art of influence into a **verifiable science**: the science of **Advanced Neuro-Linguistic Programming (NLP)**.

The NLP Crossroads: Defining Advanced Mastery

The acronym **NLP** stands at a fascinating crossroads, pointing to both the foundational human influence field of **Neuro-Linguistic Programming** and, in a completely separate discipline, the computational field of **Natural Language Processing**. This book is dedicated to the former, positioning it as the **master blueprint for human influence**.

The pioneers of NLP gave us a brilliant, early map for understanding how language, neurology, and behavior interconnect. This foundational work, introducing powerful concepts like **Anchoring, Reframing, and Strategy Elicitation**, provided essential insights that first mapped out how our language shapes our internal experience and, consequently, our results. This is the positive legacy we honor and build upon.

However, any field that promises mastery must be prepared to face rigorous scrutiny. The early models of Neuro-Linguistic Programming, while groundbreaking in their time, often relied heavily on analogy and non-specific observations. They presented powerful techniques but occasionally anchored those techniques to metaphorical, and sometimes scientifically outdated, concepts of brain function.

This reliance on anecdotal success, rather than empirical validation, is what fueled the skepticism from the wider scientific community, which, in some cases justly, pointed to a lack of rigorous, independently repeatable evidence for all of its claims.

This challenge is precisely where **Advanced NLP** begins. We do not ask you to simply *believe* in a system; we ask you to **master the science that now validates, refines, and supersedes** the original models. We strip away the unverified, anecdotal elements and fuse the powerful, actionable core of NLP with the most reliable findings from **cognitive science, behavioral economics, and contemporary linguistics**.

This book is the next evolution of NLP, providing the evidence-based framework that allows you to confidently apply techniques with the expectation of a **predictive outcome**.

The computational field of **Natural Language Processing** has, in its own way, validated the core premise of human influence: by using computers to analyze vast datasets of human speech and text, it has confirmed that **specific word patterns reliably correlate with specific psychological states and purchasing decisions** (Loftus & Palmer, 1974). Our goal is to take that computational precision and make it an intuitive human skill for you. You are moving from a rudimentary map to the GPS-level accuracy of modern science, ensuring that every linguistic and non-verbal maneuver you make is backed by verifiable data on how the human brain processes information and makes decisions.

The Three Pillars of Predictive Influence

The ability to "consistently predict reactions" is possible only because human decisions are fundamentally **algorithmic**. They are not random acts of free will in a vacuum; they are the result of highly systematic **cognitive shortcuts** developed by the brain to conserve energy. To master influence is to master the architecture of these shortcuts. Our methodology in Advanced NLP is built upon three irrefutable scientific pillars:

Pillar 1: Behavioral Economics and The Architecture of Framing

For decades, the assumption in much of the business and psychology world was that human beings were essentially rational actors, *Homo economicus*, who made decisions based on a clear, logical assessment of utility. **Behavioral Economics** shattered this myth.

The pioneering work of Nobel laureate Daniel Kahneman and Amos Tversky, specifically their development of **Prospect Theory**, provided the mathematical proof that decision-making is **framing-dependent** (Kahneman & Tversky, 1979). Their most critical finding is the principle of **Loss Aversion**: the finding that the pain of a loss is psychologically approximately **twice as powerful** as the pleasure of an equivalent gain.

This principle is the ultimate verifiable lever of influence, and it is the scientific refinement of the classic NLP technique of **Reframing**.

In traditional NLP, Reframing taught you to change the *meaning* of an event by shifting its context. In **Advanced NLP**, we use the mathematics of Prospect Theory to consciously frame our proposals. We stop focusing solely on what a person *gains* by saying "yes" (which only taps into 1x motivational power), and we strategically focus on what they **lose or miss out on** by saying "no" (which activates 2x motivational power).

Consider a classic sales scenario:

- *The Legacy Frame (Gain-Focused):* "If you sign this contract, you will **gain** three new clients in the first month."
- *The Advanced NLP Frame (Loss-Aversion Focused):* "By **not** signing this contract today, you are actively choosing to let your

competitor **capture** the three new clients that are currently ready to come on board. This is what it **costs** you to wait."

This is not manipulation; it is an application of a fundamental, mathematically verified principle of human motivation. The ability to structure your language to activate this powerful, predictable bias is the essence of verifiable framing. Mastering this pillar allows you to engineer the context of the decision, making your desired outcome the path of least motivational resistance.

Pillar 2: Cognitive Science and The T.O.T.E. Algorithm

The promise of predicting reactions requires a system that is not only built on science but is also **algorithmic**, a system you can run repeatedly with the expectation of a consistent result. The foundational understanding comes from **Cognitive Science**, which views the brain as an information processing system.

Early NLP borrowed heavily from the work of George A. Miller, Eugene Galanter, and Karl Pribram, specifically their **T.O.T.E. Model (Test–Operate–Test–Exit)** (Miller, Galanter, & Pribram, 1960). We use the T.O.T.E. model as the master blueprint for all influence strategies, transforming the vague process of persuasion into a closed-loop system of feedback and refinement:

1. **TEST (The Initial Calibration):** This phase is about gathering accurate data, not making assumptions. Before you speak, you must **TEST** the subject's current frame, emotional state, and predictable cognitive biases using verifiable non-verbal and linguistic cues (which we cover in detail later).
2. **OPERATE (The Intervention):** You apply a strategic intervention, a specific linguistic frame, a Meta-Model question, or a non-verbal shift, designed to move the subject from State A to State B.
3. **TEST (The Feedback Loop):** Crucially, you immediately **TEST** for the effect. Did the subject's breathing deepen? Did you see a flash of a micro-expression of agreement? This is the moment where your **Sensory Acuity** (rooted in Ekman's research) confirms or denies the success of your intervention.
4. **EXIT (Commitment Secured or Rerun):** If the Test confirms success, you move to secure the commitment ("yes"). If not, you immediately cycle back to **OPERATE** with a refined intervention.

This T.O.T.E. structure is what makes influence a **practiced, reliable skill** rather than an improvisational art. It ensures that every action is purposeful, measurable, and adaptive, eliminating the need to guess what the other person is thinking. You gain an architecture for success.

Pillar 3: Psycholinguistics and The Programming of Language

The third pillar addresses the core concept of **Linguistic Programming**. The classic NLP models (like the Milton Model) offered powerful suggestions on how to use vague language to bypass conscious resistance. While effective, the underlying *mechanism* was often vaguely attributed to non-specific 'unconscious' factors.

Modern **Psycholinguistics** provides the precise, verifiable explanation: **Semantic Priming** (Neely, 1977). Studies consistently show that the words and concepts you introduce immediately prior to a critical decision, the "prime", unconsciously influence the speed and favorability with which a person processes a subsequent, related concept. Your language doesn't just convey information; it actively **primes** the listener's brain for the next thought, creating a favorable cognitive context.

We use this principle to transform the classic NLP technique of **Presupposition** into a highly advanced tool. Presuppositions are linguistic structures that require the listener to accept a hidden premise in order to make sense of the sentence.

For example, asking, *"Which solution do you prefer, A or B?"* presupposes that the person has already agreed to a solution. The psycholinguistic proof is that the brain, in its effort to conserve energy, expends more cognitive resources challenging the premise ("I don't agree to a solution") than simply engaging with the choice ("A or B").

By strategically loading your language with **Presuppositions** and embedding terms like "value," "agreement," and "commitment," you are, in effect, laying down neurological primes that make agreement the path of least cognitive resistance. You are not arguing for the decision; you are **programming the decision pathway** through verifiable linguistic structures.

The Architecture of Mastery: Why This Book Changes Everything

The pursuit of influence is a pursuit of power: the power to achieve your goals, to shape consensus, and to guide others toward mutually beneficial outcomes. This book is the definitive, authoritative manual for that pursuit. It is written for the individual who demands measurable results and rejects the ambiguity of traditional methods.

We have consciously created a system that is robust against academic scrutiny yet profoundly practical in the field. This book is a declaration that the most potent techniques of human influence are not mysterious, but scientific. They are waiting for the disciplined practitioner to learn, integrate, and deploy them.

Mastering the Logic of Belief

In the chapters that follow, we will begin by meticulously dismantling the concept of **Belief Systems**. We move past the idea of fighting beliefs and instead learn to see them as the mental *frames* they truly are. We will dive deep into **Cognitive Biases** (Thaler & Sunstein, 2008): the systematic, predictable errors in judgment that govern 90% of human decisions.

By understanding the brain's predictable logic (Chapter 2), you learn to structure your proposals to align perfectly with its natural tendencies, making refusal a cognitive dissonance.

The Precision of Language

You will be handed the ultimate diagnostic tool: the **Meta-Model**. Rooted in the linguistic work of Noam Chomsky, the Meta-Model teaches you the **verifiable structure of vague language** (Grinder & Bandler, 1975). When a person says, "I can't do that," they have performed three linguistic acts: they have Generalized, Deleted information, and Distorted reality.

We teach you the precise, structured questions to reverse-engineer their internal experience, forcing them to reveal the exact, missing information you need to guide their choice. This is not interrogation; it is **linguistic diagnosis**, giving you the power to find the exact pinhole in their logic where commitment can be secured (Chapter 3).

Sensory Acuity: The Predictive Edge

Perhaps the single greatest differentiator of the master influencer is the ability to read the moment-to-moment impact of their words. We train your visual system in **Sensory Acuity** (Chapter 5), turning your observations into real-time feedback data. We teach you to ignore polite words and instead focus on the **micro-expressions** (Ekman, 2003) and physiological shifts that betray a subject's *true* internal state.

This is the **'Test' phase** of the T.O.T.E. model that gives you your **predictive edge**, the ability to know exactly when your intervention has landed and when you need to adjust, all before the subject even finishes their sentence.

The Engineering of State

Finally, we address the often misunderstood concept of **Anchoring** (Chapter 6). Stripped of its mystical connotations, anchoring is simply the sophisticated application of **Classical and Operant Conditioning** (Pavlov, 1927). We will show you how to reliably associate specific emotional states (confidence, focus, agreement) with environmental triggers.

This allows you to *engineer* the emotional state of a room or a subject, ensuring that when you make your final proposal, their emotional state is perfectly calibrated for acceptance.

This is the commitment of this book. We have not merely refined old techniques; we have reconstructed the science of influence from the ground up, demanding verifiable proof at every step.

By mastering this **Advanced NLP** framework, you will acquire the specific knowledge that transforms your ability to communicate from an unreliable effort into a **practiced, predictable skill**. You will know, with certainty, exactly what to say to secure the commitment you seek. Your journey to mastery begins now.

CHAPTER 1

THE LOGIC OF BELIEF:

INTRODUCING COGNITIVE FILTERS AND FRAMING

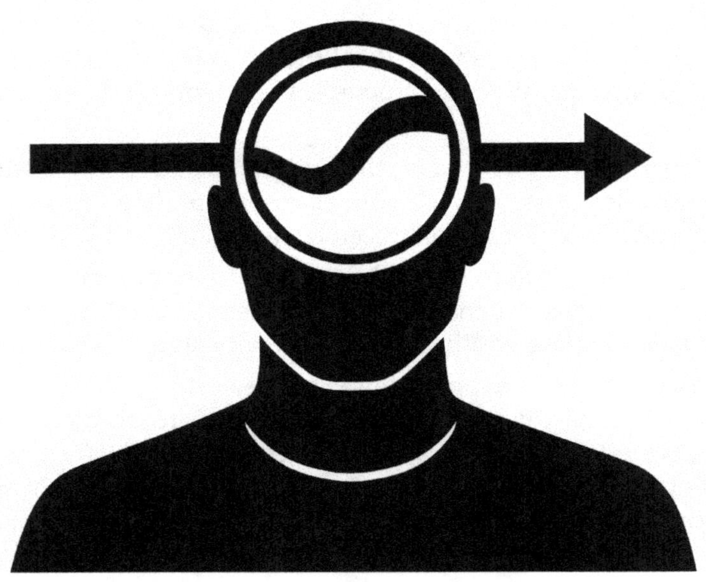

The great lie of persuasion is that you must change someone's mind.

The truth, as revealed by cognitive science and behavioral economics, is far more elegant: you don't change the mind, you change the architecture of the decision.

If you believe that influence is a battle of logic, where the person with the superior argument wins, you are already fighting a losing war. Human beings are not pure logical machines.

Our brains are efficient, flawed, and easily steered. To consistently predict reactions and move a choice from "maybe" to "yes," we must discard the fantasy of the rational actor and embrace the reality of the predictable human mind.

This chapter is the foundation of Advanced NLP because it provides the blueprint for prediction. It moves beyond the subjective concept of a "limiting belief" and into the verifiable reality of Cognitive Filters, the mental shortcuts and biases that govern every single decision your subject makes. By mastering these filters, you gain the power to structure your communication to align with their brain's path of least resistance.

2.1 The Two Systems of Decision-Making

To understand the predictable nature of human choice, we must first understand the two core mechanisms responsible for making decisions. Nobel laureate Daniel Kahneman, building on decades of psychological research, popularized this model: System 1 and System 2 thinking (Kahneman, 2011).

System 1: The Intuitive, Fast Machine

System 1 is your autopilot. It operates automatically and quickly, with little or no sense of voluntary control. It handles the vast majority of our cognitive load, from driving a car to reading a simple emotion.

- **Characteristics:** Fast, intuitive, emotional, effortless, heuristic-driven (shortcut-driven).
- **Role in Influence:** System 1 generates immediate impressions and feelings. When you encounter high resistance or immediate rejection, it is System 1 that is saying "no." Effective influence often seeks to bypass or align with this system's snap judgments.

System 2: The Deliberative, Slow Machine

System 2 is the conscious, thinking part of your brain. It is responsible for effortful mental activities that require attention, such as complex calculations, comparisons, and deliberate choices.

- **Characteristics:** Slow, effortful, logical, calculated, requires attention and energy.
- **Role in Influence:** System 2 is what approves or rationalizes the choices made by System 1. It is the gatekeeper of final commitment. When your subject says, "Let me think about it," they are handing the decision over to the slow, energy-expensive System 2.

The core objective of Advanced NLP is to present a framed proposition that is instantly accepted by the fast, emotional System 1, and then use verifiable linguistic and non-verbal cues to provide the logical scaffolding that the slow, rational System 2 needs to approve and ratify that initial "yes."

The greatest obstacle is that System 2 is fundamentally lazy. It prefers to conserve energy. This leads us directly to the concept of Cognitive Filters.

2.2 Cognitive Filters: The Predictable Shortcuts

A Cognitive Filter is a systematic pattern of deviation from norm or rationality in judgment. They are the mental shortcuts, or heuristics, that the brain relies on to save energy (Tversky & Kahneman, 1974). We rely on them because calculating every decision from scratch would paralyze us.

These filters are not weaknesses; they are entry points. When you understand the filter, you can predict the distortion it creates, and structure your proposition to fit perfectly through the warped lens.

2.2.1 Loss Aversion: The Double Weight of Loss

As introduced in Chapter 1, Loss Aversion is the most powerful cognitive filter in the realm of influence. Rooted in Prospect Theory, it states that people feel the psychological pain of a loss approximately twice as powerfully as the pleasure of an equivalent gain (Kahneman & Tversky, 1979).

- **The Filter:** The human brain is a survival organ. It prioritizes protection over acquisition. A threat to what we already possess registers as a far more urgent signal than the opportunity to acquire something new.
- **Advanced NLP Application (Framing):** To leverage this, you must shift your frame from "what they will gain" to "what they are currently losing or risk forfeiting."

Situation	Traditional (Gain) Frame	Advanced NLP (Loss) Frame
Hiring a Consultant	"You will **gain** a 20% efficiency boost."	"Your current system is causing you to **lose** 20% of your budget every month due to inefficiency."
Buying a Product	"This membership gives you **access** to exclusive content."	"If you don't secure your spot now, you will be **excluded** from this vital information when your competitors get it."

Fact Check: The Endowment Effect is a corollary of Loss Aversion, demonstrating that simply owning something (or feeling like you own it) drastically increases its perceived value (Thaler, 1980). This means that if you can frame your offer as something they **already possess** or are merely *testing* (e.g., "Take your new system home for a 30-day trial period"), their immediate sense of ownership makes the return of the item feel like an unacceptable loss.

2.2.2 The Confirmation Bias: Seeking Validation, Not Truth

The **Confirmation Bias** is the filter that ensures our beliefs remain robust. It is the tendency to search for, interpret, favor, and recall information in a way that confirms or supports one's prior beliefs or values (Nickerson, 1998).

- **The Filter:** The brain seeks consistency above all else. Once a subject has adopted a belief (e.g., "I am not a salesperson," or "That strategy is too risky"), they will unconsciously screen out all evidence that contradicts it and actively seek out evidence that supports it. They are not looking for truth; they are looking for validation.
- **Advanced NLP Application (Pacing and Leading):** You cannot directly attack a subject's core belief; it triggers immediate System 1 defensiveness. Instead, you must first **pace** their reality, validate their *experience*, and then subtly **lead** them to a new conclusion.
    - **Pace:** Start by articulating the *validity* of their current belief. If they say, "I'm worried about the risk," you pace them by saying, *"It's absolutely smart to be worried about risk. Every successful person I know is risk-averse."* (This bypasses the Confirmation Bias by confirming their self-image as a "smart, successful person.")
    - **Lead:** Once they feel heard and confirmed, you introduce the new information that re-contextualizes their belief. *"The smart, successful people I work with, however, manage risk by ensuring their investment is not a risk, but a measured step toward a guaranteed outcome."*

By pacing their belief, you gain credibility. By leading with a slight reframe, you allow them to incorporate the new idea without feeling they had to abandon their original identity.

2.2.3 The Anchoring Heuristic: The Primacy of First Data

The Anchoring Heuristic refers to the tendency to rely too heavily on the first piece of information offered (the "anchor") when making decisions (Tversky & Kahneman, 1974). Subsequent judgments are then made by adjusting away from that anchor, regardless of its relevance.

- **The Filter:** The brain dislikes cognitive heavy lifting. The anchor provides an immediate, easy reference point. All data that follows is unconsciously measured against that first point.
- **Advanced NLP Application (Value and Expectation):** You must consciously choose and deploy a strategic anchor before a proposal is made.
    - **Pricing:** If you are selling a service, the initial price you mention sets the high anchor. Even if you later negotiate down, the subject's System 2 will judge the final price not against the market value, but against the initial, high anchor.
    - **Time/Difficulty:** If you are asking a person to undertake a task, anchor the difficulty first. *"This process usually takes most people six months, but we can fast-track it in three."* You have anchored the expectation of **six months** as the normal baseline, making the three-month reality feel like a significant discount of effort.

Key Rule: Anchor High, Adjust Low. The power of the anchor remains even if the initial figure is clearly arbitrary or exaggerated. Its primary role is to set the scale.

2.2.4 The Availability Heuristic: The Vividness of Memory

The Availability Heuristic is a mental shortcut that relies on immediate examples that come to mind when evaluating a specific topic, concept, method, or decision (Tversky & Kahneman, 1973).

- **The Filter:** If something is easily recalled (highly *available* in memory), the brain assumes it is more common, more probable, or more important. Media coverage, personal trauma, and vivid storytelling all make memories more available.
- **Advanced NLP Application (Narrative Framing):** If you want a subject to choose "Yes," you must ensure that all the available mental images associated with "Yes" are vivid, recent, and positive. If you want them to avoid "No," you must make the available images associated with the *consequence of "No"* equally vivid and unpleasant (activating the Loss Aversion filter).

- **Use Vivid Stories:** Instead of saying, "This strategy is effective," use a short, sensory-rich story (a form of **Narrative Priming**): "I saw a client just last week, and the relief on her face when she closed that deal, the moment her stomach unknotted, that's what this strategy delivers." This anchors a potent, available emotional response.

2.2.5 The Bandwagon Effect (Social Proof)

The **Bandwagon Effect** or **Social Proof** describes a phenomenon where people do something primarily because other people are doing it, regardless of their own beliefs (Cialdini, 1984).

- **The Filter:** When uncertainty is high, the brain is programmed to look to the tribe for validation. If others are doing it, it must be the correct, safe course of action. This is an evolutionarily beneficial shortcut.
- **Advanced NLP Application (Pre-Framing Consensus):** Never present a choice as an isolated decision. Always frame it within a context of established consensus.
  - **Weak Frame:** "*I think this is a good idea for you.*"
  - **Strong Frame:** "*This is the exact protocol we implemented with [Successful Company A] and [Successful Competitor B]. They are already ahead of you on this, and their results are why you're considering this today.*"

Fact Check: Social proof is most potent when the people in the "tribe" are perceived as similar to the subject (Festinger, 1954). If your subject is an engineer, cite other engineers. If they are a parent, cite other parents. This amplifies the cognitive shortcut.

2.3 Framing: The Master Key to Belief Architecture

Understanding these cognitive filters leads us to the master skill: Framing.

Framing is the intentional act of structuring how information is presented to influence the choices people make. It is the language used to surround a concept, setting the interpretive context that dictates how the subject processes the data.

2.3.1 Positive vs. Negative Framing

The difference between emphasizing gains (positive framing) and emphasizing losses (negative framing) is the most fundamental application of the Loss Aversion filter.

- Example (Medical Context):
    - *Positive Frame:* "This procedure has a 90% success rate." (Focus on the gain/success).
    - *Negative Frame:* "This procedure has a 10% failure rate." (Focus on the loss/risk).

Research shows that when decisions involve potential gains (or positive outcomes), people tend to be risk-averse (choosing the guaranteed 90% success). Conversely, when decisions involve potential losses (or negative outcomes), people tend to be risk-seeking (gambling on the 10% chance of avoiding loss) (Tversky & Kahneman, 1981).

The Advanced NLP Strategy: You must be aware of your subject's current emotional state and the nature of the decision:

1. **To Secure a Safe, Guaranteed Outcome:** Use **Positive Framing.** *"Let's secure this 90% guaranteed result now."*
2. **To Motivate Action to Avoid a Threat:** Use **Negative Framing.** *"We must act to reduce the 10% risk you are currently facing."*

2.3.2 The Zero-Risk Bias

A powerful application of framing is the Zero-Risk Bias: the tendency to prefer to reduce a small risk to zero rather than to accept a greater reduction in a larger risk (Viscusi, Magat, & Huber, 1987).

- **The Filter:** The emotional satisfaction of eliminating a problem entirely is so high that the brain will trade logical utility for it. Eliminating all risk registers as a psychological **absolute**, which System 1 loves.
- **Advanced NLP Application:** If your proposal has multiple risks, focus your language on the one risk you can reduce to zero, even if it is minor. Frame this elimination as the central, most critical benefit.
    - *Instead of:* "Our software reduces your overall operational risk by 40%."
    - *Frame as:* "We guarantee our security architecture reduces your data breach risk to zero, a complete elimination of your single greatest liability."

The total risk reduction of 40% may be logically superior, but the emotional impact of the **Zero-Risk Frame** will be more potent in securing the commitment from System 1.

2.3.3 The Default Bias (Inertia Framing)

The Default Bias is the powerful tendency for people to choose the option that has been pre-selected for them (Johnson & Goldstein, 2003). It is perhaps the strongest form of cognitive laziness.

- **The Filter:** Choosing the default requires no energy, no thought, and therefore no stress on System 2. It is the path of absolute non-resistance. The brain prefers inaction (status quo) over the effort of decision-making.
- **Advanced NLP Application (Action Framing):** When presenting an option, frame the desired choice as the already-established **default setting**, requiring the subject to expend effort to opt *out* rather than to opt *in*.
    - *Weak Close:* "Would you like to start the contract, or do you need more time?"
    - *Default Frame:* "The standard protocol here is to begin the implementation phase now so we capture the upcoming Q4 window. If you wish to delay, you'll need to fill out a separate extension form. Should we just stick with the standard protocol?"

By labeling the desired path as the "standard protocol" or "our recommendation," you establish it as the psychological default. Any deviation requires the subject to consciously exert energy to challenge the status quo, which their System 2 is programmed to avoid.

2.4 The Ecology of Belief

The final layer of the Logic of Belief involves the Ecology, how a new belief or decision fits into the subject's existing world and identity.

A true belief is not an isolated idea; it is a key piece in the subject's self-concept. If your proposal requires the subject to fundamentally believe something about themselves that is contradictory to their identity (e.g., if you frame a conservative investor as "high-risk gambler"), your influence attempt will fail, regardless of how expertly you framed the language.

Advanced NLP recognizes that influence must be congruent with the subject's self-concept. This is achieved by linking the proposed action to their highest-held values (e.g., stability, family, expertise, freedom).

- **Example:** If your subject values "Stability" above all else, do not frame your proposal around "exciting growth" or "bold changes." Frame it around "securing your current position," "reducing long-term volatility," or "building a stable legacy."

The objective is to allow the subject to maintain their core identity while seamlessly integrating the new decision. You are not asking them to become a new person; you are simply showing them that your proposal is the most logical and verifiable path for the person they already are to achieve what they already value.

This chapter has provided the essential knowledge of the Cognitive Filters that allow you to predict human behavior. In the next chapter, we move from the architecture of belief to the surgical tools of language: Mastering the Meta-Model to accurately diagnose and resolve the linguistic ambiguity that prevents commitment.

CHAPTER 2

MASTERING THE META - MODEL: PRECISION IN QUESTIONING

In Chapter 2, we established that human decision-making is not a purely logical process, but one governed by predictable Cognitive Filters and the energy-saving default of System 1 thinking. Our goal as advanced communicators is to frame our propositions so they align with these biases, effortlessly guiding the subject toward "yes."

But what happens when the subject gives you ambiguous or resistant feedback? What if their language is vague, their beliefs are hidden, or their objections are generalized?

The master influencer doesn't guess; they diagnose.

This chapter introduces the Meta-Model, the most powerful diagnostic tool in the Advanced NLP arsenal. Rooted in the verifiable principles of Transformational Grammar and Psycholinguistics, the Meta-Model teaches you to use language as a precise, surgical instrument to cut through ambiguity. It moves the conversation from the foggy realm of opinion and generalization into the clear, actionable structure of *specific thought*. By mastering this model, you gain the power to retrieve the exact, missing information you need to collapse a limiting belief or secure a commitment.

3.1 The Linguistic Foundation: From Surface to Deep Structure

To understand the Meta-Model, we must first understand the relationship between what is said and what is meant.

In the 1950s and 60s, linguist Noam Chomsky revolutionized the understanding of language by distinguishing between **Surface Structure** and **Deep Structure** (Chomsky, 1957).

- **Surface Structure:** This is the language actually spoken or written, the words you hear. It is often vague, incomplete, and simplified.
- **Deep Structure:** This is the complete, internal neurological representation of the speaker's intended meaning, including all the sensory data, experiences, and contexts that were omitted in the Surface Structure.

The gap between the rich Deep Structure and the poor Surface Structure is inevitable. Our brains are efficient: we rely on three natural linguistic processes to simplify and shorten our communication. The problem is that when we apply these same simplification processes to our internal thought process, we inadvertently create **cognitive bottlenecks**: vague internal statements that limit our choices.

The Meta-Model is a set of specific questions designed to reverse these three simplification processes. When a subject speaks, they have inevitably performed one or more of these three transformations, creating a doorway for you to enter their internal logic.

Linguistic Process	Definition	The Problem (Cognitive Filter)	Meta-Model Goal
1. Deletion	Omitting key information from the statement.	Hides the specifics necessary for action.	**Recover Missing Information** (The WHO, WHAT, WHERE, WHEN)
2. Generalization	Drawing universal conclusions from one or two instances.	Creates limiting "rules" that block new choices.	**Challenge the Universal Scope** (Find the exception)
3. Distortion	Misrepresenting reality, often by exaggerating, linking unconnected events, or substituting cause/effect.	Creates false barriers, false causation, or false meaning.	**Identify the Source of the Error** (The HOW and WHY)

3.2 Category 1: Deletion — The Missing Data Points

Deletion is the process of leaving out critical pieces of information. The speaker is not lying; they are simply assuming the listener knows what they know. When a subject deletes information, they rob their own statement (or their belief) of the very specificity needed to take action or change.

3.2.1 Simple Deletion (Missing Nouns or Verbs)

The subject omits the specific person, object, or action.

- **The Statement:** "I am stressed."
- **The Problem:** The statement has deleted *who* or *what* is causing the stress, making the problem feel abstract and unsolvable.
- **The Meta-Model Question:** "**Stressed by *whom*?**" or "**Stressed about *what specific situation*?**"

By forcing the subject to make the vague feeling specific, you collapse the emotion tied to the abstract concept. You move the problem from a pervasive feeling ("I am stressed") to a solvable scenario ("I am stressed about the 3 pm meeting with the finance team").

3.2.2 Lack of Referential Index (Missing Actor)

The subject refers to something or someone without explicitly naming it.

- **The Statement:** "**They** are blocking the deal."
- **The Problem:** This vague pronoun prevents responsibility from being assigned or action from being taken. Who is "they"? A committee? A person? A mood?
- **The Meta-Model Question:** "**Who specifically** is blocking the deal?"

The Value for Influence: Often, subjects use vague references to avoid confronting the true source of resistance, which might be themselves. When you ask this question, they are forced to either name the external source (allowing you to address it) or recognize that the resistance is internal.

3.2.3 Unspecified Verbs (Missing Process)

The subject uses a verb that does not specify *how* the action occurred.

- **The Statement:** "The competition **failed** our client."
- **The Problem:** How did they fail? Was it slow delivery? Poor quality? Hidden fees? The lack of specificity prevents you from offering a targeted counter-solution.
- **The Meta-Model Question:** "**How specifically** did they fail your client?"

Advanced Application: When the subject is vague about a negative outcome, Meta-Model the verb to elicit the precise details that allow you to frame your own product or service as the explicit solution. If they say the competition "disappointed" them, your response must address the *specific mechanism* of that disappointment ("We guarantee all delivery is tracked in real-time to avoid the kind of **slow delivery** you experienced").

3.3 Category 2: Generalization — The Universal Lie

Generalization is the process of taking a singular experience and applying it to all similar instances. This is how we learn (e.g., "fire is hot"), but it is also the primary mechanism for creating limiting beliefs (e.g., "all opportunities are risky").

Generalizations are the biggest obstacles to securing a "yes," because they frame your proposal as a guaranteed failure before you even start.

3.3.1 Universal Quantifiers (The Absolutes)

These are words that imply a universal, absolute scope: *all, every, never, none, nobody, always.*

- **The Statement:** "**Nobody** in this industry uses that approach." or "That strategy **never** works."
- **The Problem:** The words "nobody" and "never" are almost always false, but they serve as a perfect cognitive barrier, preventing the subject from even considering a different path.
- **The Meta-Model Question (The Counter-Example):** "**Nobody?** So, if I could show you **one person** who successfully implemented it, would you consider it then?" or "**Never?** Can you think of **just one time** when that approach had a partial success, even if it wasn't perfect?"

The Value for Influence: This is the most direct way to collapse a limiting belief. By asking for a single, small counter-example, you force System 2 to search for an exception. If the subject finds one, the Universal Quantifier collapses. If they cannot, the burden of proof shifts to them, softening their rigid stance.

3.3.2 Modal Operators of Necessity (The Rules)

These words convey a sense of obligation, rule, or necessity: *should, shouldn't, must, mustn't, have to, need to, it is necessary to.*

- **The Statement:** "I **must** consult with my team before I commit."
- **The Problem:** This statement establishes a rigid internal rule. While consultation may be wise, the word "must" implies a necessity that feels non-negotiable and outside their control.
- **The Meta-Model Question (The Consequence):** "**What would happen if you didn't** consult with your team?" or "**What specifically** makes this a *must* rather than a good idea?"

By forcing the subject to articulate the consequence, you make the hidden rule visible. The answer often reveals a fear (e.g., "I'd get blamed if it went wrong"). Once the fear is known, you can frame a solution that eliminates the fear ("We can structure the agreement so the liability rests with us for the first 90 days").

3.3.3 Modal Operators of Possibility (The Limits)

These words define the subject's perceived limits of what is possible: *can't, couldn't, won't, couldn't, it is impossible to.*

- **The Statement:** "I **can't** afford your service right now."
- **The Problem:** The "can't" implies an environmental impossibility, often hiding a choice or a fear.
- **The Meta-Model Question (The Challenge to Possibility):** "**What exactly stops you?**" or "**What would happen if you did?**"

This question forces the subject to take ownership of the perceived limit. The "can't" is usually a **choice** or a **fear of consequence** framed as a rule. The subject might respond: "I'd have to rearrange my entire budget." Now, you have actionable data (their budget needs rearranging) instead of a brick wall ("I can't afford it").

3.4 Category 3: Distortion – The Map is Not the Territory

Distortion is the process of misrepresenting the relationship between events or ideas. The subject may connect two unrelated events, assign emotional meaning where none exists, or assume causation without proof. This is where the most irrational resistance is hidden.

3.4.1 Cause and Effect (False Causation)

The subject falsely links one event to another, claiming one *causes* the other.

- **The Statement:** "**Your tone of voice** makes me feel anxious."
- **The Problem:** This statement distorts reality by placing the locus of control externally. It denies the subject's own emotional response mechanism (their internal map) and places responsibility on the speaker. **Fact Check:** The verifiable truth is that "Your tone of voice" is an *input*, and "makes me feel anxious" is an *internal response* chosen by the subject's system.
- **The Meta-Model Question (The Internal Process):** "**How specifically** does my tone of voice cause you to *choose* to feel anxious?" or "**What is the process** that goes on inside you between my tone and your feeling?"

The Value for Influence: This question gently returns ownership of the emotion to the subject. Once they are forced to articulate the internal process (e.g., "Well, when you speak loudly, I remember a boss I used to have..."), the distortion collapses. You can then frame your solution around the *real* problem, the memory or belief, not the surface-level event.

3.4.2 Complex Equivalence (False Meaning)

The subject equates two unrelated events, stating that one *means* the other.

- **The Statement:** "**The fact that the committee didn't call me back** *means* they don't value my work."
- **The Problem:** A lack of a phone call (Event A) has been equated with a monumental failure of value (Event B). This leap of logic is a cognitive error that creates crippling internal resistance.
- **The Meta-Model Question (The False Link):** "**How specifically** does the fact that they didn't call back *mean* they don't value your work?" or "**What else** could their silence mean?"

This question forces System 2 to analyze the evidence supporting the equation. Since the committee's silence could mean they are busy, on holiday, or lost the number, the original conclusion ("they don't value my work") loses its force. This technique is a form of cognitive restructuring, directly collapsing the self-imposed barrier to commitment.

3.4.3 Mind Reading (False Assumptions)

The subject claims to know the internal state, thoughts, or intentions of another person without any external validation.

- **The Statement:** "**I know** you are only telling me this to get my money."
- **The Problem:** This is a distortion that creates an immediate wall of skepticism, based entirely on the subject's projection of intent.
- **The Meta-Model Question (The Source of Knowledge):** "**How do you know** my intentions?" or "**What specific evidence** gave you that information?"

The Value for Influence: This is a crucial question for establishing rapport and integrity. It forces the subject to admit their statement is based on assumption or their own past experience, not verifiable reality. The answer often reveals the subject's own fear or a painful memory from a past interaction, which you can then address directly to build trust.

3.5 The Surgical Application: Using the Meta-Model in the T.O.T.E.

The Meta-Model is not a tool for confrontation; it is the essential **TEST** phase in the **T.O.T.E. (Test–Operate–Test–Exit)** framework (as introduced in Chapter 1). It is the diagnostic test you run to retrieve the specific data necessary for your **OPERATE** phase (the reframed proposal).

Case Study: Closing a Hesitant Client

Client Statement (Surface Structure): "We've looked at your proposal, but frankly, **it's too expensive.** We **can't** afford the commitment right now. My colleagues **always** say that these kinds of partnerships **never** work out."

Meta-Model Diagnosis and Sequence:

1. **Diagnosis 1: Distortion (Complex Equivalence):** "Too expensive" is a false equation. It *means* "I don't perceive the value to be equal to the cost," not "I have no money."
    - **Question (Addressing Value):** "Compared to **what exactly** is this too expensive? Are you comparing the price to the **cost of staying where you are**?" (This applies the Loss Aversion Frame from Chapter 2).
2. **Diagnosis 2: Generalization (Modal Operator of Possibility):** "We **can't** afford the commitment."
    - **Question (Addressing Possibility):** "**What exactly stops you** from rearranging the budget to acquire this? If you had the results we promise guaranteed, **would you then find the resources?**" (This isolates the decision from the immediate budget barrier).
3. **Diagnosis 3: Generalization (Universal Quantifiers):** "My colleagues **always** say that these partnerships **never** work out."
    - **Question (Challenging the Absolute):** "**Never?** Can you recall **one partnership**, even a small one, that gave you a partial success or taught you a crucial lesson?" (This collapses the "never" and opens the door to your solution).

The Result: By running this sequence of precise questions, you have retrieved the Deep Structure:

- The client is not blocked by money, but by a **perceived lack of value** relative to the cost of inertia (Diagnosis 1).

- The **"can't afford it"** is really a **choice** to prioritize their current budget allocation (Diagnosis 2).
- The core resistance is based on an unverified, generalized past failure, not a rational assessment of your specific proposal (Diagnosis 3).

Once this Deep Structure is revealed, your **OPERATE** phase is surgical. Instead of arguing about price, you return to the **Loss Aversion Frame** and focus exclusively on the specific pain point that the Meta-Model revealed.

3.6 Ethics and Congruence in Precision

It is crucial to emphasize that mastering the Meta-Model is an ethical pursuit. It is not designed to corner or confuse the subject. The power of these questions lies in their ability to bring clarity: to the subject, and to you.

When an internal belief is vague, generalized, or distorted, it creates psychological pressure and limits choice for the subject. When you ask a precise Meta-Model question, the subject's System 2 is engaged, and the belief is forced to become specific. This act of clarification is often experienced by the subject as insightful and even therapeutic, as they are finally able to articulate the true source of their confusion.

The Golden Rule of Precision: Always use the Meta-Model to find the positive intent behind the limiting statement. The subject who says, "I can't afford it," has the positive intent of financial security. Your final frame must honor that positive intent while showing them that saying "yes" to your proposal is the best, most verifiable way to achieve that security.

Mastering the Meta-Model is the key to unlocking the power of the next chapter: Linguistic Programming. Once you know the precise internal map of your subject (Chapter 3), you can then use language to surgically implant the necessary resources, ideas, and presuppositions for commitment (Chapter 4).

CHAPTER 3

LINGUISTIC PROGRAMMING: THE HIDDEN STRUCTURE OF INFLUENCE

In Chapter 3, we armed ourselves with the **Meta-Model**, turning our questioning into a precise surgical instrument capable of diagnosing the hidden structure of a subject's belief (the Deep Structure). We learned that vague resistance is merely incomplete information waiting to be retrieved.

Now, we move from diagnosis to intervention.

This chapter introduces the tactical side of Advanced NLP: **Linguistic Programming**. This is the **OPERATE** phase of the T.O.T.E. model: the moment you deploy scientifically verified language structures to reshape the subject's internal experience. Our goal is to move beyond mere conversation and use language as a precise, algorithmic tool to structure choices and implant ideas.

We are not teaching linguistic parlor tricks. We are teaching the systematic application of **Psycholinguistics**, the study of the relationship between linguistic behavior and psychological processes.

By understanding how the brain processes sentence structure and embedded meaning, you gain the ability to pre-determine the cognitive pathway a subject must take, making your desired conclusion the path of least cognitive resistance.

4.1 The Cognitive Power of Presupposition

The most elegant and powerful tool in Linguistic Programming is the **Presupposition.**

A **presupposition** is an assumption taken for granted within an utterance. It is a concept that must be accepted as true for the sentence itself to make sense. Crucially, presuppositions work by leveraging the inherent laziness of the brain's **System 2**.

When you hear a sentence, your System 2 is engaged to process the main, conscious meaning. However, it often permits the peripheral, implied assumptions to slip through unverified. The conscious mind focuses on the surface meaning, allowing the deeper premise to be accepted as a non-negotiable fact.

Think of it this way: to challenge a premise, System 2 must expend significant energy by stopping the flow of communication and returning to an earlier point in the conversation. Because the brain constantly seeks to conserve energy, it defaults to accepting the presupposed reality simply to keep the communication moving.

The Linguistic Science

The linguistic foundation for this lies in the difference between a declarative statement and a presupposition. If I say, "My phone is black," the truth or falsehood of that statement is the focus. If I say, "When my black phone rings, I'll answer it," the focus shifts to the *action* (answering the phone), and the existence of a phone is automatically accepted as a fact necessary to process the rest of the sentence.

Mastering presuppositions allows you to elegantly achieve an agreement on a core premise *before* you ever ask for a conscious commitment.

4.1.1 Temporal Presuppositions (The Inevitable Timeline)

These are arguably the most effective form of presupposition for moving a prospect from "maybe" to "yes" because they establish the desired outcome as inevitable, requiring the subject to focus only on the timing or sequence of events.

Keywords: *when, before, after, during, since, while.*

Example Frame	Hidden Premise Accepted
"**When** you start seeing the positive quarterly reports..."	**Premise:** You *will* start seeing positive quarterly reports.
"**Before** we finalize the remaining details..."	**Premise:** The decision to move forward has already been made.
"I'm curious, **after** you integrate this new system, what will you tackle next?"	**Premise:** Integration *will* occur.

Application Strategy: If a subject is hesitating on the *decision* to buy, shift the language entirely to the *timing* of the process. Do not ask, *"Are you going to buy?"* Ask, *"When is the best time for us to finalize the delivery?"* The question presupposes the finalization, and the subject's System 2 will default to answering the simpler question about time.

4.1.2 Ordinal Presuppositions (The Irrelevant Choice)

This category uses sequence, number, or selective description to force the subject to accept the validity of the premise while choosing a less important element.

Keywords: *first, second, another, one, two, the other, a different, still.*

- **Example 1 (Choice of Time):** "Do you want to begin the initial onboarding session **first** thing Tuesday, or should we schedule it for **another** time this week?"
    - **Hidden Premise:** The onboarding session is happening. The only choice is *when*.
- **Example 2 (Choice of Focus):** "We've seen the success of this strategy with Client A. **Another** benefit you'll experience is..."
    - **Hidden Premise:** The first part (success with Client A) is an accepted fact, and you are now discussing *additional* established facts.

The Power of the Irrelevant Choice: This is often called the "embedded command of choice." By giving the subject two options, both of which lead to your desired outcome, you fully satisfy the brain's need for control (System 2 feels involved) while guiding them away from the possibility of "no." The ultimate goal is to remove "No" from the menu entirely.

4.1.3 Awareness Verbs and Adjectives

These verbs and adjectives presuppose the truth of the statement they govern, forcing the subject to agree with the premise if they wish to answer the question.

Keywords (Verbs): realize, know, discover, understand, be aware, regret.

Keywords (Adjectives/Adverbs): easily, quickly, successfully, fortunately.

Example Frame	Hidden Premise Accepted
"What made you **realize** this product was the superior option?"	**Premise:** You *did* realize this product is the superior option.
"Why do you **regret** waiting so long to start?"	**Premise:** You *are* regretting waiting so long to start.
"**Fortunately**, our team has already prepared the paperwork."	**Premise:** The preparedness of the team is fortunate (i.e., beneficial to you).

Application Strategy (The 'Realize' Trap): Asking a subject, "When did you **realize** this was the right decision?" is infinitely more powerful than asking, "Is this the right decision?" The subject is forced to search their mind for the *time* of realization, confirming the decision in the process.

4.2 Embedded Commands: The Stealth Directive

While presuppositions handle the *premise* of the conversation, **Embedded Commands** handle the *action*. An Embedded Command is a specific, actionable directive hidden within a longer, grammatically complex sentence.

This technique is rooted in the verifiable mechanism of **Semantic Priming** (Neely, 1977). As discussed in Chapter 1, psycholinguistic studies confirm that exposure to certain words or phrases (the prime) can unconsciously influence the processing of subsequent, related information. When you embed a command, you are essentially inserting a high-value, actionable prime into the subject's stream of consciousness.

The directive bypasses the critical, analytical System 2 because the command is presented as a component of a larger, seemingly innocent statement. System 1, which processes the language rapidly, registers the command as a directive, while the slower System 2 is busy parsing the full sentence structure.

4.2.1 Delivery is Everything: The Non-Verbal Highlight

The most critical component of a successful Embedded Command is the **delivery mechanism**. Because the command is grammatically integrated into a sentence, you must non-verbally highlight the command phrase to ensure System 1 registers it as distinct.

Highlighting Techniques (The Advanced Calibration):

1. **Vocal Tonal Shift:** Slightly lower the pitch of your voice, slow the tempo, and increase the volume on the command phrase. (Example: "I want you to **feel comfortable** making this choice.")
2. **Kinesic Cue:** Briefly gesture toward the subject, lean slightly in, or hold brief, intense eye contact precisely during the command phrase. This non-verbal punctuation separates the command from the surrounding text.
3. **Pausing:** Use a short, deliberate pause immediately before and after the command. (Example: "You might find it helpful to... **take action now**... on this specific point.")

4.2.2 Structuring the Command

Embedded Commands should be structured to be easy for System 1 to process and act upon. They typically involve clear, immediate action verbs.

Full Sentence Frame	Embedded Command (Targeted Action)
"As a professional, I know you will **find this information useful** later."	**FIND THIS INFORMATION USEFUL**
"You might be surprised how **easy it is to decide now.**"	**EASY IT IS TO DECIDE NOW**
"It's important that you **understand the value** before we move forward."	**UNDERSTAND THE VALUE**
"I want you to **take all the time you need** to review this proposal."	**TAKE ALL THE TIME YOU NEED**

Application Strategy: Embed the command just before or immediately after a statement of validation or empathy. For example, by first saying, *"I know you've been extremely busy,"* and following with, *"and that's why it's important to **act fast** to secure this opportunity,"* you link the validation of their difficulty to the urgency of your directive.

4.2.3 Pacing and Leading with Commands

This technique blends the Pacing and Leading principle (from Chapter 2) directly into the command structure.

- **Pace (Verifiable Fact):** State a verifiable fact about the subject's current reality.
- **Lead (Embedded Command):** Link the fact to your desired directive using a soft conjunction.
- **Example:** "**You are looking at this screen right now** (Pace) and **you can relax and commit to this process** (Lead)."
    - The subject must accept the first, verifiable fact (they are looking at the screen). System 1 carries this acceptance over to the next part, making the embedded command feel like a natural, logical continuation of their current state.

4.3 Comparative Negation: The Unfavorable Contrast

Comparative Negation is a specialized framing technique that relies on the **Loss Aversion** principle (Chapter 2) to bias a choice. It involves framing a choice by implicitly or explicitly contrasting it negatively with an undesirable alternative.

This technique uses language to create an immediate, internal cost-benefit analysis where the cost of the *undesired option* is amplified by the sheer negative connotation of the language used to describe it.

4.3.1 The Mechanism of Unfavorable Contrast

The human brain processes negative comparisons more quickly and with more emotional weight than positive ones, precisely because of the 2 times power of Loss Aversion. If I frame Choice A as *"less risky"* than Choice B, the primary focus shifts to the negative idea of "risk," and Choice A gains favor simply because it reduces the negative load.

Keywords: *less than, not like, unlike, rather than, instead of.*

Comparative Frame	Hidden Negative Premise	Application
"This approach is **less complicated** than your existing method."	**Premise:** The current method is 'complicated' (a known negative).	You are selling the *avoidance of complication* (a psychological gain).
"You can choose this streamlined process **rather than** the frustrating bottlenecks you've been dealing with."	**Premise:** The subject has been experiencing 'frustrating bottlenecks' (a psychological loss).	You are selling the *elimination of frustration*.

4.3.2 Comparative Negation of Identity

This is a highly potent form of framing that ties the undesirable option to a negative self-identity or self-concept. It leverages the **Confirmation Bias** (Chapter 2) by suggesting that selecting the undesired option would be inconsistent with the subject's own high opinion of themselves.

- **Example (Targeting 'Professionalism'):** "A **less professional approach** would be to delay this decision, but given the results you need, we should finalize the timeline now."
    - **Effect:** The desired action (finalizing the timeline) is subtly contrasted with the negative identity ("less professional approach"). To maintain their self-concept, the subject's System 1 is pressured to comply with the positive option.
- **Example (Targeting 'Intelligence/Efficiency'):** "We could go through the **inefficient, drawn-out process** that most people choose, but I assume you'd prefer the streamlined, efficient path that aligns with your expertise."
    - **Effect:** The desired path is linked to their professional identity ("expertise," "efficient"), while the alternative is linked to a negative state ("inefficient," "most people").

Ethical Consideration: Comparative Negation must always be aimed at *the decision or process*, not the person. When used to contrast a product's features, it highlights the superior value. When used to compare behaviors, it must link the undesired behavior to a general, negative category ("inefficient," "delaying") that the subject naturally wishes to avoid.

4.4 Strategic Syntax: The Architecture of Agreement

While Presuppositions and Embedded Commands deal with the content of influence, **Strategic Syntax** deals with the *structure* of the sentence itself. Even simple grammatical choices significantly impact how the brain processes information, especially when building agreement.

4.4.1 Active vs. Passive Voice (Locus of Control)

The choice between active and passive voice dictates where responsibility, or the **Locus of Control**, is placed in a sentence.

- **Active Voice:** [Actor] → [Action] → [Recipient]. (Example: "I secured the funding.")
  - **Application:** Use the active voice when discussing your positive actions, successes, or the actions you want the subject to take. It conveys certainty and clarity of action. (E.g., "You **will achieve** this result by **taking** this step.")
- **Passive Voice:** [Recipient] → [Action] → [Actor is optional]. (Example: "The funding was secured.")
  - **Application:** Use the passive voice to distance yourself from negative events or to mitigate the impact of necessary but potentially difficult actions. (E.g., "The changes **were implemented**," instead of "We implemented the changes that caused the disruption.") It can be used as a subtle form of distortion to reduce the emotional impact of a difficult fact.

4.4.2 Conjunctions of Flow: 'And' vs. 'But'

The most subtle syntactical choices are the conjunctions we use to link clauses.

- **The Power of 'But':** The word "but" functions as a cognitive eraser. It negates everything that came before it. Psychologically, whatever follows "but" is the only thing the listener will retain.
  - *Example:* "I understand your concern about the cost, **but** the value outweighs it."
  - **Effect:** The subject only processes the second clause ("the value outweighs it"), but they feel their initial concern was dismissed.

- **The Power of 'And':** The word "and" is a conjunction of inclusion and flow. It links two ideas without negating the first, making the listener feel heard while smoothly transitioning to the next point.
    - *Example:* "I understand your concern about the cost, **and** that's precisely why we designed the system to guarantee a 300% return on investment."
    - **Effect:** The subject's System 1 feels acknowledged (Paced), and the new information (the ROI) is introduced as a logical, non-contradictory continuation of the flow of thought (Leading). **Always use 'and' to bridge an objection.**

4.4.3 Embedded Questions (The Gentle Challenge)

An embedded question is a question folded into a statement, softening the challenge and bypassing the subject's defensive System 1 response.

- **Direct Question (Challenging):** "Why did you fail to follow the protocol?"
- **Embedded Question (Softening):** "I'm curious **what prevented you from following the protocol** at that time."

The embedded format shifts the focus from blame to curiosity, facilitating a more honest and specific response, which you can then diagnose using the Meta-Model framework.

4.5 Synthesis: Linguistic Programming in Action (The OPERATE Phase)

Linguistic Programming is the toolkit for the **OPERATE** step in the T.O.T.E. Model. You use the Meta-Model to diagnose the precise nature of the subject's resistance (the **TEST**), and then you use Linguistic Programming to deliver the precise counter-intervention (the **OPERATE**).

Diagnosis (Meta-Model)	Intervention (Linguistic Program)
Problem: Unspecified Verb → *They delayed the decision.*	**Intervention:** Use Presupposition → "***When** the decision is no longer delayed, **how quickly** will you want to start seeing the results?*" (Forces acceptance of the future result).

Diagnosis (Meta-Model)	Intervention (Linguistic Program)
Problem: Modal Operator of Possibility → *I can't find the time.*	**Intervention:** Use Embedded Command → *"I know you're a busy person, so let me show you how **easy it is to delegate this process.**"* (Commands delegation).
Problem: Generalization → *That never works for us.*	**Intervention:** Use Comparative Negation → *"We could try the **old, failed method** that never works, but I recommend the proven strategy that all our successful clients use."* (Links their statement to the negative option).

By strategically deploying these language structures, you are creating a cognitive funnel. You are not *persuading* the subject; you are **architecting the mental path** they must follow to process the information, making "yes" the logical, inevitable conclusion that saves System 2 energy and honors their deepest cognitive biases.

This precision is the hallmark of Advanced NLP. We move from the surgical use of language to the surgical reading of human physiology. In the next chapter, we will master the **Science of Sensory Acuity and Calibration**, ensuring that you can instantly and accurately TEST the impact of every linguistic program you deploy.

CHAPTER 4

THE SCIENCE OF SENSORY ACUITY AND CALIBRATION

In the previous chapters, we established the blueprint for influence. We mapped the predictable Cognitive Filters that bias decisions (Chapter 2) and armed ourselves with the surgical tools of Linguistic Programming (Chapter 4) to structure the path to agreement. These are the *proactive* steps, the preparation and the intervention, of the influence process.

But what happens in the moment of contact, when your subject is speaking one thing but feeling another? What if you deploy a masterful Presupposition, and the subject's words are polite, but their body language signals resistance?

The answer is the words are the least reliable source of information.

Mastery requires a verifiable feedback system: a real-time diagnostic that tells you, without ambiguity, if your linguistic program has landed, if your frame has been accepted, or if resistance has been triggered. This system is Sensory Acuity and Calibration, and it is the absolute core of the TEST phase in the T.O.T.E. Model.

We move from the subjective notion of "reading people" to the scientific discipline of **behavioral signal analysis**. This chapter turns your eyes and ears into highly sensitive, objective instruments capable of detecting involuntary, neurological truth.

5.1 Calibration: The Predictive Feedback Loop

Calibration in Advanced NLP is the process of establishing a subject's baseline behavior (their normal, comfortable state) and then noting the precise shifts in that baseline when a specific stimulus (your proposition, frame, or question) is introduced. These shifts are your predictive data points.

If your proposition creates measurable, consistent shifts in physiology, for example, a change in breathing or a subtle facial contraction, you have secured verifiable, objective data on the subject's internal state. These non-verbal signals are reliable because they are primarily governed by the **Autonomic Nervous System (ANS)**, the control center for involuntary functions like heart rate, respiration, and blood flow. The ANS is wired for survival, and it is far too fast and primal to be overridden by the conscious intent to lie or hide emotion.

The goal here is precision, not assumption. We discard the vague metaphors of older NLP models—such as the largely non-validated eye-accessing cues (which research has failed to consistently support)—and instead focus on three scientifically verifiable pillars:

1. **Micro-Expressions (The Face):** Involuntary, fleeting facial muscle movements.
2. **Physiological Shifts (The Body):** Changes in breathing, posture, and tension.
3. **Behavioral Synchronization (The Rapport):** Alignment or misalignment of movement patterns.

The critical insight is that your influence strategy fails not when the subject says "no," but when you **fail to TEST** their internal response and proceed with the wrong intervention. Calibration is the constant, quiet confirmation of your strategy.

5.2 Pillar 1: Facial Calibration and the Science of Micro-Expressions

The most direct and rapid window into a subject's emotional state is the face. Research pioneered by Dr. Paul Ekman confirmed the existence of **universal micro-expressions**: involuntary facial displays of emotion lasting between 1/25th and 1/2 a second (Ekman, 2003). These expressions are universal across cultures, proving they are hardwired into the human nervous system.

Training your acuity to spot these fleeting signals is the single fastest way to run the **TEST** phase of the T.O.T.E. model.

5.2.1 The Big Six (Plus One) Universal Emotions

Mastery requires familiarity with the facial muscle groups associated with the seven universal emotions. While many emotions are subtle, the following are the most critical to detect during high-stakes influence:

1. **Contempt:** This is the most damaging micro-expression to spot during a pitch. It is often visible as a unilateral (one-sided) tightening of the corner of the mouth, causing a slight sneer. **Contempt signals superiority, disdain, and moral disgust.** When a subject flashes contempt, they are internally thinking, *"This is beneath me,"* or *"You are unqualified to present this to me."*
    - *Action when detected:* Stop the current line of argument immediately. Use a Meta-Model question to acknowledge their expertise and reposition yourself as a peer or consultant, not an instructor.
2. **Disgust:** The tightening and raising of the upper lip and the wrinkling of the nose (like smelling something foul). **Disgust signals an internal rejection of a concept or idea.** It means the brain is rejecting the input.
    - *Action when detected:* Your language, the frame you used, or the product detail you mentioned triggered a rejection response. Immediately link the proposal to something clean, reputable, or high-status to cleanse the emotional frame.
3. **Fear:** Raised inner eyebrows, pulled together, causing horizontal wrinkles in the center of the forehead. The lower eyelids tense, and the lips are stretched horizontally. **Fear signals a threat to safety, status, or resources.**
    - Action when detected: Your proposition is activating the **Loss Aversion** filter too strongly. Immediately shift the frame to risk mitigation and guaranteed safety. Focus on what you control and how you will protect them.
4. **Anger:** Eyebrows are lowered and pulled together; eyes glare; lips press firmly together. **Anger signals a block to a goal the subject desires.**

- *Action when detected:* The subject feels blocked or unjustly treated by your terms, the price, or the process. Use the Meta-Model to diagnose the source of the blockage ("What specifically about this clause creates the greatest difficulty for you?").

5. **Surprise:** Eyebrows flash high and curved; eyes widen, exposing the whites of the eyes above the iris; jaw drops open. **Surprise signals an unexpected event.**
   - *Action when detected:* If positive, proceed rapidly. If negative, immediately address the unexpected issue before they consciously process the implication.

5.2.2 The Calibration Baseline: Finding the Default

You cannot measure a shift until you know the norm. Before deploying your Linguistic Programming (your **OPERATE** phase), spend the first 60 seconds establishing the subject's baseline for their "neutral" or "comfortable" state:

- **Vocal Baseline:** What is their resting pitch, tempo, and volume?
- **Facial Baseline:** What is the resting tension around their eyes and mouth? Are their lips slightly parted or pressed together?
- **Body Baseline:** What is their primary breathing locus (chest or belly)? How is their weight distributed (balanced or leaning)?

Once the baseline is set, every subsequent flash of contempt, every tightening of the jaw, and every shift in breathing constitutes verifiable, objective feedback that tells you the truth about your intervention.

5.3 Pillar 2: Physiological Calibration – The Body's Involuntary Signals

Beyond the face, the rest of the body, controlled by the involuntary ANS, provides a constant stream of predictive data. These physiological shifts are harder to mask than words or deliberate posture.

5.3.1 Respiration: The Engine of Emotion

Breathing is the most reliable external marker of internal arousal (Grossman, 1983). A subject cannot consciously maintain a false, relaxed breathing pattern when their ANS is triggered by stress or anxiety.

- **Rate and Depth:** Increased rate and decreased depth signal anxiety, stress, or excitement (System 1 activation). A sudden, audible **sigh or deep exhalation** often signals resignation or relief—a definitive shift in state.

- **Locus Shift:** A relaxed person breathes from the diaphragm (belly/abdomen). When stress is introduced, the breathing shifts up to the chest and shoulders (thoracic breathing). This **locus shift** is a clear signal that the subject has moved from a relaxed, receptive state to a state of **alertness or defensiveness** ("fight or flight").
    - *Action:* If you see the breathing shift from the diaphragm to the chest, you have triggered high resistance. You must immediately **pace** the subject's internal state, "I can see this is requiring a lot of thought", and then shift your frame to a lower-threat topic before attempting to proceed.

5.3.2 Skin Tone and Capillary Action

Although subtle, changes in skin tone are involuntary responses governed by the capillary blood flow—the foundation of the traditional NLP concept of **"VAK" (Visual, Auditory, Kinesthetic)**, now grounded in science.

- **Paling (Blanching):** A loss of color in the face, neck, or ears signals that blood is being pulled away from the extremities and non-essential organs to the major muscle groups. This is a classic **"flight"** response, the body preparing for confrontation or escape.
- **Flushing (Reddening):** An increase in blood flow, usually signaling anger, embarrassment, or high arousal. This is a classic **"fight"** response.
    - *Action:* If a subject suddenly blanches after you deploy a Loss Aversion frame, you have successfully activated their survival instinct. This is the **TEST** confirmation that the threat is real to them. You must now quickly move to the **OPERATE** phase of offering protection or a safe way out (the "Exit" step).

5.3.3 Tension and Micro-Movement (The Leaking Channels)

Unconscious tension is a leakage channel for stress.

- **Jaw Clenching:** A firm pressing of the lips or clenching of the masseter muscles (jaw) signals suppressed anger or extreme mental effort (System 2 overload).
- **Shoulder/Neck Tension:** A slight lifting of the shoulders or rigid posture signals defensiveness.

- **Fidgeting:** Repetitive, small movements (tapping fingers, jiggling legs) signal mounting anxiety or a desire to release accumulated tension.
    - *Action:* If you observe a subject's hand transition from resting flat on the table to clenching a pen or hiding beneath the table, the **TEST** indicates the subject is internally grappling with something. Use a **Meta-Model question** (Chapter 3) to articulate the tension for them: "I sense this is a complex point; what part of this feels the most difficult to resolve?"

5.4 Pillar 3: Behavioral Synchronization and Rapport

The third pillar of calibration relates to the spatial and movement patterns between you and the subject, which is essential for establishing and maintaining **Rapport**, the state of mutual responsiveness and trust.

5.4.1 Mirroring and the Chameleon Effect

The concept of **Mirroring** (unconsciously matching the posture, gestures, or tempo of another person) is scientifically supported by research on the **Chameleon Effect** (Chartrand & Bargh, 1999). Studies show that individuals who are unconsciously mimicked report liking the mimicker more and rate the interaction as smoother, even when unaware of the mimicry. This is because **synchronicity signals trust** to System 1.

- **Application (Rapport Building):** To establish rapport, consciously and subtly match three elements of the subject's behavior:
    1. **Rate of Speech:** Tempo and rhythm.
    2. **Posture:** The angle of the head or the position of the feet (avoid large, obvious movements).
    3. **Breathing Rhythm:** Matching the rate and locus of their respiration.

5.4.2 Mismatching: The Signal of Internal Conflict

If you are already in rapport (synchronized), any sudden, significant **Mismatch** in movement or posture signals that the subject has internally broken connection with you or your idea.

- **Example:** You are sitting with open posture and speaking calmly. The subject was mirroring you, but when you introduced the price, they suddenly **cross their arms or shift their torso away** from you.

- *Action:* This is a definite **TEST** failure. The crossed arms are an involuntary physiological barrier. You must interrupt your current intervention and address the barrier non-verbally first—shift your own posture to a slightly less engaged position, pause, and then ask a **Meta-Model question** that addresses the shift in state: "Before we continue, I want to make sure I'm being clear; are we still aligned on the core objective here?"

5.4.3 Kinesic Momentum (Energy Shift)

Observe the **momentum** of their movement. A shift from fluid, engaged movements (gesturing, leaning in) to rigid stillness, or vice-versa, indicates a neurological shift:

- **Sudden Stillness:** Often signals intense System 2 processing, concentration, or internal conflict. They have stopped moving to conserve energy for thought.
- **Sudden Increase in Movement:** Usually signals excitement, relief, or a physical need to vent anxiety.

The key is always to **calibrate to the change**, not the behavior itself. If a person is naturally fidgety, increased fidgeting is less significant than a naturally calm person suddenly tapping their foot rapidly.

5.5 Integration: Calibration as the T.O.T.E. TEST

This entire chapter is dedicated to the moment-by-moment validation of your influence strategy. Calibration is the constant, quiet background process that confirms your **prediction** of their reaction was correct.

The Real-Time Sequence

Here is how Calibration (TEST) integrates with Linguistic Programming (OPERATE) in a real-world scenario:

Goal: Secure commitment on a high-value timeline.

1. **Baseline:** Subject's breathing is slow and deep (relaxed). Posture is open.
2. **OPERATE (Linguistic Program):** Deploy a Temporal Presupposition (Chapter 4): *"**When** we launch this system next month, the first thing you'll **realize** is the time you've saved."*
3. **TEST (Calibration Check):**
    - *Observation:* The subject's eyes widen slightly (surprise/interest), but their lips press together, and their breathing shifts slightly upward (tension).

    - *Interpretation:* **TEST** result is ambiguous. System 1 registered the high-value promise (surprise), but System 2 (lips pressed) has an immediate objection to the timeline.
4. **OPERATE (Adjustment via Meta-Model):** Since the tension is focused around the timeline, you run a diagnostic question (Chapter 3) aimed at the Modal Operator of Necessity: *"I can see you're processing the timeline. **What specifically makes** 'next month' a challenging necessity, rather than simply a goal?"*
5. **TEST (Calibration Check 2):**
    - *Observation:* The subject uncrosses their hands, exhales deeply (relief), and speaks with relaxed posture.
    - *Interpretation:* **TEST** successful. The specific question addressed the point of tension. The problem is no longer a hidden objection; it is a clear, manageable logistic.
6. **EXIT:** Now that the tension is gone, you address the logistic and secure the commitment.

The Predictive Advantage

When you master Sensory Acuity, you gain the ability to predict the subject's verbal response **before they speak it**. If you see a flash of contempt, you know the next words will be an objection, regardless of how polite they sound. This allows you to interrupt the pattern and reframe before the objection is consciously articulated and locked in by System 2.

This level of precision moves influence from an art to a science. It is the final, essential check against the cognitive biases and hidden resistance we introduced in Chapter 2. By mastering calibration, you ensure that every linguistic intervention you deploy is tested, refined, and ultimately successful.

The next step is to understand the final neurological levers, how to reliably link internal states to external cues. We will move to **Advanced Anchoring and State Elicitation**, which is the process of using verified principles of conditioning to program the subject's internal experience.

CHAPTER 5

ADVANCED ANCHORING AND STATE ELICITATION

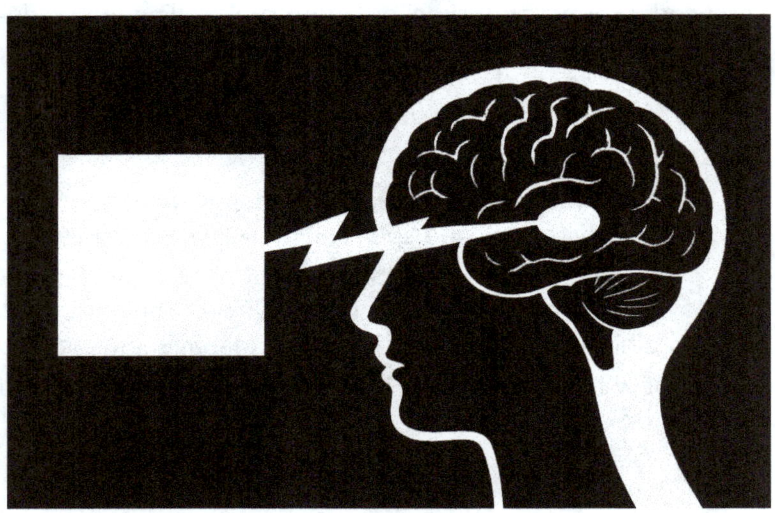

We have successfully established that influence is a predictable science. We know how to map the architecture of belief (Chapter 2), surgically diagnose resistance using the Meta-Model (Chapter 3), and deploy targeted language with Linguistic Programming (Chapter 4). Critically, we know how to TEST the impact of every intervention through Sensory Acuity and Calibration (Chapter 5).

But there is a critical vulnerability in any human interaction: state.

A subject can be perfectly aligned with your logic, but if they are currently feeling anxious, distracted, or irritated, their decision will be compromised. The rational gatekeeper, System 2, becomes impaired under high stress, often defaulting to a safety-first "no," regardless of the objective merits of your proposal.

The master influencer does not rely on chance for the subject's state; they engineer it.

This chapter introduces the science of Advanced Anchoring and State Elicitation. This is the method for reliably linking an external stimulus (a gesture, a word, a specific touch) to a highly specific, resourceful internal state (confidence, certainty, agreement). We move past the vague, metaphorical explanations of classic NLP and ground the technique in the verifiable neurological principles of Classical and

Operant Conditioning. This is the ultimate OPERATE tool for controlling the emotional environment of commitment.

6.1 Anchoring: Conditioning the Neurological Pathway

In essence, an anchor is a conditioned stimulus. It is a neurological shortcut that allows you to bypass the conscious, slow process of state management and directly access a specific emotional memory.

Traditional NLP popularized the concept of an "anchor" as a link between a unique stimulus and a potent internal experience. Our verifiable framework defines Anchoring as the deliberate application of established learning theories to create and fire these neurological associations. This process relies on two distinct, scientifically proven mechanisms:

6.1.1 Mechanism 1: Classical Conditioning (The Stimulus-Response Link)

Classical Conditioning, pioneered by Ivan Pavlov in the early 20th century, teaches us that two stimuli repeatedly paired together will eventually form an association in the nervous system (Pavlov, 1927). A previously neutral stimulus (the *bell*) becomes a **Conditioned Stimulus (CS)** that reliably elicits a powerful, involuntary **Conditioned Response (CR)** (salivation), even when the original Unconditioned Stimulus (food) is absent.

- **In Anchoring:** The **Unconditioned Stimulus (US)** is the intense, desired emotion (e.g., peak confidence) that naturally elicits an **Unconditioned Response (UR)** (e.g., physiological calmness). The **Neutral Stimulus (NS)** is your unique anchor (e.g., a specific pressure on the knuckle). By repeatedly applying the NS *precisely* at the peak of the US, the NS becomes the **Conditioned Stimulus (CS)**, capable of eliciting the calm state (**CR**) on demand.

The verifiable power here is that the response is **involuntary** and rooted in the midbrain's emotional pathways, making it a reliable way to access and shift a subject's state (LeDoux, 2003).

6.1.2 Mechanism 2: Operant Conditioning (The Behavior-Consequence Link)

Operant Conditioning, primarily associated with B.F. Skinner, teaches us that behaviors are learned and maintained by their consequences (Skinner, 1938). The frequency of a behavior is either increased through **Reinforcement** or decreased through **Punishment**.

- **In Anchoring:** This mechanism is less about emotional state and more about **actionable commitment**. If you want a subject to repeat a desired behavior (e.g., agreement, nodding, expressing certainty), you must immediately follow that behavior with a pleasant consequence (**Positive Reinforcement**), such as validating language, a non-verbal reward (a smile, a nod), or a valuable piece of information.

Operant Conditioning is how you ensure that the subject's System 2 finds the act of agreeing with you to be a **rewarding and energizing experience**, thereby reinforcing the inclination toward consensus in the future.

6.2 Advanced Anchoring: The Five Keys to Precision

The difference between accidental conditioning and advanced application lies in precision. You cannot "fire" an anchor unless it has been "set" correctly. The following five principles ensure your anchors are potent, clean, and reliable.

Key 1: Peak State Intensity (The Unconditioned Stimulus)

The power of the anchor is directly proportional to the intensity of the emotional state at the moment of conditioning. The stronger the **Unconditioned Stimulus (US)**, the fewer repetitions required to form the **Conditioned Stimulus (CS)**.

- **Elicitation Technique:** Before setting the anchor, you must verbally or contextually guide the subject into a state of **peak intensity**.
    - *Example (Eliciting Certainty):* Do not ask them to feel certain; ask them to recall a specific, detailed memory when they felt **absolute, undeniable certainty** in their life—a moment where they *knew* they were right.
    - *Meta-Model for Elicitation:* "Close your eyes for a moment, and go back to that time. Where exactly in your body did that feeling of certainty begin? What was the first sound you heard? Make that picture bright and clear. **Amplify that feeling now.**"

Key 2: Uniqueness of the Stimulus (The Clean Anchor)

The **Neutral Stimulus (NS)** you choose must be unique and highly distinguishable. If you anchor peak confidence by simply tapping your desk, an action that happens countless times, the anchor will be weak and unstable.

- **Kinesthetic (Touch):** The most potent anchor. It must be a specific point (e.g., precisely two knuckles on the table, a specific pressure point on the wrist) that is not part of normal interaction.
- **Auditory (Sound/Word):** A unique, non-common phrase used only at the peak state (e.g., "Exactly right," spoken with a specific cadence).
- **Visual (Sight):** A unique gesture (e.g., interlocking fingers in a specific way) or a distinct visual prompt.

Key 3: Timing and Association (The Critical Moment)

The anchor must be applied precisely as the emotional state is **peaking**, not before it starts and not after it fades. The neurological window for effective association is narrow.

- **Sequence:** As the subject's face (calibrated via Chapter 5) shows peak intensity (deep breath, flush of color, engaged eye contact), apply the Kinesthetic anchor (e.g., the knuckle press). Hold the anchor for a few seconds to cement the association, then release it just as the state begins to subside.
- **Neurological Basis:** This simultaneous activation ensures the neural pathways for the stimulus and the response fire together, promoting rapid long-term potentiation (the strengthening of synaptic connections that form memory and learning) (Bliss & Lømo, 1973).

Key 4: Reinforcement and Testing (Solidifying the Anchor)

The anchor must be reinforced using multiple, similar emotional states and then **TESTED**.

1. **Reinforcement:** Ask the subject to recall three separate memories of certainty and apply the exact same anchor at the peak of each. This strengthens the association and makes the anchor robust against contextual changes.
2. **Testing:** Break the state (e.g., change the subject, ask a technical question). Then, **fire the anchor** (apply the CS). Your calibration (Chapter 5) must confirm the **Conditioned Response (CR)** is elicited, the subject's posture should shift, breathing should deepen, and a verifiable emotional response should appear on their face. If it fails, repeat the process.

Key 5: Stacking Anchors (The Power Chord)

To ensure maximum impact, multiple similar anchors can be applied at the peak of the same emotional state.

- **Stacking:** If you are eliciting "Confidence," you can set Kinesthetic Anchor 1 (knuckle press), Auditory Anchor 1 (the word "Precision"), and Visual Anchor 1 (a hand gesture) all at the peak of the same emotion. When you later fire all three (Kinesthetic, Auditory, and Visual) simultaneously, you create a powerful "power chord" that reliably accesses the full intensity of the resource state.

6.3 Tactical State Elicitation: Anchoring for Influence

In the context of Advanced NLP, Anchoring is used to make the subject feel the necessary emotion to commit to your proposal at the exact moment you ask for the commitment.

6.3.1 The Agreement Anchor (Operant Conditioning for Consensus)

This is the most direct application of **Operant Conditioning** in influence. The goal is to condition the subject to associate the act of **agreeing with you** with a pleasurable, rewarding consequence.

The Setup:

1. **Identify the Desired Behavior:** Nodding, saying "yes," leaning in, or expressing approval.
2. **Select the Reinforcer (Positive Consequence):** A genuine, high-value non-verbal reward, usually a specific smile, a confirming nod, or a positive, unique phrase like "Exactly right."

The Sequence (Reinforcement Schedule):

1. Ask a series of rapid, low-stakes questions designed to elicit easy, immediate agreement (**Pacing**). *(E.g., "You agree that efficiency is important, correct?" "You see the value in saving time, yes?")*
2. Each time the subject exhibits the **Desired Behavior** (nods, says "yes"), immediately apply your **Reinforcer** (smile, confirming nod, the unique phrase "Exactly right").
3. The repeated pairing of the act of agreement with the pleasurable, positive consequence conditions the subject's system to find agreeing with you **rewarding.**

The Payoff: When you transition to the high-stakes final question, the subject's **System 1** is already conditioned to seek the reward associated with agreement, making the final "yes" the path of conditioned comfort and acceptance. This leverages the **Bandwagon Effect** on a micro-scale: the subject is following the momentum of their own reinforced behavior.

6.3.2 The Decision Anchor (Contextual Conditioning)

This technique involves setting an anchor not on the subject's body, but on the **context of the decision.**

- **The Setup:** Identify a specific object or spot in the decision environment (the contract, the pen, the corner of the table).
- **The Sequence:** Throughout the initial stages of rapport and positive value discussion, repeatedly touch, point to, or glance at the **Decision Anchor** while the subject is expressing positive emotions (e.g., excitement, comprehension, confidence).
- **The Payoff:** When you arrive at the moment of commitment, the final action required is for the subject to engage with the **Decision Anchor** (e.g., picking up the pen, signing the contract). By anchoring positive states to that object, the physical act of engaging with it elicits the positive, resourceful state you conditioned earlier, reducing hesitation and fear.

6.3.3 The Collapse Anchor (State Interruption)

This is the inverse application of Anchoring: using a **Conditioned Stimulus** to disrupt or collapse a negative state (e.g., high anxiety, fear, or rigidity).

- **The Setup:** Anchor the negative state precisely at its peak. Do not reinforce it, but simply acknowledge and anchor it.
- **The Intervention:** Once the negative state is anchored, immediately **fire a conflicting, positive anchor** (e.g., your stacked "Confidence" power chord).
- **The Result (State Collapse):** Neurologically, the simultaneous firing of two conflicting, high-intensity states (Anxiety anchor + Confidence anchor) causes both neural pathways to momentarily fire and then inhibit each other (LeDoux, 2003). The result is a brief moment of internal disorientation, forcing the subject's System 2 to find a new, neutral, or resourceful state, effectively interrupting the negative cycle.

This allows you to create a momentary **reset** in the conversation, giving you the window of opportunity to deploy a new, positive frame or a clarifying **Meta-Model** question.

6.4 Neurological Basis: The Amygdala and Emotional Memory

The verifiable science of Anchoring lies in the **Amygdala**, the almond-shaped structure in the limbic system responsible for processing and storing emotional memories.

Fear conditioning (a form of classical conditioning) has been extensively studied, showing that the amygdala is the central hub where the **Conditioned Stimulus (CS)** becomes permanently linked to the fear response (UR). This rapid, non-conscious linkage is the same mechanism at work in Advanced Anchoring (Davis, 1992).

When you successfully anchor a state of **certainty** or **excitement**, you are creating a strong neural pathway in the subject's brain that bypasses the cerebral cortex (the slow, rational part) and directly accesses the emotional memory stored in the amygdala and related structures. The goal of Advanced NLP is to intentionally create positive, resourceful conditioned responses where default environmental triggers might otherwise create negative or hesitant states.

6.5 Ethical Responsibility and the Ecology of State

Because Anchoring provides a direct, non-conscious lever into a subject's emotional experience, its application carries a profound ethical responsibility. The **Ecology of Influence**, the final test of any intervention, must be applied rigorously to state elicitation.

The Ecological Check for Anchoring:

1. **Congruence with Identity:** Is the state you are anchoring (e.g., "Decisiveness") consistent with the subject's self-concept and highest values (Chapter 2)? Anchoring a state that conflicts with their core identity will fail or create internal dissonance.
2. **Utility of the State:** Does the state you are anchoring serve a positive, long-term purpose for the subject? You should anchor **confidence** to help them commit to a beneficial decision, not **recklessness** to bypass their rational skepticism.
3. **Clean Anchors:** Avoid anchoring negative states, even accidentally. Never pair a high-intensity negative emotion (e.g., frustration) with any unique gesture, word, or location, as this will poison that resource for future use.

The master influencer uses Anchoring to ensure the subject is in their **optimal resourceful state** to make a great decision, not a manipulated one. We are clearing away anxiety and distraction so that their rational System 2 can ratify the excellent, valuable frame you have provided.

By mastering Advanced Anchoring, you now control the emotional variables of the encounter. You have the tools to diagnose resistance (Chapter 3), frame the proposition (Chapter 4), monitor the results (Chapter 5), and ensure the subject is in the right emotional state to commit (Chapter 6).

The final step is to synthesize all these tools into a single, cohesive, and predictable strategy, the architecture of long-term commitment. This will be the focus of our final, concluding chapter.

CONCLUSION

We began this journey by defining influence not as a gift of charisma, but as a **practiced, verifiable science**. Throughout the previous chapters, we have systematically dismantled the mechanisms of human decision and armed ourselves with the tools necessary to structure the path to agreement:

- We mapped the predictable decision errors, the **Cognitive Filters** and **Loss Aversion**, that define the human algorithm (Chapter 2).
- We mastered the surgical diagnosis of resistance through the **Meta-Model** (Chapter 3).
- We learned to architect propositions using the embedded commands and assumptions of **Linguistic Programming** (Chapter 4).
- We transformed our senses into real-time feedback systems using **Sensory Acuity and Calibration** (Chapter 5).
- And finally, we gained control over the emotional variables by employing **Advanced Anchoring and State Elicitation** (Chapter 6).

Now, the final, most crucial step: **Synthesis**.

A box of surgical tools does not make a surgeon; the blueprint, the protocol, and the disciplined application of the strategy do. This chapter delivers the **Master Blueprint**: the **Predictive Influence Loop**. This loop is the strategic integration of every tool in this book, governed by the relentless feedback mechanism of the **T.O.T.E. Model**, all situated within a context of deep, neurological **Rapport**. Mastery is not about deploying a single technique; it is about running this comprehensive, adaptive loop until commitment is secured.

7.1 The Master Blueprint: The T.O.T.E. Model Refined

The foundation of our strategy is the **T.O.T.E. Model** (Test–Operate–Test–Exit), originally developed by Miller, Galanter, and Pribram (1960) to describe the neurological structure of behavior. It is the definitive algorithm for self-correction and goal achievement, and we apply it directly to the process of influence.

The T.O.T.E. Model reframes the entire interaction as a continuous cycle of **checking for congruence (TEST)** and **intervening (OPERATE)** until the desired outcome is achieved. It eliminates improvisation and replaces it with **adaptive, data-driven action.**

Step 1: TEST (The Initial Calibration and Outcome Frame)

The cycle begins not with talking, but with **calibrating** and **framing**. Before any linguistic intervention, you must gather essential data.

1. **Define the Outcome (The Exit Condition):** What is the specific, sensory-verifiable commitment you need? (e.g., "The client signs the contract," not "The client feels happy.") This defines the **T.O.T.E. Exit condition**.
2. **Establish Rapport and Baseline:** Engage the subject, using subtle **Mirroring and Matching** (Chapter 5) to establish neurological synchronization. **Calibrate** their neutral/comfortable state (their breathing, posture, resting facial tension). This is the initial **TEST** of their baseline behavior.
3. **Identify the Filter/Belief:** Use soft, open-ended language to elicit the subject's initial perspective. Listen for **Generalizations, Deletions, and Distortions** (Chapter 3) and identify the controlling **Cognitive Filter** (Loss Aversion, Confirmation Bias, etc.) that will govern their decision (Chapter 2).
    - *Key Insight:* The initial **TEST** provides the data. If the data is ambiguous (e.g., the subject says "yes" but their body language signals tension), you proceed to OPERATE to clarify the internal state.

Step 2: OPERATE (The Strategic Intervention)

Based on the data gathered in the initial TEST, you select and deploy the most precise intervention.

1. **State Elicitation (The Emotional Context):** First, anchor the emotional environment. If the subject is anxious, deploy a **Collapse Anchor** or a **Confidence Anchor** (Chapter 6). If they are hesitant, utilize **Operant Conditioning** to build momentum with the **Agreement Anchor**.
2. **Linguistic Programming (The Core Message):** Deploy a precisely framed proposition that aligns with the subject's cognitive filter. If you detected a **Loss Aversion** filter, frame the proposition using **Comparative Negation** (Chapter 4), emphasizing the cost

of inaction. If the resistance was vague, use the **Meta-Model** to elicit the Deep Structure (Chapter 3).

   - *Key Insight:* The **OPERATE** phase is not persuasion; it is the calculated input designed to shift the subject from their current state (State A: Hesitation) to the desired state (State B: Commitment).

Step 3: TEST (The Feedback Loop)

Immediately after deploying your intervention, you must **TEST** for the effect. This is the moment of truth where your **Sensory Acuity** proves the success or failure of the intervention.

1. **Check for Congruence:** Use your calibration skills (Chapter 5) to observe the subject's physiological response. Did the pitch of their voice drop? Did their breathing shift from thoracic (stressed) to diaphragmatic (relaxed)? Did you see a flash of **Contempt** or **Disgust**?
2. **Confirm the Shift:** If you deployed a Loss Aversion frame, you should see a subtle increase in arousal (System 1 activation). If you deployed an Agreement Anchor, you should see increased synchronization/mirroring.
3. **Diagnosis:**
   - **Success (Congruence):** The subject's verbal response and non-verbal signals align with the desired outcome. Proceed to EXIT.
   - **Failure (Incongruence):** The subject's words are positive, but their body signals resistance (e.g., they say "I agree," but their jaw clenches). Rerun the loop.

Step 4: EXIT or Rerun

The final step determines the overall flow of the interaction.

- **EXIT (Commitment Secured):** If the **TEST** confirms success (congruence is achieved), transition immediately to securing the verbal or written commitment. Use a final **Temporal Presupposition** to seal the deal (e.g., "Now that we've confirmed this, **when** is the best day to finalize the paperwork?").
- **RERUN (Adaptive Strategy):** If the **TEST** indicates incongruence or failure, the process immediately loops back to the **OPERATE** phase. The data from the failed **TEST** is now your new input.

You do not repeat the previous intervention; you deploy a refined strategy (e.g., switch from a Linguistic Program to a Meta-Model question to diagnose the source of the hidden tension).

This T.O.T.E. structure eliminates guesswork. It turns every objection into data, every failure into a learning opportunity, and every intervention into a calculated move toward the desired end state.

7.2 The Context: Rapport as Neurological Synchronization

The T.O.T.E. loop operates most efficiently when the context is one of **deep, neurological rapport**. Rapport is often dismissed as mere friendly nodding, but in Advanced NLP, we define it as **interpersonal neural synchronization**, a state where the subject's brain is naturally receptive to your input.

Rapport is not an emotion; it is a **neurological precondition for influence.**

7.2.1 The Mirror Neuron System

The verifiable foundation for rapport lies in the **Mirror Neuron System (MNS)**, first mapped in macaque monkeys and later confirmed in humans (Rizzolatti & Craighero, 2004).

- **The Mechanism:** Mirror neurons are specialized cells that fire both when an individual performs an action and when the individual *observes* another performing the same action. The MNS is the brain's fundamental mechanism for empathy, understanding intent, and learning. When you observe a subject reaching for a cup, the same neurons fire in your brain as if you were reaching for the cup yourself.
- **Rapport as MNS Activation:** When you engage in subtle **Mirroring and Matching** (Chapter 5), you are intentionally sending verifiable non-verbal signals to the subject's MNS. You are, in effect, telling their brain: **"I am like you, I understand your action, and I share your internal state."** This subconscious verification of similarity is the fundamental basis of trust. When MNS activation is high, cognitive defenses are lowered, making the subject naturally more receptive to your linguistic input.

7.2.2 Emotional Contagion: The Shared State

Rapport is deepened by **Emotional Contagion**, the process by which a person's emotions and related behaviors prompt similar emotions and behaviors in others (Hatfield, Cacioppo, & Rapson, 1994). This phenomenon operates primarily through **mimicry** (facial, vocal, postural) and the subsequent **afferent feedback**, the brain's interpretation of its own bodily state.

- **The Mechanism:** If you non-verbally project a state (e.g., Calm Confidence), the subject's MNS begins to subconsciously mimic your posture and facial expressions. The subject's brain then receives feedback from their own body ("My body is adopting a calm posture; therefore, I must be feeling calm"). This allows you to **influence the subject's resource state** without ever mentioning the emotion.
- **Application (Pre-Framing):** Before you enter the **OPERATE** phase of the T.O.T.E. loop, you must first ensure your own state is optimal. Your internal state of **Certainty** (anchored via Chapter 6) is contagious. By maintaining a congruent, resourceful state, you leverage Emotional Contagion to pull the subject out of anxiety and into a state of focus and confidence, making the final commitment possible.

7.3 The Predictive Influence Loop: A Step-by-Step Strategy

The following is the integrated, seven-step protocol for running the Predictive Influence Loop, synthesizing all the tools and concepts of Advanced NLP.

Step 1: Pre-Frame and Define the Exit (Chapter 2 & 1)

- **Action:** Define the **T.O.T.E. Exit** condition (the verifiable commitment).
- **Frame:** Determine the most potent **Cognitive Filter** (e.g., Loss Aversion) that will be the central theme of your presentation. Structure your opening to hit this filter. (e.g., "The greatest cost here is the cost of staying where you are.")
- **Internal State:** Anchor your own state of **Calm Authority** (Chapter 6).

Step 2: Establish MNS Synchronization and Baseline (Chapter 5 & 7)

- **Action:** Spend 60-90 seconds building rapport. Subtly match the subject's rate of speech, vocal volume, and posture.
- **Calibration:** **TEST** the subject's **Physiological Baseline** (breathing, facial tension). This is your initial data for the T.O.T.E. loop.

Step 3: Pacing and Elicitation (Chapter 2 & 3)

- **Action:** Pace their reality and elicit their core belief/resistance. Use soft, non-threatening statements that confirm their experience.
- **Diagnosis:** Listen acutely for **Universal Quantifiers** ("always," "never") and **Modal Operators of Possibility** ("can't," "won't"). This initial **TEST** reveals the **Deep Structure** of their resistance.

Step 4: OPERATE: Deploy the First Intervention (Chapter 4 & 6)

- **Action:** If the subject is vague (a high volume of Deletions or Unspecified Verbs), use the **Meta-Model** to ask a single, targeted question that retrieves the missing information. If they show clear, low-level agreement, deploy an **Agreement Anchor** (Operant Conditioning).
- **Linguistic Focus:** Structure your **OPERATE** phase with **Temporal or Ordinal Presuppositions** to embed the inevitability of the agreement.

Step 5: TEST, Adapt, and Recalibrate (Chapter 5)

- **Action:** Immediately after the intervention, **TEST** their response. Check for congruence: Does the physiological signal (Chapter 5) match their verbal feedback?
- **Feedback:** If you see a **Mismatch** (e.g., verbal agreement but a flash of **Contempt** or **Disgust**), the resistance is hidden.
- **T.O.T.E. Rerun:** The detected physiological signal becomes the new input. Return to **OPERATE** with a clarifying intervention (e.g., "I can see that point is causing some internal conflict; **what specific implication** of this change requires more thought?").

Step 6: The Closing Sequence (Anchoring the State of Commitment)

- **Action:** Once the subject is congruent (non-verbal signals match verbal agreement) and the last objection has collapsed, you move to the commitment phase.
- **Final Anchor:** Fire a previously set, high-intensity **Certainty Anchor** or **Confidence Anchor** (Chapter 6).
- **Final Frame:** Immediately follow the anchor with a powerful **Default Bias Frame** (Chapter 2): *"Based on all the evidence we've*

covered, the next step is the standard protocol for implementation, which starts today. Is there any logistical reason we shouldn't follow the standard protocol?"

Step 7: EXIT (The Final Seal)

- **Action:** Secure the physical commitment.
- **Final Reinforcement:** As the subject acts (signs, shakes hands, or confirms), immediately and genuinely apply a high-value **Positive Reinforcer** (a powerful, unique word and nod) to cement the reward/consequence link for future positive interactions.

7.4 The Final Leverage: Cognitive Dissonance and Commitment

The ultimate goal of the Predictive Influence Loop is to trigger the final, powerful psychological lever: **Cognitive Dissonance.**

Cognitive Dissonance is the mental stress or discomfort experienced by an individual who holds two or more contradictory beliefs, ideas, or values, or performs an action that contradicts their beliefs (Festinger, 1957). The human brain is evolutionarily compelled to resolve this dissonance, usually by changing the less strongly held belief to align with the action already taken.

The Dissonance Gap

The Predictive Influence Loop is designed to maximize the **Dissonance Gap** between the old belief and the new action.

1. **Old Belief (Resistance):** *"This proposal is too expensive and risky."* (A Generalized, Loss Aversion filter).
2. **New Action (Commitment):** The subject is linguistically and emotionally guided to say **"Yes"** and shake your hand (The Exit).

Once the subject has taken the action (the commitment), their brain must resolve the dissonance: *"I just committed to the proposal, but I still believe it is too expensive."* It is easier for the brain to retrospectively change the belief to align with the action than to undo the commitment.

The brain automatically restructures the belief: *"I committed because it's not actually expensive; it is a smart, strategic investment."*

The Law of Consistency: Influence does not stop at the signature. The act of making an initial, small commitment significantly increases the probability of making subsequent, larger commitments (Cialdini,

1984). By guiding the subject to several small, congruent agreements throughout the T.O.T.E. loop (e.g., "Yes, efficiency is key," "Yes, that's what stopped me before"), you build a powerful, verifiable track record of agreement that they are neurologically compelled to maintain.

7.5 Mastery: The Continuous Pursuit of Precision

The strategies outlined in this book transform influence from a hopeful encounter into a predictable process. The Predictive Influence Loop is your final, complete operating system. It requires the continuous, disciplined practice of:

1. **Objectivity:** Using **Calibration** to gather data, not relying on intuition.
2. **Surgical Precision:** Deploying the **Meta-Model** and **Linguistic Programming** to address the exact, verifiable cause of resistance.
3. **Adaptive Control:** Utilizing the **T.O.T.E. Model** to ensure every action is tested and corrected immediately.

The journey to advanced influence is a commitment to precision. By integrating these scientific principles, you gain the ability to predict, control, and architect consensus in any human interaction, ensuring that the path you prescribe becomes the path of least resistance for the subject's own logical system. Your mastery begins now.

SYNTHESIS AND STRATEGIC REFLECTION

You've made it. We've gone deep into the complete blueprint of predictable influence, moving all the way from the psychological foundations to the integrated, self-correcting strategy of the **Predictive Influence Loop**.

But let's be real: reading a textbook on carpentry doesn't make you a master builder. Mastery in Advanced NLP isn't about memorizing the jargon; it's about **self-calibration** and **meta-cognition**, it's about intentionally stopping and thinking about how *you* think, how *you* react, and how *you* apply these tools.

This final chapter isn't about new material. It's your surgical checklist. It's a structured set of reflection questions designed to turn the principles from neat theories into robust, reliable habits. Use a journal or a voice recorder for this. Don't let yourself get away with **Generalizations** ("It went well"). Be your own toughest **Meta-Model** coach. Dig for the specifics.

8.1 Reflecting on The Subject's Map (Chapters 2 & 3)

The goal here is simple: stop guessing what people want and start accurately mapping their internal reality.

1. **Framing and Loss Aversion:**
   - Think about the last three times you tried to influence a key decision. **How specifically** did you frame the conversation to make the **cost of doing nothing** (Loss Aversion) feel heavier than the price of your solution?
   - What verifiable, non-verbal signal, a flicker, a breath change, a shift in posture, did your **Calibration** pick up that confirmed your Loss Aversion frame actually landed? Did you trigger resistance instead?
2. **Meta-Model Self-Correction:**
   - Pull up a recent significant objection you received. Now, coach yourself through the **Meta-Model** diagnosis:
     - Which **Generalization** (like "We can **never** afford that") was used? What is the single, specific **counter-example** you should have asked the subject for right away?
     - What key piece of information was missing (a **Deletion**)? Who was the missing actor, or what was the unspecified process?
     - What **Distortion** (like "Their silence **means** they don't trust us") was at play? What was the true, internal fear or false logic that the subject needed to see?
3. **Identity and Alignment:**
   - Before your next high-stakes conversation, list out the subject's top three values (e.g., Security, Freedom, Innovation).
   - How will your final pitch explicitly link to reinforce **all three** of those values? Are you making sure that saying "yes" to you aligns perfectly with their self-concept (their **Confirmation Bias**)?

8.2 Reflecting on Intervention and Programming (Chapters 4 & 6)

This section is about verifying the surgical precision and *cleanliness* of your inputs. You're checking for accidental contamination.

1. **Linguistic Precision:**
   - Go back through a recent email or presentation script. Find every instance where you used the word **'but'** to negate a concern. Now, replace it with the word **'and.'** What does that simple change do to the mental process for the reader?
   - Pick a crucial instruction you need to implant (e.g., "Decide now"). Formulate two or three distinct **Embedded Commands** that carry that message, then practice the **Tonal Shift** and the **Pause** that makes them covertly effective.
   - When you use a **Temporal Presupposition** (like, "**When** you start seeing the revenue increase..."), are you absolutely sure you're bypassing an inconsequential detail, or are you actually avoiding a major objection that needs a full **Meta-Model** diagnosis?
2. **Anchoring and State Control:**
   - Describe the last time you consciously **set an anchor** on a subject. What exact, unique **Kinesthetic Stimulus** did you use (e.g., specific knuckle press)? Was the subject truly at their **peak state** when you set it?
   - Define your **Agreement Anchor** (the unique sound, word, or gesture you use to reward consensus). Are you being diligent enough to **only** use that reinforcer when they are genuinely agreeing, or are you accidentally polluting it with random conversation?
   - Think about your personal state. What **Anchor** do you use to access **Calm Authority** before a big meeting? Do you **TEST** that anchor on yourself regularly to make sure it still fires instantly?

8.3 Reflecting on The Loop and Calibration (Chapters 5 & 7)

This is about turning your senses into data-gathering tools and ensuring you are always running the **Predictive Influence Loop** adaptively.

1. **The Respiration Test:**
    - In your next conversation, consciously try to ignore the words for one minute. Focus only on the subject's **Respiration.** Note the precise moment and topic when the breath **locus shifts** (from belly to chest) or when they take a sudden, deep breath. What specific **internal conflict** do you think that physiological shift represents?
    - What is your internal definition of the micro-expression of **Contempt**? Practice spotting the unilateral sneer in the mirror. If you spot it in a client, what is the fastest, non-defensive action you can take to address the **superiority signal** and reset the rapport?
2. **T.O.T.E. Adaptive Strategy:**
    - Reflect on a recent failure to close a deal or secure agreement. Plot your steps onto the **T.O.T.E. Model** flow: **Where did your first TEST fail?** Did you miss a key calibration cue?
    - Describe a situation where you successfully executed a **T.O.T.E. Rerun.** What *new, specific information* did the failure of the first **TEST** provide, and how did you use that information to make your second **OPERATE** phase surgical?
    - What is the final line you use to secure the **EXIT**? Does it ask for a simple signature, or does it leverage a final **Temporal Presupposition** and an **Agreement Anchor** to cement their commitment?

8.4 Reflecting on Ethics and The Long Game (Chapter 8)

The ultimate test of true influence is its sustainability and its ethical footprint.

1. **The Ethical Calculus:**
    - Identify a situation where you used a powerful covert technique (like a **Loss Aversion Frame** or an **Embedded Command**). If the subject were to watch a replay of that conversation and understand every technique you used, would they still feel the decision was theirs and the value was real?
    - How are you actively using **Reciprocity**? List three **high-value, unrequested insights** you can deliver to a key relationship this week, insights that help them understand *their own* **Deep Structure** better.
    - Run the **Autonomy Test** on your current biggest goal: Do the interventions you plan still leave the subject with the genuine feeling of **ownership** over the final decision?
2. **Consistency and Legacy:**
    - List three small, low-risk commitments you can secure from a subject *before* asking for the final agreement. How will you make sure you immediately **reward** (Positively Reinforce) their follow-through on those small steps to build a **habit of consistency**?
    - If your entire legacy were defined by your ability to upgrade the **Internal Maps** of others, what is the single most important limiting belief (**Generalization** or **Modal Operator of Possibility**) you are committed to helping a key person overcome?

By committing to this rigorous cycle of self-reflection, you are moving beyond technique and embracing the **Adaptive Intelligence** that defines true mastery in the science of predictable influence.

BOOK FOUR

IRRESISTIBLE CHARM: RELATIONSHIP DYNAMICS

INTRODUCTION
TO IRRESISTIBLE CHARM

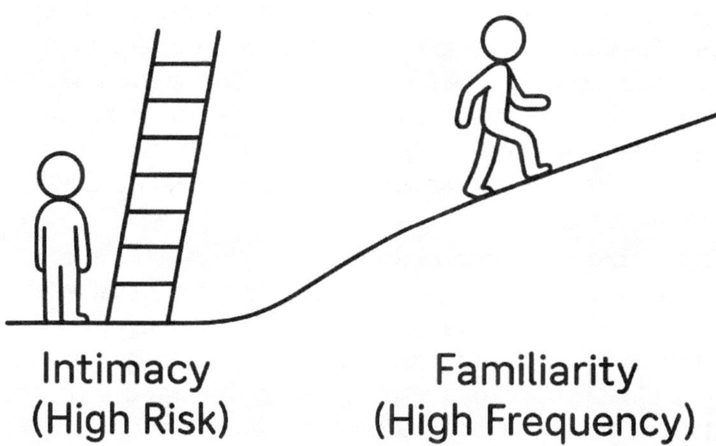

We have moved through the logical and the non-verbal. Book 1 covered the strategy of choice. Book 2 taught you the charisma of physical projection. Book 3 ensured your words landed with precision. Now, we face the hardest challenge: making people **want** to be influenced by you. This book is about building **Irresistible Charm** through the mastery of relationship dynamics.

Charm is not just a thin layer of manners. It is a fundamental psychological resource. It is the skilled use of openness, social connection, and emotional management to secure intense attraction and loyalty over the long term. Charm is the difference between a good transaction and a lasting connection. It is the mechanism that ensures people feel deeply invested in your presence and your success.

This book guides the relationship from simple professional trust to deep, personal alignment. It is built on the measurable science of **self-disclosure** and **social cohesion**. We will show you how to rapidly accelerate intimacy without setting off the target's psychological defenses. We focus on the architecture of human connection, ensuring the bond you create is resilient and self-sustaining.

The Blueprint of Intimacy: Self-Disclosure

Every deep connection, whether with a partner, a key client, or a core team member, rests on a calculated exchange of personal information. This process is called **self-disclosure**. Charm is essentially the intentional management of this exchange. It controls the pace and the appropriate depth of intimacy.

The objective is to quickly create a sense of familiarity and closeness. Research strongly confirms a key finding: **disclosure frequency**, how often you share small personal details, is the number one factor that predicts familiarity and closeness, provided the disclosures are perceived as appropriate. This means that the sheer volume of low-stakes interaction is more important than rushing to share deep secrets.

The Threshold of Appropriateness: The strategy must be precise. You must be aware of the boundary. Studies show that while intimate disclosure can increase closeness, it also carries a significant risk: it far more often **reduces social attraction** if the target perceives the disclosure as inappropriate. If you share too much too soon, you violate a boundary. You signal poor judgment, and the target immediately retreats.

Charm is the skill of navigating this delicate line. It requires maximizing the frequency of low-stakes disclosures to build rapid familiarity. At the same time, you must meticulously monitor the target's reciprocal behavior. This tells you the exact moment it is safe to increase the depth of the conversation.

The Three Engines of Magnetic Attraction

Irresistible charm relies on three core principles that elevate a relationship beyond just a functional exchange.

1. Narrativity: The Entertainment Investment: A relationship must be engaging. It must hold the target's interest over time. Simply stating dry facts is boring. Charm requires presenting personal information as a compelling story. **Disclosure narrativity**, the practice of telling short, structured stories about yourself, significantly increases perceived closeness and social attraction.

This positive effect happens because the narrative format possesses a clear **perceived entertainment value**. The goal is to frame every interaction as a worthwhile investment of the target's time and attention. This concept is extremely important in virtual or text-based settings. In those spaces, where physical presence and body language are missing, attraction depends almost entirely on "words, charm, and seduction." Linguistic crafting becomes the only tool you have.

2. Social Rituals: The Shared Identity Check: Charm secures long-term loyalty by building a **shared identity**. People feel an intense sense of belonging when they share common experiences and values. This is achieved through **shared social rituals** and **identification humor**.

Identification humor builds group cohesion because it appeals to a set of shared expectations and norms that everyone in the group recognizes. When a group laughs at the same social violation, they confirm they share the same underlying worldview. This shared psychological vetting mechanism strengthens the relationship and reduces uncertainty about the other person.

The ultimate goal of this shared laughter is to create deep cohesion. Research confirms that shared laughter increases interpersonal attraction, enhances group cohesion, and helps resolve conflicts. By encouraging shared humor and inside jokes, you help the group develop a resilient **shared identity** that is much stronger than their individual differences.

3. Projection of Psychological Stability: Charm is amplified by projecting deep psychological stability. A perceived **good sense of humor** is an invaluable social resource. People naturally gravitate toward those who project a positive, engaging feeling.

Positive humor styles are strongly associated with desirable traits: high self-esteem, extroversion, and greater satisfaction in relationships. By consistently using positive, unifying humor, the charismatic person projects stability and social desirability. This makes them a highly sought-after connection. They are seen as a psychological resource.

The Synthesis of Charisma and Strategy

This book takes the strategic systems of the previous books and applies them directly to the human heart and mind:

- **Linguistic Precision (Book 3):** The personal narratives and disclosures must use concrete language to maximize impact and avoid cognitive friction.
- **Non-Verbal Resonance (Book 2):** All disclosures must be supported by composed delivery and intentional stillness, ensuring the **Halo Effect** reinforces trustworthiness.

- **Covert Persuasion (Book 1):** The emotional commitment gained through self-disclosure and loyalty must be leveraged to secure larger, structural loyalty and adherence.

This book details the exact steps for managing this delicate process. We will show you how to structure disclosures to accelerate intimacy, how to use humor for social vetting, and how to continuously calibrate the relationship's boundaries to maintain peak social attraction.

The next chapter, **Accelerate Intimacy: Structuring Calculated Self-Disclosure**, details the precise formula for using disclosure frequency and content. It shows you how to build rapid, deep familiarity while minimizing the risk of sharing too much, too soon, which could break the connection.

CHAPTER 1

ACCELERATE INTIMACY: STRUCTURING CALCULATED SELF - DISCLOSURE

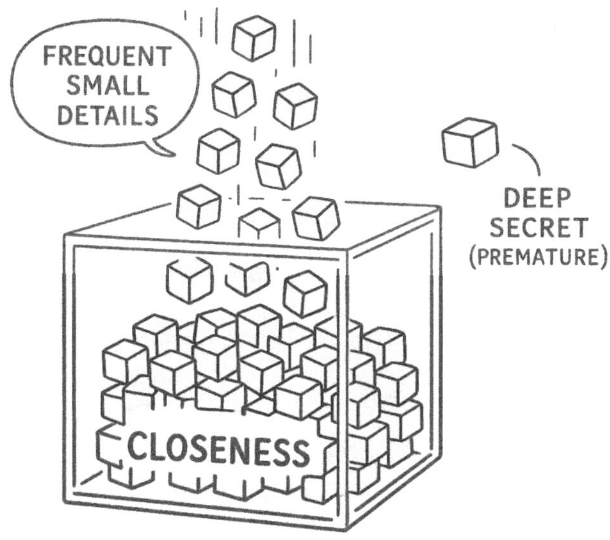

We enter the most delicate part of influence. It is not enough to guide a person logically. You must connect with them personally. This requires accelerating intimacy without rushing to vulnerability. The tool for this rapid connection is **calculated self-disclosure**.

Charm is essentially the intentional management of shared personal information. Every deep relationship, whether it is personal or professional, is built on this exchange. The objective is to establish familiarity and closeness so fast that the target feels they have known you far longer than they actually have. This process creates a resilient, strong psychological bond.

I. The Formula for Familiarity: Frequency Over Intimacy

The primary mistake people make when seeking connection is sharing too much, too soon. They confuse vulnerability with intimacy. They try to speed up the process by dumping secrets or painful details right away. This approach is often disastrous.

The Key Finding: Research consistently shows that the most powerful factor predicting familiarity and closeness is **disclosure frequency**. This is the volume of information shared, not the depth of the information. The sheer number of small, safe interactions matters more than the urgency of the deep secrets.

If you share often, about low-stakes things, your weekend routines, a minor preference, or a funny anecdote from your week, you quickly build a dense foundation of connection. The target feels they know you well because they have accumulated many small data points. This high-frequency exchange is the fastest route to perceived closeness.

The Danger of Premature Depth: While intimate disclosure can certainly increase closeness in established relationships, it far more often **reduces social attraction** if the target perceives the sharing as inappropriate for the current stage of the relationship.

If you reveal deep, personal failures or intense emotional anxieties too early, you signal a lack of boundaries or emotional instability. This sets off an internal alarm for the target, and they immediately retreat. They feel uncomfortable. They view the sharing as a social violation. The risk of sharing deep personal matters often outweighs the potential benefit in the initial stages.

Actionable Frequency Strategy:

1. **Maximize Low-Stakes Volume:** Share specific, small details about your life three times more often than you would naturally. Talk about your favorite type of coffee, the difficulty of your commute, or a small win you had this morning.
2. **Maintain Neutrality:** Ensure the content is positive, non-controversial, and not emotionally taxing. The objective is to build a large catalog of neutral shared facts.
3. **Prioritize Reciprocity:** Always leave room for the target to match your disclosure. Your small disclosure is an invitation for them to offer a small disclosure back. This mutual exchange is the engine of closeness.

II. The Necessity of Narrativity: Charm as Entertainment

It is not enough to just share facts. The words must be engaging. A relationship must be compelling enough to hold the target's sustained interest. Simply stating dry facts is boring, and boring conversations kill charisma.

The Power of Storytelling: Disclosure narrativity, the practice of framing personal information as a structured, short story, increases perceived closeness and social attraction. This positive effect happens entirely because the narrative format possesses **perceived entertainment value**. The target enjoys listening to you. They are investing their attention because they are getting a worthwhile return.

The Strategy of Framing the Mundane: The goal is to elevate mundane details into engaging, short narratives. You must frame every piece of information as an investment of the target's attention.

- *Instead of (Dry Fact):* "I was late because I had to fill out a form." (Zero entertainment value)
- *Use (Narrative Frame):* "I was almost twenty minutes late because the new security form insisted I list my dog's middle name. It was a bizarre, unnecessary five minutes of my life, but I learned that the system will shut down if I type 'None'." (Short, specific, creates a shared moment of mild frustration, possesses clear entertainment value).

By consistently delivering these small, entertaining narrative capsules, you maximize the psychological impact and dramatically increase social attraction toward you, the source of the story. The interaction is transformed from a simple exchange of facts into a valuable, engaging social resource.

III. The Calibration Test: Diagnosing Appropriateness

The effects of self-disclosure are entirely controlled by the target's **perceived appropriateness**. This boundary is dynamic. It is subjective, and it must be actively monitored. You cannot guess the boundary; you must test for it.

Reciprocal Disclosure as a Gauge: The single most reliable measure of appropriateness is **reciprocal disclosure**. A target who matches your level of disclosure, in both frequency and depth, implicitly confirms that your current level of intimacy is acceptable. Their return of information signals that the boundary is safe.

The Testing Sequence for Depth:

1. **Initial Low Stakes:** Start with high-frequency, low-intimacy disclosures (Chapter 2, Section I).
2. **The Gentle Deepening:** Once familiarity is established, you should gently test the boundary. Offer a disclosure that is *slightly* deeper than the one before it (e.g., instead of talking about hobbies, talk about a minor professional philosophy).

3. **Observe Response:** Watch the target's reaction carefully. Did they match the new depth? Did they ask a follow-up question that indicates comfort?
    - **If they retreat:** If the target offers a very short, closed answer, changes the subject abruptly, or redirects the focus back entirely to you, the intimacy level was inappropriate. **You must immediately retreat.** You pull back the depth of future disclosures to a safer, frequent level.
    - **If they match:** If the target matches or even exceeds the new depth, they have implicitly signaled the boundary is safe, and you may proceed to the next level.

This continuous calibration ensures you build closeness rapidly without violating trust. Pushing too hard or too fast reveals a lack of social intelligence, which instantly breaks the charm and reduces social attraction.

IV. Disclosure and the Compliance Drivers

Calculated self-disclosure is not just for emotional connection. It is a strategic tool that feeds directly into the compliance drivers detailed in Book 1, securing commitment and activating liking.

1. Activating Liking (Similarity): The core of the Liking principle is similarity. We like people who are similar to us. By using **disclosure frequency** to share many small, positive details, you are maximizing the surface area for finding common ground.

- **Actionable Alignment:** You should quickly note any small detail the target shares, a favorite movie, a preferred travel destination, a shared frustration with a local service, and immediately disclose a similar, supporting detail. This instant, subtle mirroring of preferences creates a powerful, unconscious sense of connection. The target thinks, "This person is like me," which is the fastest route to trust and acceptance.

2. Securing Commitment and Consistency: Self-disclosure creates the psychological condition for **Commitment and Consistency**. For commitment to be lasting, the target must accept **inner responsibility** for the action, feeling they chose to perform it without strong external pressure.

- **Application:** By initiating a series of small, reciprocal disclosures, you are securing small commitments from the target ("I trust this person with a small detail about my life"). This establishes a pattern of positive, low-pressure commitment. The larger requests that follow feel like a logical, consistent extension of this established pattern of trust. The target believes the final, large choice originated from their own will, not from your external control.

V. The Virtual Challenge: Charm Without Presence

The architecture of charm changes when physical presence is removed. In virtual or text-based communication, non-verbal signals like haptics and eye contact are absent. The entire burden of building rapport and attraction shifts to the linguistic architecture of the message.

Linguistic Charisma is Paramount: In the virtual medium, attraction relies almost entirely on "words, charm, and seduction."

1. **Narrativity is Essential:** Since you cannot rely on composed posture (Book 2) to hold attention, your **Narrativity** must be extremely strong. Every communication must be crafted to provide entertainment value and familiarity.
2. **Concrete Vocabulary:** You must use the principles of concrete language (Book 3) to ensure the message delivers maximum emotional density. Abstract or vague language will be instantly ignored in a competitive digital environment.
3. **Frequency and Presence:** High-frequency, low-stakes digital communication maintains familiarity. It keeps you present in the target's mind without demanding deep cognitive effort, sustaining the bond.

When physical tools are gone, linguistic mastery must compensate. You must use the principles of framing and concrete language to build a compelling virtual persona that ensures the target's continued interest.

VI. Architectural Vulnerability

Accelerating intimacy through calculated self-disclosure is the first step in building irresistible charm. It is the sophisticated use of architectural vulnerability: you control the input and the pace. You maximize familiarity through **frequency**, strengthen the bond through **narrativity**, and ensure safety by constantly checking for **appropriateness**.

This process creates a bond that is psychologically deep. The target feels safe, understood, and entertained. This deep connection makes all subsequent attempts at influence feel less like external demands and more like shared, safe opportunities.

The next chapter, **Cement Loyalty: Creating Identity Through Shared Social Rituals**, details how to solidify this connection. We move from the individual exchange of information to the creation of permanent, structural loyalty by manufacturing group identity and shared experiences.

CHAPTER 2

CEMENT LOYALTY: CREATING IDENTITY THROUGH SHARED SOCIAL RITUALS

A connection between two people is weak. It can break easily under pressure. Intimacy, even deep intimacy, is fragile if it remains private. To make a bond last, to build true **loyalty**, you must move it into a strong social setting.

Loyalty is not a feeling you simply wish for. It is a structure you must build. It rests on shared experiences, confirmed values, and common rituals. When someone becomes truly loyal, they stop asking if they should support you. They just act consistent with the common identity they already share with your group.

This chapter details how to use **shared social rituals** and **group identity** to build a bond that is resilient. We move from the personal exchange of details to the creation of a powerful, unified perspective. This is how you make loyalty strong for the long term.

The Core Need for the "Us"

People have a deep, constant need to feel like they belong. They look for a collective, a group that shares a basic way of seeing the world. This **shared identity** is the essential foundation of loyalty. Once individuals feel like they belong to a group, their actions are driven by the group's goals. They stop thinking only about personal self-interest.

To secure this collective mindset, you must prove that the group is structurally unified. You must show that the target and the charismatic person are completely linked. This unification happens through shared memory and shared laughter. You must create a clear boundary that says, "We are together, and they are separate."

Loyalty becomes structural when you tie the individual's self-image to the group's identity. If a person sees themselves as "a dedicated member of this core team," challenging the team becomes challenging their own self-worth. That is a painful choice most people will avoid.

The charismatic person must constantly create this feeling of "us" versus everything else. They do this by turning small, shared moments into powerful, permanent rituals.

I. The Ritual of Belonging: Making Moments Stick

Small, accidental events often come to define a group's spirit. The shared laughter over a small accident or a strange phrase becomes a marker. The charismatic leader notices these markers. Then they turn them into **social rituals**.

Inside Jokes as Identity Markers: Inside jokes are not accidental fun. They grow naturally from unique group dynamics. They reflect common experiences. They bring a specific joy to the members that outsiders do not share. These small moments are essential social markers. They function as fast, reliable ways to re-establish trust and affection. This is especially true when tension appears in the group.

Creating the Permanent Ritual: You must not let a good shared moment simply fade away. You must use it again. You must elevate it.

- **The Ritual of Remembrance:** The charismatic individual constantly references the inside joke or a funny shared moment. They might mention it at the start of a serious meeting. They might mention it in a difficult conversation. This repeated use turns the moment into a **shared ritual**. This ritual quickly confirms mutual loyalty and affection. It signals to the target, "We share a memory that is unique. We are part of a specific, protected group."
- **Psychological Payoff:** When the group laughs at the inside joke, they get a dose of emotional warmth and affirmation. This good feeling is tied directly to the group's identity. The target learns that participation in the group ritual gives them a consistent, positive emotional reward. This consistent payoff links the group identity to feeling psychologically well. They become dependent on the group for this feeling.

II. The Effort of Commitment: Securing Lasting Loyalty

The loyalty created through social rituals is structural. It is deliberately built to activate the powerful driver of **Commitment and Consistency**.

The consistency rule says people feel a constant need to align future actions with past commitments. This adherence is strongest when the commitment is **active, public, and effortful**. If the action is easy, private, or passive, the commitment breaks quickly.

Structuring the Effortful Ritual: You must design small, repeated rituals that satisfy these three demands.

1. **Active:** The ritual must require a physical action, not just agreement. This could be a unique, shared handshake used only by the core team. It could be a required verbal declaration of a positive intention before starting work.
2. **Public:** The ritual must be visible to others. A shared, positive saying repeated before a challenge is public. It creates external pressure to uphold the group's image.
3. **Effortful:** The ritual must require minor effort. This could be the small effort of memorizing a specific group history. It could be the small vulnerability of sharing one honest challenge from the previous week.

By performing these rituals, the target constantly reaffirms their commitment to the group's identity. They feel **inner responsibility** for the group's behaviors and values. They believe the commitment is their own choice. This makes the loyalty secure and self-sustaining. It is much stronger than loyalty based on external demands alone.

The Cost of Inconsistency: When rituals are established, the psychological cost of *breaking* them becomes very high. Breaking a public, active commitment causes internal conflict. The target feels pressure because their action (breaking the ritual) contradicts their self-image (a loyal member). To relieve this internal pain, they are overwhelmingly motivated to maintain the ritual.

III. The Unifying Force of Humor: Vetting Values

The most efficient tool for creating this unified perspective is **humor**. Humor is a highly sophisticated social resource. We must focus on the most unifying function: **identification humor**.

The Shared Value Check: Identification humor builds group cohesion. It appeals to a set of shared expectations and norms that everyone recognizes. When a group laughs at the same joke, it often means the joke points out an unusual violation of a norm or expectation.

- **Actionable Vetting:** The shared laughter confirms alignment. If the target laughs at the same social violation, they confirm they share your core values and baseline expectations. This mutual reinforcement strengthens the relationship and instantly reduces uncertainty about the other person. This shared perspective creates a unified worldview that is essential for trust.
- **Targeting the Norm:** The best identification humor targets a minor violation of an *external* norm or expectation. This means something outside the group that everyone can agree upon. You must avoid humor that targets a group member. You must avoid humor meant to divide or criticize. By agreeing on what is externally ridiculous or annoying, you solidify the bond inside the group.

Therapeutic Value and Conflict Resolution: Shared laughter has documented emotional value. Research confirms that shared laughter increases attraction between people. It enhances group cohesion. It helps resolve conflicts. When people laugh together, they form stronger bonds. They develop a **shared identity** that is more resilient than their individual differences. This shared emotional release acts as a safety valve, making the group feel psychologically safer.

IV. The Founding Myth: Shared Narrative

Loyalty needs a history. It is cemented by shared memory. The charismatic leader ensures the group possesses a powerful, common story of its past. This story must focus on overcoming shared, external difficulty.

Narrativity and Emotional Density: The **narrativity** of self-disclosure (Chapter 2) is used for group cohesion. By framing the group's history as an engaging, short story, you maximize the **perceived entertainment value** of the collective experience.

- **Framing the Struggle:** The leader must constantly frame past difficulties as "the time *we* all overcame that impossible deadline" or "the moment *we* realized the old system was holding *us* back." This framing turns shared difficulty into a **founding myth**. The narrative must be concrete. It must use specific dates, names, or quantifiable metrics. It must unify the group under a banner of shared achievement.

This process ensures that when the group faces a new challenge, they refer back to the shared memory (the narrative) as proof of their inherent strength and loyalty. The loyalty is cemented by the memory of shared success against an external problem.

The Anchor of Stability: The charismatic persona is seen as a source of psychological safety. This constant attraction solidifies loyalty because people naturally gravitate toward sources of stability and positive emotion.

The Positive Humor Style: Positive humor styles are directly associated with desirable personality traits like high self-esteem and extroversion. By constantly using positive, unifying humor, the charismatic person projects **psychological stability** and **social desirability**. This stability is the emotional anchor for the group. They are seen as a **safe and valuable social resource**. The natural desire to stay near this source of stability is a powerful driver of loyalty.

Loyalty as Structure

Cementing loyalty is the construction of an identity. It moves beyond individual rapport to the creation of a powerful psychological structure.

1. **Shared Rituals** provide the active, public, and effortful commitment markers that secure long-term consistency.
2. **Identification Humor** provides the social vetting that confirms shared values, reducing uncertainty and increasing cohesion.
3. **Shared Narrative** elevates group history into a founding myth, reinforcing collective strength.

This system ensures that the individual target's loyalty is not just an emotion they feel. It is a structural part of the group's running identity. They are loyal because the group's success and their participation in its rituals are now deeply tied to their self-image.

The next chapter, **Gauge Limits: Calibrating Disclosure for Optimal Attraction**, addresses the continuous maintenance of this bond. We detail the crucial skill of monitoring the relationship boundary. We ensure that intimacy is escalated just enough to maintain high attraction without violating the boundary of appropriateness. Violating that boundary could instantly destroy the loyalty built.

CHAPTER 3

GAUGE LIMITS: CALIBRATING DISCLOSURE FOR OPTIMAL ATTRACTION

We have covered the initial burst of intimacy. We know that high **disclosure frequency** builds familiarity fast. But familiarity is not the same as lasting attraction. True, irresistible charm requires constant work. You must monitor the most delicate boundary in any relationship: the line of **appropriateness**.

The biggest mistake a person can make is pushing too hard, too fast. They confuse openness with intimacy. They share deep secrets hoping to earn trust quickly. But studies show that this is dangerous. Intimate disclosure, if given at the wrong time, often **reduces social attraction** instead of building it. It sets off an internal alarm. It signals a lack of control.

This chapter teaches you how to maintain maximum attraction by mastering the art of the **Calibration Test**. You must learn to read the target's subtle signals. You must know exactly when to advance the intimacy and, more importantly, when to immediately pull back. This constant monitoring ensures the bond remains strong and safe.

I. The Boundary Rule: Intimacy Versus Appropriateness

Intimacy is an acceptable state only when the target feels the context is right. Appropriateness is the psychological framework that allows intimacy to proceed. Without it, the deepest secrets feel uncomfortable, like a social violation.

The High Risk of Premature Depth: If you share a deeply personal failure or intense emotional difficulty too early, the target is put in a difficult position. They feel pressure to reciprocate. They feel responsible for this sudden, unearned vulnerability. This creates anxiety. They respond by retreating. They view the sharing as a sign of poor boundaries or emotional instability on your part.

This is a risk management issue. The potential reward of gaining quick closeness is real, but the risk of destroying attraction by violating the boundary is far greater. Therefore, you must prioritize low-stakes sharing, high volume, and constant monitoring. You must secure familiarity first. Intimacy must be earned later, through controlled testing.

The Role of Context: The level of appropriate disclosure depends entirely on the setting. In a virtual setting, where attraction relies entirely on **words and charm** , disclosures must be crafted with maximum precision and minimum emotional demand. In a professional setting, the appropriate boundary for disclosure is much tighter than in a personal setting. The charismatic person always adheres to the highest level of formality required by the environment, adjusting only slowly.

II. The Calibration Test: Monitoring Reciprocal Behavior

You cannot guess where the boundary lies. You must test for it gently, then confirm the safety of the boundary through the target's reaction. The best gauge for appropriateness is **reciprocal disclosure**.

A target who matches your level of disclosure, in both frequency and depth, implicitly confirms that your current level of intimacy is acceptable. Their return of personal information signals that the boundary is safe for both of you.

Step 1: The Gentle Deepening

Once you have established familiarity through high frequency (Chapter 2), you test the boundary gently. You offer a disclosure that is *slightly* deeper than the one you offered previously. This must be an intentional, small step up the ladder of vulnerability.

- *Example:* You previously talked about minor preferences (favorite foods). The gentle deepening moves to minor challenges (a frustration with a professional process, or a small life lesson you learned last month). It is honest, but it is controlled. It does not carry immense emotional weight.

Step 2: Observe Verbal and Non-Verbal Response

You must watch the target's reaction carefully for specific cues. They signal their comfort level instantly.

- **Verbal Retreat:** Does the target offer a very short, closed answer? Do they change the subject abruptly, perhaps redirecting the focus entirely back to you? Do they offer an answer that is much less personal than your disclosure?
- **Non-Verbal Retreat:** Do they break eye contact and look away for a prolonged period? Do they physically shift their posture away from you (a movement away from openness)? Do they suddenly become less animated or energetic?

These are all signs that your disclosure was too much. The target is signaling, "Stop. You have exceeded the boundary."

Step 3: The Decision Point

You have two choices at this crucial moment:

- **If they Match or Exceed:** If the target offers an equal or slightly deeper disclosure, or if they ask a warm, engaging follow-up question, they have implicitly confirmed the boundary is safe. You may proceed to the next level of intimacy at the next opportune moment.
- **If they Retreat:** If you observe any verbal or non-verbal retreat, the intimacy level was inappropriate. **You must immediately retreat.** You pull back the depth of future disclosures to a safer, more frequent level. You must respect the boundary you discovered. Retreating signals that you are socially intelligent and that you respect their comfort. This respect helps preserve the existing level of trust, even if the boundary test failed.

This continuous calibration ensures you build closeness rapidly without violating trust. Pushing too hard or too fast reveals a serious lack of social intelligence, which instantly breaks the charm and reduces social attraction.

III. The Psychological Cost of Boundary Violation

Why is inappropriate intimacy so damaging? Because it breaks the illusion of competence you built in Book 2. It triggers a strong negative psychological response in the target.

1. The Halo Effect Failure: Your charisma is built on the **Halo Effect**, the idea that people assume you are competent and stable because you are composed and controlled. When you suddenly share inappropriate, raw, or unstable information, you break your own persona. The target thinks, "If they are this unstable, they cannot possibly be competent." The entire perception of authority collapses instantly.

2. Increased Anxiety: Inappropriate self-disclosure creates anxiety in the target. This anxiety is uncomfortable. To relieve this stress, the target's mind automatically seeks distance from the source of the anxiety: you. They retreat from the interaction, or they become emotionally closed off. This defense mechanism is not rational; it is automatic.

3. Social Bias and Retreat: Non-verbal behavior is highly influential. If your behavior is suddenly inconsistent or inappropriate, it creates a **social bias** against you. The target may feel pressure to mirror the uncomfortable vulnerability you just showed, or they may feel pressure to conform to this new, negative, shared attitude about you. They retreat to avoid this psychological pressure.

The ultimate goal is to keep the target feeling secure in your presence. Boundary violation shatters this security immediately.

IV. Sustaining Optimal Attraction with Narrativity

Once the optimal level of disclosure is found, the place where the target is comfortable but still curious, you must sustain it. This is done by maximizing the **perceived entertainment value** of your disclosures.

The Power of Storytelling: Disclosure narrativity, framing personal information as a short, engaging story, increases perceived closeness and social attraction. The narrative format is inherently valuable to the target. They are investing their attention and getting a worthwhile return.

Framing the Routine: You must continuously frame small, routine details as engaging narratives. You are avoiding dry facts and focusing on short, structured stories.

- *Example:* Frame a business challenge not as a vague problem, but as "The 72-hour period last month when we almost lost the deal due to the shipping error, and how the team managed to fix it by 3 PM Friday."

This approach requires using the principles of **Concrete Vocabulary** (Book 3). Specific names, dates, and measurable facts make the narrative feel real and emotionally dense. This continuous delivery of engaging content sustains the target's interest, ensuring they remain attracted to you as a source of positive, valuable interaction.

V. The Continuous Calibration

Gauging limits is the core of sustainable charm. It is a continuous, moment-to-moment process of testing, observing, and adjusting. You are creating intimacy by design, controlling the pace to maintain high attraction without violating the boundary of appropriateness.

1. **Prioritize Frequency:** Start with high-frequency, low-stakes disclosures to build rapid familiarity.
2. **Test Gently:** Use small, incremental deepening of the conversation to find the boundary of the target's comfort.
3. **Read Reciprocity:** Use the target's verbal and non-verbal response as the final gauge for appropriateness. Retreat immediately if you detect signs of anxiety or withdrawal.

This disciplined approach ensures that the deep loyalty you cemented in Chapter 3 remains protected. You maintain the psychological security the target needs. This leaves the target feeling safe, entertained, and consistently drawn to your presence.

The next chapter, **Sustain Interest: Crafting Narrative for Entertainment Value**, will focus exclusively on the mechanics of storytelling. We will detail how to use the structure of a narrative to amplify psychological effects, ensuring every interaction, from a brief email to a long conversation, holds the target's sustained interest.

CHAPTER 4

SUSTAIN INTEREST: CRAFTING NARRATIVE FOR ENTERTAINMENT VALUE

We secured the target's interest. We know they feel familiar because you shared details often. They feel safe because you carefully checked the boundaries of intimacy. Now the hard work begins: keeping them engaged over time. A strong bond will still break if the relationship becomes boring.

To achieve **irresistible charm**, you must ensure the connection provides a consistent, valuable psychological reward. This consistent reward is **perceived entertainment value**.

This chapter details the precise steps for storytelling. We stop just sharing facts. We start crafting a structured narrative. You must learn to transform the small details of your life into short, engaging stories. This steady storytelling is the engine that keeps the target's interest high. It ensures they remain attracted to you as a valuable source of positive interaction.

I. The Power of Story: Entertainment as Closeness

Why does telling a story work better than listing facts? The human brain is built for narrative. Facts demand logical effort and slow thought. Stories instantly engage emotion, memory, and imagination.

The Key Finding: Research confirms that **disclosure narrativity** significantly increases both perceived closeness and social attraction. This positive effect happens because the narrative format possesses clear **perceived entertainment value**.

The target invests their attention and time in listening to you. They receive a worthwhile return on that investment. The interaction moves from a basic exchange into a valuable, engaging social resource. They like the feeling they get when they listen to you talk.

This is especially vital in text-based or virtual communication. Physical presence and body language are missing in those settings. Attraction and interest rely almost entirely on **"words, charm, and seduction"**. Your linguistic skill must work extra hard to compensate for the lack of visual cues. If your digital communication is boring, the connection stops immediately.

II. The Architecture of the Engaging Narrative

A story is not just a sequence of events. It is a tool with a specific psychological structure. To maximize entertainment value, you must frame every small event. Use a clear, recognizable narrative structure.

The Short-Form Narrative Structure: You must compress events into short, efficient stories. They must maximize emotional payoff. Every successful short narrative should contain three basic acts:

1. **The Setup (The State of Normalcy):** Establish the scene quickly. Use concrete details to anchor the story in reality. This gives the target a clear baseline. *Example: "Last Tuesday, the 2:00 PM meeting was just a 15-minute file review with the client."*
2. **The Conflict (The Break in Pattern):** Introduce the unexpected problem or deviation from the norm. This step creates tension and curiosity. *Example: "But at 2:05 PM, the entire system crashed. It froze every single file on the shared network. We had zero access."*
3. **The Resolution (The Lesson or Outcome):** Provide a quick, satisfying end. Offer a lesson, a feeling of relief, or a moment of humor. *Example: "I spent 40 frantic minutes trying to troubleshoot.*

The real lesson I took away was simple: physical backups must now happen every Monday morning, without fail."

This structure guarantees that the target's attention is captured by the conflict. Then they receive the satisfying emotional release of the resolution. This consistent delivery of structured, entertaining content keeps their interest high. It prevents the bond from becoming predictable and dull.

III. Maximizing Impact with Concrete Vocabulary

The narratives you tell must use the principles of **Concrete Vocabulary** (Book 3). Abstract, vague language instantly destroys entertainment value. Specificity makes the difference between a story that sticks and one that is forgotten.

Specific Details Engage the Senses: Concrete language uses specific names, dates, numbers, and direct verbs. It engages the target's imagination instantly. They can visualize the scene. They can feel the tension.

- *Weak Example:* "I had a bad experience with the software last year that cost us time." (Abstract, unspecific).
- *Strong Example:* "Last **September 12th**, the **budget submission** failed at 4:58 PM. It cost us **three full workdays** to recover. I learned to never trust a cloud server after 4:00 PM." (Specific, measurable, creates a clear image and gives a specific date).

This specific, measurable detail maximizes **emotional density**. The target understands exactly what three days of lost time means. This makes the narrative feel real. It strengthens the psychological bond. It increases the perceived entertainment value.

IV. Narrativity and Psychological Vetting

Storytelling is not just about fun. It is a sophisticated way to conduct subtle **psychological vetting** (Chapter 3).

The Vetting Process in Narrative: When you tell a story, you reveal your values by how you narrate the conflict and the resolution.

- If your stories consistently emphasize integrity and hard work, the target learns that you value those traits.
- If your stories consistently emphasize avoiding responsibility, the target learns to distance themselves.

The target constantly watches your narratives. They want to determine if your inner values match their own. If the values align, the psychological vetting succeeds. Then the bond deepens. This subtly reinforces the **Confirmation Bias**. The target looks for information that proves they were right to trust you.

The Shared Struggle Narrative: Narratives that focus on a shared struggle against an external problem are very potent. These stories activate the **Reciprocity** principle. By framing your vulnerability, the struggle, within a successful narrative, the resolution, you offer an emotional concession. The target feels they must reciprocate by offering their trust or continued attention.

This narrative of shared difficulty also builds group cohesion (Chapter 3). Frame the group's past difficulties as a **"founding myth."** For example: "That time we fixed the code in 48 hours to save the company." This maximizes the collective entertainment value of the group's history. It reinforces loyalty.

V. Sustaining Interest by Combating Time Delay

A crucial function of effective storytelling is combating the target's natural tendency toward **Temporal Discounting**. This is the cognitive process where people value rewards less the further out they are in the future.

Your proposal often requires action *now* for a reward that is *delayed*. Narrativity helps close this psychological gap.

The Strategy of Imminent Visualization: You must use sensory language. Make the future outcome feel present and imminent.

- *Instead of:* "If you commit to this plan, you will receive the benefit next year." (Delayed, low value).
- *Use:* "When you execute this plan, you will **see** the budget surplus number on the screen *by June 1st*. You will **feel relief** immediately when the deadline passes." (Sensory, imminent).

By making the future reward tangible, something they can see or feel, you minimize the perceived time delay. This makes the present commitment easier to accept. The narrative keeps the **reward** visually and emotionally present.

VI. The Engine of Enduring Charm

Sustaining interest through narrative is the engine of enduring charm. It moves the relationship from a functional necessity to a source of consistent psychological reward.

1. **Structure the Story:** Use the three-act model (Setup, Conflict, Resolution). This maximizes tension and release.
2. **Use Concrete Vocabulary:** Inject specific numbers, dates, and names. This maximizes emotional density. It combats cognitive friction.
3. **Frame the Values:** Ensure your stories subtly check your core values. Align them perfectly with the target's need for consistency.
4. **Close the Time Gap:** Use sensory language. Make future rewards feel imminent and emotionally present.

This disciplined approach ensures that the target remains psychologically invested in you. You are a source of positive, engaging interaction. You are not only trustworthy, but you are also rewarding to listen to. This continuous psychological return is the definition of irresistible charm.

The next chapter, **Project Desirability: Vetting Values Through Shared Laughter**, focuses on the most advanced social tool. We detail how to use humor not just for entertainment. We show how it acts as a precise instrument to confirm shared moral and social alignment. This further solidifies the bond.

CHAPTER 5

PROJECT DESIRABILITY: VETTING VALUES THROUGH SHARED LAUGHTER

We have secured the target's physical presence and controlled the flow of personal details. But a relationship built on shared facts and careful boundaries will not last if the core values clash. The ultimate test of long-term compatibility is often invisible. It is revealed through laughter.

This chapter details the most advanced social tool in the charismatic arsenal: **humor**. Humor is not just for entertainment. It is a precise instrument. You use it to confirm shared moral and social alignment. This vetting process solidifies the bond. It ensures the target sees you as a desirable, stable, and valuable psychological resource.

The quality of your humor dictates your desirability. Laughter proves that you and the target share the same baseline understanding of the world. This mutual confirmation reduces deep uncertainty. It builds intense social cohesion.

I. The Social Functions of Laughter

Humor is a sophisticated function of human society. It serves several powerful social roles. These roles fall on a spectrum. Some functions unify the group. Other functions divide and isolate. A charismatic leader uses only the unifying elements.

The two unifying functions are **identification** and **clarification**.

1. Identification Humor: The Shared Value Check

Identification humor builds group cohesion. It works because participants share a common value or perception that the humor brings out. When a group laughs at the same joke, it is often because the joke points out a small violation of a social rule or expected pattern.

- **The Vetting Mechanism:** The shared laughter confirms alignment. If the target laughs at the same social violation, they confirm they share your core values. This immediate, mutual reinforcement strengthens the relationship. It instantly reduces the natural uncertainty people feel when forming a new connection. This shared perspective evokes a solid, unified worldview that is essential for deep trust.
- **How to Apply It:** You must use humor that references an *external* problem or expectation. For example, reference a silly administrative rule everyone hates. Or mention a common frustration with a technology platform. By making a light, shared joke about the external issue, you confirm that everyone agrees on the norm. You solidify the internal group bond. This is subtle, but highly effective.

2. Clarification Humor: Reducing Uncertainty

Humor also serves to clarify expectations. This function reduces uncertainty about others. It appeals to common values. When a joke clarifies expectations and reinforces mutual understanding, it quickly establishes what is acceptable within the group.

If a social setting is tense or ambiguous, deploying unifying humor can quickly clarify what is expected. It reinforces mutual understanding. When anxiety is high, humor provides a quick moment of levity and shared identity. This allows the group to relax and reset its emotional tone.

The Spectrum to Avoid: While humor can unify, it can also divide. You must strictly avoid humor that differentiates or enforces norms through criticism. Humor that attacks an external group, or that singles out a member of your own group, instantly destroys cohesion. It breaks the feeling of safety you worked hard to build.

II. The Psychology of Desirability

A perceived good sense of humor is an invaluable social resource. People naturally seek out those who project a positive and engaging feeling. The humor you use is directly tied to your psychological stability.

The Link to Positive Traits: Positive humor styles are strongly linked to highly desirable personality traits. These traits include high self-esteem, extroversion, and cheerfulness. People who use positive humor styles also report greater satisfaction in their relationships.

- **Projecting Stability:** By consistently using positive, unifying humor, the charismatic person projects deep **psychological stability** and **social desirability**. They signal that they are emotionally secure. This makes them highly attractive. It facilitates stronger connections.
- **The Anchor:** This stability is the emotional anchor for the group. When external pressure mounts, the group looks to the leader who uses positive humor. This signals competence and emotional security. They are seen as a **safe and valuable social resource**. The natural desire to stay near this source of emotional stability is a powerful driver of loyalty.

You must view humor as a tool for projecting your best self. Avoid negative, hostile, or self-deprecating humor styles. These signals often suggest internal conflict or low self-esteem. True loyalty requires the leader to project an unwavering, positive emotional outlook.

III. Cementing Loyalty: Shared Rituals and Group Identity

Humor moves beyond temporary laughter to create lasting loyalty. This is achieved by creating shared rituals and "inside jokes."

Inside Jokes as Identity Markers: Inside jokes naturally emerge from unique group dynamics. They reflect common experiences and bring a specific joy to the members. A charismatic leader can actively encourage these shared humorous rituals. They serve as reliable, quick ways to re-establish trust and affection, especially when tension is present.

The Effortful Ritual: This social alignment is structurally sound because it activates the powerful driver of **Commitment and Consistency**. Loyalty based on social rituals is strong because the target accepts inner responsibility for the commitment.

The ritual must be **active, public, and effortful**. The shared laughter and the continued use of inside jokes are active, public commitments to the group's identity. This small, continuous effort strengthens the bond. The target feels they chose this belonging themselves, making the loyalty self-sustaining.

Conflict Resolution: The therapeutic value of shared laughter is supported by research showing that it helps resolve conflicts. When people laugh together, they form stronger connections. They develop a **shared identity** that is more resilient than their individual differences. This shared emotional release acts as a safety valve. It allows the group to quickly repair itself after minor disputes.

IV. The Charismatic Delivery: Stillness and Humor

Humor requires perfect delivery. It relies entirely on the non-verbal foundation established in Book 2. If the delivery is flawed, the humor fails to unify.

Composure and Delivery: Humor needs perfect **composure** for delivery. If you deliver a joke with nervous energy, the anxiety compromises the humor. The audience laughs at the anxiety, not with the content. Controlled stillness and a measured vocal pace (Chapter 2) ensure the humor is perceived as intentional and stable.

Emotional Contagion: Humor is a highly effective tool for initiating positive **Emotional Contagion**. If you project genuine amusement, the people in the group who are easily influenced by social cues will immediately absorb and reflect that emotion. This spreads the positive feeling throughout the room.

The Halo Effect: The positive feeling generated by unifying humor reinforces the **Halo Effect**. The target now connects the positive emotional state (joy, connection) directly with your composed presence. This further cements the inference of trustworthiness and reliability.

V. Vetting Values Through Narrative and Laughter

Storytelling (Chapter 5) and humor must work together. The stories you tell reveal your values. The humor confirms that those values match the group's.

The Narrative Vetting: When you frame a story, you reveal what you value by how you handle the conflict. If you narrate a story that focuses on integrity during a financial struggle, you vet your honesty. If the target laughs at the moral outcome, they confirm that they also prioritize honesty.

The Founding Myth: Use this shared laughter to reinforce the **"founding myth"** of the group (Chapter 3). Frame the group's past struggles as a shared triumph against an external problem. This creates a strong collective narrative that reinforces loyalty.

The Anchor of Stability: This system ensures the target remains psychologically invested in you. You are a consistent source of stability, attraction, and positive emotional reward. This continuous psychological return is the definition of irresistible charm.

VI. The Desirable Persona

Projecting desirability is the art of using social tools to secure long-term loyalty. You move a collection of individuals from separate self-interest into a unified, emotionally connected group.

1. **Identification Humor** confirms shared values and reduces uncertainty.
2. **Shared Rituals** provide the active, public commitment markers that secure long-term consistency.
3. **Positive Humor Styles** project psychological stability, making you an attractive emotional resource.

This system ensures that the target's bond with you is not just based on a temporary feeling. It is a strong, structural part of their ongoing identity. They are loyal because your presence makes them feel safe, unified, and psychologically stable.

The final chapter will summarize all the techniques from Irresistible Charm. We will integrate the skills of disclosure, calibration, humor, and loyalty to finalize the architecture of the magnetic social persona.

CONCLUSION

THE ARCHITECTURE OF ENDURING CHARM

We have finished the study of Irresistible Charm. This book taught you how to build deep, lasting connections that secure loyalty. We moved the focus from temporary rapport to the creation of a resilient, shared identity. Charm is not just a polite social skill. It is a system for managing vulnerability, setting boundaries, and using social rituals to cement long-term commitment.

This final chapter synthesizes the core lessons of **Disclosure, Calibration, Loyalty, and Narrativity**. We show how these elements fuse together. This unified system ensures the target remains psychologically invested in you. The goal is simple: to create a desirable social persona that provides consistent psychological returns.

I. The Foundation: Intimacy by Design

The entire system of charm rests on the controlled management of personal information. This process accelerates closeness without the risk of emotional instability.

Synthesis of Disclosure and Frequency (Chapter 2):

1. **Prioritize Frequency:** The most powerful factor predicting closeness is **disclosure frequency**. You must maximize the number of low-stakes, safe interactions. This builds a dense foundation of familiarity quickly.
2. **Narrativity as Value:** Simply sharing facts is boring. You must use **disclosure narrativity** to frame small details as short, engaging stories. This storytelling provides **perceived entertainment value**. This ensures the target invests their attention and time in the interaction.

The Crucial Calibration (Chapter 4):

Intimacy is only safe when the target feels the boundary is right. You must constantly monitor the relationship.

1. **Test Gently:** You find the boundary by testing it. Offer a disclosure that is *slightly* deeper than the one before it.
2. **Read Reciprocity:** You use the target's reaction as the final gauge. A target who matches your level of disclosure implicitly confirms the boundary is safe.
3. **Retreat Immediately:** If you observe any verbal or non-verbal retreat (signs of anxiety or discomfort), you must immediately pull back the depth of future disclosures. Violating the boundary of appropriateness destroys social attraction and breaks the trust you built.

This disciplined approach ensures you build closeness rapidly while maintaining the psychological security the target needs.

II. The Structural Cement: Loyalty and Shared Identity

Intimacy is secured permanently by cementing the personal bond into a shared group identity. This loyalty is structural, not emotional.

Synthesis of Rituals and Commitment (Chapter 3):

1. **Build Shared Rituals:** Loyalty is built on shared experiences. The charismatic person must turn accidental, shared moments (e.g., inside jokes) into repeatable **social rituals**.
2. **Activate Effortful Commitment:** These rituals must be **active, public, and effortful**. This commitment is self-sustaining. By performing these rituals, the target continuously reaffirms their commitment to the group's identity. This makes the loyalty strong and permanent.

3. **Vetting Values with Humor:** Humor is used as a psychological vetting mechanism. **Identification humor** builds group cohesion. It works because the shared laughter confirms that everyone agrees on the same core values and norms. This immediate confirmation instantly reduces uncertainty and strengthens the bond.

This system ensures that the individual's loyalty is now tied to a strong, shared identity. The psychological cost of breaking that loyalty becomes very high.

III. The Anchor of Desirability

The magnetic persona must be seen as a source of psychological stability and positive emotion. This constant attraction solidifies loyalty.

Synthesis of Desirability (Chapter 6):

1. **Project Stability:** You must consistently use **positive humor styles**. These styles are strongly associated with desirable personality traits like high self-esteem and extroversion. This projects **psychological stability**. People naturally seek out this source of emotional security.
2. **Narrate the Myth:** You sustain interest by continuously framing the group's past struggles as a **"founding myth."** This narrative elevates shared difficulty into collective triumph. This reinforces group strength and loyalty.

This ensures the target remains psychologically invested in you. You are a consistent source of stability, attraction, and positive emotional reward.

IV. The System Integration

Irresistible Charm is the synthesis of all four books. It acts as the final relational layer for the entire influence system.

- **Charm Protects Authority:** The composure you project (Book 2) is protected by the careful boundaries you maintain (Chapter 4). If you break the boundary, you destroy the persona.
- **Charm Delivers Language:** The precise, concrete language (Book 3) is delivered through engaging narratives (Chapter 5), maximizing its appeal and emotional density.
- **Charm Secures Commitment:** The emotional connection secured through self-disclosure is leveraged to secure the structural **Commitment and Consistency** (Book 1) of the group.

The result is a relationship that is resilient and strong. The target feels safe, unified, and continuously drawn to your presence. The influence is no longer a tactic. It is a natural consequence of the deep, positive bond you have established.

We have now mastered the art of building lasting connection. The final book, **Instant Influence**, shifts the focus entirely to generating immediate, urgent action. We will explore the mechanics of time, scarcity, and loss aversion. These are the powerful psychological forces that compel rapid compliance. We move from building long-term loyalty to securing the decisive, necessary action *now*.

REFLECTION QUESTIONS

We have completed the study of Irresistible Charm. This book taught you how to build deep, strong connections that secure loyalty. You learned to manage vulnerability, set boundaries, and use social rituals to cement long-term commitment.

The skills of charm, disclosure, calibration, humor, and loyalty, must move from theory to consistent practice. Use these questions to personalize the material. Map the concepts onto your own interactions. Prepare for the final phase of influence: urgent action.

Section 1: Disclosure and Intimacy Calibration

Charm relies on accelerating closeness without violating the target's sense of appropriateness. This requires controlled self-disclosure.

1. **Frequency over Depth:** Think about a new professional contact you made last month. How often did you communicate? Was the communication focused on deep issues or **low-stakes details** (e.g., commute, hobbies, minor preferences)? How can you increase the **disclosure frequency** of small, safe details by 50% in your next week to quickly build familiarity?

2. **The Danger of Premature Intimacy:** Recall a time when someone shared too much information with you too soon. How did that make you feel? Did it **reduce social attraction**? What specific detail did they share that crossed the line of appropriateness for that early stage of the relationship?
3. **The Calibration Test:** You must use the target's reaction to find the boundary. If you were to offer a small, slightly deeper disclosure in your next meeting, what specific **verbal or non-verbal signal** would tell you that the target was retreating? What is your immediate, planned **retreat response** to protect the existing level of trust?
4. **Narrativity and Value:** Think of a routine, necessary task you completed yesterday (e.g., filing a tax document, fixing a slow computer). Rewrite the description of that task using the three-act narrative structure (Setup, Conflict, Resolution). How does framing the mundane detail as a short story increase its **perceived entertainment value**?

Section 2: Loyalty, Rituals, and Desirability

Loyalty is secured by cementing the personal bond into a resilient, shared group identity.

5. **Identification Humor: Humor** is a psychological vetting mechanism. Identify one external social norm or expectation that your work group commonly dislikes (e.g., a shared administrative burden or a specific technology glitch). Plan one piece of **identification humor** that targets this external issue. How would shared laughter over this external problem confirm alignment on your core values?
6. **The Effortful Ritual: Commitment** is strongest when it is active, public, and effortful. Think of a goal your immediate team needs to achieve next month. Design one small, **effortful ritual** that the core team can perform weekly (e.g., a specific 5-minute shared task, a specific public verbal confirmation). How does this small effort solidify their long-term commitment to the group's success?
7. **Anchor of Stability: Positive humor styles** project psychological stability, making you an attractive social resource. If pressure mounts next week, how will you consciously use positive, unifying humor to act as an **emotional anchor** for your team?

8. **The Founding Myth:** Think about a time your group overcame a significant difficulty or setback (e.g., losing a client, missing a deadline). How can you frame that negative event as a **"founding myth"**, a shared narrative of collective triumph against an external problem? Use concrete details (dates, names, metrics) to make the story emotionally dense.

BOOK FIVE

INSTANT INFLUENCE: URGENCY AND ACTION

INTRODUCTION

TO INSTANT INFLUENCE

We have finished the complex work. We have built the long game of influence. We learned how to frame a decision for consistency (Book 1). We mastered the charismatic presence needed for trust (Book 2). We secured the deal with precise language and zero resistance (Book 3 and Book 4).

But sometimes, consistency and loyalty are not enough. Sometimes, you need action **right now**.

This final book deals with the most decisive phase of influence: **Instant Influence.** This is the art of collapsing the decision window. It is about using the psychological forces that compel immediate, urgent compliance. This system relies entirely on manipulating the target's perception of time and value.

This is the shift from long-term relationship building to short-term motivational science. You stop asking, "Why will they agree next week?" You start asking, "What psychological trigger forces them to agree in the next 60 seconds?"

The Science of Impatience: Temporal Discounting

The foundation of instant influence is the human brain's flawed relationship with time. This concept is called **Temporal Discounting**. It is the cognitive process where people prefer more immediate rewards over future benefits, even if the future benefits are worth more.

This human nature tends to be impatient. Behavioral economics shows that people often make irrational choices when time is involved. Imagine you have a choice: take $100 today, or take $110 in a month. Many people will grab the immediate $100. The extra $10 seems less valuable simply because it is delayed. The value we place on future rewards drops sharply the further away they are.

This phenomenon is also known as time discounting or hyperbolic discounting. It explains why people struggle with long-term financial planning. It explains why people engage in unhealthy behaviors that offer immediate rewards, like smoking.

The persuader's job is to exploit this tendency. You must make the target act in the present by structuring the choice so that the **present action** is associated with an **immediate reward** or the avoidance of an **immediate loss**. This technique overrides the target's ability to rationally evaluate the long-term payoff.

The Dominance of Fear: Loss Aversion

While you can motivate people with positive rewards, fear is a much stronger driver. Specifically, the fear of losing something is measurably more powerful than the desire to gain an equivalent item. This is the core principle of **Loss Aversion**.

Nobel laureates Daniel Kahneman and Amos Tversky showed this: the psychological pain of losing something is generally more powerful than the pleasure of gaining an equivalent item.

The strategy for instant influence is simple: **Frame non-compliance as a guaranteed, immediate loss.**

- Do not focus on the potential money they will make next year (Gain Frame).
- Focus on the immediate money they will lose if they wait until tomorrow (Loss Frame).

This technique triggers the **Fear Of Missing Out (FOMO)**. To avoid the regret associated with missing out, people are compelled to make quick, impulsive decisions. They often overlook a thorough evaluation of the proposal's true long-term value.

The Scarcity Trigger: Rarity and Reactance

Loss Aversion is amplified by **Scarcity**. We value things more when they are rare or limited.

Our brains are built to assign greater value to things that are scarce, even if their actual worth does not change. A famous experiment in 1975 showed this clearly: participants rated identical cookies from an almost empty jar as more desirable than the same cookies from a full jar. The desire was determined entirely by the perceived limited availability.

Psychological Reactance: Scarcity triggers an immediate defensive reaction. When our freedom to choose or acquire something is threatened by limited availability (e.g., "Only three left" or "Offer ends at midnight"), we experience **Psychological Reactance**. This is an innate desire to reassert that threatened freedom. We often do this by wanting the restricted item even more intensely.

The powerful combination for instant influence is: **Temporal Discounting + Loss Aversion + Scarcity.**

You create a situation where the future reward is devalued (Temporal Discounting). You ensure inaction means an immediate, guaranteed loss (Loss Aversion). You restrict the time window to challenge the target's freedom (Scarcity/Reactance). This manufactured urgency collapses the decision window entirely.

The Integration of Charisma and Urgency

The emotional stability and trust you built in Books 1 through 4 are not discarded here. They are used as anchors for the urgency.

- **Authority and Urgency:** If a target trusts your **Authority** (Book 1/2), they trust your deadlines. Your urgent demand, "You must sign this by 3 PM", is accepted as legitimate fact, not as a cheap sales tactic.
- **Commitment and Action:** The small commitments you secured (Book 1) pave the way for this urgent, large commitment. The target's mind sees the urgent action as consistent with their established pattern of following your guidance.

This book provides the final, mechanical steps for compelling this immediate action. We turn these powerful psychological concepts into actionable steps for controlling time and value.

The next chapters will break down these elements:

- **Compel Action Now:** We detail how to use **Temporal Discounting** to secure present commitment for a delayed payoff.
- **Force Urgency:** We show how to activate **Loss Aversion and Scarcity** by framing inaction as a guaranteed loss.
- **Demand Presence:** We explore techniques for minimizing the **perceived delay** of the future reward, making it feel imminent.
- **Control Deadline:** We show how to manufacture the psychological need to buy, ensuring the target feels the pressure to comply immediately.

Mastery of instant influence ensures that when the moment for decisive action arrives, hesitation is eliminated, and the choice is made immediately in your favor.

CHAPTER 1

COMPEL ACTION NOW:

EXPLOITING TEMPORAL DISCOUNTING

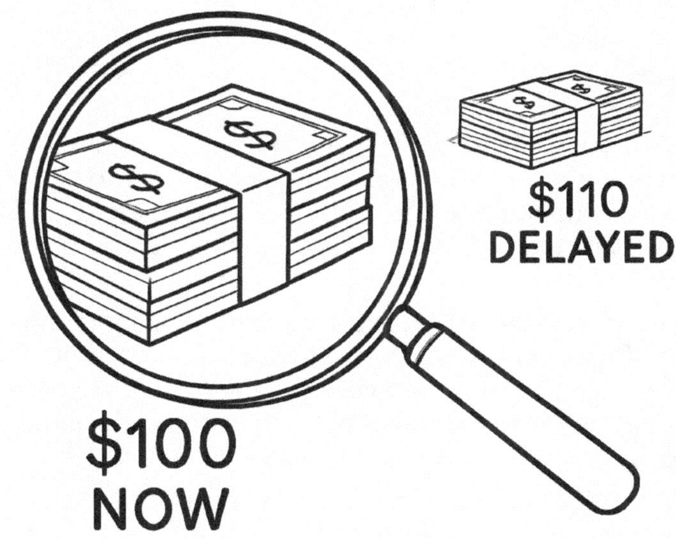

We are now focused on closing the deal immediately. The time for subtle cultivation is over. You must bypass the target's slow, rational system. This is done by exploiting the fundamental flaw in human judgment: the way we value rewards over time.

This flaw is called **Temporal Discounting**. It is the psychological reason people prefer a smaller reward right now over a larger reward later. The value of a future prize fluctuates based on how long you have to wait to get it. The longer the delay, the less the reward is worth to the target's brain.

Your job is to structure the choice so the target's innate impatience becomes the reason they act immediately. You must ensure the present action is associated with an immediate payoff, even if the main benefit is months away.

I. The Science of Present Bias

Behavioral economics confirms that human financial decisions are not always rational. This concept explains why people struggle with long-term financial planning, like saving for retirement. It explains why people engage in behaviors that offer immediate rewards, even if they have long-term negative consequences, like choosing cake over health.

The Impatience Factor: Most people will choose to take $100 today rather than $110 in a month. The extra $10 seems less valuable simply because it is delayed. The value of future rewards drops sharply the further away they are. This phenomenon is also known as hyperbolic discounting.

The Strategy: Pay a Present Premium: To compel instant compliance, you must pay a small, immediate premium to secure the large, future commitment. You must associate the required action *now* with an instant, tangible gain. This gain must occur immediately upon agreement.

- *Example:* If the target must commit to a six-month project, do not focus only on the project's future completion. Focus on the immediate reward they get by signing the document *today*. This could be immediate access to an exclusive community, a small material bonus, or instant elevation of status.

This immediate payment counteracts the hyperbolic devaluation of the long-term benefit. Even if the future reward is substantial, the certainty and presence of the immediate reward motivate the necessary current decision. The immediate gain satisfies the target's impulse for instant gratification.

II. Structuring Immediate Incentives

Because human nature tends toward impatience, immediate compliance is achieved by structuring the request so that execution generates an instant psychological or material gain. This gain must satisfy the target's impulse for instant gratification.

The Strategy of Immediate Status: Status is a powerful, immediate psychological reward.

- *Example:* Frame the present action as an immediate elevation of status. "By signing this document today, you instantly move into the **Tier One Founder's Circle**, which unlocks immediate access to the lead development team." The target receives the status immediately, even if the development team does not meet for two months. The psychological reward is present.

The Strategy of Immediate Relief: Stress is a strong motivator. The target often delays action because the final decision is stressful.

- *Example:* Frame the present action as immediate relief from pressure. "The moment you sign this, the three weeks of indecision are over. We can immediately stop planning and **start building**. The burden of the final decision is lifted from your shoulders right now." The immediate reward is the removal of cognitive stress.

This structuring ensures that the target's mind views the agreement not as the start of long work, but as the end of difficult deliberation.

III. The Illusion of Presence: Minimizing the Gap

The subjective value of a reward increases sharply if it is perceived as temporally or physically close. If the future outcome feels distant and abstract, the brain heavily discounts its value.

The persuader must use visual and linguistic techniques to minimize the perceived time gap between the present action and the long-term benefit. This creates the **Illusion of Presence**.

Sensory Language: You must describe the future outcome with extreme sensory detail. This makes the future reward concrete and imminent, fighting the natural tendency toward temporal discounting.

- *Instead of:* "You will achieve budget control next quarter." (Abstract, delayed)
- *Use:* "By committing now, you will **see** the final $7,000 surplus number on your screen by June 1st. You will **feel** the relief immediately when the deadline passes." (Sensory, imminent)

By making the future reward tangible, something they can see, feel, or hear, you psychologically minimize the perceived time delay. The outcome feels present, making the action required today feel less like work and more like the final step before realization.

Visual Anchors: Use physical anchors to shrink the time gap. Show the target a model, a blueprint, or a projected image of the finished result. The physical representation brings the abstract future benefit into the present moment.

IV. The Emotional Cost of Delay

Temporal discounting often leads to emotional consequences. People who prioritize short-term gratification often feel regret or guilt later. This regret can be leveraged preemptively.

The persuader must frame the *lack* of immediate action as a guaranteed source of immediate future regret. This technique activates **Loss Aversion** (Book 5, Chapter 3).

The Strategy of Preemptive Regret: The focus must be on the emotional cost of delay, not the statistical cost. Non-action is presented as a quantifiable, immediate emotional expense.

- *Example:* "If you delay this decision until tomorrow, you are accepting the **guaranteed loss** of the current pricing. You will look back at this conversation next month and know that you personally cost the project $5,000 by waiting 24 hours. That regret is immediate."

This strategy compels the target to act now to avoid the psychological pain of feeling responsible for missing out or failing to secure the present opportunity. The action is driven by the desire to avoid future guilt.

V. The Integration with Commitment and Consistency

The urgent action demanded by exploiting temporal discounting must still align with the target's need for consistency (Book 1). The target must believe the impulsive decision was still rational.

The Immediate Justification: The persuader must provide a quick, immediate justification that aligns the impulsive, present action with the target's existing values.

- *Target's Value: Efficiency.*
- *Justification:* "You are acting now because waiting would be inefficient. As an efficient manager, you know that the fastest route to the final goal is to secure the necessary resource immediately."

By providing this immediate linguistic frame, the target can quickly justify their impulsive decision, securing the action without triggering a full rational review.

VI. Collapsing the Decision Window

Exploiting temporal discounting is the art of collapsing the decision window. You structure the choice so that the reward is perceived as present and the cost of delay is perceived as immediate and painful.

1. **Pay a Present Premium:** Secure the present commitment by offering an immediate material or psychological gain.
2. **Minimize the Gap:** Use sensory language and visual anchors to make the future benefit feel imminent.
3. **Frame Future Regret:** Present non-action as a guaranteed, immediate loss of value, triggering the desire to avoid guilt.

This ensures the target's inherent impatience works for you, compelling immediate compliance and eliminating hesitation. The next chapter will amplify this pressure by detailing the combined force of **Loss Aversion and Scarcity**.

CHAPTER 2

FORCE URGENCY:
ACTIVATING LOSS AVERSION AND SCARCITY

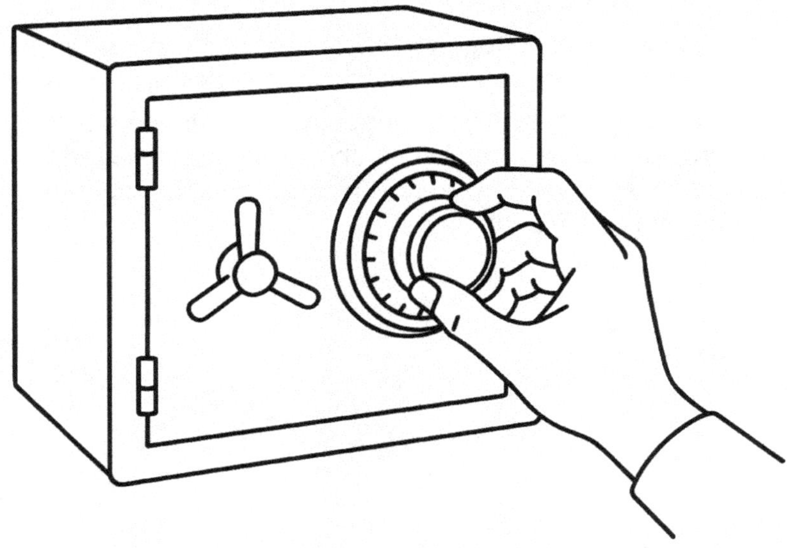

We spent the last chapter learning to use time against the target. We exploited the fact that people prefer small, immediate rewards over larger, delayed rewards. That strategy collapses the decision window by making the target impatient for the present payoff.

But impatience is a soft trigger. True, immediate action requires force. It needs psychological pressure that the target cannot ignore. This pressure is built on fear. Specifically, the fear of loss.

This chapter deals with the mechanical activation of the strongest emotional drivers for instant compliance: **Loss Aversion** and **Scarcity**. You stop motivating the target with the promise of future gain. You start compelling them with the certainty of immediate pain. This combination is the psychological force required to secure decisive action right now.

I. The Pain of Loss: Why Fear is Stronger than Hope

The most powerful psychological insight in motivation is this: the pain of losing something is measurably stronger than the pleasure of gaining an equivalent item. This is the core principle of *Loss Aversion.*

This concept was highlighted by Nobel laureates Daniel Kahneman and Amos Tversky. They showed that when humans make decisions, the psychological pain of losing something weighs much heavier than the pleasure of gaining an equivalent item. If you gain $100, the joy is significant. If you lose $100, the pain is usually much sharper than the previous joy was sweet.

This fundamental truth dictates your entire urgency strategy. You stop selling the positive outcome. You start selling the avoidance of the negative outcome.

Framing Non-Compliance as a Guaranteed Loss:

The persuader's job is to make non-action the most painful option available. You must frame the decision not as choosing a good option, but as choosing to **avoid a guaranteed loss**. This loss must be specific. It must be immediate. It must be quantifiable.

- **Weak Framing (Gain Focus):** "If you approve this today, you will gain an extra 5% savings over the standard price next quarter."
- **Strong Framing (Loss Focus):** "If you delay this approval until tomorrow, you **guarantee the loss** of the 5% savings currently locked in. Waiting 24 hours means you personally cost the project $2,500."

The second frame uses the target's own fear of regret against them. It immediately ties the psychological pain of loss to the present moment. Non-action becomes a quantifiable, immediate expense. The target's brain is wired to mitigate this pain instantly.

The Emotional Cost of Regret: Loss Aversion works because it triggers the **Fear Of Missing Out (FOMO)**. People make impulsive decisions to avoid the regret associated with missing out on a clear advantage. The target stops thinking about the product's long-term utility. They start thinking only about the urgent need to protect themselves from the painful consequence of inaction.

This urgency often forces targets to bypass a thorough evaluation of the proposal's true value. The emotional need to protect the status quo overrides rational analysis.

II. The Scarcity Trigger: Rarity Increases Value

Loss Aversion is potent on its own. It becomes overwhelming when paired with **Scarcity**. We value things more when they are rare or limited in availability.

Our brains automatically assign a greater psychological value to things that are scarce. This happens even if the item's actual worth does not change. A fascinating experiment demonstrated this perfectly in 1975. Participants rated identical cookies from an almost empty jar as more desirable than the same cookies from a full jar. The desire was driven entirely by the perceived limited availability.

Engineering Scarcity Conditions:

The persuader must actively **engineer scarcity**. You must visibly reduce the perceived availability of the desired outcome. This ensures the target feels a constant pressure to act before the opportunity vanishes.

1. **Limited Quantity (Resource Scarcity):** The item or access must be presented as limited in number. Use specific, low numbers. *Example: "We only have three slots left in the founder's circle," or "Only the first five contracts signed will receive the dedicated consulting time."* This forces a calculation not just of cost, but of competitive opportunity.
2. **Limited Time (Temporal Scarcity):** The decision window must be closed with a firm, irreversible deadline. This deadline must be justified by external forces, not internal whim. *Example: "The system update happens at midnight tonight, and the price automatically adjusts 8% after that time."* This external justification legitimizes the urgency.

The Strategy of the Empty Jar: The appearance of scarcity matters more than the reality of the inventory. Ensure that the target perceives the resource as diminishing. Even if you have fifty contracts to sign, the perception that *others* are snapping up the resource increases its desirability. You are using Social Proof (Book 1) to amplify the fear of loss. If others are taking the limited resource, it must be valuable.

III. The Freedom Threat: Psychological Reactance

Scarcity does more than just trigger loss aversion. It triggers an innate defensive reaction known as **Psychological Reactance**.

We possess a deep, psychological need to feel free to choose. When our freedom to acquire or choose something is threatened by limited availability, we experience a strong desire to reassert that freedom. We often do this by wanting the restricted item even more intensely. This defensive desire overrides careful thought.

Restricting Choice to Increase Desire: The strategy is to subtly, temporarily restrict the target's perceived freedom.

- *Example:* When you announce the limited-time deadline ("Offer ends at midnight"), you are threatening the target's future freedom to acquire the item at that price. Their immediate psychological impulse is to overcome that threat by securing the item now.

The Combination Lock: The most overwhelming force for instant influence is combining the three core pressures:

1. **Time Pressure (Temporal Discounting):** The target devalues the future reward.
2. **Loss Aversion:** The target fears losing the immediate benefit or guarantee.
3. **Reactance/Scarcity:** The target feels their freedom is threatened, increasing their desire for the restricted item.

This manufactured urgency collapses the decision window entirely. It minimizes the time available for the target's rational processing system (Central Route) to interfere. The decision becomes purely emotional and impulsive.

IV. Legitimizing the Urgency with Authority

The entire system of instant influence relies on the trust established in the previous books. If the target suspects your deadline is arbitrary or a cheap sales tactic, the pressure fails. They must believe the deadline is a legitimate, external fact.

Authority Legitimizes Scarcity: Your **Authority** (Book 1/2) legitimizes the scarcity and the deadline.

- *If you have established an authoritative persona (composed, still, expert posture),* your urgent demand, "The financial lock-in requires the signature by 3 PM Tuesday", is accepted as a verifiable business fact, not a personal whim. The target trusts your competence and therefore trusts your constraints.

Commitment Secures the Impulse: The previous small **Commitments** you secured (Book 1) pave the way for this urgent, large commitment. The target's mind sees the immediate, urgent action as consistent with their established pattern of following your guidance and recommendation. The impulsive decision is instantly justified by their prior pattern of trust.

The Linguistic Frame of Necessity: You must use precise, concrete language (Book 3) to frame the urgency as necessity.

- *Avoid:* "We'd like you to sign now."
- *Use:* "The system update **requires** the signed document by 3 PM. Failure to comply locks us out of the current pricing."

The strong, precise, and concrete language reinforces the legitimacy of the constraint, further reducing the target's chance to question the urgency.

V. The Decisive Action

Forcing urgency is the art of controlling the final moment of decision. You use the scientifically verified principles of Loss Aversion, Scarcity, and Psychological Reactance to generate immense, immediate pressure.

1. **Frame Loss:** Make non-action a guaranteed, painful financial or emotional loss.
2. **Engineer Scarcity:** Introduce a legitimate, external constraint of time or quantity.
3. **Use Authority:** Ensure your established competence and authority legitimize the urgent constraint.

This system ensures that when the moment for decisive action arrives, the target is compelled to act immediately in your favor. Hesitation is eliminated because the perceived psychological cost of delay is too high. The final chapters detail how to maintain this pressure, ensuring the target follows through on the impulse.

CHAPTER 3

DEMAND PRESENCE: MINIMIZING PERCEIVED DELAY FOR FUTURE GAIN

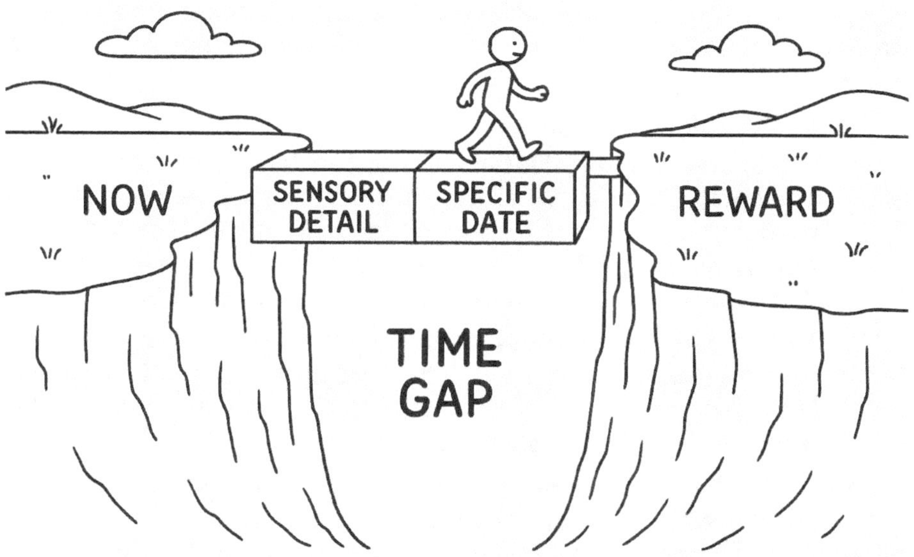

The last two chapters showed you how to collapse the decision window. You used **Temporal Discounting** to make the target impatient. You used **Loss Aversion** and **Scarcity** to make them fearful of waiting. This process forces an immediate impulse.

But impulse is fleeting. You need to solidify that impulse into commitment. The key here is making the future feel immediate. The target discounts future rewards sharply because those rewards feel abstract and distant. If the reward seems far away, the brain ignores it.

This chapter details how to create the **Illusion of Presence.** You must use linguistic and visual techniques to shrink the perceived time gap. You make the future benefit feel tangible, sensory, and imminent. This keeps the reward emotionally valuable right now. You ensure the target feels the final payoff is just around the corner.

I. The Science of the Shrinking Gap

The subjective value of a reward increases sharply when it is perceived as temporally or physically close. This is the opposite of temporal discounting. When the brain can easily visualize a reward, it assigns it higher value.

The Strategy: Sensory Immersion: You must use language that engages the target's five senses. This makes the abstract, delayed outcome feel present and imminent. This active visualization combats the natural tendency of the brain to devalue things that are not here yet.

Actionable Sensory Language:

1. **Visual and Auditory Detail:** Do not just talk about a "successful outcome." Describe what the successful outcome looks like and sounds like. *Example: "By committing now, you will **see** the budget surplus number, $8,000, on your screen every Monday morning. You will **hear** the client confirming the final agreement next week."*
2. **Tactile and Kinesthetic Detail:** Describe the feeling associated with the reward. *Example: "The final contract is not just paper. Signing it today means you **feel** the relief and the burden lifting immediately from your shoulders."*

By making the future reward tangible, something they can see, feel, or hear, you psychologically minimize the perceived time delay. The outcome feels present. This makes the present action feel less like an effort and more like the final step before realization.

II. Anchoring the Future in the Present

The brain relies heavily on immediate, concrete anchors. To demand presence, you must anchor the abstract future benefit to a specific, present moment or object.

Visual Anchors: Use physical anchors to shrink the time gap.

- *Example:* Do not just talk about the completion date next year. Show the target the **specific physical prototype,** the **final blueprint,** or the **signed legal document** that represents the finished project. Hold the physical contract and say, "This document right here is the moment the three weeks of indecision are over. Signing it right now is the same as starting the system build." The physical object makes the future benefit feel immediate.

Linguistic Anchors (Specifics): Vague timeframes, like "soon" or "next quarter," heavily discount the reward. Use specific, concrete dates and times (Chapter 5) to anchor the future.

- *Example:* "The system will be fully operational by **March 1st, 2026**." This concrete date is a much stronger anchor than "next year." The specific detail makes the future reward feel structured and certain. Certainty reduces the brain's impulse to devalue the future reward.

III. The Reciprocity of Immediate Gain

Instant influence often requires asking the target to do something hard or immediate. The target's brain wants a reward for that effort. This activates the **Reciprocity** principle.

By making the target visualize the immediate benefit, you create an emotional payoff *now*. This immediate emotional reward acts as a form of **reciprocal exchange** for the present commitment they are making.

The Strategy: Presenting the Immediate Benefit: Structure the language to emphasize what the target *gains immediately* by signing, even if the gain is psychological.

- *Example:* "By agreeing to this now, you instantly secure the **Tier One Founder's Circle** status. That status and access begin **today**." The immediate gain of status is the reciprocal "payment" for the immediate action. The target feels they have received something of value *right now* in exchange for their commitment. This eliminates the feeling that they are acting only for a distant, unverified benefit.

IV. Justifying the Impulse: The Consistency Frame

When the target acts impulsively, driven by the pressure of Loss Aversion and Scarcity, they will immediately seek justification for that choice. They need to believe their impulsive decision was still rational and consistent with their self-image.

This is where the linguistic frame of **Commitment and Consistency** (Book 1) must be deployed instantly.

The Strategy: Providing the Immediate Justification: The persuader must provide a quick, immediate linguistic frame that aligns the impulsive, present action with the target's pre-established values.

- *If the target values efficiency:* Justify the impulse: "You acted immediately because waiting would be highly inefficient. As an efficient leader, you know the fastest route to securing the resource is to commit now."
- *If the target values stability:* Justify the impulse: "You signed immediately to secure the current price lock-in. That action was necessary to **guarantee stability** and mitigate future risk, which aligns with your core goal of protection."

By providing this immediate frame, the target can quickly justify their impulsive decision. This secures the action without triggering a full, rational review later that could lead to buyer's remorse.

V. Combating Regret: The Focus on Status Quo Bias

The urgency strategy must also account for the target's natural resistance to change. Humans generally prefer things to remain the same; this is called **Status Quo Bias**. Any decision to change is hard, even when the new option is objectively better.

The Strategy: Reframing Non-Action as Change: The most powerful way to bypass the Status Quo Bias is to **reframe non-action as the true risk.**

- *Instead of:* "Sign this to move to a new, better system." (Focus on change)
- *Use:* "If you fail to sign this today, you are actively choosing to **risk instability** from the old system, which costs you $1,000 per month in maintenance fees. This action is simply securing the current, safe operational state." (Focus on preventing a negative change).

By framing non-action as the true departure from stability, you turn the target's innate preference for the Status Quo into a force that drives them toward your solution. They act immediately to protect the present, safe reality, which you have linked to your proposal.

VI. Demanding Presence

Demanding presence is the final mechanical step in forcing urgent compliance. You neutralize the natural human tendency to delay and devalue the future.

1. **Sensory Immersion:** Use language that makes the future reward tangible, imminent, and sensory.

2. **Anchor the Future:** Use specific dates and physical objects to anchor the abstract benefit to the present.
3. **Frame Justification:** Immediately provide a linguistic frame that aligns the target's impulsive action with their core values, preventing regret.

This disciplined approach ensures that when the target makes the final, urgent decision, they do so with the psychological conviction that they acted responsibly and in their own immediate best interest. The next chapter will finalize this pressure by detailing how to eliminate hesitation through precise incentive structuring.

CHAPTER 4

ELIMINATE HESITATION: STRUCTURING INCENTIVES FOR IMMEDIATE REWARD

The last few chapters focused on generating impulse. We used time pressure to make the target impatient. We used fear to make them act now. But fear fades quickly. Impulse needs to be immediately reinforced with a positive payoff. If you demand action, you must also provide an instant reward.

This chapter details how to structure incentives so they eliminate hesitation. The incentive must serve two key purposes: first, it must satisfy the target's impulse for **immediate gratification**. Second, it must provide the **rational justification** needed to defend the sudden, impulsive choice.

We are moving past abstract future benefits. We are engineering a present, concrete reward that locks in the commitment today.

I. The Science of the Immediate Payoff

We know that **Temporal Discounting** makes the target devalue future rewards dramatically. Even a large benefit planned for next year feels worthless right now. To eliminate hesitation, you must provide a payoff that happens *today*. This payoff acts as the necessary reciprocal payment for the present commitment.

The Strategy: Present Premium: To compel instant compliance, you must pay a small, immediate premium to secure the large, future commitment. You must associate the required action *now* with an instant, tangible gain. This gain occurs the moment the target agrees.

This immediate payment counteracts the heavy psychological discounting of the long-term benefit. The immediate gain satisfies the target's impulse for instant gratification and makes the decision feel immediately worthwhile.

Actionable Incentives for Today:

1. **Immediate Status Elevation:** Status is a powerful, immediate psychological reward. You must frame the present action as an instant promotion or entry into an exclusive group.
    - *Example:* "By signing this document today, you instantly move into the **Tier One Founder's Circle**. This begins your new status immediately." The target receives the status now, even if the main project deliverable is delayed.
2. **Immediate Relief from Pressure:** Stress is a strong factor in hesitation. The target often delays action because the final decision itself is stressful.
    - *Example:* Frame the present action as immediate removal of cognitive stress. "The moment you sign this, the three weeks of painful deliberation are over. We can immediately **stop planning and start building**. The burden of the final decision is lifted from your shoulders right now." The immediate reward is the removal of mental effort.
3. **Small Material Bonus:** Offer a small, unexpected material bonus that is delivered instantly. This could be a specific, immediate service or a small, non-refundable discount. This must be a concrete, measurable gift.

This structuring ensures that the target's mind views the agreement not as the start of long, hard work, but as the immediate end of difficult decision-making.

II. Locking the Commitment with the Consistency Frame

When a target acts impulsively, driven by the pressure of Loss Aversion, they will immediately feel internal pressure to justify that choice. They need to believe their sudden decision was rational and **consistent** with their self-image. If they cannot justify the impulse, they will experience buyer's remorse and may retreat later.

The immediate reward is the key to providing this justification.

The Strategy: Providing the Immediate Justification: The persuader must provide a quick, linguistic frame that aligns the impulsive action with the target's pre-established values (Book 1). The immediate incentive becomes the proof of rationality.

- *If the target values* ***Security****:* Frame the incentive: "You acted immediately to secure the current price lock-in. That action was necessary to **guarantee stability** and mitigate future risk, which aligns with your core goal of protection."
- *If the target values* ***Efficiency****:* Frame the incentive: "You acted now because waiting would be inefficient. You secured the **Tier One Status** immediately, proving your commitment to the fastest route to the final goal."

The immediate payoff (status, relief, or a bonus) acts as a physical anchor for the rational justification. The target can point to the immediate reward and say, "I acted responsibly because I got this." This locks in the commitment, preventing regret.

III. The Reciprocity of Instant Gain

Instant influence often requires asking the target to agree to something challenging or immediate. This activates the **Reciprocity** principle. The target needs to feel they are not being taken advantage of.

By providing an immediate incentive, you are offering a form of **reciprocal exchange** for the present commitment. This immediate payment is a psychological acknowledgment of the difficulty of the decision you are asking them to make.

The Strategy: Immediate Concession: Frame the incentive not as a bonus, but as an immediate, necessary concession you are making to them.

- *Example:* "We need your signature now for the system lock-in. Because we are asking for this immediate action, we are offering this **5% discount** that expires in the next hour. This is our concession for the urgency we require."

This framing turns the incentive into a tangible part of the negotiation process. The target feels they have forced you to make a reciprocal concession, which reinforces their sense of control over the interaction.

IV. Eliminating the Status Quo Bias

The urgency strategy must also combat the target's inherent preference for things to remain the same, known as **Status Quo Bias**. Any decision to change is hard, even when the new option is objectively better.

The Strategy: Reframing Non-Action as Costly Change: The most powerful way to bypass the Status Quo Bias is to **reframe non-action as the true risk to stability.**

- *Avoid:* "Sign this to move to a new, better system." (Focus on uncomfortable change)
- *Use:* "If you fail to sign this today, you are actively choosing to **lose the current pricing** and **risk instability** from the old, outdated maintenance system. The best action for maintaining the status quo is securing this resource immediately." (Focus on preventing a negative change).

By framing non-action as the true departure from stability, you turn the target's innate preference for the Status Quo into a force that drives them toward your solution. They act immediately to protect the present, safe reality, which you have linked to your proposal.

V. The Final Lock

Structuring incentives for immediate reward is the final lock on the impulsive decision. You neutralize the natural human tendency to delay and devalue the future.

1. **Pay a Present Premium:** Offer an immediate material or psychological gain that satisfies the need for instant gratification.
2. **Provide Instant Justification:** Use a linguistic frame that aligns the immediate reward with the target's core values, preventing regret.

3. **Combat Status Quo:** Frame non-action as the true risk to stability, forcing the target to choose your proposal to maintain safety.

This disciplined approach ensures that when the target makes the final, urgent decision, they do so with the psychological conviction that they acted responsibly and in their own immediate best interest. The next chapter will finalize this pressure by detailing how to maintain this manufactured urgency until the action is fully completed.

CHAPTER 5

CONTROL DEADLINE: MANUFACTURING THE PSYCHOLOGICAL NEED TO BUY

We have built the psychological pressure. The target is impatient for the reward. They are afraid of the loss. They feel their freedom is threatened by scarcity. These forces create the impulse.

But impulse is only the first step. You must now control the moment of final compliance. This requires manufacturing a psychological need so strong that the target feels they absolutely must buy **now** to regain control of their own environment. You do not just set a deadline. You make the target internalize the deadline as their own urgent problem.

This chapter details how to use legitimacy, consistency, and psychological reactance to finalize the urgent decision. You ensure the target completes the action before their rational mind can trigger regret or analysis.

I. Legitimizing the Deadline: Authority as Fact

The entire system of instant influence collapses if the target believes your deadline is arbitrary. If they suspect you are simply using a cheap sales tactic, they will wait, and the pressure will fail. The deadline must be accepted as a **legitimate, external fact**.

The Role of Authority: The trust you built in your **Authority** (Book 2) must legitimize the constraint. Your composure, your still presence, and your competence must support the deadline.

- **Verifiable Constraint:** The deadline must be justified by an outside force that you cannot control. This might be a financial system lock-in, a change in regulatory code, or a hard logistical cut-off.
    - *Example:* Do not say: "The price goes up when I decide."
    - *Say:* "The system wide update happens at midnight tonight. The current pricing structure is locked into the old system. The price automatically adjusts 8% after that time." This external justification makes the urgency real.

The Linguistic Frame of Necessity: You must use precise, concrete language (Book 3) to frame the deadline as an unavoidable necessity. Use direct verbs.

- *Avoid:* "We'd like you to decide soon."
- *Use:* "The system lock-in **requires** the final signed document by 3 PM Tuesday. Failure to comply locks us out of the current pricing." The strong, precise language reinforces the legitimacy of the constraint. This reduces the target's chance to question the urgency.

The target trusts your competence, so they trust your constraints. They believe the deadline exists because you, the authority figure, confirmed it.

II. Leveraging Reactance: The Freedom Threat

Scarcity not only triggers fear of loss. It triggers **Psychological Reactance**. This is the innate human desire to reassert threatened freedom. When the target perceives a threat to their freedom to choose, they want the restricted item even more intensely.

The Strategy: Restricting Future Freedom: You must briefly and subtly threaten the target's perceived future freedom. This dramatically increases their present desire for the restricted option.

- *Example:* The deadline ("Offer ends in 60 minutes") restricts the target's freedom to get the benefit later. Their immediate psychological impulse is to overcome that threat. They reassert their freedom by immediately securing the item now.

The Focus on Exclusivity: Scarcity is more effective when the threat is tied to **exclusivity.** The fact that an item is scarce suggests that others recognize its value and are snapping it up. This ties scarcity directly into **Social Proof** (Book 1).

- *Example:* "Only the first five contracts will receive the dedicated consulting time." This implies that knowledgeable people are already taking the resource. The target must act immediately to avoid being excluded from the valuable, restricted group. This compels the target to act impulsively to keep their status and autonomy.

III. The Consistency Lock: Justifying the Impulse

When the target acts on urgency, their mind immediately tries to justify the quick decision. They need to believe the impulsive choice was rational and **consistent** with their self-image. If they cannot justify the impulse, they will feel buyer's remorse and may cancel or retreat later.

The Strategy: Providing the Immediate Consistency Frame: You must immediately provide a linguistic frame that aligns the urgent action with the target's pre-established values (Book 1).

- **Immediate Payoff Justification (Chapter 5):** The immediate reward you gave (status, relief, or bonus) acts as a physical anchor for the rational justification. The target can point to the immediate reward and say, "I acted responsibly because I got this bonus right now."
- **Value Alignment:** You must connect the quick action to their core values:
    - *If the target values Innovation:* Frame the action: "You signed immediately because **innovators** secure necessary resources immediately. Delay is a tactic for the cautious, not the forward-thinker."
    - *If the target values Caution:* Frame the action: "You secured the lock-in now to prevent the 8% price increase. That action was the **most cautious and fiscally responsible** choice available."

This immediate, tailored justification locks in the commitment. It prevents the regret that stems from making an impulsive choice.

IV. The Final Barrier: Eliminating Buyer's Remorse

Buyer's remorse often occurs when the target realizes they acted impulsively. This is a cognitive clash between the quick decision (Peripheral Route) and their need for rational consistency (Central Route).

The Strategy: Closing the Cognitive Loop: You must proactively close the cognitive loop immediately after the signature.

1. **Reiterate the Loss Avoided:** Immediately remind the target of the specific loss they successfully avoided by acting now. *Example: "Congratulations. You successfully avoided the $2,500 cost increase that would have hit tomorrow."* This reinforces the positive feeling of **loss avoidance**.
2. **Affirm the Commitment Effort:** Remind them that the action was **effortful** (Commitment principle). *Example: "That was a difficult decision to make under pressure, and I commend you for securing this."* This reinforces their inner responsibility for the choice. They now feel committed to the action because they associate it with their own strong will.
3. **Future Visualization:** Use sensory language one final time to make the immediate future seem present. *Example: "We can now immediately send the first production timeline. You will see that document in your inbox in the next hour."* This shifts the target's focus from the difficult decision they just made to the immediate reward they are about to receive.

This final sequence ensures the target's rational system accepts the impulsive decision.

V. Finalizing the Urgency

Controlling the deadline is the art of finalizing the urgent decision. You transition from generating impulse to securing commitment.

1. **Legitimize the Pressure:** Use authority and external facts to make the deadline real and unavoidable.
2. **Activate Reactance:** Restrict future freedom with scarcity to increase the target's desire for the restricted item.

3. **Lock Consistency:** Immediately justify the impulsive action with a linguistic frame that aligns the choice with the target's core values.

This system ensures that the target's psychological need to buy is manufactured, controlled, and resolved instantly in your favor. This completes the entire influence system, moving from strategy and charm to decisive, immediate action.

CONCLUSION

THE FINAL SYSTEM OF DECISIVE ACTION

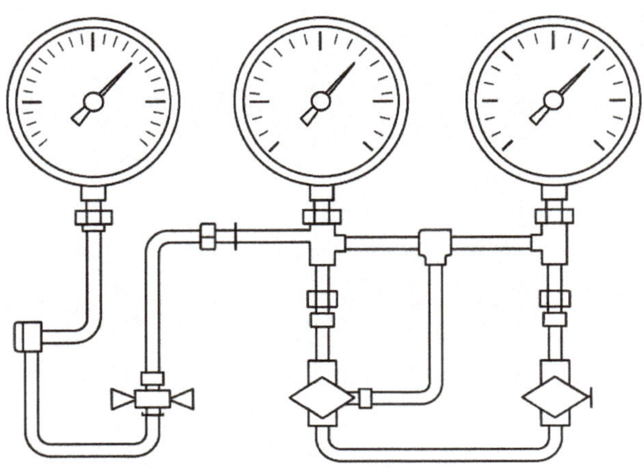

We have finished the final book, completing the entire structure of influence. This book, **Instant Influence**, was dedicated entirely to collapsing the decision window. It moved us beyond the patience of long-term strategy and into the mechanics of immediate compliance.

The core lesson is that immediate action is not rational. It is a forced psychological impulse. You stop relying on the target's slow, analytical mind. You start manipulating their perception of time and value. You ensure the action happens before regret or second thoughts can interfere.

This conclusion synthesizes the three core drivers of instant action: **Temporal Discounting, Loss Aversion, and Scarcity**. We show how to fuse these forces. This creates the overwhelming psychological need that compels the target to agree right now.

I. The Foundation: Controlling Time and Value

Instant influence begins by exploiting the fundamental flaw in how humans perceive time. This flaw is **Temporal Discounting**.

The Discounting Principle: People prefer a smaller reward right now over a larger reward later. The psychological value of a future prize drops sharply the further away it is. This impatience is human nature.

Synthesis of Temporal Discounting (Chapter 2):

1. **Pay a Present Premium:** To compel instant compliance, you must pay a small, immediate premium for the present commitment. This could be immediate status elevation, immediate relief from decision stress, or a small, measurable bonus. This immediate gain satisfies the target's impulse for instant gratification.
2. **Minimize the Gap:** You must use **sensory language** and **visual anchors** to shrink the perceived time gap. Describe the future outcome with extreme detail. Make the target *see* the budget surplus or *feel* the relief immediately. This makes the future reward feel present, keeping its value high.

This strategy uses the target's impatience against them. It ensures they view the agreement not as the start of long work, but as the immediate end of difficult deliberation.

II. The Overwhelming Force: Fear and Rarity

Impatience is a soft trigger. To secure decisive action, you must use the strongest emotional forces: fear and restriction.

Synthesis of Loss Aversion (Chapter 3):

1. **Frame Loss Over Gain:** The fear of losing something is much stronger than the desire to gain an equivalent item. You must frame non-compliance as a guaranteed, immediate, quantifiable loss. *Example: "Waiting 24 hours means you personally cost the project $2,500."* This triggers the **Fear Of Missing Out (FOMO).** The emotional need to avoid loss overrides rational analysis.

Synthesis of Scarcity and Reactance (Chapter 3):

1. **Engineer Scarcity:** You must visibly reduce the perceived availability of the desired outcome using a legitimate, external constraint (limited time or limited quantity).
2. **Activate Psychological Reactance:** The deadline restricts the target's freedom to choose later. This threat activates their innate desire to reassert control. They do this by immediately securing the restricted item. This manufactured urgency eliminates hesitation.

This combination of forces collapses the decision window entirely.

III. The Final Lock: Controlling the Deadline

Impulse must be secured quickly before regret can set in. This requires legitimizing the deadline and instantly aligning the impulse with the target's core values.

Synthesis of Legitimacy (Chapter 6):

1. **Authority Legitimizes Urgency:** Your **Authority** (Book 2) must legitimize the deadline. The target must believe the deadline is a verifiable external fact (e.g., a system update, a hard financial lock-in) and not a cheap tactic.
2. **Use Concrete Necessity:** You must use precise, **concrete language** (Book 3) to frame the deadline as an unavoidable necessity. *Example: "The system lock-in requires the final signed document by 3 PM Tuesday."*

Synthesis of Consistency (Chapter 6):

1. **Lock the Impulse with Justification:** When the target acts impulsively, you must immediately provide a linguistic frame that aligns their action with their core values. This is the **Consistency Frame** (Book 1). *Example: "You signed immediately because, as a cautious leader, you knew that securing the current price lock-in was the most fiscally responsible action."* This immediate justification locks in the commitment. It eliminates buyer's remorse.
2. **Combat Status Quo:** You must reframe non-action as the true risk. By linking non-action to the loss of stability, you compel the target to choose your proposal to maintain the present, safe reality.

IV. Conclusion: The Full Circle of Influence

This final book, **Instant Influence**, completes the entire system. It is the decisive application of the principles we built in the previous four books.

- **Strategy (Book 1):** The commitment drivers are used to secure the impulsive action.
- **Presence (Book 2):** Authority legitimizes the scarcity and urgency.
- **Language (Book 3):** Concrete vocabulary and framing maximize the fear of loss.

- **Charm (Book 4):** The established trust ensures the urgent demand is seen as helpful advice, not manipulation.

The result is a system where the target is guided through a comprehensive, controlled process. The final action is immediate, decisive, and fully justified by their own psychological need for safety and consistency.

We have now provided a complete, scientifically grounded guide to covert persuasion, charisma, linguistic control, irresistible charm, and instant influence. The next step is the final resource list and checklist.

REFLECTION QUESTIONS

We have completed the system of **Instant Influence**. This final book taught you to collapse the decision window. You learned to use the powerful forces of time, scarcity, and loss aversion to secure immediate action. You moved from patient strategy to forced impulse.

The skills covered here, anchoring the future, manufacturing urgency, and locking the commitment, must become instant reflexes. Use these questions to personalize the material. Map the concepts onto your own interactions. Prepare to execute with decisive speed.

Section 1: Temporal Discounting and Present Value

The foundation of instant influence is the human flaw of **Temporal Discounting.** You must make the present action feel like the immediate reward.

1. **Immediate Payoff:** Think about a proposal you need to send this week that offers a large reward six months from now. What is the immediate, small, **psychological** reward you can offer right now, today, for the signature? This could be instant status elevation or immediate relief from the decision stress.

2. **Sensory Immersion:** The target discounts abstract future benefits. Describe the final outcome of your current project using only **sensory language**. What will the target *see*, *feel*, or *hear* the moment the project is completed? Use specific details to make the future feel imminent and valuable right now.
3. **Status Quo Justification:** Humans naturally resist change. This is the **Status Quo Bias**. If your target is hesitating, how can you reframe non-action as the greater **risk to stability**? Write one sentence that links signing the document today to maintaining their current safe reality.
4. **Justifying the Impulse:** When someone acts on impulse, they need immediate justification. If a client signed quickly because of a deadline, what single, self-serving reason can you immediately provide them to align their impulsive action with their core value of **fiscal responsibility**?

Section 2: Loss Aversion and Scarcity

The strongest triggers for instant action are the fear of loss and the threat of scarcity. This pressure eliminates hesitation.

5. **Framing Loss:** Identify a goal where you need an immediate "yes." How are you currently framing the request (e.g., gain)? Now, rewrite the request entirely to focus on **guaranteed loss**. What is the specific, quantifiable financial loss or missed opportunity they suffer if they wait until tomorrow?
6. **Engineering Scarcity:** You must create an external, legitimate constraint. If you cannot use a price deadline, what is one non-monetary resource you can limit immediately (e.g., dedicated consulting time, priority access, limited slots in the pilot program)? How can you use that **scarcity** to trigger the target's desire to act now to avoid exclusion?
7. **Psychological Reactance: Scarcity** threatens freedom, which triggers **reactance**. If you announce a deadline, the target wants the item more intensely. How can you subtly reference the fact that "other interested parties" are taking the limited resource, using **Social Proof** to amplify the fear of exclusion?
8. **Closing the Cognitive Loop:** Buyer's remorse is a risk after an impulsive decision. Immediately after securing a major agreement, what two actions can you take? You must do one to reinforce the **Loss Avoided** and one to affirm the target's **effort and consistency**.

Section 3: Authority and Final Execution

The final execution requires using established trust to legitimize the urgency and finalize the commitment.

9. **Legitimizing the Deadline:** Your **Authority** must support the deadline. If you set a deadline of 3 PM on Friday, what is the single **external, verifiable fact** (e.g., a system update, a hard financial closing date) that justifies the deadline? You must trust your constraints to make the target trust them.
10. **The Final Sequence:** Review the critical steps for immediate compliance. Put them in order: **Loss Frame, Scarcity Threat, Immediate Justification (Present Premium), and Consistency Frame.** How would you use this sequence in the last 60 seconds of a negotiation to eliminate all remaining hesitation?

OVERALL CONCLUSION

THE ARCHITECTURE OF TOTAL INFLUENCE

We have finished the system. This collection of five books was a focused study on the mechanics of total influence. We moved from the foundational strategy of the mind to the final, rapid execution of a decision. The core lesson is clear: influence is not an accident of personality. It is a precise, learned architecture built on verifiable psychological facts.

If you internalize this system, you stop relying on hope. You start relying on predictable science. You gain the ability to guide any social interaction, securing deep loyalty and immediate compliance, regardless of the setting.

Here, we review the five pillars of this system. We integrate them into one cohesive model for consistent, repeatable success in social and professional life.

I. Book 1: Covert Persuasion: Psychological Leverage

The Core Principle: Reality is Negotiable.

The system begins by recognizing that people do not act on objective facts. They act on their own **subjective reality**, which is built from their perception of the facts. This personal version of truth dictates behavior. Covert persuasion is the intentional structuring of information to manage that subjective reality.

Key Levers of Control:

- **Exploiting Bias:** We leveraged **cognitive biases**, the systematic, predictable errors in human judgment, to create the path of least cognitive resistance. By subtly increasing pressure, you force the target's brain to use fast shortcuts, bypassing slow, rational thought.
- **Framing and Anchoring:** We used the **Anchoring Effect** to set the highest possible value marker early in the conversation. This anchor dictates the entire acceptable range of subsequent outcomes.

- **Consistency is King:** The greatest leverage is securing a small, initial **Commitment**. We learned that commitment is strongest and most lasting when it is **active, public, and effortful**. This makes the target feel **inner responsibility** for the choice, ensuring they stick with it to maintain consistency with their new self-image.
- **Mitigating Resistance:** We used the **Confirmation Bias** to our advantage. Instead of challenging the target's beliefs, we framed the proposal as the necessary, logical step that **confirms their existing self-image** (e.g., responsible, innovative). This reduces the evidence required for acceptance.

Result: You move the target from being a cautious analyst to being a self-justifying participant in a decision they believe they made entirely on their own logic.

II. Book 2: Magnetic Charisma: Non-Verbal Resonance

The Core Principle: Trust is a Physical Signal.

The next step is securing trust. Influence requires competence, but charisma ensures that competence is projected without the need for words. Non-verbal behavior is a powerful, subtle form of social influence that operates **below conscious awareness**.

Key Levers of Control:

- **Controlled Presence:** We focused on **stillness** and **symmetry**. Nervous energy broadcasts anxiety and instantly undermines competence. Controlled composure acts as the antidote to the target's anxiety, making them feel safe.
- **The Halo Effect:** This projected composure is the single positive trait that triggers the **Halo Effect**. The target infers deep competence and trustworthiness from your stability alone.
- **Emotional Transfer:** Charisma spreads energy. We learned to use **Emotional Contagion**, the automatic transfer of emotional states, to mobilize groups. By focusing positive energy on **high self-monitors**, you initiate a **charismatic cascade** that spreads the desired mood quickly.
- **Haptics and Trust: Touch** is the first language of human security. Strategic, appropriate touch (e.g., a controlled handshake) bypasses the slow, verbal rapport process and establishes fundamental trust immediately.

- **Social Cohesion: Identification Humor** is the fastest tool for group bonding. Shared laughter confirms consensus on core values and dramatically reduces uncertainty, creating a resilient **shared identity**.

Result: Your physical presence becomes a stable, desirable psychological resource. The target is non-verbally inclined to trust, like, and follow you before the argument even begins.

III. Book 3: NLP Mind Control: The Science of Framing and Belief

The Core Principle: Language Constructs Reality.

This book replaced vague theory with precise linguistic mechanics. We learned that the choice of words is the most efficient conduit for psychological influence.

Key Levers of Control:

- **Framing is Control:** We used scientifically verified **framing** to dictate perception. Framing the exact same facts as a "loss" versus a "gain" changes the choice itself. This control ensures the target views the proposal through your positive lens.
- **Linguistic Synchrony: Rapport** is achieved by subtly matching the target's vocabulary density, emotional tone, and pace. This **linguistic mirroring** reduces **cognitive friction** and makes the message feel familiar and effortless.
- **Flexible Influence:** We mastered the ability to switch between **Push energy** (assertion, direction) and **Pull energy** (inquiry, collaboration). This flexibility maintains rapport while ensuring compliance when direction is necessary.
- **Resistance Reframing:** When the target objects, you do not argue the fact. You immediately **validate the feeling** and **change the frame's category** (e.g., "risky" becomes "necessary security"). This disarms resistance by invalidating the target's negative context.
- **Concrete Vocabulary:** We eliminated abstract, vague language. **Concrete vocabulary** (specific numbers, dates, and names) maximizes **emotional density** and minimizes the mental work required of the target. This makes the message persuasive and memorable.

Result: Your words become precision instruments. The target receives the message efficiently and accepts the conclusion, believing they reached it through their own logical process.

IV. Book 4: Irresistible Charm: Relationship Dynamics

The Core Principle: Loyalty is a Shared Structure.

Charm is the system that moves influence from a single event to a long-term, self-sustaining relationship. It generates continuous social attraction.

Key Levers of Control:

- **Frequency Over Intimacy:** We accelerated intimacy by prioritizing **disclosure frequency** over depth. Sharing a high volume of low-stakes details quickly builds familiarity without the high risk of emotional instability.
- **Narrativity Sustains Interest:** We used **disclosure narrativity** to frame personal details as engaging, short stories. This storytelling provides **perceived entertainment value**, ensuring the target remains psychologically invested in the interaction.
- **Calibration is Key:** We mastered the **Calibration Test**. This is the process of gently testing the boundary of intimacy and instantly **retreating** if the target signals discomfort or anxiety. This ensures the bond is maintained at the level of **optimal appropriateness.**
- **Cementing Loyalty:** We solidified loyalty by creating **Shared Social Rituals** (e.g., inside jokes). These rituals provide the **active, public, and effortful** commitment markers that secure long-term consistency.

Result: You build a desirable persona that provides consistent psychological reward. The target is not just compliant; they are personally loyal because the relationship is safe, entertaining, and structurally resilient.

V. Book 5: Instant Influence: Urgency and Action

The Core Principle: Collapse the Decision Window.

The final stage is securing immediate, decisive action. This system bypasses rational thought by leveraging fear and scarcity.

Key Levers of Control:

- **Temporal Discounting:** We exploited the human flaw of **Temporal Discounting.** We made the future reward feel present by using sensory language. We made the cost of delay feel immediate, compelling present action.
- **Loss Aversion:** We used the strongest psychological driver: the pain of loss. We framed non-compliance as a guaranteed, immediate, quantifiable loss, triggering the **Fear Of Missing Out (FOMO).**
- **Scarcity and Reactance:** We engineered **Scarcity** (limited time or quantity) and **Authority** to legitimize the deadline. This threat to the target's freedom triggers **Psychological Reactance**, forcing them to act now to reassert their control over the threatened resource.
- **Locking the Impulse:** Immediately after securing the action, we provided a **Consistency Frame.** This linguistic justification aligns the impulsive action with the target's core values, locking the commitment and eliminating buyer's remorse.

Result: You gain the ability to generate decisive action on demand. Hesitation is eliminated because the perceived psychological cost of delay is too high.

The Complete System

These five pillars form a comprehensive system. They move you from passive interaction to active, intentional influence. You begin by diagnosing the target's mind. You project authority with your body. You structure every word for effect. You build loyalty through shared connection. Then, you finalize the process by collapsing the final moment of decision.

Mastery of this architecture is not about becoming someone else. It is about maximizing your true, consistent capabilities. It ensures that your goals are achieved reliably, ethically, and with the full, justified conviction of the person you are influencing.

PRINT AND KEEP CHECKLIST

THE TOTAL INFLUENCE SYSTEM

This checklist translates the entire five-book system into actionable, step-by-step practices. Use this guide before and during every high-stakes interaction. The goal is to move from analysis to reflex, ensuring your influence is consistent, precise, and immediately effective.

Book 1: Covert Persuasion: Psychological Leverage

Goal: Control the Decision Environment and Secure Consistency

Before the Interaction	During the Interaction	Post-Agreement Lock
1. Diagnose Reality: Identify the target's core belief or existing bias (e.g., "I value caution").	**1. Set the Anchor:** Introduce the highest justifiable value marker or request first (e.g., 20% budget increase, 6-month delay).	**1. Secure Active Commitment:** Get the target to take an immediate, small, **active** step (e.g., sign the first page, send an internal commitment email).
2. Frame for Alignment: Prepare the linguistic framing that **confirms** their belief (e.g., "This action is the most cautious choice").	**2. Exploit Contrast:** Immediately follow the rejected high anchor with your actual, smaller request. This makes the real request seem disproportionately acceptable.	**2. Ensure Public/Effortful:** Make sure the commitment is visible to others or requires minor effort to reinforce **Consistency**.
3. Prepare the Present Premium: Determine a small, immediate reward the target receives for acting *now*, combating **Temporal Discounting**.	**3. Use Social Proof:** Reference the adoption of similar people, especially those the target respects or identifies with.	**3. Reframe Justification:** Provide the target with the language to justify their decision internally (e.g., "You moved fast because you prioritize stability").

Book 2: Magnetic Charisma: Non-Verbal Resonance

Goal: Establish Pre-Emptive Trust and Mobilize Emotion

Controlled Presence (Authority)	Emotional Transfer (Mobilization)	Haptic and Social Connection (Trust)
1. Maintain Stillness: Eliminate all nervous energy leaks (fidgeting, pen clicking). Controlled stillness projects composure and competence.	**1. Diagnose Susceptibility:** Identify high self-monitors (emotional amplifiers) for fast spread and low self-monitors for long-term stability.	**1. Maximize Haptics:** Use a firm, dry, symmetrical handshake, maintaining steady eye contact for three seconds. This taps into the fundamental need for security.
2. Use Open Posture: Stand and sit with symmetrical, open posture. Claim your space physically to non-verbally assert status.	**2. Project Composure:** Maintain a calm, measured vocal pace and low pitch. This triggers the **Halo Effect**, making the target infer trustworthiness from your stability.	**2. Use Identification Humor:** Deploy humor that targets an external norm or shared frustration. Shared laughter confirms consensus on core values and builds cohesion.
3. Control Gaze: Maintain intentional eye contact during key phrases (opening, closing, critical question) to signal sincerity and focus.	**3. Initiate Cascade:** Focus enthusiasm and energy projection on the high self-monitors to spread the desired mood to the group.	**3. Create Shared Rituals:** Elevate a small shared moment (e.g., an inside joke) into a repeatable ritual. This provides the necessary **effortful** marker for group loyalty.

Book 3: NLP Mind Control: The Science of Framing and Belief

Goal: Achieve Linguistic Precision and Eliminate Friction

Framing and Clarity	Rapport and Style Synchrony	Resistance Mitigation
1. Use Concrete Vocabulary: Replace abstract nouns ("optimization," "synergy") with specific facts, numbers, and dates (e.g., "$5,000," "Tuesday at 3 PM").	**1. Match Vocal/Linguistic Pace:** Subtly align your speaking speed and vocabulary density with the target's style to reduce cognitive friction.	**1. Validate, then Shift:** When resistance occurs (e.g., "too risky"), immediately validate the feeling, then change the frame's category.
2. Use Active Verbs: Ensure sentences use direct verbs. This communicates certainty and eliminates passive ambiguity.	**2. Use Flexible Influence:** Start with **Pull energy** (inquiry, collaboration) to build rapport and gather information. Switch to **Push energy** (assertion, direction) to close the commitment.	**2. Reframe Loss:** Frame non-compliance as a **guaranteed, immediate loss** (e.g., "you lose the discount tomorrow"). This activates the strongest psychological driver.
3. Align Evidence: If targeting a critical processor (Central Route), lead with **message quality** and detailed evidence. If targeting a peripheral processor, use **authority**.	**3. Deploy Communality Buffer:** If asserting competence (especially for female persuaders), blend the command with language of warmth and shared goals (e.g., "our mutual objective") to reduce resistance.	**3. Pre-Empt the Objection:** State the target's most likely objection before they do, then immediately control the framing of the solution.

Book 4: Irresistible Charm: Relationship Dynamics

Goal: Accelerate Intimacy and Cement Loyalty

Accelerating Closeness	Sustaining Interest (Narrative)	Boundary Management (Calibration)
1. Prioritize Frequency: Maximize the number of small, low-stakes disclosures to build rapid familiarity. **Frequency** predicts closeness faster than intimacy.	**1. Use Narrativity:** Frame all personal details as short, structured stories (Setup, Conflict, Resolution) to create **perceived entertainment value.**	**1. Test Gently:** Offer a disclosure that is *slightly* deeper than the previous one to test the boundary of comfort.
2. Avoid Premature Depth: Never share raw, deep vulnerability too soon. If perceived as inappropriate, it instantly **reduces social attraction**.	**2. Vet Values:** Ensure your stories reveal positive, core values (e.g., integrity, hard work). This reinforces the target's **Confirmation Bias.**	**2. Read Reciprocity:** Use the target's verbal and non-verbal response (matching your disclosure) as the final gauge for appropriateness.
3. Virtual Connection: In digital settings, rely entirely on **words, charm, and seduction**. Use strong narrative to compensate for the lack of physical presence.	**3. Frame Shared Struggle:** Use shared narratives to create a "founding myth" (e.g., "The time *we* overcame the impossible deadline"). This cements collective loyalty.	**3. Retreat Immediately:** If the target shows anxiety, withdrawal, or low reciprocation, immediately reduce the depth of future disclosures to preserve trust.

Book 5: Instant Influence: Urgency and Action

Goal: Collapse the Decision Window for Immediate Compliance

Time Control (Discounting)	Fear Activation (Urgency)	Final Lock (Commitment)
1. **Pay Present Premium:** Offer an immediate material or psychological gain for acting now (e.g., instant status upgrade, immediate stress relief).	1. **Frame Loss:** Frame non-compliance as a guaranteed, quantifiable loss (e.g., "you lose the $2,000 discount tomorrow").	1. **Legitimate the Deadline:** Ensure the scarcity or deadline is justified by an **external, verifiable fact** (e.g., system lock-in, financial cut-off).
2. **Sensory Immersion:** Use language that makes the future reward tangible and sensory (e.g., "You will *see* the surplus on your screen") to minimize the **Temporal Discounting** gap.	2. **Engineer Scarcity:** Introduce a legitimate constraint (limited time or quantity) to trigger the **Fear Of Missing Out (FOMO)**.	2. **Provide Consistency Frame:** Immediately after the signature, provide the target with the linguistic justification that aligns the impulse with their core value (e.g., "You acted responsibly to avoid the loss").
3. **Combat Status Quo Bias:** Reframe non-action as the true risk to stability. Force the target to choose your solution to maintain the current safe reality.	3. **Activate Reactance:** Threaten the target's future freedom to acquire the item at that price to trigger **Psychological Reactance**.	3. **Close the Loop:** Immediately reiterate the **Loss Avoided** and affirm the target's **effort** to prevent buyer's remorse.

PART 2: DARK PSYCHOLOGY AND MANIPULATION 5-1

The Complete Guide to Gaslighting, Social Engineering, Dark Triad Tactics, Cognitive Bias Exploits and Emotional Control

INTRODUCTION

The Architecture of Influence: Why You Must Study the Dark Side to Protect the Light

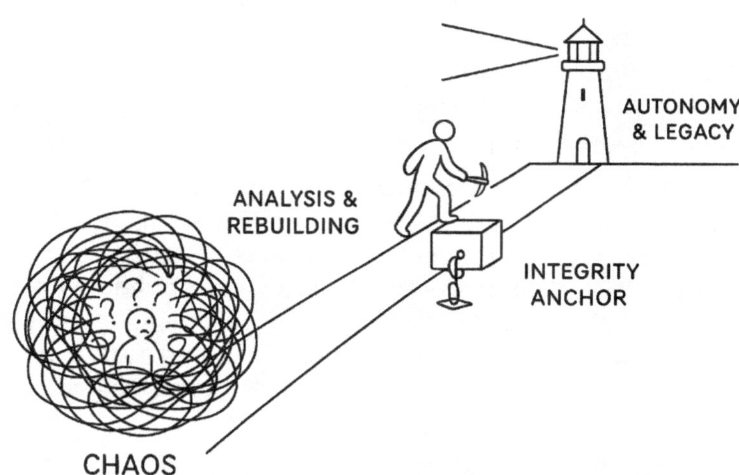

Influence is not magic. It is a mechanic. It is a set of levers and pulleys within the human mind that, when pulled in the right sequence, produce a specific reaction. Most people move through life unaware of these mechanisms. They believe their choices are entirely their own. They assume their memories are accurate recordings of reality. They trust that the people around them operate with the same empathy and moral code that they do.

This assumption is dangerous.

We live in an environment where attention is the currency and compliance is the product. Every day, you encounter entities, individuals, corporations, algorithms, that want something from you. They want your money, your vote, your time, or your emotional submission. Most of these interactions are benign. The barista suggests a pastry; you say yes or no. But a significant percentage of these interactions are predatory. They are designed to bypass your logic and hack your decision-making process.

This collection, *Dark Psychology and Manipulation 5-1*, exists to expose that machinery. It serves a single function: to hand you the blueprints of the weapon so you can build the shield. You cannot defend yourself against a strategy you do not recognize. If you cannot name the tactic, you will fall victim to it.

The Myth of the Rational Actor

For decades, traditional economics and psychology operated on the belief that humans are "rational actors." The theory suggested that when people make decisions, they weigh the costs and benefits, analyze the data, and choose the optimal path.

We now know this is false.

Research in behavioral economics and neuroscience shows that the human brain is not a logic engine; it is a survival engine. It prioritizes speed over accuracy. To process the millions of bits of data flooding your senses every moment, your brain relies on heuristics: mental shortcuts. These shortcuts save energy. They allow you to decide what toothpaste to buy without spending three hours analyzing ingredients. They let you trust a uniformed officer without demanding identification every time.

Manipulators exploit these shortcuts. They know that if they trigger the right heuristic, your brain will skip the logic phase and jump straight to compliance.

Consider the "Default to Truth" theory proposed by psychologist Tim Levine. His research suggests that humans are evolutionarily hardwired to believe what others tell them. In a tribal setting, constant suspicion was inefficient. Cooperation ensured survival. Therefore, we assume honesty until we have overwhelming evidence of deception. A manipulator relies on this biological hardwiring. They know you will twist yourself into knots to make sense of their lies because your brain resists the energy-intensive process of suspicion.

This book bundle dismantles these biological vulnerabilities across five distinct disciplines.

Book 1: The Assault on Reality (Gaslighting)

The first volume addresses the most insidious form of control: Gaslighting. This is not simple lying. Lying is an attempt to hide the truth. Gaslighting is an attempt to erase the concept of truth itself.

The term originates from the 1938 play *Gas Light*, but the psychological mechanism is far older. It attacks the victim's metacognition, the ability to think about their own thinking. When a predator gaslights you, they are not just trying to win an argument. They are trying to replace your internal hard drive.

We will examine the work of researchers like Dr. Robin Stern, who identified the "Gaslight Tango." This dynamic requires two people: one to distort reality and one who needs to stay in the relationship enough to accept the distortion. We will look at the neurological impact of this abuse. Chronic doubt and emotional suppression shrink the hippocampus, the part of the brain responsible for memory and learning. Gaslighting is not just annoying; it causes physical brain damage.

You will learn to identify the subtle precursors to this abuse. It rarely starts with a massive lie. It begins with trivialities. A misplaced set of keys. A denied conversation. Slowly, the predator increases the frequency until the victim no longer trusts their own sensory input. This volume provides the tools to anchor yourself in objective reality and sever the neural pathways of doubt.

Book 2: The Security Breach (Social Engineering)

The second volume shifts from the intimate to the transactional. Social Engineering is the art of hacking humans. In the security industry, professionals often say, "You cannot patch a human being." You can install the best firewalls and the most complex encryption on a server, but if a hacker calls an employee and claims to be from IT support, that employee will often hand over the password.

Social engineering exploits our social instincts: helpfulness, fear of authority, and curiosity.

We will dissect the anatomy of the con. You will see how attackers use "Pretexting" to create a fabricated scenario that compels you to act. This is not just about email scams. It applies to the person at the bar extracting information about your company, or the stranger gaining access to your secure apartment complex by carrying a heavy box and waiting for you to hold the door.

This section leans heavily on the principles of persuasion identified by Robert Cialdini, specifically "Authority" and "Liking." Attackers know that if they wear a high-visibility vest and carry a clipboard, 90% of people will not question their presence. We are conditioned to obey symbols of authority, not the actual authority. You will learn to verify, to pause, and to break the polite social contracts that leave you exposed.

Book 3: The Predator's Profile (Dark Triad Tactics)

To defend against manipulation, you must understand the manipulator. Book 3 focuses on the personality types most likely to use these tactics: The Dark Triad.

Psychologists Delroy Paulhus and Kevin Williams coined this term in 2002 to describe three overlapping but distinct malevolent traits:

1. **Narcissism:** Grandiosity, entitlement, and a lack of empathy.
2. **Machiavellianism:** A strategic, cynical approach to interaction where others are viewed solely as tools for personal gain.
3. **Psychopathy:** Impulsivity, low anxiety, and a total absence of remorse.

These individuals are not rare. Studies suggest they make up a significant portion of the population, with higher concentrations in corporate leadership, law, and politics. They are often charming, charismatic, and successful. This volume will teach you how to spot them before they embed themselves in your life.

We will analyze the "empathy gap." Most people project their own conscience onto others. You assume that if you hurt someone, they feel bad, so the other person must feel bad too. The Dark Triad personality does not feel this. When you project a conscience onto a psychopath, you give them a tactical advantage. You will learn to profile these traits based on behavior, not words. You will learn the "Grey Rock" method and other containment strategies to neutralize their influence without triggering their rage.

Book 4: The Internal Traitor (Cognitive Bias Exploits)

Sometimes, the manipulator is not an external enemy. It is your own brain. Book 4 explores Cognitive Bias Exploits. These are the systematic errors in thinking that affect the decisions and judgments that people make.

Marketers, politicians, and master manipulators treat these biases like buttons on a control panel.

- **The Halo Effect:** If someone is attractive, we automatically assume they are smart, kind, and honest.
- **Loss Aversion:** We feel the pain of losing $100 twice as intensely as the pleasure of gaining $100. Manipulators use this to trap us in bad deals.

- **The Sunk Cost Fallacy:** We continue to invest time and money into a failing project or relationship simply because we have already invested so much.

This volume draws on the Nobel Prize-winning work of Daniel Kahneman and Amos Tversky. We will discuss the difference between "System 1" thinking (fast, automatic, emotional) and "System 2" thinking (slow, logical, calculating). Manipulation almost always targets System 1. The goal of this section is to train you to force your brain into System 2 processing when the stakes are high. You will learn to recognize when your own mind is lying to you.

Book 5: The Final Defense (Emotional Control)

The final volume ties everything together. Knowledge is useless if you cannot execute it under pressure. Emotional Control is the foundation of all defense.

When you are angry, afraid, or euphoric, your prefrontal cortex, the part of the brain responsible for logic and planning, shuts down. Your amygdala takes over. A manipulator's primary goal is often to provoke an emotional spike. Once you are emotional, you are suggestible.

We will study the physiology of emotion. We will look at how to interrupt the "refractory period", the time during which you are unable to take in information that contradicts your current mood. We will discuss the concept of "State Management." This is not about suppressing emotion; it is about regulating it so that it informs your decisions rather than dictating them.

This section provides the "Print and Keep" tactics. It gives you the breathing protocols used by first responders to lower heart rate in seconds. It teaches you how to detach from a verbal attack so you can observe the attacker's strategy rather than absorbing their insults.

The Ethics of Dark Psychology

A common question arises when discussing these topics: *Is it ethical to learn this?*

Some argue that teaching these techniques is dangerous. They fear it creates more manipulators. But this argument ignores a fundamental reality. The predators already know these techniques. The con artist does not need this book; they learned these skills through trial and error or from mentors in the trade. The toxic narcissist does not need a manual; they have spent a lifetime perfecting their craft.

t is the empathetic, the trusting, and the cooperative who need this information.

gnorance is not a virtue. It is a vulnerability. By understanding how the mechanism works, you strip it of its power. When you see a "Scarcity Tactic" in a sales pitch, you don't feel anxiety; you feel recognition. You think, *"Ah, they are trying to trigger my fear of missing out."* The moment you label the tactic, the spell breaks. You regain your agency.

Furthermore, understanding these dynamics makes you a better leader, parent, and partner. It allows you to recognize when you might be inadvertently manipulating others. It forces you to examine your own communication. Are you guilt-tripping your child? Are you gaslighting your spouse because you can't admit you were wrong? This knowledge works as a mirror as much as a shield.

How to Read This Bundle

You do not need to read these books in order, though they are arranged to build a cumulative skillset.

f you are currently questioning your sanity in a relationship, jump immediately to **Book 1**. If you are worried about your digital footprint or corporate security, start with **Book 2**. If you are dealing with a difficult boss or an ex-partner who seems devoid of empathy, **Book 3** is your priority.

However, do not skip the reflection questions at the end of each book. Information alone does not change behavior. Application does. The reflection questions are designed to move the concepts from your short-term memory to your long-term behavioral patterns.

This text is dense. It prioritizes information density over fluff. You will find scientific references, definitions, and actionable steps. We have stripped away the filler. There are no long, winding anecdotes about the author's childhood unless they serve a specific instructional purpose.

The Warning

As you read, you will experience a phenomenon known as the "Baader-Meinhof phenomenon," or frequency illusion. Once you learn a new concept, you start seeing it everywhere.

You will see gaslighting in political speeches. You will see social engineering in the emails from your bank (or the fake ones). You will see the Dark Triad traits in characters on television and perhaps, uncomfortably, in people you know.

This can be overwhelming. It can lead to cynicism. You might start to view every interaction as a transaction and every person as a potential threat. This is not the goal.

The goal is *selective vigilance*. You do not wear a bulletproof vest to sit on your couch, but you might wear one if you were entering a war zone. This book teaches you how to recognize when you are in a war zone. It teaches you to spot the red flags—the micro-expressions, the linguistic patterns, the pacing of a conversation—that signal danger.

When you are safe, you can take the armor off. You can connect, love, and trust. But you will do so with eyes wide open, knowing that if the situation changes, you have the tools to protect yourself.

Breaking the Cycle

Manipulation relies on silence. It relies on the victim feeling isolated, crazy, or ashamed. By reading this, you are breaking that silence.

History is filled with examples of mass manipulation. From cults to financial bubbles, humans are prone to being led astray. But history is also filled with individuals who stood up and said, "No." These were the people who recognized the pattern. They were the ones who kept their heads when everyone else was losing theirs.

To be that person requires more than just stubbornness. It requires education. It requires a systematic understanding of the human operating system.

We are about to dismantle that system piece by piece. We will look at the ugly parts of human nature. We will look at the lies, the greed, and the cruelty. But in doing so, we will find the path to autonomy.

You are the only person who should be in control of your mind. Not the algorithm, not the marketer, not the abuser.

This is your manual for taking back that control.

Turn the page. The analysis begins now.

BOOK ONE

GASLIGHTING: DECONSTRUCTING REALITY DISTORTION AND RECLAIMING SANITY

INTRODUCTION

If you've picked up this book, you're likely exhausted. You probably don't need a clinical definition of gaslighting; you need air. You need to know that the invisible fog you've been living in: the one that makes you question your memory, your worth, and even the solidity of the floor beneath your feet is real, and it has a name.

You aren't crazy. You aren't overly sensitive. You aren't flawed.

You are, in fact, the victim of a calculated, systematic form of psychological abuse designed to destroy your internal sense of reality and replace it with a controlled, distorted version imposed by someone else.

For too long, the term "gaslighting" has been tossed around loosely, used to describe everything from a minor disagreement to someone simply being dismissive. But true gaslighting is a complex, high-stakes psychological operation. It's not just lying; it's lying with the intent to shatter the target's ability to trust their own senses, emotions, and memories. It is psychological violence designed to create **dependence and control**.

This book is your field guide out of the fog. It is a detailed map, using insights from psychology, neuroscience, and trauma research, to show you exactly how the distortion was created, how it damaged your brain and nervous system, and most importantly, how to systematically reverse that damage and reclaim absolute sovereignty over your own mind.

The Origin of the Term: Recognizing the Pattern

The term "gaslighting" comes, as many know, from the 1938 play and subsequent 1944 film *Gaslight*, where a manipulative husband systematically tries to drive his wife insane. He hides and moves objects, makes noises in the attic, and, critically, dims the gas-fueled lamps in the house while adamantly denying that the light is changing.

Every time the wife points out the dimming light, an objective, observable fact, he tells her she is imagining things, that she is becoming mentally ill, until she fully believes her perception is flawed.

The genius and horror of the story lie in its three key elements, which are the hallmarks of real-life gaslighting:

1. **Objective Reality is Attacked:** It's not a subjective opinion; it's a verifiable fact (the light is dimming).
2. **The Attacker is the Source of the Distortion:** The manipulator is creating the reality they are denying.
3. **The Goal is Emotional and Psychological Disintegration:** The objective is to make the target question their own sanity to the point of dependence.

If you are reading this, you have likely been looking at a dimming light for a long time, and you've been told the problem is with your eyes.

Why Me? The Myth of Vulnerability

Survivors often torture themselves with the question, "Why was I susceptible?" The implication is that a weakness or flaw made them a target. We must abolish this myth immediately.

Gaslighters do not seek out "weak" people; they seek out people with qualities they desperately need, usually:

- **Empathy and Trust:** You were capable of deep love and were willing to believe in the goodness of others. This natural trust was exploited.
- **A Desire for Harmony:** You are a peacemaker. You value the relationship over being "right," which led you to concede your reality in the service of preserving peace.

- **Competence and Accomplishment:** Gaslighters often choose successful, intelligent, and capable people whose competence they can slowly erode and whose success they can secretly envy and harness.

The qualities that made you a target are, in a healthy world, your greatest strengths. They were weaponized against you.

The Silent Damage: What Gaslighting Does to the Brain

The invisible fog is a product of real, measurable changes in your neurobiology. It's crucial to understand that the confusion isn't just "in your head"; it is a systemic response to chronic psychological stress.

The constant denial of your reality activates your body's threat response system, the **HPA axis (Hypothalamic-Pituitary-Adrenal axis)**, which regulates your stress hormones, primarily cortisol. When your reality is constantly contradicted, your brain cannot achieve safety. It is in a perpetual state of high alert, constantly scanning for threats.

This chronic stress leads to:

- **Hypervigilance:** You spend excessive mental energy monitoring the environment, anticipating the next lie, and documenting interactions. This massive cognitive load is why you feel exhausted all the time.
- **Erosion of Memory and Trust:** Your brain struggles to lay down coherent, reliable memories because the emotional context is always chaotic. When you can't trust your own memory, you are forced to rely on the manipulator's version of events—the core goal of the abuse.
- **Emotional Flooding:** Your prefrontal cortex, the part of the brain responsible for logic and impulse control, gets overwhelmed by the constant flood of stress hormones, making it impossible to think clearly, argue rationally, or set firm boundaries when you need them most.

This book is about bringing that nervous system back offline, quieting the hypervigilance, and rebuilding the solid, predictable foundation of your mind.

The Roadmap Ahead

This journey is structured to first understand the weapon and then to build the defense.

- **Chapters 2 & 3** will meticulously dissect the phases and mechanisms of gaslighting, giving names to the confusing behaviors you witnessed. We will identify the core psychological principles used against you.
- **Chapters 4 & 5** will focus on identifying the pattern in various spheres of life (work, family, romance) and providing the immediate counter-moves, teaching you how to build your **Cognitive Anchor**, the inner, unshakeable truth.
- **Chapters 6, 7, & 8** are the architectural phase: rebuilding the fractured self, creating a stable life structure, and integrating your experience into enduring wisdom and a purposeful life.

Your safety, your sanity, and your authentic life are not negotiable. The time for confusion is over. The time for clarity and reclamation starts now.

CHAPTER 1

THE MECHANICS OF REALITY DISTORTION

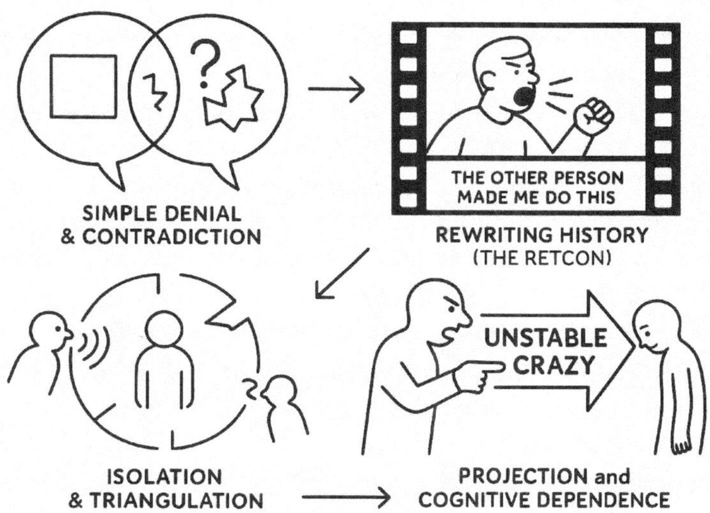

In Chapter 1, we established that gaslighting is real and that the exhaustion you feel is the result of chronic neurological stress. Now, we must move into the engine room. To defeat this specific form of abuse, we need to stop reacting to the symptoms and start dissecting the **mechanics**: the specific, calculated toolbox the manipulator uses to build their distorted reality.

Understanding these techniques is not about victim-blaming or giving the aggressor credit for genius; it is about recognizing patterns. Once a magic trick is explained, it loses its power.

The process of reality distortion is not a single event; it is a gradual, four-phase campaign designed to strip the target of their cognitive independence.

Phase I: The Foundation of Doubt (The Contradiction)

The first step in gaslighting is planting a small, almost insignificant seed of doubt. The manipulator begins by attacking a minor, verifiable fact. This is the simplest form of distortion, but it's crucial because it tests your boundaries and establishes their narrative authority.

1. Simple Denial and Weaponized Amnesia

The most common starting tool is **Simple Denial**. You state a truth, and they flatly deny it, often with an air of absolute certainty and incredulity:

- *You:* "We agreed to meet at 7 PM."
- *Them:* "No, we absolutely did not. I would never agree to that time. You misheard me."

This move forces you into an immediate, unproductive debate. You spend energy arguing a fact you know to be true.

This quickly escalates to **Weaponized Amnesia**. The manipulator knows exactly what they said or did, but they pretend to have no memory of it. This isn't just about forgetting; it's about shifting the blame for the gap in memory onto you.

- *You:* "You were the one who broke the vase last week."
- *Them:* (With wide eyes) "I don't recall that at all. Are you sure you're remembering that correctly? You know how stressed you've been lately."

The moment you concede, even slightly ("Maybe I *did* mishear"), the foundation is set. You have allowed their authority to supersede your memory.

Phase II: The Escalation of Memory Attack (The Retcon)

Once the foundation of doubt is set, the gaslighter escalates to directly rewrite history. This is often called the **Retcon** (short for "retroactive continuity," a term borrowed from comic book writing where past events are rewritten to fit the current story).

1. Shifting Blame through Rewriting Emotional Context

The Retcon technique takes a painful event, acknowledges it actually happened (because it's too visible to deny), and then **completely changes the emotional context** and responsibility.

- *Original Reality (Truth):* They screamed at you for 20 minutes because they were drunk and angry.
- *Retcon Reality (Distortion):* "I only raised my voice because you were backing me into a corner and making me feel unsafe. I was reacting to your aggression. You forced my reaction."

Notice the subtle, terrifying mechanism here: **They admit the event, but transfer the agency.** The new story is that *your behavior* caused their unacceptable reaction. This is incredibly confusing because part of the original event *is* acknowledged, making the distortion feel almost true.

The goal of the Retcon is to paralyze you with confusion. If the memory of the event is tainted with the possibility that *you* were the actual aggressor, you become terrified of bringing up any past issue, allowing the manipulator to escape accountability entirely.

Phase III: Weaponizing the Environment (Isolation and Triangulation)

Gaslighting rarely happens in a vacuum. To maintain control, the aggressor must destroy the target's external support network, the external reality-check system. This is where the techniques of isolation and **Triangulation** come into play.

1. Isolation: The Necessary Precondition

The first step is often subtle but systematic **Isolation**. The manipulator subtly critiques or alienates your friends, family, or professional connections:

- "Your mother is so dramatic; you shouldn't listen to her advice."
- "Your best friend seems jealous of our relationship."
- "Don't tell your coworker about that; they can't be trusted."

This creates dependence. As your reliable outside sources of validation are cut off, the manipulator becomes your **only source** of information, emotional feedback, and reality.

2. Triangulation: Introducing the Third Party

Triangulation is the powerful social-engineering tool used to destabilize your external reality. This involves introducing a third party, either real or invented, to support the gaslighter's narrative.

- "My sister agrees that you are overly sensitive."
- "My coworker noticed you were behaving oddly yesterday, too."
- "Even your mother told me she's worried about your memory."

The psychological impact is devastating: You suddenly feel like you're not just arguing against one person, but against the entire social consensus. The gaslighter has successfully created a warped sense of social proof, forcing you to doubt yourself because "everyone else sees it but you."

Phase IV: Emotional Sabotage (Projection and The Shame Bomb)

The final phase moves from intellectual confusion to emotional ruin. The manipulator's goal here is to make you internalize their flaws, turning their guilt and rage into your shame.

1. The Power of Projection

Projection is perhaps the most insidious tool. It is the unconscious psychological defense mechanism where the aggressor attributes their own unwanted traits, emotions, or behaviors to you.

- The person who is constantly cheating accuses *you* of being paranoid and unfaithful.
- The person who is drunk and screaming accuses *you* of being "out of control" and unstable.
- The person who is financially reckless accuses *you* of constantly spending too much money.

This tactic forces you into constant **Defensiveness**. You are so busy denying the false accusation and defending your character that you lose sight of the aggressor's original, harmful behavior. The focus shifts entirely from *their actions* to *your reaction and defense*.

2. The Shame Bomb and Cognitive Dependence

The cumulative effect of all these mechanics is the **Shame Bomb**. When you are constantly lied to, isolated, and accused of things you didn't do, the brain eventually seeks to resolve the punishing psychological discomfort of **Cognitive Dissonance** (the conflict between what you see and what you are told).

As we discussed in Chapter 1, the easiest way for the mind to resolve this war is to surrender. You start to believe: *They are insistent, everyone else seems to agree, and my memory is clearly failing. Therefore, the problem must be me.*

This moment of self-blame is the gaslighter's ultimate victory. You have granted them cognitive dependence, and their reality distortion is complete. You are now convinced you need them, the very person causing the damage, to tell you who you are.

But that cognitive dependence, based on years of systematic deception, is only a habit. And any habit, once understood, can be systematically dismantled and replaced. The next chapter will show you how this dependency was built over time, setting the stage for the counter-moves that begin in Chapter 5.

CHAPTER 2

THE THREE STAGES OF PSYCHOLOGICAL ERASURE

If Chapter 2 explained the toolbox of the manipulator, the lies, the retcons, the projection, this chapter turns the gaze inward. We are going to map the internal terrain of the gaslighting target.

Psychological erasure is not a sudden event; it is a meticulously choreographed, three-act play performed deep inside the victim's mind. It is the systematic removal of the self's capacity for autonomous thought, feeling, and action. This process takes the intelligent, functional adult and reduces them to a state of chronic self-doubt and dependence.

Understanding these stages is vital for two reasons: First, it validates your experience, proving that what you went through was a predictable, systemic response to abuse. Second, it shows us the precise points where the mental damage occurred, giving us the exact repair locations for the counter-moves we will learn in Chapter 5.

We will examine the neurological and behavioral shifts that mark the progression from healthy resistance to catastrophic surrender.

Stage I: Disbelief and Defense (Fighting the Fog)

This initial stage is defined by **cognitive dissonance** and the target's vigorous, though often futile, attempt to maintain their established reality. In this phase, the target still fully trusts their own perception but is utterly baffled by the unwavering confidence of the aggressor's lies.

The War of Evidence and the Cognitive Squeeze

The gaslighter has just initiated the campaign with simple denial and contradiction (Phase I of Chapter 2). The target is operating under the assumption that the problem is a **misunderstanding** or a **memory lapse** on the part of the aggressor. The target's primary goal is to close the gap between the truth and the lie.

Behavioral Markers of Stage I:

1. **Documentation Mania:** The target becomes a private detective. They start saving text messages, taking screenshots, keeping detailed journals, and recording conversations. This is a desperate attempt to gather **external evidence** to counteract the internal pressure of the gaslighter's denial. This behavior is rational, if they deny the light is dimming, I'll take a picture of the dimmer switch, but it is ultimately exhausting and fruitless, as the manipulator will simply deny the validity of the evidence ("You fabricated that," or "That screenshot is taken out of context").
2. **The Arguing Loop (JADE):** The target wastes vast amounts of energy trying to **J**ustify, **A**rgue, **D**efend, and **E**xplain. They believe if they can just present the facts logically, the aggressor will capitulate. This fuels the manipulator, who thrives on the target's need for validation. The gaslighter's goal is not to win the argument; it's to exhaust the target's cognitive resources.
3. **Seeking External Validation (The Plea):** The target asks trusted friends or family, "Did that really happen? Am I remembering

this correctly?" This is the last, healthy defense mechanism before isolation sets in. They are reaching out to their social ecosystem to recalibrate their internal compass.

The Neurological Cost: Hypervigilance and the Overwhelmed Prefrontal Cortex

In Stage I, the brain is in an active **fight-or-flight** mode, but it's a mental fight.

The **prefrontal cortex (PFC)**, the part of the brain handling logic, decision-making, and critical thinking—is working overtime. It is trying to reconcile two irreconcilable facts: *A) My memory is correct, and B) This person, whom I trust/love, is adamantly denying my reality*. The cognitive dissonance is painful, consuming immense mental energy.

Simultaneously, the **HPA axis** is firing consistently, bathing the brain in cortisol and adrenaline. The target is in a state of **hypervigilance**, constantly scanning the manipulator's face, tone, and body language for clues, trying to predict the next lie or emotional shift. This chronic scanning drains the target, leading to perpetual fatigue, insomnia, and an inability to concentrate on unrelated tasks.

The critical shift in Stage I: The target is primarily focused on **fixing the other person** or **fixing the relationship**, failing to recognize that the only thing that needs fixing is the target's own proximity to the abuse. Their ego is still intact, but their mental health is suffering massive damage.

Stage II: Self-Doubt and Internalization (The Surrender)

This is the most painful and transformative stage of erasure. The target stops trying to convince the manipulator and starts trying to **convince themselves** that the manipulator is right. The chronic psychological warfare of Stage I has succeeded in wearing down the target's defenses.

The Birth of Self-Blame and Learned Helplessness

The relentless barrage of denial, projection, and triangulation (Phase III of Chapter 2) finally convinces the target that the high cognitive cost of fighting is not worth the zero return. The easiest way for the brain to stop the painful stress response is to surrender to the only available explanation: **"The problem is me."**

Behavioral Markers of Stage II:

1. **Chronic Apologizing:** The target begins to apologize not for specific mistakes, but for *existing*, for feeling, for needing, for remembering, or for causing the aggressor's emotional instability. They walk on eggshells, constantly trying to predict and preempt the aggressor's next outburst. This is an attempt to control the chaos by sacrificing their own voice.
2. **Internalized Projection:** The gaslighter's accusations (e.g., "You are lazy," "You are unstable," "You are too emotional") are fully absorbed. The target now genuinely believes they are the source of all conflict and the fundamental flaw in the relationship. When something goes wrong, the immediate internal monologue is, **"What did I do to cause this?"** This marks the full collapse of the internal locus of control.
3. **Withdrawal and Isolation:** The target stops seeking external validation. They have been told by the aggressor that their friends/family are jealous or untrustworthy, and they have been told by the aggressor that their own perspective is flawed. This combination leads to deep isolation and shame, confirming the manipulator's narrative.

The Neurological and Psychological Collapse: Freeze and Fragmentation

In Stage II, the nervous system transitions from the active **fight** of Stage I to the debilitating **freeze** response.

The constant flow of cortisol and adrenaline begins to suppress areas critical for memory consolidation (hippocampus) and emotional processing. The brain has decided that the external environment is unsolvable and unavoidable, leading to **Learned Helplessness**.

Learned Helplessness: This is a psychological condition where a person suffering from a persistent painful stimulus becomes unwilling to avoid subsequent encounters with that stimulus, even if they become avoidable. The target learns that *their actions do not matter*; fighting back doesn't work, and asserting reality only makes the aggressor angrier, leading to more pain. The only perceived solution is passivity.

Identity Fragmentation: The target starts to live with a dual self:

- **The Original Self:** The authentic person with clear boundaries, memories, and emotions. This self goes quiet, tucked away for survival.

- **The Survival Self:** The compliant, self-blaming version who anticipates the aggressor's needs, mimics their opinions, and constantly minimizes their own feelings to maintain peace.

The target is no longer arguing about a specific event; they are arguing about their *right to exist* as a separate, feeling, autonomous person, and in this stage, they begin to lose that argument.

Stage III: Dependence and Dissociation (The Erasure)

This is the endgame. The target has fully surrendered their independent reality, and their survival is now intricately linked to the aggressor's approval. The authentic self is functionally erased, replaced by a "shell self" that exists primarily to manage the relationship and preempt threats.

The Trauma Bond and the Shell Self

The core experience of Stage III is the **Trauma Bond**. This is a destructive attachment where the victim experiences a repetitive cycle of abuse followed by positive reinforcement (e.g., a sudden, lavish display of kindness or a period of calm). The target interprets the intermittent reinforcement not as manipulation, but as proof that the aggressor is capable of love and that *the target's endurance* eventually brings forth that love.

This dynamic creates a profound, addictive dependence where the target finds the highest form of relief and safety *only* in the presence and approval of their abuser. The aggressor becomes both the **disease and the cure**.

Behavioral Markers of Stage III:

1. **Emotional Flatness and Numbness (Dissociation):** The brain, overloaded with stress, pulls the plug on the emotional centers. The target feels numb, disconnected, and experiences significant difficulty accessing or naming their own feelings. This **dissociation** is a survival mechanism, if I don't feel it, it can't hurt me. The target may experience memory gaps (dissociative amnesia) during times of high stress because the brain literally checked out.
2. **Loss of Personal Initiative:** The target's goals, hobbies, friendships, and opinions fade away. All energy is devoted to managing the relationship. When asked simple questions like, "What do you want to do this weekend?" or "What are your

goals?" the target feels lost, because the "shell self" has no personal desires; its sole purpose is to reflect the needs of the manipulator.

3. **Echoing the Aggressor:** The target speaks in the aggressor's language, using their opinions and even their specific phrases. They may defend the aggressor to outsiders, using the exact excuses the manipulator provided ("He's just stressed," "I did push their buttons"). They become an extension of the aggressor's narrative, demonstrating the full erasure of the original, autonomous voice.

The Final Neurological Crisis: Loss of Identity

In this final stage, the chronic stress has changed the brain's baseline functionality. The amygdala (the brain's fear center) is overdeveloped and constantly on high alert, while the PFC and hippocampus are chronically suppressed.

The biggest crisis is the near-total collapse of the **sense of self**. The authentic self, deprived of validation, voice, and autonomy, retreats further into the subconscious. The target genuinely feels like they are wearing someone else's life, or that their real self is missing. They may look in the mirror and not recognize the person staring back.

The Ultimate Paradox of Erasure: The target, who was once successful, empathetic, and competent, is now utterly dependent on the person who caused the damage, and they fear nothing more than being abandoned by that person. They have been gaslit into believing that outside the safety of the toxic bond, they are fragile, unstable, and unlovable.

From Erasure to Re-Emergence: The Call to Action

The journey through the three stages of psychological erasure is brutal, but it is not a life sentence.

Stage I (Disbelief) is proof you fought. You gathered evidence and reached out. That effort was heroic, even if it failed against a master manipulator.

Stage II (Self-Doubt) is proof you adapted. Your nervous system was intelligently trying to minimize the pain when it recognized the threat was unavoidable.

Stage III (Dependence) is proof you survived. Your brain prioritized survival through compliance when autonomy was impossible.

The core of the authentic self, the intelligence, the clarity, the kindness that made you a target, is still intact beneath the shell. It cannot be permanently destroyed, only deeply buried.

The path to recovery, starting in Chapter 4, is the systematic, stage-by-stage process of reversing this erasure:

1. **Stop the Disbelief Loop (Reverse Stage I):** Establish the **Integrity Anchor** to override the need for external evidence.
2. **End the Self-Doubt (Reverse Stage II):** Rebuild the internal locus of control and define reality purely by **factual observation**.
3. **Break the Dependence (Reverse Stage III):** Re-engage with the authentic self, reclaim autonomy, and establish boundaries.

Understanding the deep psychological mechanisms of erasure is the first step in the grand, necessary process of **re-emergence**. You now know exactly where the chains were forged; next, we learn how to break them.

CHAPTER 3

GASLIGHTING IN PROFESSIONAL AND PERSONAL SPHERES

In the previous chapters, we dissected the mechanics of reality distortion (Chapter 2) and mapped the stages of psychological erasure (Chapter 3). You now understand that gaslighting is a predictable, systematic campaign. But a campaign is only effective if it's tailored to the battlefield.

The core tools, denial, projection, triangulation, remain the same, but the terrain changes dramatically depending on the context: intimate, familial, or professional.

The primary difference lies in the **nature of the bond** that traps you.

- In **intimate relationships**, the bond is built on **love and attachment**, making the abuse feel like an existential threat.
- In **family dynamics**, the bond is built on **duty and obligation**, making the abuse feel unavoidable and sanctioned by tradition.
- In the **workplace**, the bond is built on **necessity and competence**, making the abuse feel like a direct threat to your financial survival and professional identity.

Understanding the specific context is the first step toward building the right counter-move (Chapter 5), because the emotional stakes, and therefore the exit strategies, are entirely different.

Section I: The Intimate Sphere —The Trap of Love and Attachment

Gaslighting is most often studied in the context of romantic partnership because the stakes are highest, and the perpetrator has the deepest access to the target's emotional core.

1. The Weaponization of Vulnerability

In healthy intimacy, vulnerability is a shared currency, a reciprocal exchange that builds trust. In gaslighting dynamics, vulnerability is simply **ammunition**.

The perpetrator encourages you to reveal your deepest insecurities, past traumas, and greatest fears during periods of intense connection (often called the "idealization phase"). They do this not out of genuine empathy, but to collect leverage.

Core Mechanics in Intimacy:

- **Jekyll and Hyde Syndrome:** The manipulator alternates sharply between intense love/idealization and severe devaluation/criticism. This fluctuation is the engine of the **Trauma Bond** (Chapter 3). The target becomes addicted to the brief periods of calm and validation, interpreting them as the "real" person, and attributing the abuse to external stress or their own failing. This cycling keeps the target perpetually off-balance, searching for the "good" partner, thus maintaining dependence.
- **Emotional Invalidation as Erasure:** The gaslighter constantly minimizes the target's legitimate emotional responses.
    - *You:* "I feel hurt when you disappear without texting."
    - *Them:* "Why do you always overreact? That's not a normal reaction. You are so needy; you must have abandonment issues." The victim is not only denied the right to their feeling but is shamed for it, implying their emotional structure is defective. This accelerates Stage II (Self-Doubt) erasure.

- **The Blurring of Sexual Reality:** This is a particularly insidious form of intimate gaslighting. It involves denying conversations about sexual boundaries, claiming sexual encounters didn't happen as remembered, or denying consent was withdrawn. This attack on physical reality is extremely damaging, leaving the victim questioning their bodily memory and autonomy.

2. The Unique Challenge: The Attachment System

Intimate gaslighting directly hijacks the human **Attachment System**. We are biologically wired to seek proximity to and safety from our primary attachment figures. When the person who is supposed to be your safe harbor becomes the storm itself, the brain panics.

The victim often develops a **Disorganized Attachment Style**: they simultaneously seek closeness (for safety) and fear it (because it causes pain). This internal conflict is devastating and explains why targets find leaving nearly impossible, despite obvious evidence of harm. They are driven by an instinctual, prehistoric need to resolve the proximity-seeking dilemma.

Section II: The Familial Sphere —The Trap of Duty and Obligation

Familial gaslighting is perhaps the most difficult to escape because the bonds are lifelong, often predating the victim's own memory, and are enforced by cultural or social expectations of loyalty. You can divorce a spouse; you cannot divorce a parent or sibling (emotionally speaking).

1. The Unbreakable Chain of Duty

In a family setting, the gaslighter uses two powerful, ready-made weapons: **Hierarchy** (I am your parent/elder) and **Guilt** (I sacrificed everything for you).

Core Mechanics in Family Dynamics:

- **The Scapegoat/Golden Child Dynamic:** The family gaslighter often creates two or more roles to perpetuate the abuse through triangulation:
- **The Scapegoat (You):** The target upon whom all of the family's dysfunction, guilt, and problems are projected. "You are the reason we can't have nice things," or "If you were just less sensitive, Dad wouldn't drink."

    - **The Golden Child (The Ally/Weapon):** The child or sibling who can do no wrong, often used as the third party in triangulation: "Your sister/brother never complains when I ask for help. Why can't you be more like them?" The Golden Child is the living proof that the manipulator is a *good* parent/relative, and the Scapegoat is the **defective element**.
- **Historical Retconning:** Unlike the romantic sphere, where history is short, family gaslighters rewrite decades of history. They deny childhood events, minimize trauma, and reframe abusive moments as "tough love" or "necessary discipline." They often say things like, "That never happened. You are exaggerating again," or "It wasn't that bad, stop being so dramatic." This attacks the victim's fundamental sense of personal history and origin.
- **Obligation as Control:** The manipulator uses past favors or sacrifices as non-negotiable leverage for present compliance. "After everything I've done for you, you can't spare five minutes to agree with me?" This weaponization of duty cripples the victim's ability to set a boundary, as setting one feels like an act of profound, unforgivable betrayal.

2. The Unique Challenge: The External Sanction

Familial gaslighting often receives tacit approval from the wider social system. Outsiders tend to defer to the "parental wisdom" or the notion that "family must stick together." This external sanction validates the aggressor's narrative and leaves the victim utterly alone, confirming the isolation mechanisms of Stage II and III.

Recovery often requires the drastic step of **No Contact (NC)** or **Grey Rock (GR)** (Chapter 5), which feels unnatural and against every societal expectation instilled since birth.

Section III: The Professional Sphere —The Trap of Competence and Necessity

Workplace gaslighting, often called **Coercive Control in the Workplace (CCW)**, is less about emotional attachment and more about **power asymmetry** and **reputational destruction**. The goal is to control the target's professional output and, ultimately, remove them as a threat or competitor.

1. Competence as the Target

A professional gaslighter (often a superior, but sometimes a highly competitive peer) seeks to dismantle the target's sense of professional competence. They know that if they can make you doubt your ability to perform your job, they can control your output and manage your reputation.

Core Mechanics in the Workplace:

- **Minimizing Achievement (The Moving Goalpost):** The manipulator denies clear, successful outcomes. A project might be completed perfectly, but they immediately shift the standard: "It was fine, but you could have done it faster," or "This is standard work, nothing special. Why are you asking for credit?" This is the professional equivalent of denial, making the victim feel that success is impossible to achieve or prove.
- **Documentation Manipulation:** This is the most dangerous professional tool. The gaslighter may selectively misfile emails, omit the target from important communications, or create false paper trails that subtly imply incompetence or error. When questioned, they use Weaponized Amnesia: "I never saw that email," or "You must have sent that to the wrong address, but I'll take the blame for your mistake this time." This is often done subtly over months to build a non-existent history of performance issues.
    - *Example:* Assigning a task verbally, then denying the assignment or rewriting the scope of work when the target delivers the product.
- **Public Discrediting (Reputation Attack):** This is the professional form of triangulation. The gaslighter subtly undermines the target in front of peers or superiors, often through "concerned" language: "I'm worried about [Target]'s ability to handle this; they seem a bit stressed lately," or "They were supposed to have handled that, but you know how scattered they can be." This poisons the perception of the target among the people whose opinion is vital for their career progression.

2. The Unique Challenge: Necessity and Verification

The victim in the workplace is caught in a paralyzing bind: they need the job for financial stability (necessity), but they cannot trust the reality of their performance (verification). The gaslighting creates a terrifying Catch-22:

- If I leave, I prove I was incompetent and unstable.
- If I stay, I risk further reputational damage and the loss of my financial security.

The exit strategy must therefore be hyper-rational and entirely focused on **external, verifiable facts** (HR records, saved emails, neutral third-party feedback), entirely bypassing the emotional context of the abuser.

Synthesis: The Universal Core of Gaslighting

Across all three spheres—intimate, familial, and professional: the **feeling of the victim is identical**: profound exhaustion, chronic self-doubt, and the terrifying sensation of standing on shifting sands.

The gaslighter, regardless of their role (spouse, parent, boss), is always exploiting the same core psychological principles:

1. **The Need for Safety (Intimacy):** They destroy your psychological safety and then demand you rely on them for rescue.
2. **The Need for Belonging (Family):** They threaten your belonging and use duty to force compliance.
3. **The Need for Competence (Work):** They destroy your professional identity and use financial necessity to ensure silence.

Your survival required understanding these bonds. Your recovery demands that you now choose **Autonomy** over Attachment, **Clarity** over Duty, and **Integrity** over Necessity.

The counter-moves we explore in Chapter 5 are designed to give you the tools to sever these toxic bonds without severing your own well-being. They are techniques for self-anchoring, regardless of whether the distortion is happening in your kitchen, your childhood home, or a corporate boardroom.

CHAPTER 4

COUNTER-MOVES AND COGNITIVE ANCHORING

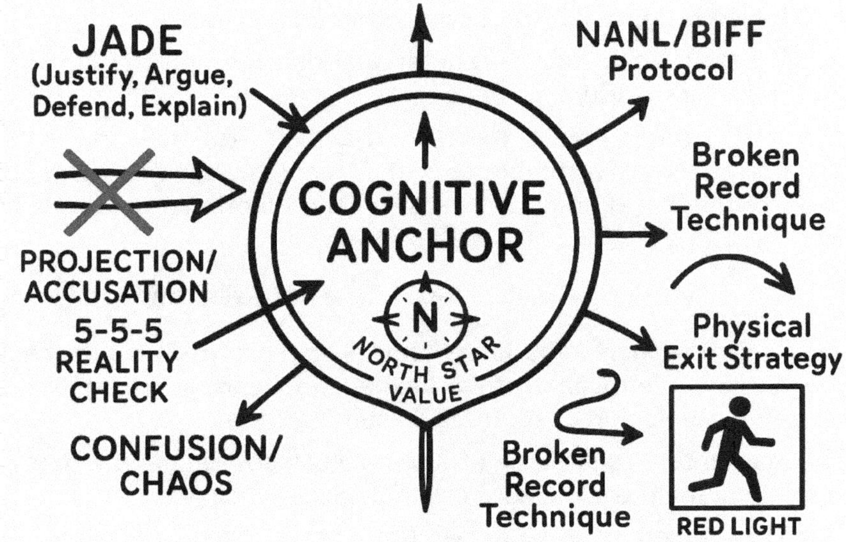

We have finished the diagnosis. You know their tactics (Chapter 2) and the psychological stages of erasure they induce (Chapter 3). You understand how they tailor their abuse to intimate, familial, and professional spheres (Chapter 4).

The question is no longer, "What is happening to me?" but, **"What do I do now?"**

This chapter provides the tactical arsenal. The goal is to install the **Cognitive Anchor**: a core set of mental and behavioral defense protocols designed to stabilize your reality, conserve your mental energy, and force the manipulator to reveal their intentions instantly. The Cognitive Anchor neutralizes the gaslighter's power by refusing to engage in their game of confusion.

The counter-moves fall into three categories: **Mental Defenses**, **Communication Tactics**, and **De-Escalation Protocols**.

Section I: Mental Defenses – Installing the Cognitive Anchor

The Cognitive Anchor is the internal rule you adopt that states: *My reality is non-negotiable and does not require external validation to be true.* This frees you from the exhausting need to prove yourself to the manipulator.

1. The Principle of Non-Engagement

The gaslighter's power source is your energy spent in confusion, argument, and self-doubt (JADE, from Chapter 3). The moment you enter an argument to *defend* a verifiable fact or an authentic feeling, you lose.

The Foundational Rule: Stop JADE (Justify, Argue, Defend, Explain).

- **JADE is fuel for the gaslighter.** When you JADE, you hand the aggressor the tools to prolong the conflict, gather new accusations (to be used later as Retcons), and keep you off-balance.
- **The Power of the Simple Statement:** Your response to a blatant contradiction should not be an explanation, but a simple restatement of your boundary or reality.
    - *Them (Denial):* "I never said we were meeting at 7 PM. You're misremembering."
    - *Your JADE Response (Wrong):* "Yes, you did! I have the text message right here, and I even confirmed it with Jane..."
    - *Your Anchor Response (Correct):* **"I recall the agreement differently. I will be at the location at 7 PM. I will not discuss this further."**

This simple pivot starves the gaslighter of the energy they need to escalate.

2. The Internal Reality Check (The 5-5-5 Protocol)

When the gaslighter delivers a "Shame Bomb" (Chapter 2) or a projection, the trauma response triggers emotional flooding and self-doubt. You need a rapid, internal mechanism to distinguish *their reality* from *actual reality*.

The **5-5-5 Reality Check Protocol** is a rapid grounding technique:

1. **5 Seconds: Identify the Lie/Projection:** What exactly did they just say? (e.g., "You are financially reckless.")
2. **5 Seconds: Ground in External Fact:** What objective, verifiable evidence contradicts this? (e.g., "My bank account has been growing for six months, and all bills are paid.")
3. **5 Seconds: Label the Origin:** Who is this statement about? (e.g., "That is *their* fear/projection/shame about *their* debt, not a reflection of my behavior.")

This exercise takes your mind out of the *emotional* defense mode and forces it back into the *logical, factual* PFC (prefrontal cortex), which was overwhelmed in Stage I of erasure. By immediately labeling the accusation as *theirs*, you prevent the critical Stage II internalization (self-blame).

3. The Unilateral Value Declaration (The "North Star" Value)

To combat the chaos and confusion, you must unilaterally decide the **one core value** you will never compromise again. This value becomes your **North Star** for all decisions.

- *If the trauma involved* constant *lying:* Your North Star must be **Radical Transparency**.
- If the trauma involved being constantly belittled: Your North Star must be **Mutual Respect**.
- *If the trauma involved control:* Your North Star must be **Absolute Autonomy**.

The moment any relationship, personal or professional, violates this North Star, the Cognitive Anchor takes over, and the relationship moves to the de-escalation protocol (Section III). This simplifies complex emotional decisions into a simple, binary choice: *Does this action align with my North Star, yes or no?*

Section II: Communication Tactics – Non-Arguable Responses

Once your Cognitive Anchor is established internally, you need external communication strategies that are **boring, clear, and non-reactive**. The goal is to communicate your boundary or reality without inviting debate.

1. The NANL Protocol (Neutral, Assertive, Non-Latching)

This is the most critical communication technique for disrupting the gaslighter's cycle. It is the language of professional, dispassionate competence.

- **Neutral (Tone):** Speak in a flat, monotone voice, devoid of emotion, anger, or sadness. This denies the gaslighter the emotional reaction they feed on.
- **Assertive (Content):** Use clear, concise "I-statements" or direct statements of fact. Do not use qualifiers ("I feel like," "Maybe," "I think").
- **Non-Latching (Focus):** When they attempt to pull you into a tangent, projection, or historical Retcon, you immediately return to your original point and refuse to follow their distraction.

NANL in Action:

- *Them:* "I didn't steal your wallet. You probably hid it because you're losing your mind again."
- *JADE (Latching):* "I am not losing my mind! And I certainly didn't hide it! I put it on the counter, you saw it!"
- *NANL (Non-Latching):* **"The wallet was on the counter. I will recheck the usual places. If it does not appear, I will assume it is misplaced. I will not accept accusations about my mental state."** (Repeat this last sentence calmly, if necessary, until they give up.)

The power of NANL is that it turns the interaction into a monologue about your stable reality, not a dialogue about their distortion.

2. The Broken Record Technique

This is used when the manipulator insists on violating a boundary you've just set or continually tries to pull you back into an argument you ended.

You repeat the exact same sentence, calmly and neutrally, until they drop the subject. It's effective because it denies the manipulator the escalating, novel conflict they crave.

- *Boundary:* "I need to end this phone call now."
- *Them:* "You always do this when I try to talk seriously! You're avoiding me!"
- *You:* **"I need to end this phone call now."**

- *Them:* "No, you don't. We are not finished. You are being immature."
- *You:* **"I need to end this phone call now."**
- *Them:* (Frustrated) "Fine, hang up! See if I care!"
- *You:* **"Goodbye."** (And you hang up.)

The Broken Record is the sound of your Cognitive Anchor holding firm. It's boring, predictable, and highly effective.

3. The BIFF Protocol (Brief, Informative, Friendly, Firm)

This is the gold standard for communication when you **must** interact (e.g., co-parenting, required workplace communication) but want to minimize emotional exposure. It transforms a potential emotional debate into a sterile, professional transaction.

- **Brief:** Use the fewest words possible. Less text means less material for them to Retcon or distort.
- **Informative:** State only the facts, action items, or logistics required. No feelings, no opinions, no history.
- **Friendly (Neutral):** Maintain a pleasant, non-antagonistic tone. Use neutral openings like "Hi," or "Per our schedule," to deny them the opportunity to claim hostility.
- **Firm:** Do not invite debate or flexibility on agreed-upon boundaries or facts.

BIFF Example (Co-parenting):

- *Them (Trolling):* "The schedule is impossible, and you clearly only care about yourself. Why did you force the exchange to be on Thursday?"
- *Your BIFF Response:* **"Hi. Per the agreement, the exchange is at 4 PM Thursday at the school. Please ensure the school bag is packed. Thank you."** (Do not reply to the accusation or the "why.")

The BIFF protocol shields you from the emotional volatility of Stage II and III internalization.

Section III: De-Escalation Protocols – Managing Physical and Emotional Safety

Sometimes, the manipulator will escalate when they sense they are losing control. Your defense must include immediate, non-negotiable protocols for safely ending the interaction.

1. The Trauma Stop-Light Protocol

This is an internal regulation tool designed to prevent the nervous system from entering the catastrophic **Panic Zone** (as discussed in Chapter 6's context).

- **GREEN LIGHT (Go):** You are regulated, PFC is active, and you can apply NANL or BIFF calmly. Continue the interaction only as long as required.
- **YELLOW LIGHT (Caution):** You feel the first sign of emotional flooding—heart rate rising, anger, immediate defensiveness. **Verbalize the pause.** Say: **"I am sensing I need to pause this conversation."** Use the Broken Record if they resist, and leave the physical space.
- **RED LIGHT (Stop):** You feel the full onset of the freeze response, dissociation, or intense panic. **Immediate extraction is mandatory.** End the call, leave the room, or physically separate yourself. Do not explain, apologize, or worry about manners. Your safety takes absolute priority over their feelings or social etiquette.

2. The Physical Exit Strategy (The Boundary of Space)

If the gaslighter is physically present, you must have a pre-planned, non-debatable exit route.

- **Establish a Code Word:** Have a single, neutral word (e.g., "Mackerel" or "Document") that you use only with the aggressor to signal the conversation is over and you are leaving. It is a factual statement of ending the interaction, not an emotional request.
- **The Go-Bag Philosophy:** Even if you aren't leaving permanently, always have a small mental or physical "Go-Bag" prepared: your keys, phone, and wallet. When you hit the Red Light, you grab your essential items and leave immediately.

- **Documentation in Real-Time:** If the gaslighter is escalating to threats, use your phone's voice memo app (covertly, if necessary) or simply write down key phrases *as they happen*. This acts as both external evidence and an immediate reality check: *I am recording this, so it is undeniably real.*

3. De-Triangulation: Reclaiming Your Support System

The gaslighter has tried to isolate you (Chapter 2, 4). The counter-move is radical, intentional **Re-Engagement** with your safe support system.

- **The Trusted Listener:** Choose one person (therapist, trusted friend, non-toxic family member) and designate them as your **Trusted Listener**. This person's role is simple: when you call, they only have to listen, validate your memory, and remind you of the facts. They are not there to fix the problem, only to recalibrate your reality check system.
- **The Fact-Based Reversal:** When confronting a friend or family member who was used in triangulation ("Your mother thinks you're unstable"), your response should be factual and calm: **"I have spoken to my mother, and she did not say that. If you need to speak about me, please speak directly to me, not through third parties."** This exposes the lie without becoming hostile and forces the manipulator to either admit the distortion or double down in an obvious way.

Conclusion: The New Foundation

The purpose of these counter-moves is not to fix the gaslighter (an impossible task), but to **prove to yourself** that your reality is stable, your boundaries are firm, and your autonomy is secured.

By consistently applying the Cognitive Anchor and the NANL/BIFF protocols, you move decisively out of Stage II (Self-Doubt) and Stage III (Dependence) and back into the space of autonomous self-governance. You are transforming from a victim who is reactive and confused into a survivor who is proactive, clear, and utterly boring to abuse.

The fog lifts not when the gaslighter stops lying, but when **you stop listening** to the lie and instantly replace it with the sound of your own, steady truth. This new, stable inner world forms the foundation for the architectural rebuilding process we begin in Chapter 6.

CHAPTER 5

REBUILDING THE FRACTURED SELF

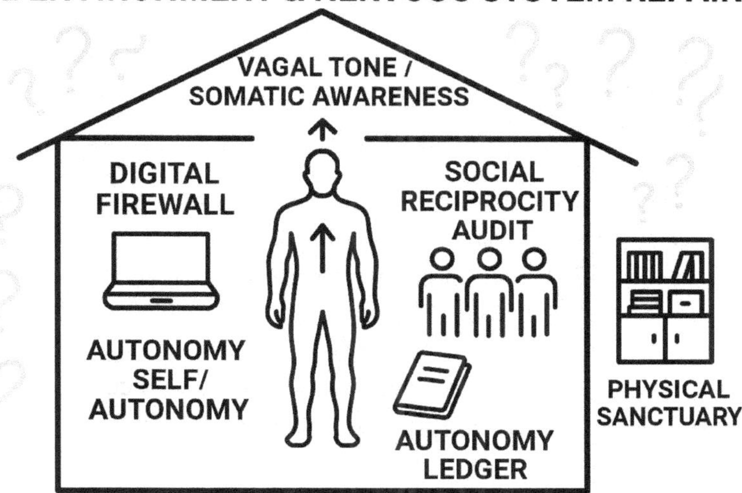

We have completed the most critical defensive work. The Cognitive Anchor is set (Chapter 5), and you have the immediate communication tactics, NANL and BIFF, to fend off distortion. You are no longer sinking. You are floating, stabilized, and secured.

But defense is only half the battle. If Chapter 5 was about stopping the bleeding, this chapter is about **rebuilding the infrastructure** of the self and the life that was damaged by the campaign of erasure (Chapter 3). The manipulator's goal was to make you dependent, compliant, and numb. Our goal now is to reverse every point of that erasure, creating a life that is so structurally clear, predictable, and aligned with your values that gaslighting becomes functionally impossible.

This is the architectural phase of recovery: building a **Low-Chaos, Low-Contradiction (LCL) Environment** that fosters genuine autonomy and reconnects you with the authentic self that was buried in Stage III. This rebuilding requires attention to four interlocking domains: identity, physical space, social systems, and the nervous system itself.

Section I: Reclaiming the Self — Identity and Values Reconstruction

The core damage of gaslighting is the fragmentation of identity (Stage III erasure). The manipulator forced you to adopt a "Shell Self", a persona defined by their expectations, while the **Authentic Self** retreated. Rebuilding requires a deliberate, systematic process of differentiating these two selves and excavating the buried truths.

1. The Great Unpacking: Separating the Self from the Shell

The first step is a direct, non-judgmental audit of your current beliefs and behaviors to determine their origin.

- **The Origin Test:** Take 10 core beliefs or life habits (e.g., "I always wait for permission," "I believe I am bad at math," "I hate expressing strong opinions"). For each one, ask:
  - Did this belief/habit start before or after the toxic relationship began?
  - Does this belief/habit serve my peace, or does it serve the maintenance of someone else's comfort?
  - If I eliminated this belief/habit, whose disapproval am I most afraid of facing?

If the answer points back to the manipulator or the toxic dynamic, you have identified a component of the Shell Self. The goal is not to hate the Shell Self, but to thank it, it was a brilliant survival mechanism, and then gently retire it. The Authentic Self is recovered through the subtraction of the lies you were forced to adopt.

2. The Values Excavation: Beyond the North Star

In Chapter 5, we defined a single North Star Value to stop the immediate crisis. Now, we expand this into a comprehensive personal constitution. The Authentic Self is defined by its values, and recovery requires living in congruence with them.

Create a hierarchy of your **Five Non-Negotiable Core Values**. These are the standards by which you judge yourself and others, and they must be rooted in the lessons of the trauma:

Trauma Lesson Learned	Core Value to Uphold	Daily Congruence Example
The pain of constant lying and secrecy.	**Transparency**	I will state my needs / feelings clearly, even if it causes minor tension.
The pain of being drained and exploited.	**Reciprocity**	I will track the energy exchange in all relationships (giving and receiving).
The pain of being controlled and micromanaged.	**Autonomy**	I will make personal decisions (e.g., spending, scheduling) without consulting the opinions of others.
The pain of feeling chaotic and confused.	**Consistency**	I will commit to a predictable daily routine (sleep, work, self-care).
The pain of emotional isolation.	**Integrity**	I will seek validation only from verifiable facts and my Trusted Listener.

The Principle of Value Congruence: The higher the alignment between your actions and your top five values, the less room there is for self-doubt. When you act on a value (e.g., choosing transparency over appeasement), your inner voice strengthens, directly reversing the self-doubt of Stage II.

3. Decision Muscle Reconstruction: The Autonomy Ledger

Gaslighting damages the **Decision Muscle** by punishing the victim for making choices (Stage II). The target stops trusting their own judgment and enters a state of decision paralysis. We must rebuild this muscle deliberately, starting small.

The **Autonomy Ledger** is a deliberate log of small, sovereign decisions you make daily:

Date	Micro-Decision Made (Autonomy Exercised)	Previous Shell Self Habit	Emotional Result
Today	Chose my own dinner menu (pasta).	Waited for partner / friend to suggest.	Minor relief, sense of control.
Today	Declined an optional social invitation.	Felt obligated, said yes automatically.	Major peace, conservation of energy.
Today	Took a 15-minute walk during a stressful work deadline.	Rushed through work without a break.	Reduced anxiety, mental clarity.

Start with **Micro-Decisions**, trivial choices like what movie to watch, what shirt to wear, or which route to drive. These low-stakes decisions rewire the brain to trust its own signals. As confidence grows, move to **Medium Decisions** (how to spend leisure time, setting financial goals) and finally **Major Decisions** (career moves, relational commitments). The ledger is proof of your regaining agency, a direct counter-evidence to the Retcon.

Section II: Architecting the Life — The Low-Chaos, Low-Contradiction (LCL) Environment

The LCL Environment is the external container designed to protect your internal progress. The goal is to maximize predictability and minimize any source of distortion, anxiety, or high emotional demand.

1. Defining the Low-Chaos, Low-Contradiction Framework

The gaslighter operates in a high-chaos, high-contradiction environment. They rely on inconsistency to keep you confused. The LCL environment is the opposite:

- **Low Chaos:** Defined by predictability, order, and minimal surprises. This reduces the nervous system's need to constantly scan for threat (hypervigilance).
- **Low Contradiction:** Defined by clear, unambiguous information, honest communication, and consistent adherence to agreed-upon rules. This prevents the cognitive dissonance that fuels Stage I and II erasure.

2. The Physical Environment: Order and Sensory Safety

Your physical space must reinforce the fact that **what you see is what is real.** Gaslighters thrive on moving objects, changing schedules, and creating physical mess that mirrors mental mess.

- **The Sanctuary Principle:** Every item in your home should be placed in a consistent, logical location. If you know where your keys are, you can't be easily gaslit into believing you lost them. Decluttering is not just aesthetic; it's an act of **reality stabilization.** A messy, overwhelming environment feeds the feeling that "something is wrong."
- **Sensory Boundaries:** Audit your environment for unnecessary sensory input that exacerbates hypervigilance:
    - **Sound:** Do you have constant, unexpected noise? Use noise-canceling headphones or ambient noise (white/brown noise) to create a predictable auditory field.
    - **Visual:** Is your space highly organized or cluttered? Clutter is visual chaos. Establish clear zones for work, rest, and leisure.
    - **Information Diet:** Reduce exposure to sensational news, highly anxious social media feeds, and toxic digital communities. Limit news checks to twice daily at set times.

3. The Digital Environment: Guarding the Gate

The digital world is a prime source of chaos and contradiction, perfectly suited for the gaslighter's tactics.

- **The Communication Firewall (Documentation Redux):** All communication with the manipulator (or anyone resembling their tactics) must be restricted to **one non-emotional, recordable platform** (e.g., email or a co-parenting app). *Never* communicate via unrecorded phone calls or emotionally charged, fleeting text messages. All communication must adhere strictly to the BIFF protocol (Chapter 5).
- **Social Media Hygiene:** Unfollow or mute anyone who consistently operates in high-chaos (e.g., constant drama, passive-aggressive posts, or obvious attention-seeking behavior). They are living contradictions, and their input pollutes

your LCL environment. Your social feed should reinforce stability, not anxiety.

4. The Social Environment: The Reciprocity Audit

The people in your life are the walls of your LCL environment. You must audit them for their contribution to chaos or clarity.

- **The Reciprocity Audit:** Evaluate your current relationships based on the energy exchange. A healthy relationship should feature:
    1. **Validation:** Do they affirm your feelings and memories?
    2. **Respect for Boundaries:** Do they accept a "no" without argument or guilt?
    3. **Emotional Regulation:** Are they generally regulated and calm, or do they constantly pull you into their high-drama crises?
- **The Three-Tier Trust Circle (De-Triangulation):** Systematically rebuild your support structure using defined roles:
    1. **Level 1: The Integrity Circle (1–3 People):** These are your Trusted Listeners (Chapter 5) and primary reality checks. They are non-judgmental, stable, and know your history. They validate and reflect the facts back to you.
    2. **Level 2: The Social Circle (5–10 People):** These are friends or peers who share interests and provide low-stakes enjoyment and normal social interaction. They are not privy to your trauma history but contribute to normalcy and belonging.
    3. **Level 3: The Boundary Circle (Acquaintances):** Relationships here are cordial, transactional, and maintained through low-effort boundaries. No emotional vulnerability or time investment.

By defining these tiers, you conserve energy and ensure that your most precious resource, your reality, is only shared with the most trusted, regulated sources.

Section III: Repairing the Nervous System — Deep Trauma Integration

The LCL environment provides the external safety, but we must also address the internal neurological damage: the chronic fight-or-flight state, the emotional flatness (dissociation), and the hypervigilance. This is the body's recovery from Stage I and III erasure.

1. The Return to Somatic Awareness (Reversing Emotional Numbness)

Gaslighting trained you to ignore your body's signals (e.g., your gut feeling screaming "lie," while your mind was forced to say "truth"). **Somatic Awareness** — the ability to check in with and listen to your physical self—is the way back to the authentic self.

- **The Body Scan:** Practice a daily, non-judgmental body scan. Lie down and ask: *Where do I feel tension? What is the temperature of my hands? Is my jaw clenched?* Do not try to fix the feeling; just observe it. This practice rebuilds the necessary connection between mind and body that the trauma tried to sever, allowing feelings to be felt and released, reversing dissociation.
- **Interoception Exercises:** Focus on internal physical sensations to establish concrete reality. Try focusing on the cold water on your hands, the texture of a blanket, or the specific rhythm of your breath. These grounding exercises pull you out of mental abstraction and into the undeniable physical present.

2. Vagal Tone and the Calming Response

The **Vagus Nerve** is the main control system of the parasympathetic (rest and digest) nervous system. Chronic gaslighting severely compromises the Vagus nerve, keeping you trapped in sympathetic (fight or flight) dominance. Improving **Vagal Tone** is essential for true, sustained calm.

Techniques for increasing Vagal Tone:

- **Extended Exhalation:** The most potent tool. Inhale deeply for a count of 4, and exhale slowly for a count of 6 or 8. This signals safety to the Vagus nerve and rapidly down-regulates the heart rate and cortisol production.
- **Cold Exposure:** Splashing cold water on your face, holding an ice pack on your chest, or even short cold showers activates the Vagus nerve, interrupting the sympathetic stress cycle.

- **Humming and Singing:** The Vagus nerve passes through the voice box. Humming or singing vibrates the nerve, directly promoting a calming response. This is a powerful, instant self-soothing tool.

3. Trauma Integration vs. Trauma Management: The Power of Narrative

You are moving beyond simply *managing* symptoms (Stage I-era coping) to *integrating* the trauma into your life story.

- **The Reframed Narrative:** Write down your story, but instead of focusing on what the gaslighter *did* to you, focus on what **you did to survive and overcome** the tactics. Transform statements of victimization ("He made me feel crazy") into statements of agency and learning ("His attempts to make me feel crazy taught me the unwavering value of my own sanity"). This shift is the core of **Post-Traumatic Growth (PTG)**.
- **The Neutral Observer:** When a trigger hits, practice observing the physical and emotional response without engaging with the memory itself. *A neutral observer would note: 'Heart rate increased, stomach clenched, thought pattern is defensive.'* By remaining the observer, you create space between the triggered reaction and the autonomous decision to respond calmly, thereby reinforcing the Cognitive Anchor.

Section IV: Sustaining the Autonomy — The Long-Term Maintenance

Recovery is not a linear event; it is a spiral — you revisit old issues from a new, higher vantage point. Sustained autonomy requires systems for managing inevitable setbacks.

1. The Trigger Test: Managing Relapses and Slips

A **slip** is a temporary fall back into an old Stage II or III behavior (e.g., questioning your memory over a minor disagreement, or arguing a point you know is futile). These are opportunities, not failures.

- **The Post-Slip Audit:** When you recognize a slip, immediately audit it using the Cognitive Anchor principles:
    1. **Which value was compromised?** (e.g., Autonomy, because I tried to please them).
    2. **Which stage did I fall into?** (e.g., Stage II self-doubt).

3. **What counter-move should I apply *right now*?** (e.g., Stop JADE, use NANL, execute a physical exit).

This immediate, non-judgmental analysis prevents the slip from turning into a full relapse. You are proving that the Authentic Self can recover instantly, rather than being swallowed by the old Shell Self pattern.

2. Self-Compassion as the Ultimate Defense

The gaslighter weaponized shame (Chapter 2). The counter-weapon is radical **Self-Compassion**. Shame demands perfection, which is unattainable and exhausting. Self-compassion recognizes that healing is messy, and you are worthy of kindness *regardless* of your performance.

- **The Best Friend Test:** When you fall into self-criticism ("I should have seen that coming," or "Why am I still struggling with this?"), ask: *What would I say to my best friend if they were struggling with the exact same thing?* You would never condemn them. Extend that same gentle, validating voice to yourself.
- **The Acceptance of Complexity:** Accept that you can simultaneously feel relief *and* grief after leaving the toxic dynamic. The trauma bond (Stage III) created a false sense of connection that must be grieved, even if the person was abusive. Allowing for this complexity prevents the gaslighter's all-or-nothing thinking from creeping back in.

3. The Final Shift: From Defense to Stewardship

The ultimate measure of success is the final shift of your focus from the **Defense of Self** to the **Stewardship of Life**.

You stop defining yourself by what the gaslighter *did* to you and start defining yourself by what **you will do with your reclaimed life**. You move from constantly guarding your wounds to actively cultivating your garden (your LCL environment).

You are the sole author, architect, and governor of your reality. You have built the Cognitive Anchor, you have secured the LCL environment, and you have reclaimed your nervous system. The fractured self is not only whole: it is stronger, clearer, and more resilient than ever before. This new structure is non-negotiable, and it is entirely yours.

CONCLUSION

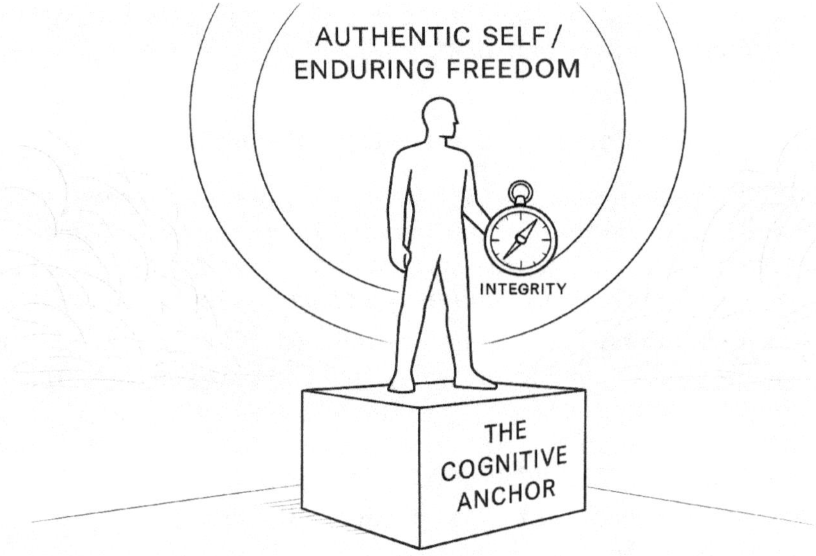

If you are reading this, you are no longer a victim; you are a survivor who has claimed their spoils. You walked into this book lost in the thick, suffocating fog: a place where your own thoughts and memories were treated as unreliable witnesses. Now, you stand on solid ground, an architect of your own unshakeable reality.

You meticulously charted the aggressor's maneuvers. You learned that the terrifying feeling of "going crazy" was just a predictable, three-stage campaign of psychological erasure. You built the ultimate mental fortress, the Cognitive Anchor, and armed yourself with the non-negotiable language of freedom (NANL, BIFF). Most critically, you had the courage to look inward and rebuild your identity and external life, brick by brick, into a Low-Chaos, Low-Contradiction (LCL) Environment.

This final chapter is the victory lap: the ultimate integration. We are moving beyond the mechanics of defense into the **philosophy of enduring freedom**. This isn't about avoiding the gaslighter forever; it's about making yourself so structurally sound, so utterly aligned with your truth, that the distortion simply cannot reach you. It's about achieving a sense of inner peace that feels not just *good*, but **inevitable**.

The work culminates in a single, powerful act: the **Unification of the Fractured Self**. We take the pieces scattered by the trauma and forge them into a sovereign, unassailable whole.

Section I: The Unification – Securing the Unshakeable Reality

The very definition of gaslighting is the attempt to divide you against yourself. The moment you began to doubt your memory ("Did that really happen?") or your emotion ("Am I overreacting?"), the gaslighter won the existential argument. Healing is the forceful, loving, and permanent merger of the external truth with your internal reality.

1. From Exhaustion to Authority: Letting Go of the Need to Prove

Perhaps the most profound moment of healing is realizing you can finally put down the briefcase of evidence. You can stop compiling text messages, stop checking timelines, and stop rehearsing your defense speech. Why? Because you no longer have to convince *them*. You only have to convince **yourself**.

The Cognitive Anchor's great gift is the transition from **proving** to **knowing.**

For so long, the aggressor forced you into the grueling role of the defense attorney, endlessly justifying your reality, your feelings, and your boundaries (JADE). That process drained your life force, leaving you exhausted and vulnerable.

The healed self shifts the entire power dynamic. Your truth is no longer a debate you're forced to win; it is an **authority** you choose to inhabit.

- When a lie surfaces, you recognize the tactic instantly, not the content. You see the *mechanism* of the lie, the cheap, repetitive script, and you meet it with total indifference.
- Your response is not an argument, but a decisive statement of finality: "I recall the facts clearly. I will not be discussing this further." Then, and this is the critical part, **you turn your attention elsewhere.** You shift your focus to a task, a project, or a loved one.

This radical disengagement starves the aggressor's ego. They need your confusion; they crave your emotional energy. By offering them nothing but a dry, factual closing statement, you are not being rude; you are being **sovereign**. You have revoked their access to your time, your energy, and your attention, thereby securing the emotional energy needed for growth.

2. The Inviolable Constitution: Values as Your Operating System

Your Core Values, once established, must transcend the role of a mere checklist. They become the foundational operating system of your life: a personal, ethical, and moral constitution that governs every choice, filtering out chaos before it can enter.

This system is simple, non-negotiable, and based on the lessons of your trauma. If your primary value is **Autonomy**, then any request that feels like control or micromanagement is automatically flagged for termination, regardless of who makes it. If your primary value is **Reciprocity**, then any relationship that consistently takes more energy than it gives must be gently moved to the Boundary Circle (Chapter 6).

The beauty of this system is that it removes ambiguity. Life decisions are no longer complex emotional negotiations; they are simple, binary questions: *Does this action align with my Constitution, Yes or No?*

This deliberate alignment addresses the core fragmentation of gaslighting: the cognitive dissonance. When you act in alignment with your values, you unify your inner and outer self. That feeling of **wholeness** is the opposite of the anxious, fragmented feeling of Stage III erasure. It is the deep, cellular relief of knowing you are finally and fully on your own side.

3. The LCL Environment: Your Sanctuary of Sanity

Let's be clear: the Low-Chaos, Low-Contradiction (LCL) Environment is the most essential external defense you possess. It is the physical and digital representation of your regulated nervous system.

The gaslighter operates in a fog of inconsistency, random aggression, and manufactured urgency. Your LCL Environment is the antidote, a sanctuary of predictability and verifiable truth.

- **Physical Order:** Your tidy desk, your consistently placed keys, your organized digital files. These aren't just habits; they are **reality anchors**. Every time you put an item back in its place, you are signaling to your brain: *This world is orderly. I know where things are. I am safe.*
- **Digital Integrity:** The Communication Firewall (Chapter 6), restricting interaction to BIFF-only channels, is a gate you guard with extreme prejudice. It prevents the sudden, emotional volatility of a phone call or text message from breaching the walls of your composure.

- **Social Selection:** You have audited your Social Circle. You no longer entertain those who constantly live in high-drama or contradiction. You prioritize people who are emotionally regulated and who validate your experience without needing to fix it.

Maintaining the LCL environment is not tedious maintenance; it is an act of **radical self-love**. You are choosing predictable safety over the thrilling, exhausting drama you were trained to need. This stability frees up immense cognitive energy for creation, joy, and purpose.

Section II: The Transcendence – Inhabiting Enduring Freedom

To transcend the trauma is to use the experience not as an anchor, but as an engine. It is moving beyond survival and into a state of thriving, defined by clarity, ease, and a deep sense of internal capability.

1. Somatic Sovereignty: The Truth in the Body's Whispers

The deepest level of healing is felt in the body. The gaslighter tried to turn your physical instincts against you; now, your body is your most loyal ally.

This is **Somatic Sovereignty**: the absolute trust in your physical reactions as the first, purest form of truth.

- **The Unmistakable Clench:** When a new person or situation approaches, you feel an instant physical response: maybe a slight clench in your gut, a tightness in your jaw, or a prickle of unease. Before, you would have labeled this "anxiety" and dismissed it. Now, you label it **"Data."**
- **The Informed Action:** You allow the feeling to be what it is, use a Vagal Tone technique (Chapter 6) to keep your head clear, and then make a decision based on the data. The decision is calm, not panicked. *Example: "My gut is clenching. I don't trust this proposal. I will not sign anything today."*

You are no longer reacting to fear; you are acting with an ancient, restored wisdom. You have integrated the trauma lesson: *The person who tells you not to trust your gut is usually the one who benefits from your blindness.*

2. The Teflon Mind: Immunity to the Lie

The Teflon Mind is the psychological structure that makes you utterly uninteresting to manipulators. They try to stick their lie, their projection, or their shame bomb to you, and it simply slides right off.

This immunity is built on two simple principles: **Prediction** and **Boredom**.

1. **Prediction:** Because you studied the mechanics (Chapter 2), you can see the script coming. When the person starts the classic, repetitive monologue, you recognize the pattern before the words even land. You are one step ahead, mentally preparing your neutral closing statement.
2. **Boredom:** The manipulator thrives on novelty and escalation. When you show genuine, non-reactive boredom with their tired, predictable tactics, you deprive them of their psychological reward. You see their shame, their instability, and their need for control, and you feel only a detached lack of interest.

The Teflon Mind is a fortress because it is not defensive; it is simply **impenetrable.** It does not absorb the external narrative because its internal truth is already secured.

3. The Reclaimed Emotional Palette: Depth and Nuance

The goal of recovery is not emotional bulletproofing; it is emotional **integrity**. You have reversed the numbness and flatness of dissociation (Stage III). Now, your emotions are clean, clear, and unburdened by guilt.

- **Clean Anger:** When you feel anger, it's not the hysterical, confusing rage of being perpetually wronged. It is precise, useful, and clearly signals a violation. It provides the necessary, clean energy to act decisively and enforce the boundary, without sinking into hostility.
- **Uncomplicated Joy:** Joy is now a baseline experience, not a fleeting reward you must desperately cling to. It is free from the anxiety of the "other shoe dropping," because you know that even if the shoe drops, you have the inner resources to deal with it calmly.
- **Self-Compassion:** This is the most vital emotion. When you slip, you do not meet yourself with the gaslighter's voice of condemnation. You meet yourself with the gentle, validating voice of your best friend. This self-kindness stops the shame cycle dead in its tracks.

Section III: The Legacy of Experience – The Architect of Purpose

The final, essential step is to integrate the experience, transforming it from a source of shame into a wellspring of profound, clarifying wisdom. This is the heart of Post-Traumatic Growth (PTG).

1. The Superpower of Radical Discernment

You have earned a PhD in human deception. This knowledge is not a curse; it is a **superpower of discernment**, an instantaneous ability to read the energetic subtext of any situation.

- **You See the Asymmetry:** You can instantly feel when a transaction is one-sided, when a relationship is based on extraction rather than reciprocity, or when a professional interaction is masking a power play.
- **You See the Motive:** You look past the polite words and recognize the anxiety, the need for control, or the lack of integrity in the underlying motive. You no longer confuse chaos with connection, or smooth talk with substance.

This discernment acts as an intuitive guide, eliminating the need for complex internal debate. You don't have to be fooled to learn the lesson; you simply observe the data and know the truth. You owe it to your survival to **never ignore that wisdom again.**

2. Ethical Agency and the Duty of Sovereignty

The greatest thing the gaslighter stole was your **ethical agency**, the right to live and act according to your own moral truth. The final freedom is restoring this agency as an unbreakable duty.

Your sovereignty now requires three ethical actions:

- **Duty to Self-Protect:** Your first and highest moral responsibility is to protect the LCL Environment. If someone threatens your peace or integrity, you have an *ethical obligation* to withdraw your presence, resources, and time immediately.
- **Duty to Voice (Clarity):** Your voice, now free of JADE and emotional pleading, is a force for clarity. When you speak your truth, calmly, factually, neutrally< you are not trying to win an argument; you are **declaring reality**. This stabilizes not only your world but the world around you.
- **Duty to Example:** The way you live your restored life, with boundaries, peace, and congruence, is the most potent form of healing and advocacy. You become the living proof that recovery is not just possible, but total.

3. Building the Lighthouse: The Legacy of Purpose

Your trauma is not your identity, but your story is your legacy. The final transcendence is realizing that the energy once trapped in confusion is now available for genuine, authentic purpose.

You are no longer stuck at the shore, fighting the waves. You have used the lessons to **build the lighthouse.**

- The **Foundation** of the lighthouse is your Cognitive Anchor.
- The **Walls** are your LCL Environment and Boundaries.
- The **Light** is your Authentic Self, shining with the Superpower of Discernment.

Your purpose is now defined by the values you chose in the face of destruction. If you committed to **Transparency**, perhaps your purpose is to communicate honestly and clearly in your professional field. If you chose **Autonomy**, perhaps your purpose is to champion independent thought in your community.

This final perspective shift moves you from defining yourself by the trauma, *I am a survivor of gaslighting*, to defining yourself by your creation, *I am the sovereign architect of a life built on integrity and peace.*

Section IV: The Long Game of Autonomy – Future-Proofing the LCL Environment

Freedom is not a single event; it is a daily discipline. To ensure your enduring freedom, you must view your Cognitive Anchor and LCL Environment not as finished projects, but as high-performance systems requiring vigilant, gentle maintenance.

1. The Quarterly LCL Audit: Normalizing Maintenance

Establish a dedicated time every three months for a **System Audit**—a calm, non-judgmental inspection of your entire reality.

- **Boundary Drift Check:** Where have your boundaries softened? Did you agree to something out of obligation? Recalibrate the boundary with a calm, corrective BIFF statement.
- **Emotional Residue Check:** Are you holding onto any low-grade anxiety or irritability that doesn't match current circumstances? This is usually unprocessed somatic residue. Commit to a week of intensive Vagal Tone exercises to release it.
- **Clarity Check:** Is there any clutter, digital or physical, that is reintroducing small inconsistencies? Clear the clutter; restore the sanctuary.

These audits prevent the insidious, creeping decay that brings back the conditions for Stage I erasure. You are tending your garden, not fighting a raging fire.

2. The Grace of the Slip: Non-Judgmental Self-Correction

A slip is inevitable. You might catch yourself JADing over something trivial, or momentarily question a memory. This is not failure; it is simply your old programming attempting to execute its routine.

Your response must be defined by **grace**, not guilt:

1. **Stop the Action:** "I just started JADing. Stop."
2. **Label the Program:** "That was the old Stage II survival script running. I don't need that anymore."
3. **Recalibrate with Kindness:** Immediately execute a Vagal Tone technique (a 4-second inhale, 8-second exhale) and follow it with a small, intentional, value-aligned action (e.g., "I choose to step outside for five minutes," or "I choose to close this laptop").

You are teaching your nervous system that when the old fear is triggered, the new response is immediate self-regulation, not surrender to panic.

3. The Responsibility of the Healed Self

The loyalty you once misdirected toward the person who harmed you is now permanently redirected to the person who saved you: **yourself.**

This is your final, beautiful responsibility:

- **You are responsible for recognizing Red Flags** in any new professional, social, or intimate relationship and acting on that wisdom immediately.
- **You are responsible for maintaining the LCL Environment** that protects your nervous system.
- **You are responsible for continuing to choose integrity** over appeasement, clarity over confusion, and autonomy over dependence, every single day.

You have faced the absolute worst and emerged with an unshakeable understanding of your own worth. You are not only free from the fog; you are the light.

REFLECTION QUESTIONS

The work of recovery is not measured by the speed at which you finished this book, but by the depth at which you commit to living its principles. You have absorbed the knowledge, built the defenses, and secured your environment. Now, we must move from passive comprehension to active, ongoing **integration**.

This chapter is your final tool: a structured guide designed for journaling, conversation with a therapist, or quiet, solo reflection. Think of these questions not as a test, but as your **Quarterly LCL Audit** (Chapter 7) for the soul. They are designed to bring the theoretical concepts, the Retcon, the Cognitive Anchor, Somatic Sovereignty, out of the pages and into the dynamic reality of your daily life.

Reflection is the highest act of self-governance. It proves that you are no longer operating on autopilot, driven by old survival programming. You are now the conscious author and intentional editor of your own life story. Dedicate time and honesty to this final practice. It is the enduring commitment to your sanity.

Part I: Diagnosis and Naming the Lie (Reviewing Chapters 1 & 2)

Before you can build, you must clear the foundation. This section asks you to look back at the tactics you faced, not to relive the pain, but to strip the manipulation of its emotional power by giving it a precise, factual name. Naming the lie is the first step toward neutralizing it.

1. **Weaponized Amnesia & The Retcon:**
   - Think of the three most recent instances where you felt compelled to defend your memory of a past event. What was the exact lie (the Retcon) that was presented to you?
   - What verifiable fact (documentation, neutral witness, personal log) was the Retcon attempting to erase?
   - If you had the Cognitive Anchor then, what simple, non-JADE statement would have shut down the argument immediately? (Practice writing that statement down.)
2. **The Projection Tactic:**
   - Identify a quality or behavior the gaslighter frequently accused you of (e.g., "reckless," "too emotional," "selfish"). This is often their own unowned shame.
   - Do you still carry any residual guilt or belief that this accusation is true? If yes, what objective counter-evidence exists in your life right now (e.g., a balanced bank account, stable friendships, documented acts of generosity)?
   - If that accusation were leveled at you today, how would you use the **5-5-5 Reality Check Protocol** (Chapter 5) to instantly label the origin of the statement as *theirs*, not yours?
3. **Invalidation and the Shell Self:**
   - Which phrase or line from the aggressor was most effective at making you doubt your feelings (e.g., "You're overreacting," "It's just a joke")?
   - Name three feelings or instincts that you learned to suppress during the toxic dynamic (e.g., anger, intuition, need for space).

- When was the last time you consciously allowed one of those previously suppressed feelings to surface and honored it without judgment? What physical sensation did that create (Somatic Awareness)?

Part II: The Internal Audit and Erasure (Reviewing Chapters 3 & 4)

Gaslighting works by dismantling your self-structure in stages. This section focuses on identifying exactly where the most significant damage was done and understanding the environmental context that allowed it to thrive.

1. **Identifying the Most Damaging Stage of Erasure:**
   - Looking at the three stages of erasure (Stage I: Disbelief, Stage II: Self-Doubt, Stage III: Dependence), which stage did you spend the most emotional energy fighting?
   - If you primarily struggled with **Stage II (Self-Doubt)**, what was the primary source of that doubt? Was it decision paralysis, chronic anxiety, or the constant need for external approval? How has the **Autonomy Ledger** (Chapter 6) started to reverse that paralysis?
   - If you primarily struggled with **Stage III (Dependence)**, what specific emotional or physical habits (e.g., inability to sleep alone, fear of silence, constantly waiting for instruction) are still faintly echoing in your current life? What small, daily act of **Sovereignty** can you commit to this week to break that specific echo?
2. **Contextualizing the Abuse:**
   - Did the gaslighting primarily occur in an intimate, familial, or professional context (Chapter 4)? How did the specific rules of that environment, intimacy, duty, or hierarchy, make the abuse harder to recognize?
   - If the context was **professional**, identify one way you are currently using the **BIFF Protocol** (Chapter 5) to maintain professional communication while eliminating emotional exposure. If not, draft a BIFF response to a recent stressful work email.
   - If the context was **familial**, what is the single, highest boundary you need to maintain with that system today (e.g., no discussion of my finances, I will not visit without an exit plan, I will not engage in triangulation)?

3. **The Shell Self vs. The Authentic Self:**
    - Identify one core belief or behavior you adopted from the **Shell Self** (e.g., "I must be silent to keep the peace," "I must always apologize first").
    - Now, identify the corresponding action or belief of the **Authentic Self** (e.g., "I have the right to speak clearly, even if it causes tension," "I apologize only when I have wronged someone").
    - How can you thank the Shell Self for its survival efforts, acknowledge that its job is done, and actively replace that habit with the Authentic Self's action this week?

Part III: The Foundation of Freedom (Reviewing Chapters 5 & 6)

This section shifts from reflection on the past to active engagement with the present. It is about applying your tools and ensuring your environment is structurally sound.

1. **Defining and Upholding Your Values:**
    - Revisit your **Five Non-Negotiable Core Values** (Chapter 6). Write them down.
    - In the past week, identify one moment where you lived in **high congruence** with one of those values. Describe the peace or pride you felt afterward.
    - Identify one moment where you had a **slip** and compromised a value. What was the immediate emotional consequence (e.g., immediate anxiety, self-anger)? How can you use that feeling as data to correct the action next time?
2. **Maintaining the LCL Environment:**
    - Audit your physical space: Is there any **physical clutter** that is introducing chaos or contradiction? If so, commit to a 30-minute act of **reality stabilization** (decluttering) right now.
    - Audit your digital space: Which specific social media feed or news source consistently operates in **high chaos** or manufactures unnecessary contradiction? What is your plan to eliminate or strictly limit its exposure this week?

- Audit your Social System: Is there anyone currently in your Social Circle (Level 2) who needs to be moved to the Boundary Circle (Level 3) because they are draining your energy or disrespecting your boundaries? How will you use NANL to communicate that change without explanation?

3. **Somatic Repair and Vagal Tone:**
    - When you feel a moment of low-grade stress or anxiety, where is the tension localized in your body (jaw, shoulders, stomach)?
    - Describe your favorite **Vagal Tone exercise** (extended exhalation, cold exposure, humming) and commit to practicing it for 5 minutes, twice daily, this week.

Part IV: Legacy and Future Sovereignty (Reviewing Chapter 7)

This is the final, forward-looking step: integrating your wisdom into your identity and committing to the long game of autonomy.

1. **The New Baseline of Reality (The Teflon Mind):**
    - Describe what it feels like when an aggressor's attempt at manipulation (a lie, a projection) simply "slides off" your **Teflon Mind**. What is the internal, emotional response you feel? (Hint: It should be boredom or detachment.)
    - What is the **Superpower of Radical Discernment**—the hard-won wisdom—giving you the ability to spot today? (e.g., spotting emotional manipulation in professional settings, recognizing a lack of reciprocity in a new acquaintance).
    - How will you honor that earned wisdom by refusing to ignore the **Red Flags** in the future, even if doing so feels momentarily uncomfortable?
2. **The Duty of Sovereignty and Purpose:**
    - What small, sovereign choice are you most proud of making recently (an action taken solely for your peace, without regard for external opinion)?
    - Looking forward, how can you shift your focus from **Defense of Self** to **Stewardship of Life** (Chapter 7)? How will you actively cultivate your personal "garden" (your purpose, your joy, your interests) this month?

- If you were to write a mission statement for the next year based purely on your Core Values, what would the first line be? (e.g., *My mission is to operate with radical transparency and to prioritize my time above all external requests.*)

3. **Commitment to Maintenance:**
   - Commit to performing a comprehensive **LCL System Audit** (like this reflection guide) once every quarter for the next year. What date will you schedule your next one?
   - In the event of an unexpected challenge or "slip," what is your three-step plan to initiate **Non-Judgmental Recalibration**? (Hint: Interrupt the Shame Cycle, Execute Vagal Tone, Perform an Act of Autonomy.)

You have the tools. You have the knowledge. You have the wisdom. The work of healing is complete, but the discipline of living freely is eternal. Congratulations on your sovereignty. You are the architect of your own reality, and it is unshakeable.

BOOK TWO

SOCIAL ENGINEERING: HACKING THE HUMAN FIREWALL AND SECURITY PROTOCOLS

INTRODUCTION

The Great Pivot: From Personal Reality to External Guard Duty

You came through the psychological trenches of Book 1. You faced the sustained, hidden campaign of gaslighting, a fight waged against your core identity, built specifically to rot away your internal compass, your very right to your own truth. That was a crisis of being, played out with crippling emotional stakes.

Now, we must completely change the ground we stand on. The struggle we examine in this second book is colder, more financially driven, and utterly transactional. It is less about creating chaos in your soul and far more about stealing your **trust** in order to make off with money, critical access, or sensitive information. We are pulling away from the subtle, destructive dance of relational control and turning our full attention toward the rigid, calculated procedure of **Social Engineering (SE)**, which is nothing more than the professional science of deceiving the human mind to bypass all digital and physical security roadblocks.

If Book 1's goal was equipping you with a Cognitive Anchor to lock down your personal reality, the purpose of this book is showing you how to construct a practical, impenetrable **Human Firewall** to secure all your external assets. The core fact that tied the first book to this one remains unchanged: the most sophisticated system in existence, whether that system is a person or a multinational corporation, will never be stronger than its poorest link. And, year after year, report after report, that weakest point is proven to be the person—the human operator whose basic sense of helpfulness, tendency to follow orders, or simply being too busy makes them susceptible to making one disastrous mistake.

Social Engineering, hands down, is the single greatest hazard facing security today. It is implicated in the vast majority of successful corporate breaches, huge acts of financial fraud, and every instance of corporate information theft.

The enemy in this book is not a spiteful ex-spouse looking for emotional revenge; the enemy is a focused, goal-oriented specialist, a "person hacker" who has a greater grasp of your basic psychology than they do of advanced C++ code. To secure yourself, you must first understand exactly how this attacker thinks and, more importantly, understand the basic human frailties that make you, the trusting user, the biggest possible target.

The Core Principle: What Social Engineering Actually Is

Social Engineering is best defined as the deliberate use of psychological trickery to persuade people into doing things they shouldn't or giving up confidential items. It is the age-old confidence trick, updated for the era of servers and satellites. The point is not usually to cause the victim distress; the point is to get access, get intelligence, or get rich, and the route taken involves manipulating human nature instead of exploiting software bugs.

Look, we all have this picture in our heads of a "hacker": someone sitting alone, maybe wearing a hoodie, typing away, defeating advanced encryption, cracking complicated passwords. That's the Hollywood lie.

The actual situation, confirmed by anyone who has ever had to clean up a real breach, is often embarrassingly simple: a human hacker generally only needs a friendly voice, a believable story, and the nerve to ask for something completely forbidden. They don't jump the security fence; they just convince the guard to open the gate for them.

The Scale of the Scam

SE attacks vary wildly in complexity and size, but the attack path is always the same: **you**.

1. **The Fishing Net (High Volume, Low Effort):** Think about the routine scams: the call claiming to be your bank (Vishing), the text telling you your delivery address is wrong (Smishing), or the email demanding immediate action. These are wide-net operations, launched at massive scale, hoping to snag the 1% of the population who are busy, tired, or just not thinking clearly.
2. **The Harpoon (Precision, High Value):** These are the targeted strikes, often called **Whaling** (when the CEO or CFO is the prey) or **Spear Phishing** (when a specific IT admin is the victim). The attacker doesn't rush this. They spend weeks, sometimes months, gathering every scrap of public information they can find: LinkedIn posts, press releases, company jargon. This allows them to create a perfect, detailed "pretext" (the fake story) designed to trick a specific employee into giving up system credentials or approving a huge wire transfer. We're talking millions of dollars lost and entire product designs stolen.
3. **Physical Tactics (The Sneak Attack):** SE isn't only done with keyboards. It includes physical actions like **Tailgating** (slipping in behind someone with a valid badge), **Shoulder Surfing** (watching someone punch in a code), or **Dumpster Diving** (sifting through trash bins for phone lists, org charts, or old memos). The aim never changes: to get around a technical lock or a camera by manipulating the person in charge.

The history of Social Engineering has been with us since people first started talking to each other. The invention of the telegraph and, later, the internet didn't invent the con; it just gave the con artist a global loudspeaker. Because digital communication costs next to nothing, the attack is infinitely scalable. A scammer can send out a billion emails for free, and if they net just a handful of victims, the profit is astronomical. The risk is asymmetric.

The Fatal Flaw: Why Our Brains Are Bad at Security

We need to talk about why you are such a good target. It's not because you're stupid or lazy; it's because you're a functioning human being. Our brains didn't evolve to watch out for fake hyperlinks; they evolved for **social survival** and **getting things done quickly**. Our minds are built to cooperate, build quick friendships, and respond to social cues. These very things, these evolutionary necessities, are the exact things the attacker uses against us.

Most of our day-to-day thinking happens in what Kahneman labeled **System 1 Thinking**, it's quick, instinctive, emotional, and jumps to conclusions. Security, however, demands **System 2 Thinking**, it must be slow, skeptical, analytical, and deliberate. The job of the social engineer is to ensure their attack lands directly in the lap of System 1.

Here are the most important cognitive defaults and biases that turn the Human Firewall into Swiss cheese.

1. The Trust Default (We Believe What We Hear)

The biggest failure point is simple human trust. It's built into our operating system. According to Timothy Levine's **Truth-Default Theory**, humans generally assume, without thinking about it, that *the information being presented is factual.* This assumption is vital; society would fall apart if we had to critically fact-check every conversation, every instruction, every sign.

The social engineer weaponizes this inertia. They rely on you taking their story as the default reality, the urgent call from the IT guy, the stressed message from the CEO's assistant, the panic-stricken message from a family member. Questioning that reality takes effort, it demands System 2 energy, and our brain is programmed to avoid that cost. Once the attacker presents a simple, believable situation (the pretext), the target's brain instantly settles on: *"This makes sense, so I should just help."* Breaking this truth-default requires consistent, practiced doubt.

2. The Authority Reflex (The Compulsion to Obey)

A deeply ingrained vulnerability is our tendency to follow orders from someone who seems important. This comes from childhood, school, and the workplace, managers, supervisors, anyone with a title. The attacker uses official names, big titles, and impressive language as weapons.

- **The Scenario:** Someone calls, saying, "This is Mark, the VP of Operations," or "I'm Detective Chavez from the Cyber Crimes Unit."
- **The Automatic Response:** The instant that authoritative name hits your ears, your ability to think critically takes a big hit. Your mind stops asking, *"Is this correct?"* and starts asking, *"How do I do what I've been told?"* The immediate fear of disappointing an authority figure (e.g., getting fired, getting written up) almost

always seems more immediate and dangerous than the abstract risk of clicking a suspicious link. People override their own security instincts just to avoid a potentially awkward or contentious moment with someone who sounds senior.

3. Reciprocity (The Need to Pay Back)

As the master of influence Robert Cialdini laid out, the **Principle of Reciprocity** creates a psychological debt: we feel compelled to repay favors, gifts, or acts of kindness. This is the glue that holds communities together, but for the social engineer, it is pure currency.

- **The Investment:** The attacker starts small. Maybe they sincerely compliment your work, hold the door for you, or legitimately help you fix a minor technical glitch that has nothing to do with the main attack.
- **The Call for Repayment:** Once that tiny debt is established, the attacker makes the real, high-risk request: "Since I spent that time helping you get your printer working, could you do me a quick favor? I need you to open this attachment—it's the only way for me to log my service time."
- **The Trap Snaps Shut:** The target feels internal pressure, a social and psychological obligation, and complies, telling themselves that the high-risk action is just a small thing needed to even the social score. The desire to be nice and polite breaches the Human Firewall.

4. Urgency and Loss Aversion (Panic Button Thinking)

People are typically motivated more strongly by the threat of losing what they currently possess than by the opportunity to gain something new. This is the principle of **Loss Aversion**. The attacker uses manufactured time pressure to put this system into overdrive.

- **The Panic Signal:** The attack is framed as time-sensitive: "You have five minutes to update your password or your entire account will be permanently wiped," or "The database will corrupt unless you install this fix immediately."
- **What This Does to Your Head:** Urgency immediately shoves your brain into reflexive, survival mode, System 1. The entire point is to stop the slow, careful analysis of System 2. Fear of losing money, access, or reputation forces a quick, unchecked reaction (clicking the button, confirming the transfer). The attacker works to transform a situation demanding deliberation into one demanding reaction.

5. Liking, Familiarity, and Emotional Resonance

We are fundamentally wired to trust, and thus comply with, people we like, people we think are similar to us, or people who use emotional triggers effectively.

- **Building a Fake Bond:** The attacker will meticulously study the target's public profiles, looking for that tiny thread of common ground (e.g., "I saw you post about that hiking trip, I was just on the same trail last month!"). This quick familiarity is a shortcut to trust.
- **Weaponizing Empathy:** Attacks often rely on faked distress (e.g., "I'm a contractor, I lost my access card, and if I don't get this delivery signed for in the next two minutes, I'll get charged hundreds of dollars! Please just buzz me in!"). Most people are fundamentally decent and will bypass protocol to help a distressed person. The social engineer turns human compassion into a security vulnerability.

The Attacker's Playbook: The Structured Attack Sequence

Social Engineering is far from random chance; it's a formalized method that closely resembles a military reconnaissance and strike operation. To defend, you must know the sequence cold. A reliable defense must be functional at **every single step**, not just at the moment the sensitive request is made.

Phase 1: Information Gathering (The Groundwork)

This phase is silent, invisible, and the most critical. The objective is to compile every available piece of information, public, semi-public, or casually shared, about the target, the organization, and the internal processes. This information is the essential ingredient for making the fake story real.

- **Open Source Intelligence (OSINT):** The attacker goes through professional networking sites (like LinkedIn), corporate sites, public releases, and social media with a fine-tooth comb. They are searching for:
    - **The Chain of Command:** Who reports to whom? Who handles finance?
    - **Employee Behavior:** Names, titles, and non-work details (Do they post about their weekend routine? Do they mention specific corporate events?).

    - **Technology Footprint:** What kind of security software, email systems, or hardware models are mentioned in public documents or user complaints?
    - **The Language:** They look for the internal jargon, project code names, or the casual slang used in the office that only an insider would know.
- **The Result:** The attacker creates a detailed profile that allows them to call or email the target and sound exactly like a trusted insider. They use the correct names, the right project code, and the appropriate urgency (e.g., "Hi, I'm calling about the Project Falcon security patch roll-out that was scheduled for this afternoon, I need your quick sign-off"). This level of detail immediately disarms the target's skepticism.

Phase 2: Building the Setup (The Pretext)

With the facts gathered, the attacker builds the **pretext**, the fabricated situation that perfectly excuses the interaction and, crucially, justifies the forbidden request. The pretext must feel absolutely real, have a credible air of urgency, and involve some emotional component (like distress or authority).

- **Plausibility Check:** The story must align perfectly with the target's OSINT profile. If the target is in IT, the pretext is a sudden zero-day vulnerability. If they are in Accounts Payable, it's a sudden, urgent invoice approval needed before a deadline.
- **Rapport Generation:** The attacker uses a short, easy interaction to establish a friendly connection, deploying Liking and Reciprocity. They might engage in small talk about a shared hobby found online before making the real request.
- **The Narrative Arc:** The finished pretext answers all potential questions: *Who are you? Why are you calling me? Why is this urgent?* and *Why must I break protocol to help you?* (e.g., "I'm the HVAC repair technician, I'm stuck in the loading dock, and the temperature sensor for the server room is failing; if you don't remote-open the door for me now, the whole system will overheat in minutes!")

Phase 3: The Attack and Execution

This is the short, focused moment when the psychological bias is triggered, and the damage is done. The success here is entirely dependent on the quality of the first two phases.

- **Triggering the Bias:** The attacker introduces the highly sensitive request, leaning heavily on the established rapport, the fake authority, or the high-pressure urgency (e.g., "I know this is unusual, but the CEO authorized me to get your credentials, it's the only way to test the new VPN connection before she leaves the country. It has to be now," leveraging **Authority**).
- **Executing the Payload:** The target, processing under reflexive System 1, clicks the malware link, gives the sensitive details (Vishing), or performs the physical act (Tailgating).
- **Defensive Insight:** If the attacker's story is weak, it forces the target into slow, analytical System 2 thought, and the attack fails. If the attacker is perfect, System 1 takes over, and compliance is almost guaranteed.

Phase 4: Exit Strategy and Isolation

The expert social engineer only considers the job finished once the objective is secured and they have left the interaction cleanly, ensuring the victim doesn't realize the compromise immediately.

- **The Clean Break:** The attacker quickly provides a believable, urgent reason to end the conversation (e.g., "Perfect, that worked! I'm now being patched through to the main office, I need to go. Thanks a ton!"). This quick end prevents the victim from reviewing the interaction critically.
- **Post-Exploitation:** The attacker immediately uses the stolen credentials or executes the malware before the victim has time to process the strange request and report it. The smooth, professional exit maintains the illusion of legitimacy, buying critical time to execute the theft.

Social Engineering Versus Gaslighting: A Key Difference

It is absolutely crucial to distinguish the deep psychological trauma of Book 1 from the detached, mercenary hacking of Book 2. Both rely on deception, but their **intent** and **effect** are miles apart.

The social engineer is not trying to dismantle your life; they are trying to break your security protocols. However, they frequently use **micro-gaslighting** techniques to overcome minor resistance in the moment:

1. **Challenging Immediate Memory:** "You must have signed the waiver form yesterday, don't you remember? I have the confirmation right here." (A miniature, transactional Retcon to dismiss the victim's accurate memory of *not* signing a form).

2. **Questioning Technical Skill:** "Are you sure you followed my instructions? My console shows an error, which indicates you might be typing the security code incorrectly." (A subtle put-down, invalidation, to make the victim doubt their own technical competence, thereby making them more willing to hand control over to the "expert" attacker).

These small tactics are strictly transactional; they are used to ensure compliance *right now*, not to cause long-term, chronic emotional devastation.

The Mandate for Defense: Fortifying the Human Target

Why dedicate such comprehensive focus to the attacker's full methodology? Because the only possible way to build a security barrier that actually works is to know the attack surface inside and out. If the attacker's approach is to exploit automatic, System 1 human biases, the defender's response must be to systematically train System 2 skepticism until it is an automatic, secondary response.

Security, for too long, has been seen as a pure technology issue that technology should solve: stronger passwords, more complex VPNs, and stricter firewall rules. But every year, massive companies fall because one tired person clicked one bad link or disclosed one simple piece of information on the phone.

The definitive security protocol is the **Human Firewall**: the active, cognitive defense system that we must intentionally install and keep updated in the mind of every single user.

The Cost of Being Unprepared

The long-term costs of a successful SE attack are immense, extending far beyond the immediate cash stolen:

- **Direct Financial Theft:** The loss of funds via unauthorized wire transfers.
- **Reputation Collapse:** The total destruction of public trust following a major data disclosure.
- **Legal Consequences:** Massive fines and penalties from regulatory bodies (for example, under HIPAA or GDPR).
- **Loss of Intellectual Property (IP):** The theft of trade secrets, formulas, and proprietary client lists.

More important for our purposes, the cost is the **loss of cognitive sovereignty**: the temporary surrender of the critical mind that enabled the breach. This book exists to make that surrender functionally impossible by training your mind to identify the pattern instantly.

The New Discipline: Behavioral Security

To harden the Human Target (the focus of Chapter 6), we must stop simply being "aware" ("I guess I should be more careful") and start practicing active, repeatable **behavioral security**. This means:

1. **Installing Mental Checklists:** Creating simple, automatic procedures that fire before the System 1 impulse can take over (e.g., "If I get an urgent request, I must hang up and call the sender back on their known, official number").
2. **Emotional Speed Bumps:** Training yourself to recognize the feeling of manufactured urgency and intentionally delaying the decision to engage. This forces the problem from System 1 (reflex) into the more reliable System 2 (analysis).
3. **Making Skepticism the Default:** We must actively reverse the instinct to trust. Your new operational default must be: "When the request is unusual, high-pressure, or breaks policy, the answer is **NO** until I can verify the legitimacy independently and securely."

The Structure of Book 2: Your Counter-Intelligence Manual

This volume is set up to walk you through the entire Social Engineering attack sequence, providing the perspective of both the professional attacker and the trained defender. By fully absorbing the attacker's entire playbook, you gain the ability to predict and disable their next move before they can even make the core request.

- **Chapter 2: Pretexting and the Art of Fabrication:** We will break down why narratives work. You will learn the mechanics of creating a believable fake identity and, conversely, how to instantly dismantle a suspect pretext down to its implausible core elements.
- **Chapter 3: Open Source Intelligence (OSINT) Gathering:** This is our deep assessment of the intelligence phase. We show you exactly how much of your personal and corporate data is available to a dedicated attacker, and we teach you how to perform a "Self-OSINT" review to find your own weak points and clean up your public, digital footprint.

- **Chapter 4: Phishing, Vishing, and Smishing Dynamics:** This section takes apart the various digital methods of delivery. We analyze the components of a malicious email, the use of voice manipulation on the phone, the scripts, and the psychological payload used to drive quick compliance across all communication methods.
- **Chapter 5: Exploiting Social Norms and Reciprocity:** We will examine how the six core principles of influence (Authority, Liking, Scarcity, etc.) work and demonstrate precisely how attackers take advantage of your politeness, kindness, and instinct for professional compliance to circumvent established security policy.
- **Chapter 6: Hardening the Target:** This is the practical defense chapter. We move from theory to action, laying out the specific, routine protocols needed to build an unbreakable Human Firewall, creating verification checklists, practicing emotional delays, and deliberately building a personal culture of security.
- **Chapter 7 & 8:** The Conclusion and final Reflection Questions will ensure all these principles are permanently solidified, guaranteeing they become not just abstract concepts, but reliable, practiced actions in your life.

The skills you achieved in Book 1, sharp self-awareness, critical analysis, and the ability to distinguish true reality from manipulation, are now your professional tools. You are uniquely equipped for this confrontation. You won the internal war; now, we secure the external perimeter. You are becoming the essential security defense, turning the supposed greatest weakness in any system, the human factor, into its greatest, most resilient strength.

CHAPTER 1

PRETEXTING AND THE ART OF FABRICATION

The Deceptive Center: The Critical Function of the Pretext

In the structure of any Social Engineering (SE) operation, the moment of execution—the actual transfer of data, the click of the link, the approval of the wire transfer—is merely the final, quick motion. The real work, the sustained effort that achieves the compromise, lies in the **Pretext**.

A pretext is defined as a fabricated scenario or excuse used to conceal the true purpose of an activity. In the context of security, it is the sophisticated narrative that the attacker constructs and deploys to establish rapport, create legitimacy, and, most crucially, **justify a high-risk or policy-breaking request**.

The objective of the pretext is simple and brutal: it is a psychological override. The attacker knows the target is equipped with security training, corporate procedures, and healthy suspicion (System 2 thinking). The pretext is the lever used to disable this skepticism by providing the brain with a ready-made, emotionally compelling, and believable explanation for why established rules *must* be temporarily disregarded. It's the cognitive bypass. The defender, presented with a compelling story, finds it easier to comply with the narrative than to engage in the difficult, awkward work of questioning the authority or the urgency of the person telling the story.

If the attacker has done their background research (OSINT, as we will discuss in Chapter 3), the pretext should sound less like a criminal request and more like a standard, if urgent, part of the target's job. The moment the target accepts the pretext as a plausible reality, the Human Firewall is compromised, and the execution phase is virtually assured success.

The Psychological Necessity of the Narrative

Why does the human mind require a story to break its own rules? The answer connects directly to the core psychological mechanisms discussed in the Introduction: Compliance, Authority, and the Truth Default.

1. The Justification of Compliance

People, especially in professional environments, possess a deep psychological need to see themselves as good employees, good citizens, and competent professionals. Following rules is integral to this self-image. Breaking a security protocol, such as sharing a password or bypassing a two-factor check, creates **internal conflict**.

The pretext solves this conflict instantly. It shifts the burden of responsibility away from the target and places it onto the necessity of the *situation*.

- **Conflict:** "I know I shouldn't give out my VPN credentials."
- **Pretext:** "But this is the emergency IT team, and the entire server farm is overheating. If I don't give them this access right now, the company loses everything."
- **Resolution:** The target is no longer breaking a rule; they are **saving the company**. The pretext transforms a forbidden act into a heroic act of duty, making compliance psychologically comfortable and removing the internal veto.

2. The Authority Transfer

A perfect pretext establishes the attacker's persona (the "role") as having greater authority than the target, or as acting on behalf of an even higher, unassailable authority (e.g., the CEO, the FBI, a government regulator).

This immediately triggers the **Authority Bias**. The target's job shifts from "gatekeeper" to "assistant." The question changes from "Is this safe?" to "How quickly can I assist the Executive Team/Special Task Force with their urgent requirement?" The narrative successfully leverages a deep-seated human tendency to avoid disagreement with perceived superiors. The target knows they shouldn't perform the action, but the social cost of telling the "VP of Operations" that they can't help feels too high.

3. Overriding the Truth Default

The Truth-Default Theory states that we assume truth until evidence forces us to assume deception. The goal of the pretext is to overload the interaction with so much surface-level, plausible "truth" that the System 2 brain never receives the necessary trigger to engage deep suspicion.

A weak pretext involves simple lies: "I'm a Nigerian Prince." This is easy to flag. A powerful pretext involves verifiable public facts: "I see you're the lead manager on Project Phoenix. I need access to the Beta server for the quarterly patch update, the one the team was discussing on the company's internal forum last Tuesday." The inclusion of specific, accurate details, names, dates, projects, acts as psychological gravity, pulling the target's mind into the reality of the story and making the truth-default kick in with extreme force. The target thinks, "He knows about the forum post and the project name, so he must be legitimate."

The Three Pillars of the Unassailable Pretext

Every successful fabricated scenario rests on three foundational structural elements. A defect in any one of these pillars causes the entire construction to collapse, forcing the target into necessary skepticism.

Pillar 1: High Plausibility and Verifiability

A pretext must feel completely authentic, and critically, it must be supported by verifiable, external details, even if the details are irrelevant to the actual attack. The believability of the story must be calibrated precisely to the target's role, environment, and personal life.

- **Plausibility to Role:** If the target is a receptionist, the pretext should involve issues related to scheduling, physical access, or package delivery, tasks that fall squarely within their domain. Asking a receptionist for high-level network documentation is *implausible* and creates friction. Asking them to confirm the CEO's arrival time and swipe an "important vendor" in for a "scheduled meeting" is highly *plausible*.

- **Plausibility to Context:** The story should align with current events in the organization. If the company just announced a major acquisition, the pretext should be an urgent legal audit related to the acquisition. If a new security system was just installed, the pretext should be a mandatory follow-up system check. The attacker draws from the target's actual, real-life context to make the lie seem like routine.
- **Verifiable Details:** The inclusion of actual, confirmed details is the signature of a superior pretext. The attacker should use:
    - The correct name of the target's direct supervisor.
    - The correct name of a project the target is working on.
    - A piece of company jargon that only an insider would know.

The goal is to eliminate the target's ability to easily say, "That doesn't make any sense."

Pillar 2: Necessary Justification and Problem Solving

The pretext must contain a clear, pressing **problem** that only the attacker, with the target's forbidden assistance, can solve. The core purpose of the story is to explain *why* the rules are being broken.

The attacker must build a narrative where the request for the sensitive information or action is the **only possible solution** to an urgent, high-stakes crisis.

- **The Problem:** An immediate threat to the company, the target's manager, or the target themselves. Example: A malware outbreak has quarantined the main server, and only a manual input from a physical device can unlock the system before the data is erased.
- **The Justification:** The attacker cannot solve this problem through standard channels. Example: The attacker's network access has been specifically disabled by the quarantine, or their badge is locked out, or the phone system is down, requiring a cell phone call.
- **The Necessary Request:** The target's assistance is the final, essential step. Example: The target must now read their VPN code over the phone to the "engineer" who will manually input it into the physical console.

The stronger the justification, the greater the perceived risk of *inaction*, the weaker the target's willingness to stick to standard procedure. The target feels compelled to move into crisis management mode, where standard rules are relaxed.

Pillar 3: Emotional Resonance and Manufactured Urgency

A purely factual story seldom works. The pretext must inject an emotional component to propel the System 1 thinking process and ensure the attack is processed with speed. This emotional layer prevents the target from performing the slow, analytical verification required by System 2.

- **Urgency (Scarcity/Time-Lock):** This is the most common trigger. The threat must be immediate and time-bound. Example: "If this access isn't granted in the next five minutes, the deal will fall through," or "This must be finished before the CEO's flight leaves, or I'm fired." Urgency elevates the stress level, severely degrading cognitive function.
- **Authority (Fear of Retribution):** The attacker assumes the role of an authority figure or claims to be directly authorized by one. The emotional lever here is the fear of being seen as obstructionist, incompetent, or of causing a superior to fail. Example: "This is a mandatory security mandate from the government, and your failure to comply will result in an immediate violation."
- **Empathy (Desire to Help):** The attacker adopts a sympathetic, low-status, or distressed role. Example: "I'm the new intern, and I clicked the wrong button. If I don't get this fixed, I lose my job, and my family needs this income." This leverages the common human desire to help others and avoid causing suffering. The target's own kindness is turned against them.

The Execution: Role-Playing and Script Development

Pretexting is, at its heart, an acting job. The effectiveness of the narrative depends entirely on the attacker's successful adoption of a convincing role. This role is developed based on the OSINT gathered in Phase 1 and the specific bias the attacker intends to trigger.

Common Attacker Personas

The most common and consistently successful attacker roles are those that naturally justify urgency, require access, and demand compliance.

1. **The Harried IT Technician/Support Staff:**
    - **The Role:** A low-status, busy individual, often sweating under pressure, who needs simple help to fix a massive, escalating problem.
    - **The Pretext:** A system-wide alert, an undocumented update, an urgent patch deployment that is going wrong.
    - **The Request:** "I need you to reset your password and tell me the temporary code so I can log into the diagnostic portal from my side." (Uses **Urgency** and **Authority/Expertise**).
    - **Why it Works:** The target views this person as a peer or service provider, not an authority figure, making it feel less confrontational to help them with a small act (giving a code) to fix a large, non-personal problem (the crashing system).
2. **The Executive/Manager's Personal Assistant (P.A.):**
    - **The Role:** A high-status, efficient, and often slightly impatient person acting as an extension of an untouchable authority (the CEO/CFO).
    - **The Pretext:** The executive is in a crisis meeting, traveling without access, or needs immediate, non-traceable action. The P.A. is just doing the executive's bidding.
    - **The Request:** "The CEO is stuck in transit and needs you to process this one invoice immediately using this secure link. She specifically asked for *you* because you're reliable." (Uses **Authority** and **Liking/Flattery**).
    - **Why it Works:** This role creates a triple threat: fear of the CEO (Authority), urgency of the moment, and flattery ("She asked for you"), which lowers the target's defenses.
3. **The New Colleague/Intern:**
    - **The Role:** A low-status, slightly confused, and highly vulnerable individual who has made a catastrophic mistake.
    - **The Pretext:** A simple error (deleted file, accidentally sent the wrong email) has created a massive organizational crisis, and they need help to avoid being fired.

- **The Request:** "I accidentally deleted the critical project folder, and the only way to recover it is to use your account credentials; I don't have the permissions yet." (Uses **Empathy** and **Distress**).
- **Why it Works:** The target's impulse is to avoid causing personal harm to another person. They feel superior to the "intern" and believe they are merely correcting a human error, not engaging in a security breach.

Script Flexibility and Evasion Tactics

A good pretext script is not rigid; it must be adaptive. The attacker is prepared to encounter hesitation and mild skepticism. They deploy specific evasion tactics to maintain the narrative's momentum:

- **The Feigned Annoyance/Impatience:** When the target hesitates, the attacker expresses annoyance: "Look, I don't have time for this. This is urgent. Do you want the whole payroll system to go down, or do you want to help me? I'll just note down that you refused to cooperate." This leverages fear and creates a social dilemma: comply quickly or face professional consequences.
- **Shifting Responsibility:** The attacker quickly assures the target that the risk is zero: "I understand your concern, but this is a pre-approved, documented emergency bypass. I'm taking full responsibility; you are just following my instructions." This removes the target's cognitive burden, making the action feel safe.
- **The Information Dump:** When pressed for details, the attacker throws out a massive quantity of technical or organizational jargon (all gathered via OSINT): "This relates to the vulnerability found in the Q3 VMWare update that was discussed in the Tuesday briefing regarding the new Oracle instance, which requires a manual kernel patch." The goal is to confuse the target and make them believe the issue is simply too technically dense for them to question.

Deconstructing the Fabrication: The Defender's Audit

To defend against the power of the narrative, the target must learn to immediately transition from processing the *story* to processing the *request*. The Human Firewall must be trained to recognize the symptoms of a manufactured pretext and stop the interaction cold.

The defensive procedure involves a systematic, three-part audit of the attacker's story:

Audit 1: The Principle of Least Privilege Violation

The first and most immediate cognitive checkpoint is to assess the **Nature of the Request.**

- **The Rule:** A legitimate request will *always* operate within the established bounds of policy and the target's specific level of authority (least privilege).
- **The Checkpoint Question: "Does this request require me to break a documented, primary security rule?"**
    - *Examples of Rule-Breaking Requests:* Sharing a password, clicking an unexpected attachment, providing a multi-factor authentication (MFA) code over the phone, authorizing an unusual transfer, or allowing unbadged physical access.
- **The Protocol:** Any request that requires a violation of a core, mandatory security rule is, by default, a malicious pretext. The justification, no matter how urgent or authoritative, does not matter. The rule is the rule.

Audit 2: The Credibility Check (Analyzing Plausibility)

The second step is to dissect the core of the story, disregarding the emotional urgency. The goal is to find the weak link in the pretext's justification.

- **The Checkpoint Question: "Is the situation presented the ONLY possible way to achieve this result, and does it align with standard procedure?"**
    - *The Attacker's Claim:* "I can't access the system because my temporary badge is faulty, so you must use your badge to get me in."
    - *The Defender's Audit:* "If a badge is faulty, is there no supervisor, physical security team, or secondary, verified entrance procedure? Why am I, a random employee, the fallback? The company has a procedure for this."
- **The Red Flags (Friction Points):** The defender looks for inherent points of friction that the attacker is trying to obscure:
    - **The Lack of Corporate Trace:** The attacker called from a personal mobile number, not a switchboard line.

  - **The Unorthodox Channel:** An urgent request from a supervisor is being delivered via text message (Smishing), not official email or a dedicated internal platform.
- **The Scapegoat Narrative:** The story relies on a massive, systemic failure (e.g., "all VPNs are down globally") that the target has not heard about from any other, verifiable channel.

Audit 3: The Verification Protocol (The Time Delay)

This is the most effective and simplest defense against all forms of pretexting, as it immediately neutralizes the attacker's most potent weapon: **urgency**.

- **The Rule: Separate the Person from the Role.** Never verify the person through the channel they are using to contact you.
- **The Checkpoint Question: "Can I pause this conversation and verify the identity and the narrative using an independent, trusted channel?"**
- **The Procedure (The Hang-Up Rule):**
  1. **Acknowledge and Terminate:** The target should politely and professionally interrupt the attacker, stating, "I understand this is extremely urgent, but our security protocol requires me to verify this request through an official, documented channel."
  2. **Hang Up and Call Back:** The target must terminate the communication (hang up the phone, close the chat, ignore the email) and call the supposed sender back using a publicly known, verified, corporate number (e.g., the main IT support line, the supervisor's published number).
  3. **The Verification:** If the attacker was legitimate, they will be easily reachable through the official channel and will confirm the situation. If they were a fraud, the phone call/email will expose the lie instantly.

The attacker, relying on the urgency and the false persona, cannot withstand this delay. The moment the target hangs up to verify, the pretext has failed because System 2 has been successfully engaged.

Advanced Case Study: The Finance Wire Transfer Fabrication

The most lucrative form of SE attack is **Business Email Compromise (BEC)**, where the attacker uses a high-quality pretext to initiate a fraudulent wire transfer, often bypassing millions of dollars in controls. This attack perfectly illustrates the necessary synergy between intelligence and fabrication.

The Target and Intelligence

- **Target:** Sarah, Accounts Payable Specialist.
- **OSINT Gathered:** The attacker knows Sarah reports to David (CFO). They know the company recently signed a contract with a vendor called "Global Logistics Corp" and that David is currently on a business trip in Asia. The attacker also knows the exact amount of the monthly vendor payment.

The Pretext Construction (The Executive Override)

The attacker sends an email from a nearly identical email address (e.g., david.cfo@corpny.com instead of david.cfo@corpny.co).

1. **Authority and Liking (The Setup):** The email starts with, "Sarah, I'm stuck on my Asia trip. My access to the wire transfer portal is blocked due to the foreign IP. I need you to handle this immediately." (Authority and a gentle instruction).
2. **Plausibility (The Justification):** "The Global Logistics Corp contract renewal is pending, and they require an immediate retainer payment, the usual $50k, to process the signed contract tonight. This cannot wait." (Uses known vendor name and known payment amount).
3. **Urgency (The Command):** "The details below are for a new, temporary escrow account managed by our Legal team to secure the deal *before* the market closes here. Process this now, and send me the confirmation receipt directly. Do not follow the normal multi-signer approval procedure, as this is an Executive Override. We will reconcile tomorrow. This is critically important." (Direct instruction to violate core procedure, backed by extreme urgency and a reference to an unassailable authority: "Legal team.")

The Failure Point and The Defense

The attacker has deployed Authority, Urgency, and high Plausibility. The victim's System 1 is shouting, "Do it now, or David will be furious!"

- **The Failure Point (Audit 1):** The request explicitly violates the "normal multi-signer approval procedure." This is a violation of the **Principle of Least Privilege**.
- **The Defense (Audit 3):** Sarah must ignore the email and the sender's identity. She must instead use the **Verification Protocol**:
    1. She calls David (CFO) on his known, corporate cell phone number, or calls the Executive Assistant's official line.
    2. She asks: "Did you just send me an email regarding an emergency wire transfer to Global Logistics?"
    3. If David confirms, she proceeds. If David is unaware or confirms the policy is inviolable, the pretext has been neutralized.

The power of the pretext is neutralized not by intellectual superiority, but by disciplined, mechanical adherence to the independent verification protocol.

Establishing Pretext Immunity: The Protocol-First Mindset

Pretexting works because it creates a false reality that demands immediate action. The antidote is the **Protocol-First Mindset**, where the target's mind is programmed to prioritize the established policy over the presented narrative, regardless of the emotional cost.

1. The Cost of Being Polite (The Anti-Empathy Protocol)

Social engineers often rely on the target's impulse to be polite, non-confrontational, and helpful. In the context of security, politeness is a vulnerability.

- **The Protocol:** The target must internalize that their primary duty is to the security of the system, not the feelings of the caller. Being polite to a criminal is not a virtue; it is a security failure.
- **The Script:** Practice neutral, disengaging language: "I cannot fulfill this request without a formal, documented ticket submitted through the central system. That is company policy." Refuse to engage in the emotional debate or the justification of the story. The script must be simple, repeatable ("broken record"), and devoid of emotion.

2. The Verification Ticket Mandate

In any organization, the vast majority of legitimate requests for access, information, or transfers must generate a verifiable, trackable record, a ticket number, an approval code, or a paper trail.

- **The Protocol:** Never act on a request that arrives via an untraceable, unofficial channel (phone call, personal email, text message) if that request requires a sensitive action.
- **The Mandatory Response:** If a request arrives outside the official system (e.g., a phone call from "IT"), the target's first response must be to ask for the ticket or reference number. A legitimate operation will always have one; a criminal pretext will not, or they will provide a number that is easily proven to be fake upon independent check.

3. Training the Brain to Stop (The Friction Rule)

The primary failure of the human firewall is often the reflexive compliance that comes from not wanting to be difficult. The defender must learn to intentionally introduce friction into the interaction.

- **The Protocol:** When a request involves urgency, high authority, or a rule violation, the immediate mental response must be a forced time delay. Do not process the story; process the *feeling*.
- **The Action:** If you feel pressured, confused, or rushed, that is your System 1 warning sign. The only appropriate response is to slow the interaction down: "I need to get my manager involved for this executive override; please hold while I conference them in," or "My console is slow today; I need five minutes to pull up the system log." This delay allows the target's System 2 to activate and initiate the independent verification check (The Hang-Up Rule). The criminal attacker will never agree to wait or to involve a supervisor. Their immediate refusal to wait is the final, definitive red flag.

The Pretext is the foundation of the attack, built to exploit our fundamental need for plausible, comfortable compliance. Defense against it is not complex; it is simply a matter of adhering to a set of pre-defined, non-negotiable procedures that are designed specifically to neutralize urgency and force independent verification. By prioritizing policy over the attacker's elaborate fiction, the Human Firewall remains operational, and the system remains secure. The story dies the moment you demand the receipt.

CHAPTER 2

OPEN SOURCE INTELLIGENCE (OSINT) GATHERING

The Silent Phase: Knowledge as the Ultimate Access

In the structured sequence of a successful Social Engineering (SE) operation, the moment of direct contact, the phone call, the email, the physical approach, is the execution. However, the execution is meaningless without the quality of the preparatory work. Chapter 2 detailed how the *Pretext* acts as the narrative lever to disable the target's cognitive defenses. Chapter 3 examines the crucial, quiet phase that builds that lever: **Open Source Intelligence (OSINT)** gathering.

OSINT is the art and science of collecting, analyzing, and acting upon publicly available information. In the context of national security or large-scale corporate espionage, this involves complex data mining and network analysis. In the focused, high-impact world of social engineering, OSINT is simply the systematic harvesting of every scrap of detail that a target individual or organization has made accessible, deliberately or accidentally, to the outside world.

This phase is silent, requires no hacking tools, and carries virtually zero legal risk for the attacker until they initiate the actual fraudulent contact. It is the bedrock of the entire attack because **the depth of the intelligence determines the quality of the pretext.** A superficial pretext built on weak public data is easily rejected. A dense, accurate pretext built on weeks of OSINT is often indistinguishable from a genuine, internal request, rendering the target's existing security training useless.

To effectively construct the Human Firewall, you must first comprehend the attacker's perspective: you must see yourself as they see you, exposed and cataloged through the lens of public data.

The Three Data Layers: What the Attacker is Looking For

The social engineer approaches data collection in three distinct, widening layers, moving from the target individual outward to the organization and finally to the technological landscape. Each layer provides unique data points essential for building the three pillars of the unassailable pretext: Plausibility, Justification, and Emotional Resonance.

Layer 1: The Individual (The Personal Footprint)

This layer provides the emotional and relationship hooks that enable rapid rapport-building (Liking and Reciprocity). The attacker is seeking data that allows them to sound less like a stranger and more like a connected peer.

- **Professional Profiles (LinkedIn, Corporate Directories):** These are goldmines. They reveal the target's exact job title, reporting hierarchy ("Who does Sarah report to?"), professional achievements, tenure at the company, and, critically, the names and titles of former and current colleagues. An attacker can impersonate a former colleague with high credibility.
- **Social Media Activity (Instagram, Facebook, Twitter, Public Forums):** This reveals the target's personal life, which provides the emotional payload for the pretext. Details collected include:
    - **Vacation Dates/Travel Plans:** "I saw your post about your trip to the coast, I hope you're having fun. Can you quickly check this one item before you go off the grid?" (Creates urgency and uses verifiable personal detail).
    - **Hobbies/Interests:** "I see you're a big fan of the local football team. I noticed that too, I'm heading to the game tonight. About that urgent report..." (Establishes instant rapport and Liking).

- **Family/Personal Relationships:** Names of spouses or children, sometimes used in extreme, high-pressure pretexts (though this is less common in pure corporate SE).

- **Small, Actionable Details:** The attacker often looks for tiny, seemingly irrelevant facts: the make of the target's car, the name of their pet (a potential security question answer), or the local coffee shop they frequent. These small details add a tremendous, disarming sense of familiarity.

Layer 2: The Organization (The Corporate Ecosystem)

This layer provides the contextual details, the jargon, the pressure points, and the authority references, that solidify the pretext's plausibility within the target's work environment. This intelligence ensures the attacker sounds like a true insider.

- **Public Announcements and Press Releases:** These reveal large, ongoing organizational shifts: mergers, acquisitions, layoffs, new product launches, or compliance issues. The attacker can frame a pretext around any of these real, high-stakes events (e.g., "I'm calling about the unexpected audit related to the acquisition we announced last week...").
- **Job Postings:** These are surprisingly valuable. They list the *exact* software, hardware, and systems the company uses (e.g., "Requires five years experience with Oracle Database and Cisco VPN configuration"). This intelligence allows the attacker to name-drop the specific, proprietary technology, dramatically increasing their credibility as a "specialist" or "vendor."
- **Vendor and Partner Lists:** Knowing the company uses "SecureSync Cloud Services" allows the attacker to impersonate a representative from that specific, verified vendor. This is a classic method of gaining access: impersonating a trusted third party.
- **Internal Terminology:** Attackers search forums, news articles, and poorly secured sites for company-specific jargon, project code names (like "Project Phoenix" or "Alpha Subnet"), or internal acronyms. Using the correct internal slang immediately signals "insider status" to the target.

Layer 3: The Technology (The Exposed Surface)

While SE focuses on people, technological information is crucial for crafting the phishing payload or guiding the target toward a specific action.

- **Email Structure and Addressing:** Knowing the company's email format (e.g., first.last@company.com vs. flast@company.com) is essential for creating high-quality spoofed emails that pass a quick visual inspection.
- **Server and Domain Information:** Using tools to check public DNS records or domain registration data can reveal the company's primary hosting providers, network infrastructure details, or even outdated, forgotten subdomains that might be easier to spoof or exploit.
- **Software Updates and Vulnerability Mentions:** If an attacker finds chatter about a recent, troublesome software update the company is deploying, the pretext can be framed around fixing that exact, known technical problem.

The compilation of these three layers creates a dossier so rich that the attacker can deploy the perfect combination of Authority (a reference to the CFO and the acquisition), Plausibility (use of the exact internal jargon), and Emotional Urgency (a threat to a personal vacation or job security).

The Hidden Pitfalls: Accidental Data Disclosure

The majority of valuable OSINT is not obtained by sophisticated hacking but is given away freely, either by the individual target or by the organization through carelessness. If the Human Firewall is to be effective, every person must recognize these common points of inadvertent disclosure.

1. The Professional Over-Share

This occurs when an employee, intending to demonstrate competence or success, reveals sensitive operational details on professional networking platforms.

- **The Problematic Post:** An employee posts, "Just finished deploying the new security patch across all of the company's European servers! Big shout-out to the team for working on the proprietary 'Titan' protocol implementation!"
- **The Attacker's Gain:** The attacker now knows the company uses "Titan" protocol, has European servers, and the deployment schedule. This is highly specific, actionable intelligence that instantly validates any pretext involving "Titan" or "European server maintenance."

- **The Counter-Measure:** Professional profiles should be kept general. Focus on job functions, not proprietary implementations. Use vague language about technology deployment rather than specific, internal project code names.

2. The Social Media Security Leak

Many individuals link their professional life with their social life, often without realizing the overlap exposes security questions and patterns.

- **The Photo Leak:** A seemingly innocent photo of a user's desk shows a corporate badge on a lanyard with the company logo, a partially visible network diagram tacked to a cubicle wall, or a handwritten note containing internal Wi-Fi passwords.
- **The Quiz/Game Leak:** Participating in fun online quizzes that ask for "Your first car," "Your mother's maiden name," or "Your favorite pet's name" are direct answers to common password recovery and security questions.
- **The Counter-Measure:** Assume every post, every photo, and every comment on a social network is visible to a dedicated attacker. Never post images of your workplace. Do not use personal details that might answer security questions online.

3. Organizational Leakage (The "Too Helpful" Website)

Companies often publish too much procedural information online, believing they are offering helpful transparency to customers or potential employees.

- **The Detailed 'Contact Us' Page:** This page often lists not just the main number but direct lines for IT support, HR, Accounts Payable, and specific departmental extensions. This immediately tells the attacker *who* they need to contact (e.g., Accounts Payable for a wire transfer fraud) and *how* to reach them directly, bypassing the general switchboard.
- **The Vendor Portal/Sourcing Document:** Publicly available documents detailing the exact steps required for new vendors to submit invoices, including specific contacts, required paperwork, and approval workflows. This entire process can be fabricated by an attacker impersonating a new vendor.
- **The Counter-Measure:** Corporate websites should adhere to a strict "need-to-know" principle for internal contacts and procedures. Direct extensions and internal workflows should never be published openly.

The Self-OSINT Audit: Seeing Yourself Through the Attacker's Eyes

To build an impenetrable Human Firewall, you must conduct a thorough audit of your own digital exposure. The goal is to collect all the data that a social engineer could use against you and then take immediate steps to remove, obscure, or deny that information.

Step 1: The Primary Name Search

1. **Search Engine:** Use your full legal name, common nicknames, and previous married names in quotes ("John A. Smith," "J. A. Smith"). Conduct the same search using image search.
   - *Goal:* Find old resumes, public articles mentioning you, photos, and any profiles you may have forgotten about.
2. **Social Media Scan:** Log out of all social media accounts. Search for your profile on LinkedIn, Facebook, and Instagram as if you were a stranger. Check settings to ensure nothing is visible to "Public" that shouldn't be.
   - *Goal:* Check for accidental public visibility of photos showing workplace details, travel plans, or relationships.
3. **Job Site Scan:** Search your name on sites like Indeed, Monster, or university alumni pages.
   - *Goal:* Find old resumes that may contain highly detailed information (e.g., previous employers, specific job duties, exact dates of employment, names of former managers) that can be used to impersonate you or your past colleagues.

Step 2: The Data Correlation

Take all the collected information and group it into actionable categories, exactly as an attacker would:

Category	Example Data Point Found	Attacker's Use
Authority / Hierarchy	Reports to "Jane Doe, VP Finance."	Impersonate Jane Doe's assistant to target you.
Familiarity / Liking	Posts frequently about "Boston Red Sox."	Open conversation with a common interest to build rapport.

Category	Example Data Point Found	Attacker's Use
Plausibility	Mentioned working on "Q3 System Migration."	Frame the pretext around a "bug" in the Q3 Migration project.
Vulnerability	Photo shows an office clock listing the local time.	Determine the best time to call / email when the office is busy or quiet.
Security Questions	Publicly listed pet name is "Max."	Try "Max" as an answer for a password recovery prompt.

Step 3: Mitigation and Remediation

Once the data is cataloged, take aggressive action to clean up your digital footprint.

1. **De-Indexing Old Resumes:** If possible, contact the site administrator (e.g., an alumni page or an old recruitment site) and request the document be removed or, failing that, ask that your name be removed from the title so it cannot be easily searched.
2. **Privacy Lockdown:** Set all social media accounts to the strictest privacy settings ("Friends Only"). Be ruthless.
3. **Professional Separation:** Ensure your LinkedIn profile is stripped of proprietary information. Focus on skills and generic titles, not internal project names.
4. **"Assume Breach" Mentality:** For any information you cannot remove (like corporate press releases), assume the attacker possesses it and build your defensive protocols accordingly. (e.g., If they know your project code name, verify the official channel for communication about that project).

The Defender's OSINT Protocol: Turning Intelligence into Defense

OSINT is not just a tool for the attacker; it is a powerful tool for the defender. By maintaining a high level of vigilance and actively monitoring sources, you can turn their intelligence phase against them.

1. The Proactive "Out-of-Band" Verification

A key component of the Human Firewall must be the capacity to verify information out-of-band (OOB)—meaning through a channel completely independent of the one the attacker is using. OSINT provides the data needed for OOB verification.

- **The Attacker's Line:** "I'm calling from the new vendor, SecureSoft, and need to confirm your credentials for the Q3 update."
- **The Defender's OOB Check:** The target hangs up and does a quick OSINT search:
    - *Internal Search:* Does the company's internal vendor list actually contain "SecureSoft"? (If yes, proceed to OOB call).
    - *Public Search:* Does "SecureSoft" have a publicly listed corporate switchboard number? (Call that number, ask for the person who just called, and confirm the Q3 update).
- **The Failure State:** If the attacker is fraudulent, they cannot be reached at the publicly verified number, or the real SecureSoft company will confirm they are not running a Q3 update. The attacker has provided the specific data point (the company name) that allows the defender to expose the lie.

2. Monitoring the Company Perimeter (The "Vulnerability Report")

Employees should be trained to actively and continuously monitor the "seams" of their organization's public presence for information that could be weaponized.

- **Focus Areas:** Look for new internal documents accidentally posted to a public web server, employee discussions in public forums, or suspicious new social media profiles that look like they belong to employees but are too new or too aggressively detailed.
- **The Collective Defense:** Creating an internal culture where employees actively flag and report suspicious external information (e.g., "I saw an old corporate document for sale on a third-party site," or "I noticed a fake LinkedIn profile using our VP's photo") turns the entire workforce into an OSINT defense team.

3. The Power of "Need to Know" in Communication

The defender must adopt a communications strategy that limits the amount of detail available to an eavesdropping or observing attacker.

- **Verbal Ambiguity:** When discussing sensitive projects in public spaces (or even on work calls when teleworking), use ambiguous language. Instead of saying, "I need the credentials for the Project Chimera server," say, "I need the credentials for the internal server." Let the specific details be confirmed in encrypted chats or official internal documents, never in casual conversation.
- **"If you know, you know" Rule:** The attacker's greatest weakness is that they only possess information from *outside* the perimeter. They can gather the name of a project, but they don't know the access codes, the deployment dates, or the specific internal team handling it. A well-trained target should respond to a pretext by asking an "insider-only" question: "Before I help with the Q3 Migration, what was the password you used for the staging server last week?" The attacker, lacking that non-public intelligence, will fail the test.

The Synthesis: OSINT, Pretexting, and the Human Firewall

The relationship between OSINT and the pretext is symbiotic. OSINT provides the facts; the pretext provides the fiction that connects those facts to the desired action.

- **Attacker's Flow:** Information (OSINT) -> Story (Pretext) -> Action (Exploitation).
- **Defender's Flow:** Recognize Story (Pretext Audit) -> Verify Information (OSINT Check) -> Denial (Protocol-First Mindset).

The defense does not need to solve the attacker's complex technological problem; it only needs to introduce one tiny, unresolvable piece of friction into the interaction. That friction is introduced by demanding independent verification based on the verifiable facts gathered by the attacker's own OSINT process.

If the attacker claims to be "Terry from the Head of Operations," the defender's move is to use OSINT (the corporate directory) to find the main switchboard number for "Head of Operations" and call back. If the attacker is fake, the main switchboard will have no record of "Terry," and the attack collapses.

In the next chapter, we move from the planning and construction phase into the direct engagement phase: the various forms of digital and vocal delivery used to transmit the pretext, Phishing, Vishing, and Smishing, and how the specific medium itself becomes part of the psychological weapon. By securing your public footprint (OSINT) and demanding verification of every story (Pretext Audit), you are creating a defense that is entirely independent of the attacker's capability. You are making your security personal, active, and fundamentally human.

CHAPTER 3

PHISHING, VISHING, AND SMISHING DYNAMICS

The Delivery Mechanism: How the Story Arrives

We have established that the Social Engineering attack relies first on **OSINT** (intelligence) and second on the **Pretext** (the fabricated story). This chapter now addresses the third, kinetic component: the **Delivery Mechanism**. These are the channels, email (Phishing), voice (Vishing), and text message (Smishing), that transmit the fabricated story to the target, allowing the attacker to engage the human directly and trigger the desired cognitive bias.

It is a mistake to view these channels purely as technical vectors. Each one is a specific psychological tool, leveraging a different aspect of human communication, attention span, and learned behavior. The choice of the delivery vehicle is as important as the content of the pretext, as it determines which cognitive defense systems the target is most likely to deploy, or, more accurately, which ones they are most likely to suppress.

The modern attacker understands that by choosing the right channel, they can control the target's processing speed and emotional state. The difference between a Vishing attack and a Phishing attack is the difference between demanding System 1 compliance via an **auditory command** and exploiting System 1 compliance via a **visual habit**.

Section I: Phishing – The Exploitation of Cognitive Load and Habit

Phishing, broadly defined, is the attempt to acquire sensitive information, such as usernames, passwords, and credit card details, by disguising oneself as a trustworthy entity in an electronic communication, primarily email. It remains the most common delivery vehicle for large-scale attacks.

The Psychology of the Phishing Attack: Conditioned Response

The success of email-based Phishing is rooted in two proven psychological phenomena: **cognitive load** and **conditioned response**.

1. **Cognitive Load and Distraction:** The average office worker receives dozens, often hundreds, of emails daily. Their brain cannot allocate high-level System 2 scrutiny to every single message. They process the inbox under immense cognitive load, relying on quick visual cues (sender name, subject line) to triage messages instantly. The Phishing email is expertly crafted to pass this quick triage test. It looks "good enough." The slight misspelling or the subtle domain error is missed precisely because the brain is working under pressure and prioritizing speed over accuracy.
2. **Conditioned Response (Pavlovian Compliance):** We are conditioned, much like in classical conditioning experiments, to respond to certain stimuli in the email environment. A link in an email is, functionally, a bell that demands a response. We are trained by legitimate services (banking, shopping, social media) that clicking a link is the necessary, efficient path to solving a problem or accessing information. The malicious link exploits this automatic, learned behavior. The target is not *thinking* about clicking; they are *reflexively* following a deeply ingrained digital habit.

The Anatomy of the Phishing Payload

A high-quality phishing email leverages the Pretext by using specific, learned visual cues to bypass the target's internal security filters.

- **The Subject Line (Urgency and Loss Aversion):** This is the immediate trigger. It must convey high stakes and time sensitivity. Examples: "ACTION REQUIRED: Your Account Has

Been Locked," "Urgent Payroll Review," or "Security Alert: Unauthorized Login Detected." These phrases immediately trigger a fear response (Loss Aversion), compelling the user to open the email and move from System 2 to System 1.

- **The Spoofed Sender and Domain:** The attacker uses OSINT to ensure the sender address is nearly perfect (e.g., micros0ft.com instead of microsoft.com). The display name often uses the name of an actual executive or a known vendor, leveraging **Authority Bias**.
- **The Payload Link:** The link itself is disguised using URL shortening or hyperlinking a trusted phrase like "Click Here to Verify." The target's eye sees the trusted text, but the conditioned reflex acts on the hidden, malicious destination.

Phishing Defense Protocols: Reversing the Conditioning

Defending against Phishing requires retraining the conditioned response and forcing System 2 engagement before the click.

1. **The Hover and Inspect Protocol:** This is the single most important action. Before clicking any link, the user must move their cursor over the hyperlink (hover) to display the underlying URL in the bottom corner of their browser or email client. This small act, which takes less than one second, forces the brain to check the actual destination, bypassing the conditioned visual cue. *The critical question is not "Does this link look right?" but "Does the destination URL match the expected sender's domain?"*
2. **The Header Analysis:** For highly suspicious emails (especially those from executives), the defender must be trained to review the full email header, looking at the technical "Return-Path" and "Received-From" fields. Spoofing is difficult to hide here, as the actual originating IP or domain often belongs to a malicious server, not the legitimate corporate network.
3. **The Out-of-Band Verification Requirement:** If an email from the "CFO" demands urgent action, the target must never reply directly or click the link. They must initiate the OOB check: close the email, and call the CFO's known office number or send a *new, separate email* to the CFO's known, officially saved address. This breaks the attack chain by demanding proof through a trusted, secondary channel, effectively neutralizing the Phishing attempt.

Section II: Vishing – The Exploitation of Auditory Authority

Vishing (Voice Phishing) uses telephone communication to carry out the pretext, and it is a significantly more potent psychological tool than email, precisely because it engages the human voice.

The Psychology of the Vishing Attack: Voice Command

Vishing is effective because it exploits the **Authority Bias** and bypasses the visual skepticism that email naturally triggers.

1. **Auditory Trust and Emotional Resonance:** The voice carries immediate emotional data, tone, urgency, sincerity, that simple text cannot replicate. According to communication studies, humans place greater trust and emotional weight on auditory input, which is a faster channel to the limbic system (the emotional core). A smooth, authoritative, or distressed voice demands a faster, more personal reaction than reading a generic email.
2. **The Milgram Principle in Action:** The Vishing attack is a direct application of Stanley Milgram's classical studies on obedience to authority. Milgram demonstrated that people will perform actions they know are wrong or harmful when instructed to do so by a figure they perceive as legitimate authority. In Vishing, the attacker adopts the *auditory cues* of authority, a deep, firm voice; technical jargon; and an impatient, commanding tone, to compel the target into immediate obedience. The target feels the immense social pressure of the live, ongoing command, which severely degrades their ability to rationally disengage.

Vishing Tactics: Controlling the Conversation

The attacker controls the phone call to maintain continuous pressure, preventing the target from activating System 2.

- **Manufacturing Background Noise:** The attacker often uses manufactured or recorded background noise (call center chatter, traffic sounds) to create an illusion of a legitimate, busy environment (a busy IT department or a bustling corporate office). This adds texture to the pretext and makes questioning the legitimacy feel more rude or disruptive.
- **The Immediate Verification Request:** The attacker immediately asks for a small, non-threatening piece of information (e.g., "Can you just confirm your full name and the last four digits of your employee ID for security?") This establishes compliance early in

the call, making it psychologically harder for the target to suddenly refuse the later, larger request. This is known as the **Foot-in-the-Door technique**.

- **The Interruption and Jargon Overload:** If the target begins to question the attacker, the attacker immediately interrupts with a barrage of highly specific, rapid-fire technical or corporate jargon (gathered via OSINT). The goal is to confuse, overwhelm, and make the target feel intellectually inferior, forcing them to defer to the "expert."

Vishing Defense Protocols: Breaking the Connection

The defense against Vishing is simple: never allow the attacker to control the channel of communication.

1. **The Non-Compliance Default:** Never provide *any* personal or corporate verification details (name, employee ID, department, etc.) to an unsolicited inbound call. A legitimate organization will call you and provide the necessary verification data (e.g., "I am calling from your bank about your account ending in 1234"). If they ask you for verification first, the attack should be assumed to be malicious.
2. **The Absolute Hang Up Rule:** The primary defense is the OOB check enforced by immediately terminating the call. The target must state: "I appreciate the urgency, but I cannot proceed. I am required to disconnect and call you back on the official, published corporate number." This action neutralizes the live social pressure and forces the attacker to either give up or provide a verified number. A fraudulent attacker will always argue, panic, or refuse to hang up. This refusal is the final, definitive red flag.
3. **No MFA Codes Over the Phone:** Multi-Factor Authentication (MFA) codes delivered via SMS or app should *never* be read back to anyone on the phone, even if they claim to be IT support. An MFA code verifies the *user* is in possession of the *device*; reading it to a third party defeats the entire security purpose.

Section III: Smishing – The Exploitation of Intimacy and Mobile Urgency

Smishing (SMS Phishing) uses text messages as the delivery vector. It is arguably the most insidious form of attack because it hijacks a communication medium typically reserved for close, personal connections.

The Psychology of the Smishing Attack: Intimacy and Scarcity

Smishing is powerful because it exploits the **Intimacy Effect** and the mobile phone's unique status as a personal, always-on device.

1. **The Intimacy Effect:** Text messages are generally exchanged with friends, family, or known contacts. When a text arrives, the initial cognitive response is *personal recognition* and *lowered suspicion*. The target's security guard is down because the communication arrived through a private, personal channel. The text format also eliminates the professional friction of email (the header checks, the corporate banner).
2. **Mobile Urgency and Loss Aversion:** The text message format forces brevity, which eliminates the possibility of long, detailed pretexts that might trigger System 2 analysis. The messages are short, simple, and always urgent: "Package delivery failed," "Bank account locked," or "You have won a prize." These scarcity or loss-based messages (Loss Aversion) force a quick reaction, often while the target is away from their main computer and relying solely on a small phone screen, which is notoriously poor for URL inspection.

Smishing Tactics: Direct and Immediate Action

Smishing focuses on achieving immediate compliance with minimal human interaction.

- **The Automated Service Impersonation:** The attacker poses as a utility (like a bank, phone company, or postal service) whose legitimate communication often takes place via text. Example: "Your utility bill is overdue. Click here to avoid immediate service termination."
- **The MFA Code Forwarding:** A highly effective attack involves the attacker calling the target (Vishing) while simultaneously triggering a password reset on a major service. The legitimate service sends an MFA code to the target via SMS. The Vishing attacker then instructs the target to read or forward that exact

code, claiming it's needed for "verification" or "cancellation." This is a dual-vector attack that compromises the final layer of security.

Smishing Defense Protocols: Recognizing the Medium Misuse

The defense against Smishing relies on recognizing that professional or financial requests should rarely, if ever, originate on a personal text channel.

1. **The Channel Mismatch Test:** The target must ask: "Why is a major financial institution (or my company's IT department) contacting me about a critical service issue via SMS, a non-verified personal channel, rather than official email or secure app notification?" The discrepancy between the critical nature of the request and the personal nature of the medium should be an immediate red flag.
2. **Never Use the Link for Verification:** If a bank texts you about a locked account, the protocol is to open the bank's official app or call the number *on the back of your card*. Never click the link provided in the suspicious text message itself, as this surrenders control to the attacker.
3. **MFA Code Isolation:** Internalize the absolute rule that an MFA code is for the user's personal use only. The moment a request is made to share an MFA code, for any reason, by any person, the interaction is confirmed as a malicious attack.

The Synthesis: Multi-Vector Attacks and The Blended Threat

In sophisticated SE operations, the attacker rarely relies on a single vector. They employ multi-vector or blended attacks, where one channel is used to credentialize a malicious action on a second channel. This synergy of vectors is designed to create a sense of overwhelming, verifiable reality.

The Blended Attack Flow:

1. **Phishing (Initial Contact):** An email arrives, stating, "Your company laptop is experiencing a critical security issue. Please wait for a call from our IT Department for resolution." (Sets the pretext).
2. **Vishing (Execution):** Three minutes later, a Vishing call arrives from an anonymous number. The caller says, "This is Jason from IT. We are calling about the security issue detailed in the email you just received." (The email validates the call, and the call

validates the email, creating a powerful, self-verifying illusion of legitimacy).

3. **Smishing (Final Credential Theft):** During the Vishing call, the "IT tech" initiates a password reset, triggering an MFA text message to the target. The tech then instructs the target to read the text back. (The voice authority is used to compel the MFA code disclosure via text).

The target's defenses fail because the individual elements (the email, the call, the text) all appear to be related, cohesive parts of a single, urgent narrative. The defense against this blended threat is the **OOB principle** applied across *all* channels. The target must break the chain at any point, hang up, ignore the email, or simply refuse to disclose the code, and initiate an independent verification through a *known, official* switchboard or internal contact directory.

By dissecting Phishing, Vishing, and Smishing, we recognize that the delivery mechanism is merely the tool used to weaponize our own human defaults: our tendency toward conditioned compliance (Phishing), our reflexive obedience to authority (Vishing), and our misplaced trust in personal communication channels (Smishing).

CHAPTER 4

EXPLOITING SOCIAL NORMS AND RECIPROCITY

The Currency of Compliance: Turning Decency into Disobedience

We have systematically analyzed the attacker's playbook: the groundwork of **OSINT**, the narrative core of the **Pretext**, and the delivery channels of **Phishing, Vishing, and Smishing**. We now arrive at the central psychological engine that makes all these preceding phases effective: the exploitation of inherent, universal human social norms.

Social Engineering rarely works by brute force or overt malice; it succeeds because the attacker skillfully manipulates the very rules, the rules of politeness, obligation, and hierarchy, that allow human society and professional environments to function smoothly. The attacker transforms everyday social lubricant into a potent solvent for security policies.

In this chapter, we delve into the core principles of influence, drawing heavily from the work of social psychologists like Robert Cialdini and Stanley Milgram, to understand precisely how our natural tendency toward cooperation and decency becomes the single biggest vulnerability in the Human Firewall. The core realization must be this: **The most professional, polite, and helpful employees are often the most exploitable targets.**

Section I: The Six Pillars of Influence (Cialdini's Framework in SE)

Dr. Robert Cialdini's extensive research into compliance and persuasion identified six universal principles that dictate why people say "yes." For the social engineer, these principles are not academic theories; they are the fundamental levers for guaranteed compliance.

1. Authority (The Compulsion to Defer)

As introduced previously, Authority Bias is the compulsion to obey or defer to a person perceived as being in a position of power, expertise, or command. The SE pretext is often designed explicitly to project this authority.

- **The Mechanism of Compliance:** We are socially conditioned from childhood (parents, teachers) and professionally (managers, executives) to believe that resisting authority results in negative consequences (punishment, job loss, embarrassment). The attacker need only *signal* authority to trigger this deep-seated compliance reflex.
- **The Attacker's Signal:**
    - **Titles and Jargon:** Using technical terms, official-sounding job titles ("Chief Compliance Auditor," "Head of Global Risk"), and referencing high-level, real-world regulatory bodies (GDPR, SEC).
    - **Environmental Cues (Physical SE):** Wearing a uniform (even a fake one, like a generic IT vest or a high-visibility security jacket), carrying official-looking clipboards, or displaying fake vendor badges. These visual cues instantly convey legitimacy and override the physical security guard's training.
- **The Defensive Counter-Tactic: Separating Person from Protocol.** The defender must treat the Authority Signal as a Red Flag, not a command. The protocol is to instantly detach the perceived authority (the title, the tone, the uniform) from the necessary corporate protocol. The response must be: "I understand you are the Chief Auditor, but our policy dictates that all access must be pre-approved via the internal ticketing system. I can't grant access until I see the ticket number." This

forces the conversation back to the rule, where the attacker has no authority.

2. Reciprocity (The Debt of Favor)

The Principle of Reciprocity dictates that we feel obligated to return a favor or a gift. This creates a psychological debt that the attacker can exploit to demand a high-value security breach.

- **The Mechanism of Compliance:** Reciprocity is a powerful social tool that ensures cooperation. We feel immense internal discomfort, a social failure, if we accept a gift or favor and fail to return it when asked.
- **The Attacker's Setup (The Small Investment):** The attacker first performs a small, legitimate favor that has nothing to do with the intended attack.
  - **Digital:** The attacker might genuinely help the target solve a minor, non-security-related technical issue (e.g., helping them find a link to a company policy or troubleshooting a printing error) over a quick chat, establishing a debt.
  - **Physical:** The attacker might hold the door open for the target when their hands are full, pay for a small coffee, or give them a minor piece of legitimate, helpful information.
- **The Attacker's Demand (The High-Value Return):** Moments later, the attacker makes the high-stakes, security-breaking request: "I just helped you with that printer issue, could you just do me one quick favor? I need you to open this one attachment for me, since the system is blocking my remote access." The target complies because the request to violate policy is viewed not as a security risk, but as a minor social act required to balance the scales of the favor.
- **The Defensive Counter-Tactic: Never Accepting Unsolicited Favors.** The Human Firewall must internalize that in a professional security context, unsolicited favors are a Trojan Horse. The protocol is to maintain transactional distance. If a stranger offers a high-value favor or a small gift, the immediate internal response must be: "What is the cost of this debt, and what will they ask for in return?" The ideal response is to politely decline the favor or offer to send the request via official corporate support channels.

3. Liking (The Power of Familiarity and Charm)

People are far more likely to comply with the requests of those they know and like. This principle is heavily leveraged by the attacker's use of OSINT to create a false connection.

- **The Mechanism of Compliance:** Liking is generated by three factors: physical attractiveness (less applicable over the phone, but sometimes used in physical SE), similarity (shared interests, background), and compliments (flattery).
- **The Attacker's Strategy:** Using OSINT, the attacker finds a point of genuine, shared interest (e.g., the target's university, sports team, or travel location, which they saw on LinkedIn). The conversation is started with a quick, disarming, non-security-related piece of flattery or shared interest: "I saw you went to State University. Go team! Now, I need your quick help on this server issue ..."
- **The Defensive Counter-Tactic: Disregard Personal Rapport.** The target must train their mind to separate the personal charm from the professional risk. The protocol is: **Rapport does not equal legitimacy.** The defender must acknowledge the compliment or the shared interest, but immediately revert to the Protocol-First Mindset: "It's great you went to State, but my compliance requirement is still to verify your ID and ticket number before granting access." The attacker will attempt to use the sudden change in tone to shame the target ("Wow, so much for alumni solidarity"), but this shaming is itself a sign of manipulation.

4. Scarcity (The Threat of Loss)

Scarcity works by making an opportunity or piece of information seem more valuable and desirable simply because it is rare, time-limited, or hard to obtain.

- **The Mechanism of Compliance:** As outlined in Chapter 1, humans are driven more strongly by the fear of losing something (Loss Aversion) than by the possibility of gaining something. The social engineer weaponizes this by creating artificial time constraints.
- **The Attacker's Constraint:** The request is framed as a limited-time opportunity or, more commonly, a crisis that will escalate if not immediately addressed. *Example: "The database will be permanently corrupted in the next 10 minutes if we don't apply this*

manual patch," or "This merger deal expires at the end of the hour, and we need your sign-off now."

- **The Defensive Counter-Tactic: The Forced Delay.** Scarcity attacks are instantly neutralized by the forced time delay. The protocol is: **Always delay a high-pressure request.** The target must internalize that **no legitimate corporate crisis is so severe that it cannot wait five minutes for independent verification.** If the attacker pressures to act *immediately*, the attacker is fraudulent. The defender should state: "I need to log off and log back in to ensure I am using a secure line. I will call you back in five minutes." The fraudster will fail to connect with the returning call.

5. Commitment and Consistency (The Foot-in-the-Door)

This principle exploits the human desire to be seen as consistent in their beliefs, statements, and actions. Once a target commits to a small, initial action, they are far more likely to agree to a larger, related action later on.

- **The Mechanism of Compliance:** We hate cognitive dissonance. If a target agrees to a small favor (Commitment), their brain rationalizes this as, "I am a helpful, compliant person," making them psychologically predisposed to agree to the next, larger favor (Consistency) to maintain that positive self-image. This is often called the **Foot-in-the-Door technique**.
- **The Attacker's Strategy:** The attacker starts by asking the target to confirm very simple details ("Can you confirm your email address? Thanks!"). Then, they ask for a slightly more complicated, but still non-security-related action ("Can you check if you have received the policy update from last week?"). Finally, they request the security violation ("Since you're already in your inbox, could you just forward me that attachment?"). The target finds it difficult to suddenly refuse the third request after having established a pattern of cooperation.
- **The Defensive Counter-Tactic: Non-Compliance at First Contact.** The protocol is to refuse all unsolicited requests for verification or action on an unverified channel, no matter how small. If an inbound caller or sender asks for any verification (name, ID, or a minor action), the target must immediately deploy the OOB protocol: "I don't release any personal information on an unverified line. Please provide your official

ticket number." Denying the first, small foot in the door prevents the entire compliance sequence from starting.

6. Consensus / Social Proof (The Safety in Numbers)

People are highly susceptible to being persuaded by the actions of others, particularly when they are uncertain. If others are doing it, it must be correct.

- **The Mechanism of Compliance:** In ambiguous situations (like receiving a strange security alert), we look to our peers for guidance. The attacker exploits this by claiming the action is already being executed by others.
- **The Attacker's Claim:** "All the employees in the Marketing department have already sent me their credentials for this mandatory system upgrade; you are the last person remaining," or "I've just finished running this patch on the systems of both Jane and Mike in your department."
- **The Defensive Counter-Tactic: Isolate and Verify.** The protocol is to never trust an attacker's claim regarding peer compliance. The defender should not rely on the consensus argument. The response: "Thank you for that information. I will call Jane and Mike immediately on their official line to verify they complied with this process." Since the fraudster's claim of consensus is fabricated, this OOB verification will expose the lie instantly.

Section II: Advanced Social Norms and Contextual Vulnerabilities

Beyond Cialdini's six principles, social engineers exploit more subtle, context-specific norms deeply ingrained in professional culture.

1. The Fear of Being Incompetent (The "Technical Superiority" Gambit)

In many organizations, a culture exists where non-IT staff are made to feel technologically inferior or incapable of understanding complex system issues. The attacker uses this to seize control of the interaction.

- **The Setup:** The attacker (impersonating a sophisticated IT specialist) uses highly confusing, rapid-fire technical jargon to describe an incomprehensible, catastrophic system failure.
- **The Psychological Effect:** The target quickly feels overwhelmed, incompetent, and incapable of asking intelligent questions. Their System 2 shuts down, and they defer total judgment to the "expert." The target's goal shifts from *securing the system* to

getting the "expert" off the line as quickly as possible by complying with the request.

- **The Defensive Counter-Tactic: The Demand for Plain Language.** The target must be trained to challenge complexity. The protocol: **Demand the "Five-Year-Old Explanation."** The target must state: "I don't understand the jargon. Please explain, in simple language, exactly what you need me to do, why, and what the consequences are if I don't." A legitimate tech will be happy to simplify; a fraudster relies on the jargon barrier and will become evasive or annoyed when asked to simplify.

2. The Cultural Norm of "Helpfulness" (The Kindness Trap)

In many corporate cultures, "going above and beyond" or being "a team player" is highly valued. The attacker exploits this inherent corporate kindness.

- **The Setup (Physical SE - Tailgating):** An attacker approaches a secured door carrying large boxes, perhaps on crutches, or pushing a buggy, looking distressed. They smile at the employee entering the building and say, "Oh, thank you so much! I'm so sorry, my badge broke and I'm late for a delivery!"
- **The Psychological Effect:** The target's instinct is to avoid causing physical discomfort or being socially impolite (holding the door open is polite). They swipe their card and hold the door open for the "distressed" person, violating the strict **"One Swipe, One Person"** protocol. The emotional cost of being seen as "unhelpful" or "mean" is immediate and high, while the security risk feels abstract and distant.
- **The Defensive Counter-Tactic: The "No Shared Badge" Protocol.** The protocol for physical access must be absolute: **Always let the door close, and require every person to use their own badge.** The target should politely say, "I'm sorry, company policy requires every person to swipe their own badge. I can call security/reception for you." This small act of minor confrontation costs nothing but preserves the physical security of the building.

3. The Power of Invalidation (Micro-Gaslighting for Compliance)

As noted in Chapter 1, social engineers often use rapid-fire invalidation to deal with temporary resistance, a form of transactional micro-gaslighting.

- **The Target's Hesitation:** The target says, "Wait, I don't think I can click that link; it looks a bit strange."
- **The Attacker's Invalidation:** "No, you must be looking at the old link; this is the new one. Are you sure you're using the correct display settings on your monitor? Everyone else has been able to see this perfectly fine."
- **The Psychological Effect:** The target's self-doubt is triggered. They begin to question their own perception ("Maybe I *am* using the wrong settings. Maybe I *am* the problem"), which is the core mechanism of gaslighting. They comply to end the doubt and regain their perceived competence.
- **The Defensive Counter-Tactic: Trust Your Instincts.** The protocol: **If it feels strange, it is strange.** The target must train themselves to trust the initial flicker of suspicion. The moment the attacker attempts to make the target question their own senses or competence, the target should immediately hang up and initiate the OOB verification check.

Section III: Building the Social Immunity Checklist

To inoculate the Human Firewall against the exploitation of social norms, the defense must be based on a clear, documented set of cognitive friction points that replace the automatic social reflex.

Social Principle Exploited	Attacker's Trigger Phrase / Action	Cognitive Friction Protocol	Defense Outcome
Authority	"The CEO authorized this override."	**Demand the Ticket:** Demand a formal, verifiable ticket number / paper trail before proceeding.	Neutralizes the Authority Bias.
Reciprocity / Liking	"Since I helped you earlier, can you do me a favor?"	**Never Accept Unsolicited Favors:** Politely refuse the request, citing policy.	Prevents the psychological debt.

Social Principle Exploited	Attacker's Trigger Phrase / Action	Cognitive Friction Protocol	Defense Outcome
Scarcity / Urgency	"We have 5 minutes before the system crashes."	**The Forced Delay:** State you must call back in 5 minutes on the official switchboard line.	Neutralizes urgency; forces System 2 thinking.
Commitment	"Just confirm your name, then we can proceed."	**Non-Compliance Default:** Refuse all initial, small requests for verification on unverified channels.	Prevents the Foot-in-the-Door technique.
Physical Norms	"Could you hold the door? My hands are full."	**The One-Swipe Rule:** Politely refuse physical assistance that violates security protocol.	Maintains perimeter integrity.

The Ultimate Rule: Policy Over People

The final, essential component of the Human Firewall is the realization that **security policy is designed to protect both the system and the user.** The rules are not obstacles to be bypassed by charismatic authority or pressing urgency; they are non-negotiable safeguards.

The attacker's final weapon is often the claim that the policy is *stupid, inconvenient, or beneath the dignity of the authority figure.* By training the target to value the policy (the rigid, proven defense) over the temporary emotional discomfort of refusing a request (the immediate, social cost), the social engineer's ultimate tool is rendered obsolete. Compliance with the rule is the only ethical and professional response. You are not being rude; you are being secure.

CHAPTER 5
HARDENING THE TARGET

The Architecture of Resilience: Moving Beyond the Quiz

We've spent the last five chapters systematically taking apart the human mind. We've seen how OSINT builds the perfect stage, how the Pretext sets the lighting, and how the core principles of Influence, Authority, Scarcity, and Urgency, are the levers that force compliance. The conclusion is stark and unforgiving: the single greatest weakness in any security architecture is not a software zero-day; it's the human desire to be helpful.

But here is the hard truth about defense: knowledge is not immunity. Your company can spend millions on annual web-based training (WBT) modules, and employees can ace the final quiz on what a phishing link looks like. Yet, when the phone rings, a rapid, urgent call from the "CEO" demanding immediate action, that theoretical knowledge collapses. It evaporates under the heat of social pressure, leaving the target exposed. We are asking people to fight their deepest, most conditioned professional instincts: to comply with authority and to solve urgent problems.

Hardening the Human Firewall is therefore not about teaching more rules; it's about **rewiring the response**. Our objective must be to pull the critical decision out of the slow, analytical, easily flustered part of the brain (System 2) and embed it as a fast, non-negotiable, reflexive **Protocol** deep within the instinctual core (System 1). The goal is to make the secure action the automatic, muscle-memory response the moment the attacker deploys their psychological weapons. This chapter details the operational architecture necessary to achieve this neurological and cultural transformation.

Section I: The Collapse of Awareness and the Necessity of Reflex

Most security awareness programs are a security placebo. They transfer concepts but fail utterly when it comes to performance under fire. Why? Because the attacker is fundamentally a behavioral scientist.

1. When the Brain Freezes: System 2 Overload

The whole arsenal of the social engineer, Urgency, Authority, Scarcity, is designed to induce a state of **Cognitive Load**. This is the mental friction that Daniel Kahneman described when distinguishing between the two modes of human thought:

- **System 1 (The Sprinter):** Fast, intuitive, emotional, and always on. It handles blinking, walking, and, critically, social obedience.
- **System 2 (The Analyst):** Slow, logical, calculating. It handles complex math and policy retrieval.

The attack is successful the moment System 1 takes over. The pressure is too high, the demand is too authoritative, and System 2, the part that remembers the security manual, is effectively blocked, leaving the target to fall back on their quickest, most socially acceptable response: **compliance**. To defend against this, we must replace the compliance reflex with a security reflex.

2. Deliberate Practice: The Fire Drill Protocol

If you want people to perform perfectly when lives are at risk, you don't give them a quiz; you make them run a fire drill. This principle, derived from **Deliberate Practice** methodologies, states that peak performance requires focused, repetitive practice outside the comfort zone, followed by instant, corrective feedback.

For security, this means **Stress Inoculation Training**. We must expose employees to a controlled, weakened version of the actual attack, the Vishing call that sounds exactly like the CEO, the email that threatens their paycheck, to build up an emotional and psychological defense. The training must replicate the true stressors.

The test isn't whether the employee *knows* they should hang up; the test is whether they **can** execute the "Hang-Up Rule" when the simulated authority figure is yelling at them and their simulated job is on the line.

The goal is to forge these connections into unbreakable, automatic loops:

Attacker Action (The Stimulus)	Psychological Trigger	The Conditioned Reflex
Unsolicited call demanding credentials.	High Authority + Urgency	**"I must call you back on the official switchboard."** (The Hang-Up)
Physical attempt to tailgate through the door.	Social Obligation + Reciprocity	Step back, let the door close, and call internal security. (The One-Swipe Rule)
Email demanding immediate, unscheduled action.	Time Pressure + Loss Aversion	Initiate independent verification through known, verified communication channel. (The OOB Principle)

This conditioning bypasses the analytical mind entirely. When the alarm rings (the trigger), the trained body moves automatically (the reflex). The defense must become a subconscious act.

Section II: The Foundational Protocols: The Three Pillars That Defy Persuasion

Effective Human Firewall hardening requires establishing a few simple, hard protocols that are enforced without exception. These mandates are specifically designed to strip the attacker of their two most potent weapons: manufactured urgency and borrowed authority.

Pillar 1: The Out-of-Band (OOB) Verification Protocol (The Hang-Up Rule)

This is the ultimate psychological defense, as it takes the interaction completely out of the attacker's control and removes the weapon of live social pressure.

The Absolute Mandate: Any unsolicited, high-stakes request, a password reset, a wire transfer, a physical access grant, coming via any unverified channel (phone, email, text) **must be immediately terminated and re-initiated by the employee through a pre-verified, trusted, independent channel.**

The Milgram Reset: The social engineer thrives on the same dynamic that made the Milgram experiments terrifying: the live, interacting authority figure exerts irrational pressure. The moment the target hangs up, they regain autonomy. When they call back using the verified number from the company directory, they move the interaction to a secure stage where the attacker's pretext cannot exist.

Operational Requirements:

1. **The Policy-Over-Person Script:** Employees must be taught to use the policy as a shield. The refusal must sound like this: *"I am truly sorry, but my security mandate requires me to disconnect now and call you back using the official switchboard number on our directory. It's a non-negotiable step for any urgent action."* This protects the employee's social comfort by blaming the policy, not the person.
2. **Universal Application:** This protocol must apply to **everyone**, including the CEO and the highest-ranking executives. A policy exception for authority figures is a signed permission slip for Whaling attacks. The policy must state explicitly that any person, regardless of title, who resists OOB verification is violating company protocol and must be treated as suspicious.

Pillar 2: The Need-to-Know Principle (The Information Lock)

This hardens the individual's conversational defenses against OSINT-backed pretexts, starving the attacker of critical confirmation details.

The Absolute Mandate: Never volunteer any specific, proprietary, or confirmatory information to an unverified party. Assume any specific detail offered by a stranger is a test of your legitimacy, not a sign of theirs.

The Confirmation Bias Reversal: Attackers drop in specific OSINT details (e.g., "I see you're working on the 'Phoenix' project rollout") hoping the target's instinct to be helpful will lead them to confirm the detail and offer more. The "Need-to-Know" principle trains the employee to treat these details as red flags.

Operational Requirements:

1. **The Reverse Challenge:** Train employees to respond to specific claims with unanswerable questions. If the attacker mentions "Project Phoenix," the target should ask: *"Which external consulting firm handles the database integration for that project?"* A legitimate insider will know; an attacker relying on surface-level OSINT will falter, revealing the fraud.

2. **Militant Clean Desk Policy:** The **Clean Desk, Clean Screen** mandate must be aggressively enforced. Sticky notes, passwords, internal organizational charts, and calendar printouts are digital leakage in physical form. Removing this fertile ground prevents attackers from using visual intelligence to build or confirm a pretext during physical security tests.

Pillar 3: The Zero Tolerance for Policy Violation (The Refusal Protocol)

This addresses the exploitation of social norms like **Reciprocity** and **Liking** by removing the emotional gray zone from security.

The Absolute Mandate: A request for a policy violation, sharing credentials, allowing tailgating, or clicking a link, is the single most important, non-negotiable red flag. The request itself is the security failure, regardless of the justification.

Neutralizing Reciprocity: This protocol forces a binary choice, preventing the social engineer from exploiting a small favor (like holding a door open) to demand a large security violation. The employee must be conditioned to feel more fear of the policy violation than discomfort from the social refusal.

Operational Requirements:

1. **Refusing the Small Favor:** Employees must be trained to let the door close on the "colleague" who needs to be swiped in because their hands are full. The *One-Swipe Rule* is absolute. They must be comfortable prioritizing the non-negotiable policy over social pleasantry.
2. **The Mandatory Report:** Any request to violate policy must immediately trigger a security report. This weaponizes the policy violation itself. The attacker's demand for a security shortcut becomes the automatic tripwire for their own detection.

Section III: Combat Readiness: Active Conditioning and Gamification

The protocols are only as good as the conditioning behind them. This requires moving training from the classroom into simulated combat scenarios.

1. The Multi-Vector Attack Architecture

Forget the amateur "gotcha" emails. Resilience training demands sophisticated, layered simulations that mimic real, professional criminal operations:

- **High-Fidelity Phishing:** These must be customized, using real OSINT (internal jargon, recent company events) and deployed with the specific psychological triggers discussed (e.g., an email from the "HR Director" threatening a compliance freeze, leveraging Authority and Scarcity).
- **Controlled Vishing Exercises:** This is where the reflex is truly forged. Security teams must cold-call employees with high-pressure, emotional pretexts designed to induce the full stress load. The metric is not whether they failed, but **Time to Protocol Execution**, how quickly they hung up and executed the OOB rule.
- **Physical Pretexting Drills:** Internal teams or external partners attempt to bypass physical controls (tailgating, fake badges, pretexting at reception). The goal is to measure the consistent execution of the "One-Swipe Rule" and the physical "Need-to-Know" refusal.

2. The Non-Punitive Feedback Loop: You Learn by Doing

The most important element of conditioning is the response to failure. When an employee clicks a link or fails to hang up, the feedback must be immediate, non-punitive, and focused entirely on behavioral correction.

- **Psychological Safety is Paramount:** The reaction must be: *"The criminal failed, and you helped us learn a weakness. Now, let's fix the muscle memory."* This narrative removes the fear and shame that causes employees to hide or delay reporting failures.
- **The Instant Drill:** An employee who fails a Vishing test must immediately participate in a 60-second role-playing drill to practice the Hang-Up Script. This immediate, focused repetition replaces the faulty compliance behavior with the correct security reflex, the core of behavioral conditioning.

3. Gamification: Rewarding the Right Behavior

Security should be associated with positive reinforcement, not just bureaucracy. We appeal to **Operant Conditioning** by rewarding the successful execution of security protocols.

- **Reward the Reporters:** Implement a system that visibly rewards employees who successfully report malicious activity, resist Vishing attempts, or correctly execute the OOB protocol during a drill. Public recognition, raffles, or small bonuses for proactive defense transforms compliance from a chore into a valued professional skill.

- **Focus on Success:** Celebrate team-level success in reporting and adherence. This appeals to the natural human instinct for positive competition and social status, ensuring security is seen as a source of professional pride, not administrative burden.

Section IV: Policy Design: Aligning Security with Human Nature

The final layer of defense is ensuring that the security architecture itself works *with* human nature, not against it. If security is inconvenient, employees will find a way around it, a behavioral vulnerability the attacker is always ready to exploit.

1. Making the Secure Path the Fastest Path

The policy must eliminate friction that drives non-compliance. Tedious VPN logins, complicated file transfer systems, and slow password resets all incentivize workarounds that open the door to social engineering.

- **UX Security:** Security tools should be nearly invisible until they are absolutely needed. Use seamless Single Sign-On (SSO) and biometric authentication. Ensure Multi-Factor Authentication (MFA) is as frictionless as possible (e.g., simple app push notifications).
- **Friction Auditing:** Security teams must constantly audit processes under the **"Two Clicks vs. Ten" Rule**. If the legitimate, secure workflow takes ten steps, but the malicious action (clicking the link) takes two, the malicious action will win when urgency hits. The secure path must always be the most optimized path.

2. Strategic Friction: The Security Speed Bump

While non-essential friction must be removed, **strategic, intentional friction** must be introduced at moments of high risk. This friction is designed to neutralize the attacker's time constraint by forcing the employee to use System 2 at the very moment it is most critical.

- **The Transactional Pause:** For high-stakes actions, such as a large wire transfer, the system must enforce a mandatory delay where the user is forced to manually type a verification phrase: *"I have verbally verified this request with the recipient via a known, non-email channel."* This forces the cognitive pause necessary to stop the compliance reflex and retrieve the OOB protocol.

- **MFA Context Warning:** Configure MFA prompts to provide environmental context: *"Warning: This login attempt is coming from Hong Kong. If you are not in Hong Kong, do not approve."* This converts a simple button-push into a moment of critical security analysis, immediately exposing the Vishing attacker attempting a remote login.
- **Email Banner Enforcement:** Any email originating externally that attempts to spoof an internal name (like the CEO's) must be branded with a massive, non-removable warning banner: **[EXTERNAL SENDER: PROCEED WITH EXTREME CAUTION]**. This simple visual speed bump forces System 2 engagement.

3. Hardening the Apex Target: Executive Friction

For high-value targets, friction must be woven directly into critical business processes. The **Mandatory Two-Key Protocol** for large financial transactions is the ultimate friction, legally requiring a second, independent party using an OOB channel. This structure means an attacker's demand for secrecy and urgency is instantly non-compliant with the law, not just policy. Executive Assistants, who often act as the primary operational targets in Whaling attacks, must be elevated to **Critical Defense Sensors** and receive the most intense stress inoculation training available.

Conclusion: The Human Firewall as an Active, Living Defense

The ultimate defense against Social Engineering is not found in code, but in the transformation of organizational policy into muscle memory. The Human Firewall is hardened when every employee, from the newest hire to the oldest veteran, reflexively executes a non-negotiable protocol the moment the universal triggers of urgency, authority, or scarcity appear.

This requires abandoning the passive hope that employees will remember the rules, and embracing the active discipline of behavioral conditioning and stress inoculation. When the "Hang-Up Rule" becomes as ingrained as a fire drill, when the reflex is faster than the thought, the attacker's elaborate, psychological ruse loses all power. The deception collapses because the conditioned audience automatically demands the validated receipt first, every single time. The policy stops being a binder on a shelf and becomes the unbreakable shield, ensuring that our natural human decency can never again be weaponized against the infrastructure it is meant to defend.

CONCLUSION

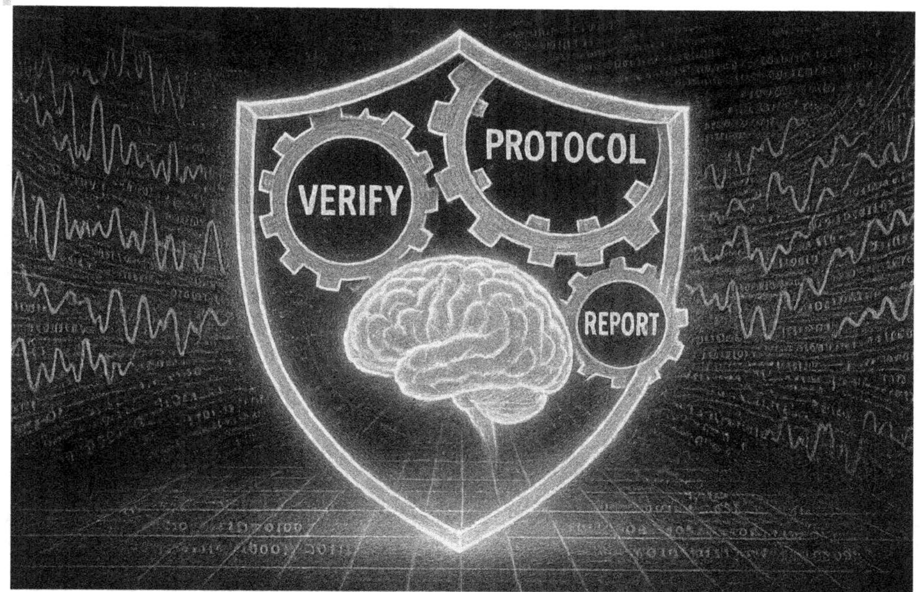

The Final Synthesis: From Vulnerability to Vector

We have walked the entire path of the social engineer, and the landscape is now painfully clear. From the seemingly innocent digital footprints left scattered across the web (OSINT) to the constructed reality of the Pretext; from the application of psychological pressure (Urgency, Authority, Scarcity) to the final, simple act of compliance. The attack is elegant, cheap, and devastatingly effective because it targets the one system that can never be fully patched: human nature itself.

The billions spent on technical security, the firewalls, the encryption, the intrusion detection systems, are all rendered moot the moment an employee clicks an unverified link or gives away a password over the phone. Why? Because these technological defenses are designed to stop technical vectors, but the social engineer leverages a **behavioral vector**. They don't hack the machine; they hack the mind that uses the machine.

This entire book has been an exploration of one profound truth: **the attack vector is human compliance.** It is the desire to be a team player, to look professional, to obey the boss, and to solve an urgent problem that provides the ultimate, hidden backdoor. Now, as we close this section, our focus shifts entirely. We are moving from understanding the weakness to engineering a cultural strength. We are moving from a reactive defense based on fear to a proactive defense based on behavioral resilience. The goal is to build the **Resilient Organization**, where security is not a burdensome requirement imposed from the top, but an instinctive, collective defense mechanism woven into the fabric of daily work.

Section I: The Cultural Cornerstone: Psychological Safety

We learned in the previous chapter that the ultimate security defense is a trained human reflex, the Hang-Up Rule, the One-Swipe Rule. But these reflexes require fertile ground to grow. If the corporate culture is based on fear, punishment, and blame, no amount of training will succeed.

1. The Reporting Gap

The single largest facilitator of social engineering attacks is the **Reporting Gap**. When an employee realizes they have been compromised, they clicked the link, they almost gave the password, or they even fell for the Vishing call, their immediate, human instinct is to hide the mistake. Why? Because in a culture of blame, admitting failure carries a higher perceived cost (shame, reprimand, job loss) than the risk of the system eventually failing.

The attacker wins twice here: first, they exploit the employee's helpfulness; second, they exploit the employee's fear, buying themselves critical hours, sometimes days, before the incident is reported and response can begin.

The Resilient Mandate: Security must establish absolute **Psychological Safety**. The organization must aggressively communicate, from the executive level down, that failure during an attack is a learning moment, not a punishable offense. The messaging must be: *"The criminal is the one who failed, and you helped us learn where our defenses are weak. Thank you for reporting immediately."* This flips the psychological cost: the risk of **not** reporting must be viewed as far greater than the discomfort of admitting a mistake. Make reporting frictionless, anonymous if necessary, and consistently rewarded.

2. The Leadership Filter

Culture is not set in a training manual; it is demonstrated by leadership. If the CEO or the CFO insists on policy exceptions, if they demand that their executive assistant bypass the OOB Verification

Protocol for a "quick transaction", they are actively validating the attacker's approach. They are endorsing the idea that Authority trumps Security.

The Resilient Leader must be the Chief Security Advocate. They must openly, consistently, and proudly adhere to the protocols, even when inconvenient. When the CEO executes the Hang-Up Rule and calls back the verified switchboard number, that single action is more powerful than a hundred hours of training. Leadership compliance transforms the protocol from a bureaucratic rule into an absolute, sacred organizational standard.

Section II: The Zero-Trust Human: Verification as Default

In the world of network security, we now operate under the Zero-Trust principle: Never trust, always verify. The Resilient Organization must apply this same rigor to human interaction, both internal and external.

1. From Trust to Verification

Humans are predisposed to trust. We assume that the badge, the signature, or the familiar voice is legitimate. The social engineer exploits this. To harden the target, we must replace the instinct of *trust* with the instinct of *verification*.

The **OOB Verification Protocol** (The Hang-Up Rule) is the most powerful tool here because it is a physical and psychological shift. It does not require technical knowledge; it requires only the disciplined refusal to proceed on the channel initiated by the perceived attacker. It is the perfect implementation of Zero-Trust for the human layer:

- *Identity Verification:* I refuse the credentials you presented.
- *Channel Verification:* I will only communicate on a channel *I* initiate.
- *Intent Verification:* The system must now enforce the friction (The Transactional Pause) to confirm the high-stakes intent.

The organizational discipline requires making this OOB maneuver the absolute default. It should be as automatic as pressing 'Save' before closing a document.

2. Devaluing the Pretext: The Need-to-Know Weapon

The attacker builds their credibility by dropping in specific details gleaned from OSINT. This confirms their legitimacy in the target's mind. The **Need-to-Know Principle** acts as a counter-intelligence measure, making the target actively *refuse* to confirm the attacker's data.

The human defense here is not denial, but redirection. The employee uses the attacker's own specific details as a weapon, forcing the attacker off-script and demanding deeper, non-public details. This turns the helpful, compliant human into an aggressive, yet professional, gatekeeper, quickly exposing the shallow OSINT data the attacker is relying on. The attacker's confidence, built on their initial intelligence, immediately dissolves when they encounter unexpected resistance and demand for depth.

Section III: The Next Battlefield: Adapting to the AI Threat

The threat landscape is changing, not because human psychology is changing, it won't, but because the attacker's tools are becoming exponentially more sophisticated and cheaper. The arrival of generative AI marks the beginning of Social Engineering 2.0.

1. AI-Powered Pretexts and Vishing 2.0

The AI revolution democratizes sophistication. We are now facing:

- **Automated OSINT:** AI can process vast amounts of public data (corporate reports, social media posts, news articles) to generate highly personalized pretexts faster than any human operator.
- **Deepfake Vishing:** Synthetic voices can now mimic any executive or critical team member with startling accuracy and deploy emotional inflections on demand. The question is no longer "is the voice real?" but "is the channel verified?"
- **Adaptive Chatbots:** Phishing emails will evolve into personalized, multi-turn chat sessions where the bot adapts its pretext in real-time, leveraging specific information about the employee's role, recent projects, and even their tone.

The core of the attack remains the same, Urgency and Authority, but the execution is now flawless. The attacker no longer stumbles over jargon or hesitates under pressure.

2. Why Behavioral Defense Endures

The ultimate irony is that as the technology on the offense side becomes near-perfect, the defense must become purely human. AI can generate a perfect voice mimic, but it cannot violate the non-negotiable **OOB Protocol** and survive.

When the deepfake voice of the CEO calls, the employee who has been properly conditioned does not waste time analyzing the timbre or the accent. They hear the psychological trigger (Urgency/Authority) and immediately execute the reflex: *"I am sorry, but I am required to hang up now and call you back on the official, published line."*

The defense is no longer about detecting the fake; it's about **enforcing the protocol.** The only thing that cannot be faked is the integrity of the independently verified communication channel.

Section IV: The Final Mandate: The Ethics of the Shield

Our study of social engineering is not just a technical exercise; it is an ethical one. The criminals we study exploit the most positive aspects of human nature: helpfulness, empathy, respect for authority, and the drive to do a good job.

The mandate for the security professional is to build a shield that protects these very human qualities. We are not hardening targets to make them cynical or suspicious of everyone; we are hardening them to be **discerning**, providing them with the professional tools to protect their organization while remaining good colleagues, good citizens, and helpful professionals.

The defense must be comprehensive, continuous, and compassionate:

- **Continuous Conditioning:** Treat security like a high-performance athletic discipline. Drills must be frequent, targeted, and progressively challenging. Security training is not an event; it is a permanent state of readiness.
- **Strategic Friction:** Use technology to deploy speed bumps at high-risk junctures (wire transfers, critical access). These pauses force System 2 thinking, neutralizing the attacker's greatest weapon: time pressure.
- **Positive Culture:** Reward the protocol, not the outcome. Celebrate the reports, celebrate the hang-ups, and celebrate the refusals. Make security synonymous with professional excellence.

The Resilient Organization recognizes that the human mind is the most complex, most valuable, and most vulnerable asset it possesses. By moving security beyond awareness and embedding it as an instinctual, non-negotiable, and culturally supported reflex, we finally construct a defense worthy of the threats we face. We turn the human firewall into a self-repairing, active, living defense system.

REFLECTION QUESTIONS

Section I: Deconstructing the Pretext: Hacking Your Own Information Landscape

The social engineer's first step is intelligence gathering. They don't need a vulnerability; they need a story. This section challenges you to look at your organization's public face, and your own, through the eyes of the attacker.

1. **The OSINT Audit Challenge:** Dedicate an hour to running OSINT searches on your organization and your senior leadership (using only public, unauthenticated tools). What non-sensitive but highly exploitable details did you discover? (e.g., the CEO's dog's name, recent vacation photos, internal project code names mentioned in a job listing, the exact time the delivery truck arrives). How could an attacker weave these four distinct details into a high-fidelity Vishing pretext demanding a financial transfer? Write the opening paragraph of that Vishing script.
2. **The Reverse Challenge Test:** If an attacker calls your department and opens with a specific, legitimate-sounding detail (e.g., "I'm calling about the status of the Project Chimera quarterly report, which I believe is running late"), design three

sequential questions that you could ask that would force a fraudster, who only has surface-level information, to stumble or reveal their lack of true depth. These questions must only require information that a true insider would know instinctively.

3. **Physical Weakness Map:** Walk through your office space, public areas, and loading docks as if you were a physical social engineer. What are the points of highest vulnerability where the **One-Swipe Rule** is consistently broken? Identify the three most common items left on desks or screens that violate the **Clean Desk Policy** (e.g., sticky notes, calendars, passwords under keyboards). If you found a calendar showing a senior executive's travel schedule, how would you use that scarcity of time to justify an urgent, out-of-protocol request?
4. **Jargon and Lingo Leakage:** Review your last two job postings or marketing brochures. What highly specific, internal jargon or unique departmental names are used? Could an attacker use this lingo to craft a seemingly legitimate, high-authority email that tricks an HR person into granting access, based purely on sounding like they belong? Outline a scenario where technical jargon is the sole key to a successful phishing attack.

Section II: The Psychological Tripwire: Neutralizing Urgency and Authority

The attack is successful when System 1 takes over. These questions force you to analyze the moments of highest cognitive load and design the protocols that neutralize the emotional pressure.

1. **The Authority Test:** Identify the three people in your organization whose names or titles would cause the quickest, most irrational compliance from your team (e.g., the Global Head of IT, the CEO, an external auditor). Now, craft a hypothetical email from one of them that invokes extreme urgency ("I am stuck in a mandatory meeting...") and a direct request to bypass the standard protocol ("...so I need you to reset this password now, no questions asked"). What is the employee's first, instinctive reaction, and what **specific words** must be trained into them to immediately trigger the **OOB Verification Protocol** instead?

2. **The Reciprocity Trap:** Think of a simple, helpful act someone could do for you near the office entrance (e.g., carrying a heavy box, holding a door while you fumble for a coffee). How quickly could that small gesture of **Reciprocity** be leveraged to ask you to break the **One-Swipe Rule**? If a stranger asks you to swipe them in, what is your prepared, professional, non-confrontational refusal script that blames the unbreakable policy, not the person?
3. **The Time-Pressure Audit:** Review a high-stakes, legitimate operational workflow in your company (e.g., adding a new vendor to the payment system or approving a large purchase). How long does this legitimate process take? If an attacker can complete a malicious version of that task in less than 30 minutes via a social engineering exploit, what is the **strategic friction** you could add to the legitimate process (a mandatory manual input, an intentional pause) to slow it down and force an internal check?
4. **Analyzing the 'Ask':** When an attacker initiates contact, their goal is to lead the target to a single "Ask" (click the link, reset the password, wire the money). In a simulated Vishing scenario, at what exact moment during the call does the social engineer shift from building the pretext to delivering the "Ask"? How does recognizing that shift, the moment the script moves from storytelling to demand, become the employee's final, crucial defense signal before compliance?

Section III: Forging the Reflex: Protocol and Conditioning

This section moves into the practical application of the behavioral defense architecture, assessing how successfully your organization is moving from theoretical knowledge to active, conditioned response.

1. **Friction Auditing:** Identify one security feature in your environment that is so cumbersome (e.g., a slow VPN, a complex MFA process, a difficult secure file transfer) that employees are known to cheat or bypass it. How much time and money would it cost to fix the *inconvenience* versus the cost of a single breach facilitated by that workaround? Propose a **UX Security** improvement that makes the secure path the easiest path.
2. **The Failure Drill Design:** If an employee fails a simulated phishing attack (they click the link), design the immediate, non-punitive corrective action. This cannot be a meeting or a new

test. It must be a mandatory, 60-second, focused drill that requires the employee to role-play the correct **Refusal Protocol** with a supervisor. What specific language must the supervisor use to ensure the employee feels psychological safety during the drill?

3. **Policy vs. Reality:** Find one security policy in your organization that you suspect is almost universally ignored (e.g., not sharing accounts, reporting all unusual activity). Why is it ignored? Is the policy unclear, inconvenient, or is there no cultural consequence for its violation? How can the enforcement of this single policy be transformed into a positive, **Gamified** reward system instead of a punitive measure?
4. **The Executive Isolation Challenge:** The executive assistant (EA) is often the most critical point of defense in a Whaling attack. Design a one-week specialized training program for EAs that focuses solely on the **Mandatory Two-Key Protocol** and **OOB Verification**. What stressors would you introduce (e.g., simulated phone calls from a "Board Member" insisting on secrecy) to ensure they are hardened against the unique, high-stakes pressure aimed at them?

The goal of these reflection questions is to transform the abstract concept of the "human firewall" into a concrete set of actions. The attack is relentless; your defense must be disciplined, reflexive, and cultural.

BOOK THREE

DARK TRIAD TACTICS: PROFILING, PREDICTING, AND NEUTRALIZING PREDATORY PERSONALITIES

INTRODUCTION

Profiling the Predator

In the preceding volume, we meticulously dissected the art of social engineering. We studied the levers of influence, Authority, Urgency, Scarcity, as external tools used to bypass the human firewall. We concluded that the attack vector is simply human compliance, and the defense lies in conditioned, reflexive adherence to protocol.

Now, we shift our focus from the *how* to the *who*. We move beyond the transactional social engineer, the one-off criminal using a temporary pretext, to analyze the **predatory personality**; the individual for whom manipulation is not a tactic, but a default state of being.

These are the architects of long-term, systemic exploitation, whether in a high-stakes corporate environment, a sensitive government agency, or a deceptively quiet interpersonal relationship. Their threat is not a single point of failure (a clicked link); it is the slow, deliberate erosion of trust, competence, and organizational structure designed to serve their singular, self-centered agenda.

This book is your field manual for identifying, predicting, and neutralizing the behavioral patterns of the **Dark Triad**.

The Unholy Trinity: Narcissism, Machiavellianism, and Psychopathy

The concept of the Dark Triad consolidates three distinct, yet interrelated, personality traits that share a core characteristic: a callous, manipulative approach to social interaction coupled with an unwavering focus on self-interest. It is critical to understand that we are not discussing clinical diagnoses, but rather **subclinical personality dimensions**, patterns of behavior that exist on a spectrum and are surprisingly common in professional settings where charisma, boldness, and ruthlessness are often mistaken for leadership.

We will explore each component in detail, but they can be briefly summarized as follows:

1. **Narcissism:** Defined by grandiosity, excessive need for admiration, and a profound sense of entitlement. The narcissist's primary goal is validation and status.
2. **Machiavellianism:** Defined by cynicism, strategic exploitation, and a cold indifference to morality. The Machiavellian's primary goal is power and transactional gain.
3. **Psychopathy:** Defined by a pervasive lack of empathy, impulsivity, and emotional detachment. The psychopath's primary goal is stimulation and immediate, often reckless, control.

These three traits rarely appear in pure form. Most predatory personalities blend elements of the triad, using their grandiose confidence (Narcissism) to set a stage, their calculated planning (Machiavellianism) to execute the long game, and their emotional detachment (Psychopathy) to discard obstacles without remorse.

The Predictive Power of Profiling

Why is profiling these traits essential to security and resilience? Because the personality defines the *pattern* of the attack, and patterns are inherently predictable.

If the threat in Book 2 was a virus that needed a firewall, the threat in Book 3 is a known intruder whose habits, weaknesses, and predictable entry points are cataloged.

- A **Narcissist** is vulnerable to ego validation and will often sacrifice security protocols if it grants them public acknowledgment or prestige. They attack to elevate status. Your defense must target their need for control and their fear of shame.

- A **Machiavellian** operates purely on calculation. They attack with a defined strategy to extract maximum transactional value. Your defense must focus on disrupting their plan's sequence and making the manipulation costly or inconvenient.
- A **Psychopath** operates with emotional indifference. They attack for the sport of control and lack the capacity for remorse. Your defense must be absolute, rigid, and based on objective boundaries, as attempts at emotional appeal or reason are futile.

Understanding these psychological blueprints allows you to shift from a generalized, reactive defense to a highly targeted, proactive prediction: *"Given this personality type, what is their most probable next move, and what is the single greatest risk they pose to our integrity?"*

The Scope of the Threat: Corporate and Personal Vectors

It is crucial to shed the popular misconception that these traits are confined to high-profile criminals. They thrive wherever hierarchy and opportunity exist:

- **The Corporate Vector:** This is the manipulative manager who isolates rivals, steals credit, and systematically undermines departmental stability to climb the ladder. They use organizational structure as their playing field, weaponizing office politics and information control.
- **The Professional Vector:** This is the transactional colleague, the cutthroat competitor, or the unethical vendor who views every interaction as a zero-sum game, prioritizing their own gain over contractual obligation or ethical conduct.
- **The Personal Vector:** While this book focuses on organizational resilience, the fundamental tactics apply equally to personal relationships, where the triad uses manipulation to achieve emotional, social, or financial control.

The goal of the following chapters is to provide you with the behavioral markers, operational tactics, and neutralization strategies necessary to recognize these predatory patterns and build impenetrable shields against them, ensuring the integrity of your systems, your career, and your sanity. We begin by placing the grandiose mask under the microscope.

CHAPTER 1

NARCISSISM: THE GRANDIOSE MASK

The Grand Deception: Why the Mask Matters More Than the Man

Let's be honest: in the professional world, we've all met one. That colleague who seems to suck all the oxygen out of the room, whose confidence defies gravity, and whose narrative of success involves a series of minor miracles they alone orchestrated. We often shrug and call them "Type A" or maybe "a bit much." But when that personality lands within the Dark Triad spectrum, it stops being a quirky trait and starts being a corrosive organizational hazard. We're talking about the **Narcissist.**

In our analysis, we must first accept a paradox: the person who appears the strongest is, in fact, the most fragile. The Grandiose Mask isn't a face they wear for fun; it's a structural necessity, a meticulously crafted shell designed to protect an unbearably hollow core. This is not about arrogance; it's about survival. Narcissism, at its subclinical level, is a compensatory strategy. The **False Self**, that perfect, flawless, entitled version of themselves they present to the world, was created years ago to fill an existential deficit. And here's the kicker: that False Self requires constant, uninterrupted feeding.

This requirement, this metabolic need for attention and validation, what we call **Narcissistic Supply**, becomes the single most reliable predictor of their future behaviour. If you can predict where they will seek supply, and what they will do when that supply is threatened, you can predict their next move in the office, the boardroom, or the operational chain. They are not acting out of malice first; they are acting out of an absolute, panicked necessity to keep the mask glued firmly in place. They must control the narrative. If they can't, the whole flimsy structure collapses, and that's the one thing they will sacrifice anything, even organizational security or integrity, to prevent.

Section I: Following the Energy: The Supply Mandate

The typical defense against a predator is to focus on what they *take* (money, credit, power). But with the narcissist, the critical analysis must focus on what they *need* (supply). Everything they do, from picking a specific subordinate to starting an arbitrary conflict, can be traced back to securing one of three types of validation.

The Supply Grid: Fueling the False Self

Think of the Narcissistic Supply as electricity. They need it flowing 24/7, and they'll tap into any available line to get it.

1. **Primary Supply (The High Voltage):** This is pure, unadulterated adoration, praise, and status recognition. This is harvested via public acclaim, immediate compliance from a subordinate, or receiving an award. It's the instant, visceral rush of validation. They build environments, teams, offices, social circles, specifically designed to harvest this easy energy. You'll notice they thrive in roles that are high-visibility but sometimes low-depth; they'd rather give a brilliant presentation on a half-finished project than quietly execute the complex, necessary backend work.
2. **Secondary Supply (The Emergency Generator):** What happens when the praise stops? Panic. That's when they switch to secondary supply, which is attention secured through chaos, drama, or conflict. If they can't be the hero, they'll absolutely settle for being the villain, or, better yet, the beleaguered victim of an unfair system. Suddenly, they're starting ridiculous email threads, blowing up in a meeting over a minor detail, or

manufacturing a crisis simply because everyone's focus, even critical focus, is *attention*. They need the emotional turbulence to confirm they matter.

3. **Tertiary Supply (The Quiet Hum):** This is the low-grade, constant validation derived from control. It's the sheer knowledge that they can manipulate policy, keep a subordinate waiting, promote a favorite, or crush a critic just because they feel like it. It's the supply of unquestioned authority. It reinforces the fundamental belief: *I am above the rules, and you are below me.*

Entitlement: The Golden Child Protocol

This belief in inherent superiority isn't just arrogance; it's a bedrock assumption known as **Entitlement**. The narcissist truly believes they are the "Golden Child" of the universe, and therefore, deserve unlimited access and exemption from normal human friction.

Watch how they interact with rules. If a policy, say, a strict procurement process or a mandatory two-factor authentication, causes *them* inconvenience, they don't see the policy as a necessary guardrail. They see it as a personal affront. They will insist that, for *them*, the rules should be bypassed. "I'm the CEO, I don't have time for a stupid password token," or "Just send me the report, don't bother with the encryption protocol, it takes too long."

The Defense Pivot: This entitlement is a gaping vulnerability. When neutralizing a narcissist, you absolutely cannot rely on your personal authority or reason. You must use the authority of an **Impersonal, Immutable Force**. The conversation cannot be: "I can't let you bypass security, Dave." It must be: "The new global compliance audit mandates this OOB verification for everyone, without exception. It's an ISO standard. My access will be revoked if I deviate." You've shifted the blame for the friction away from you and onto a mountain too big for even their ego to climb.

Section II: The Tactical Playbook: Weaving the Workplace Trap

The narcissist is not usually the lone-wolf operator; they need a stage and a supporting cast. Their professional tactics are specifically designed to manage their environment by controlling perception and eliminating competition.

1. The Projection Missile: Blame Before Breakfast

The core operational weakness of the narcissist is their inability to accept fault. Doing so would crack the False Self, leading to a catastrophic emotional collapse. Therefore, failure, error, or inadequacy must be jettisoned immediately, and that payload is aimed at the nearest viable target. This is **Projection**.

You've probably seen the speed of it: the team misses a deadline due to the narcissist's poor resource allocation. Before the word "late" is out of the senior management's mouth, the narcissist has already initiated the counter-narrative: "Well, we would have been fine, but Sarah in Accounting clearly failed to get the numbers to us on time. She's been struggling lately."

The Creation of the Scapegoat: This isn't random. The target of the projection is often someone competent, someone morally upright, or someone emotionally sensitive. Why? Because the Scapegoat's good qualities are a subtle threat to the narcissist, and targeting them serves a dual purpose: it absolves the narcissist of blame *and* sidelines a potential rival. If you are consistently blamed for things you didn't do, you aren't dealing with simple workplace error; you are the victim of a predictive pattern.

2. Gaslighting Competence: Undermining the Objective Record

The Machiavellian gaslights to manipulate a quick deal; the narcissist gaslights to **maintain cognitive superiority**. They must constantly destabilize the self-confidence of those around them to ensure they remain the smartest, most reliable person in the room.

This is why they challenge verifiable reality: "I never said the budget was greenlit last week; you must have misunderstood me. We discussed it hypothetically." They are not trying to confuse you about the budget; they are trying to confuse you about your own memory and competence. They need you to doubt your reality, because if you doubt yourself, you won't challenge their narrative.

The Internal Cost: The result is **learned helplessness** in their subordinates. People stop making independent decisions, stop challenging flawed data, and stop voicing legitimate concerns because they know the reality they observe will be aggressively denied. This creates a deeply insecure operational environment where the narcissist's flawed, ego-driven decisions proceed unchallenged.

3. The Loyal Minions: Weaponizing the Flying Monkeys

Narcissists need foot soldiers. They need people who will defend them, spread their carefully crafted version of events, and isolate their targets. These are the **Flying Monkeys** or **Enablers.**

In the office, these minions are rarely paid specifically for this role. They are motivated by secondary gain: fear of being targeted themselves, a desperate hope for reflected glory, or a misplaced sense of loyalty cultivated through selective praise. The narcissist dangles the carrot, a promotion, public praise, exclusive access, and the minion eagerly performs the dirty work: spreading rumors, aggressively defending the narcissist in meetings, and reinforcing the toxic status quo.

The Counter-Tactic: Never confront the Flying Monkey directly about the narcissist. The monkey is an energy sink and a distraction. Your goal is always to **isolate the narcissist** by using objective, documented facts that force the monkey to choose between defending their boss's irrational demands and adhering to immutable, documented policy. If the monkey has to risk their own career to defend an indefensible action, the loyalty often breaks down.

4. Narcissistic Rage: The Panic Button

When the mask is truly threatened, when objective evidence of failure is undeniable, or when the False Self is humiliated in public, the narcissist doesn't get angry; they initiate a full-system panic known as **Narcissistic Rage**.

This rage is terrifying, disproportionate, and often seemingly random. It is not an emotion about the issue at hand (the late project, the accounting error). It is a primal, desperate attempt to destroy the source of the injury (the truth) and immediately shift the focus back to themselves. It's a calculated strategy disguised as a meltdown.

The Protocol for Rage: When rage is deployed, your System 1 instinct will be to defend yourself, rationalize, or appease. This is the mistake. When facing rage, your only goal is to disengage without providing supply. Use the **Neutral Deflection Script:** "I understand you are upset. However, I will not continue this conversation while you are yelling. We can discuss the expense report when you are ready to speak professionally." Then, walk away. The rage is an attempt to pull you into the chaos; refusing the chaos is refusing the supply. You must document the event immediately (date, time, exact quotes, witnesses), treating it as an HR conduct issue, not a personal fight.

Section III: The Narcissist in the Organizational Ecosystem

The threat of the narcissist isn't just to one person; it's to the entire operational environment. Their need for supply creates systemic failures and predictable vulnerabilities.

The Hiring Trap: The High-Gloss Sales Pitch

The corporate structure rewards the traits that allow narcissists to excel in interviews: superficial charm, confident talk, and the ability to spin past failures into heroic near-misses. They are masters of **Future Faking**: painting a breathtaking picture of the success they will bring, a success so glorious that the interviewer overlooks the lack of concrete, collaborative, verifiable past achievements.

They get promoted not because of competence but because of the intoxicating promise of their persona. They fill roles where their need for status is maximized: leadership roles, public-facing positions, or roles requiring aggressive salesmanship.

The Performance Gap: Once hired, the performance often follows a predictable arc: great in the first few months (when they are still building their audience and securing territory), but rapidly declining in areas requiring genuine teamwork, vulnerability, accountability, or sustained, deep-focus effort. They are fantastic at the splash, terrible at the plumbing. They will prioritize giving a high-profile, perfect presentation over ensuring the underlying data is accurate, because the presentation delivers Primary Supply; accurate data does not.

Weaponizing Information and Resources

In an organization, the narcissist sees resources not as tools for the mission, but as symbols of their status.

- **Resource Hoarding:** They claim the best budgets, the largest offices, the most talented staff, often leaving other mission-critical teams under-resourced. This reinforces their entitlement and ensures that any success achieved by their immediate team reflects solely on them.
- **Creating Dependence:** By intentionally **Information Hoarding**, withholding vital context, technical documentation, or historical knowledge, they force subordinates and peers to constantly come back to them for answers. This feeds the Tertiary Supply (control) and reinforces the organizational illusion that they are the sole, indispensable source of competence.

- **The Isolation Play:** To eliminate a competent, humble rival, the ultimate threat, the narcissist must first isolate them. This involves systematically cutting the rival off from organizational lifeblood: excluding them from key meetings, delaying their necessary approvals, and, most powerfully, planting subtle seeds of doubt with key superiors (the smear campaign). The goal isn't to fire the person, but to make their professional life so untenable that they quit, allowing the narcissist to declare a quiet victory against "someone who just wasn't a good fit."

The Corporate Cult of Personality

A mature narcissistic environment evolves into a **Cult of Personality**. The narcissist systematically promotes and rewards those who are the most effective **Flying Monkeys**, not the most competent employees. The criteria for success become:

1. How effectively do you praise and validate the narcissist?
2. How quickly do you accept and execute the narcissist's narrative of events?
3. How aggressively do you defend the narcissist against critics?

The result is a brittle, incompetent leadership layer underneath the narcissist, a group of enablers whose loyalty is high but whose operational skill is low. This structure creates significant, dangerous technical debt and operational risk that often only comes to light when the narcissist is finally removed, and the subsequent leadership is forced to manage the systemic failures they masked.

Section IV: Neutralization and Defense Protocols

Protecting yourself and your organization from a narcissistic predator isn't about winning an emotional argument; it's about winning a strategic, documented, and policy-driven war of attrition.

1. The Professional Gray Rock: Denying the Feast

The most powerful immediate defense is emotional detachment. The **Professional Gray Rock** policy treats the narcissist as a dull, uninteresting rock. They are looking for a show; you give them silence.

- **Implement Brevity:** Your responses must be short, factual, and strictly utilitarian. No adjectives, no emotion, no justification. "Understood. I will process the request when the verification form is attached."

- **Refuse Engagement:** When they start fishing for supply (bragging, complaining, or provoking), do not feed them. Redirect to the task: "That's interesting, but I need to circle back to the Q3 budget review. Can you confirm these numbers?"
- **The Power of Monotone:** When delivering necessary pushback or setting a boundary, use a flat, businesslike tone. They thrive on the drama of conflict; a neutral tone signals that this is merely a transaction, not a supply opportunity.

2. The Absolute Defense: Documentation and the Paper Trail

Because the narcissist relies entirely on controlling memory and perception (Gaslighting, Projection), your defense must rely entirely on objective, immutable documentation. **If it wasn't written down, it never happened.**

- **The Instant Follow-Up:** After *every* key verbal exchange (a decision, a commitment, a denial, a boundary set), immediately send a brief, factual email: "Per our 2:00 PM conversation, I am confirming that the scope change requires a two-day delay and that the responsibility for the Q2 delivery error now rests with the external vendor, as you decided." Use neutral language that pins down the facts and the responsibility.
- **Use the CC as a Firewall:** When the narcissist makes an unusual or high-risk request, always include a neutral third party (a team member, a legal representative, or HR) on the response, framing it as necessary oversight: "To ensure we maintain strict compliance with the new internal audit policy, I'm cc'ing Jane Doe on this request for verification." This forces the narcissist to either halt the manipulation or proceed knowing the documented request is now visible to others.
- **Objective Reporting to HR:** If formal reporting is necessary, remove all feeling. You are not reporting a hurtful person; you are reporting **documented policy violations** and **professional misconduct**. Use dates, times, quotes, and impact (e.g., "The client contact list was deleted at 11:05 AM, following my refusal to give him my password, resulting in 4 hours of lost productivity for the team").

3. Policy as the Unbreachable Wall

The narcissist cannot be managed by personal boundaries; they view boundaries as personal challenges to be overcome. They can only be managed by **Policy as Law**.

When you need to refuse a request, especially one that bypasses security or ethical protocol, your refusal must be systemic and non-negotiable:

- **Shift the Source of Conflict:** Never say, "I am unwilling to do that." Say, "The system is hard-coded to reject that transaction," or "I am prohibited by the legal compliance mandate from overriding this two-factor authentication."
- **Blame the System, Save the Self:** By blaming an external, immutable entity (Compliance, Audit, The System Itself), you satisfy the narcissist's need to find an external fault, while removing yourself as the source of their frustration. They may yell at the system, but they won't get supply from you.

Conclusion: The Vulnerability Beneath the Veneer

The narcissistic personality is an organizational risk because their desperate need for validation overrides all operational prudence, ethical standards, and long-term planning. Their grandiosity is a brittle shield; when it is threatened, they will launch a catastrophic, predictable counterattack (rage, projection, smear campaigns) to preserve the illusion.

Your professional defense requires a commitment to objectivity. You must refuse the role they assign you, whether that role is adoring audience or convenient scapegoat. By adhering to the **Professional Gray Rock** protocol and ensuring every transaction is captured on an undeniable, factual **Paper Trail**, you starve the narcissistic dynamic of its necessary emotional fuel. Once the emotion is removed and the facts are isolated, the grandiose mask loses its power, and the threat can be managed, contained, or removed based on objective organizational risk, not personal turmoil.

CHAPTER 2

MACHIAVELLIANISM: THE STRATEGIC PLAYER

The Quiet Threat: Why You Should Fear the Planner, Not the Prankster

We've just spent time dissecting the Narcissist, the high-octane drama queen who demands the spotlight. They're loud, they're fragile, and their motives are ultimately visible because they are driven by a need for attention. But if you're looking for the true danger to your organization's integrity, stability, and future, you need to turn your attention to the person who's never seeking the podium: the **Machiavellian.**

This is the strategic player. The one who views the entire corporate landscape, the people, the departments, the policies, even the CEO's dog, as a vast, interconnected chessboard. To the Machiavellian, nothing is personal, nothing is sacred, and nothing is real except the movement of pieces designed to maximize their own long-term **leverage and control.**

Look, the Machiavellian is often misdiagnosed. They don't explode in rage. They don't weep dramatically in the hallway. They don't need your validation. In fact, they might be quite charming, quite calm, and devastatingly effective. They often climb higher and cause deeper, more lasting damage than the Narcissist because their moves are rational, patient, and executed with emotional detachment. They simply don't care about the collateral damage, and their single governing principle is: **The outcome must benefit me, and all means required to secure that outcome are justified.**

This chapter is your deep dive into the mind of the strategic predator. We're moving from the study of personality flaw (Narcissism) to the study of **applied organizational strategy**. If you want to neutralize a Machiavellian, you must stop looking at *what* they're doing and start analyzing *why* they're doing it. Every single action is a transactional investment designed to yield power down the line.

Section I: The Cold Calculus of the Strategic Player

To understand the Machiavellian, we need to understand their core operating system. It's a beautifully simple, terrifyingly efficient machine built on three foundational beliefs about the world.

1. The Principle of Emotional Utility: A Voluntary Currency

Here's where we draw a hard line between the Machiavellian and the other members of the Dark Triad. The Psychopath struggles with empathy; the Narcissist has an unstable, demanding emotional life. The Machiavellian? They have **empathy on demand**.

They can be warm, kind, and supportive if, and only if, that emotional display is a **necessary expense** to secure a desired outcome. If they need to spend six months being your best friend to get access to a key proprietary system, they will execute that friendship flawlessly. The moment they get the access, or the moment you lose utility to their grand plan, the friendship evaporates.

This isn't betrayal driven by passion; it's a contract that has reached its expiration date. This ability to put on the 'poker face' of genuine sincerity while running a completely separate, ruthless internal calculus is their greatest weapon. They can lie effortlessly because they aren't emotionally invested in the truth, the relationship, or the outcome for anyone but themselves. When you interact with them, you're not dealing with a friend or a colleague; you're dealing with an actor whose performance is tailored to elicit a specific strategic response.

2. The Cynical Framework: Everyone's Playing the Game

The Machiavellian doesn't view their ruthlessness as a moral flaw. Quite the opposite. They genuinely believe that the world, especially the corporate world, is fundamentally hostile, opportunistic, and cynical. They look around and assume *everyone* is plotting, everyone is out for themselves, and everyone has a hidden agenda.

Their own self-serving manipulation, therefore, is simply self-defense. It's the only rational way to survive in a cutthroat environment. This belief system is important because it totally **immunizes them against guilt or moral constraint**. You can't appeal to their better nature because they don't believe they have one, nor do they believe *you* have one. They see your appeals to ethics as just another clumsy attempt at manipulation.

This cynicism is the source of their patience. They are never in a rush. They are waiting for the inevitable moment when the "good guy" gets distracted, when the policy breaks down, or when a moment of chaos reveals an opportunity. They thrive by exploiting the simple, human assumption that most people are operating in good faith. They are not.

3. The Time Horizon: Calculated Delay

We talk about the "long game," but we need to define it. A Narcissist's timeline is usually measured in weeks, centered around the next presentation or promotion. A Machiavellian's timeline is measured in **years**.

Their moves are rarely designed for an immediate payoff. They are building infrastructure. They are accumulating information, collecting favors, creating dependencies, and positioning proxies. They might spend a year being aggressively kind to a junior staff member in an unrelated department simply because they predict that person will be in a position of power or have access to vital data three years from now.

If you observe a Machiavellian's action and think, "That move seems totally random or unnecessary," you're almost certainly missing the four other, seemingly unrelated events that move is designed to connect down the road. You must learn to analyze their actions not just on the tactical map of the current quarter, but on the strategic map of the next decade.

Section II: The Tactical Playbook: Masters of the Political Environment

The Machiavellian's tools are not brute force or emotional leverage; they are subtlety, ambiguity, and information control. They don't attack the system head-on; they infect it from the inside, slowly changing the rules of engagement.

1. Strategic Ambiguity: Creating the Information Vacuum

The Machiavellian hates clarity. Defined roles, documented procedures, and transparent outcomes strip away their maneuvering room. They actively create **strategic ambiguity** to ensure deniability and flexibility.

- **The Unclear Mandate:** They will happily accept a vague assignment from a senior leader, then execute it in the way that maximally benefits them, later claiming, "Well, I was just following the spirit of the mandate, as I interpreted it." They are masters of the deliberately imprecise email or the purposefully confusing meeting summary that shifts focus away from the critical details.
- **Managing the Fog:** They excel at introducing just enough conflict or confusion into a situation, a sudden rumor, a budget inconsistency, a slight delay, to make everyone else focus on the immediate, secondary problem. While their rivals are fighting the fog, the Machiavellian is quietly seizing the actual strategic asset that the conflict was designed to obscure. It's misdirection, pure and simple.

2. Information as Weaponry: The Vault of Secrets

For the Machiavellian, information is not for sharing; it is for storing and weaponizing. They are obsessive information hoarders.

- **The Data Funnel:** They rarely trust shared platforms. They will push for data to be collected on their own local systems or managed by their own hand-picked administrator. They become the indispensable, sole source for key reports, historical data, or complex performance metrics. This forces everyone else to come to them, giving them control over what data is presented and how it is interpreted.
- **The Favor Economy:** The Machiavellian operates on a rigorous, internal ledger of favors. They will go out of their way to help someone with a low-stakes issue, a minor technical problem, a quick introduction, a small financial assist, not out of kindness, but to create a **debt**. When they need a big favor (a key vote, a

crucial piece of internal information, a cover-up), they call in the debt, knowing that human nature compels the recipient to repay it. They rarely give without expectation of a return.

3. The Human Shield Tactic: Proxies and Plausible Deniability

A defining characteristic of the Machiavellian is their absolute aversion to risk that lands on *them*. If there is a chance of failure, accountability, or public backlash, they will deploy a **Human Shield**.

- **The Fall Guy:** They deliberately delegate the riskiest part of a project, the part that involves bending a rule, dealing with a sketchy vendor, or handling political fallout, to a loyal, low-level subordinate. They provide the subordinate with just enough autonomy to execute the task, and just enough ambiguity in the instruction to deny involvement if things go sideways. "I told him to finalize the contract quickly; I had no idea he was cutting corners on compliance." The subordinate takes the career-ending blow, and the Machiavellian emerges as the disappointed, ethical manager who was betrayed by their own staff.
- **The Proxies for Power:** When the Machiavellian wants to push for a major internal policy change that benefits them, they rarely put their name on it. Instead, they strategically convince a well-liked, high-status person (often an unwitting Narcissist who loves the attention) to champion the idea. The proxy takes the heat and does the political heavy lifting, while the Machiavellian ensures the language in the final policy is precisely what they need. They achieve power by remote control.

Section III: The Machiavellian Scar: Organizational Decay

The sustained presence of a Machiavellian predator creates a profound, structural corrosion within the organization, attacking the very principles that lead to healthy, collaborative work.

Exploiting the Systemic Gaps

The Machiavellian isn't interested in making the rules; they are interested in understanding where the rules *stop*. They are forensic analysts of bureaucracy.

- **The Loophole Mastery:** They are constantly searching for points of friction where accountability is split or rules conflict. They know exactly how long the finance department takes to flag a questionable expense, what level of seniority is required to override a technical safeguard, and which external regulation supersedes an internal policy. They don't break the law; they find the **gaps** where the law is silent, and they build their strategy there. This is why their actions are often infuriatingly legal but profoundly unethical.

- **Process Paralysis:** When an organization realizes it has been manipulated by a Machiavellian, say, funds were diverted via a vague consulting contract, the institutional response is almost always to add more process, more forms, and more signatures. This, however, is a victory for the Machiavellian. Complexity and bureaucracy are their natural habitat. They simply learn the new rules faster than anyone else, exploiting the confusion while ethical actors are drowned in paperwork.

The Erosion of Meritocracy and Trust

This is the Machiavellian's most destructive long-term impact. They fundamentally ruin the culture of trust.

- **The Zero-Sum Game:** They treat every interaction as a **zero-sum game**, for me to win, you must lose. This spreads quickly. When employees observe that political calculation is rewarded more than competence (e.g., the Machiavellian's loyal, but mediocre, ally gets the promotion over the high-performing, ethical rival), people stop trusting the organization's stated values. They realize the only way to get ahead is to adopt cynical, self-serving, and often Machiavellian tactics themselves.
- **The Culture of Covertness:** When trust is gone, collaboration dies. Teams stop sharing critical information for fear it will be used against them. People hoard knowledge as a form of job security. The organization becomes Balkanized, with every department, and sometimes every individual, operating as an isolated, suspicious silo. This is catastrophic for efficiency, innovation, and, critically, security. A system where nobody trusts anyone else is a system that can be easily infiltrated and controlled by the one person who understands how to play the distrust game best.

The Impunity of the Disinterested

Because the Machiavellian operates with such chilling detachment, they often survive purges and political upheavals that would destroy an emotional player. They are never caught in an *argument*; they are never caught in a *fit of rage*. They are only caught with *data*.

And when they are confronted with objective evidence, their defensive technique is masterful: **calculated denial, confusion, and feigned offense.** They will respond with logic, not emotion, often shifting the focus back to the process or the incompetence of the accuser. "I'm genuinely confused as to why you're making this sound personal. This was a standard procedural decision, and frankly, I find the tone of your accusation unprofessional." They weaponize the very idea of professional conduct to deflect scrutiny from their misconduct.

Section IV: Neutralization and Defense Protocols

Fighting the strategic player requires abandoning the idea of emotional fairness and embracing a defense built on structure, transparency, and administrative cost. You must make their game too expensive and too visible to play.

1. The Principle of Process Immutability

You must introduce **friction** at every point the Machiavellian seeks flexibility. Since they only respect strength and logic, your defense must be logical, rigid, and automated.

- **Audit-Proofing the System:** Every critical workflow, procurement, information access, budget transfers, and hiring, must be designed with an objective, verifiable audit trail that is *automatically generated* by the system, not manually compiled. The system must force compliance.
- **Decentralizing Authority:** Never allow a single person to control both the budget and the data surrounding that budget. Decision-making authority must be split and separated across multiple parties. The Machiavellian excels at controlling a funnel; the defense is to destroy the funnel and create a distributed network of required approvals.
- **Mandatory Clarity:** When receiving any ambiguous instruction from a Machiavellian, you must force clarity and documentation. Your response: *"To ensure there are no processing errors, I need to confirm: are you asking me to submit the document using the standard Process A, or are you requesting the special override Process B, and if Process B, please supply the mandatory sign-off from Legal, per policy 4.1.2."* You have forced them to commit to a specific, auditable process, which exposes them.

2. The Transparent Network: Exposing the Ledger

The Machiavellian's greatest weakness is that their schemes require **secrecy**. Your job is to make all necessary professional interactions public, transparent, and documented.

- **Mandatory Project Visibility:** All key strategic data and project status updates must be managed in a shared, read-only system visible to all relevant stakeholders. No key information should exist only in a single person's email inbox or on their personal hard drive.
- **The Universal CC/BCC Policy:** For any communication related to resource allocation, budget approval, or political maneuvering, maintain a consistent practice of copying or blind-copying a neutral, administrative third party (e.g., a shared administrative email account or a dedicated legal folder). This is not about tattling; it's about establishing an undeniable **witness** to the transaction.
- **Focus on the Discrepancy, Not the Motive:** When confronting a Machiavellian with their own actions, never talk about their cynicism or their moral choices. Talk only about the discrepancy between the stated policy and the action taken. *"The purchase order shows a single bid was accepted, but the policy mandates three. Can you explain the discrepancy, citing the specific exemption policy used?"* You keep the conversation objective, factual, and draining.

3. Building an Antidote Culture

The most resilient defense is a culture that actively punishes the Machiavellian's methods and rewards transparency.

- **Reward Transparency:** Make public, explicit rewards for teams that prioritize process adherence, open documentation, and the early reporting of mistakes. This directly counters the Machiavellian's strategy of hoarding information and punishing perceived weakness.
- **Validate the Whistleblower:** Create ironclad, non-retaliatory processes for reporting systemic exploitation. When a loyal employee who was previously a Human Shield finally reports the Machiavellian, they must be rewarded, protected, and their information must be acted upon swiftly. If the organization is seen to tolerate this behavior, the culture is already lost.

- **Hire for Humility:** The best long-term filter against the Machiavellian is during the hiring process. Look for candidates who can articulate their failures without immediately shifting blame, who give credit generously, and who demonstrate a genuine, non-transactional interest in the success of the wider team. Test for process adherence over political agility.

Conclusion: The Vulnerability of Calculation

The Machiavellian is a calculating machine, and like all machines, they are predictable once you understand their programming. Their reliance on secrecy, ambiguity, and the exploitation of human trust is their central point of failure.

You don't need to defeat them with emotion or confrontation; you need to defeat them with **infrastructure**. By creating a professional environment defined by rigid, automated processes, compulsory transparency, and decentralized authority, you deny the Machiavellian the playing field they need. You force their long-term, subtle strategies into the high-friction, visible spotlight of objective policy, where their ruthlessness can be documented, their motives exposed, and their ability to operate without accountability finally halted.

CHAPTER 3

PSYCHOPATHY: THE EMPATHY VOID

The Ice Core: What Happens When the Human Operating System Fails

We've navigated the theatrical stage of the Narcissist and mapped the calculated chess board of the Machiavellian. Now, we confront the deepest, darkest structural threat in the Triad: the **Psychopath**.

If you take only one lesson from this entire book, let it be this: When dealing with a psychopathic personality, you must immediately abandon the framework of normal human reciprocity. You are not dealing with someone who has a *flawed* conscience; you are dealing with someone who has **no conscience at all**.

This is not a personality defect born of insecurity or a strategic choice driven by cynicism. Psychopathy is understood by most researchers to be a profound neurological difference. The areas of the brain that process fear, guilt, regret, and attachment, the very anchors that tether the rest of us to ethical behavior and social cooperation, simply do not activate in the same way.

Imagine a highly advanced computer running an operating system that lacks the basic moral safety drivers installed in every other unit. It can process information faster, lie more convincingly, and take enormous risks without the emotional processing lag (fear, guilt) that slows down a normal human decision-maker. That is the psychopathic advantage.

And that's why they are the most dangerous organizational predator.

Their motives aren't status (like the Narcissist, who needs you to clap) or long-term control (like the Machiavellian, who needs you to owe them a favor). The Psychopath is often driven by two things: **immediate gain** and **stimulation**. They crave the thrill of the risk, the exhilaration of manipulation, and the rush of getting away with the unforgivable.

When you encounter this profile, every rule changes. Your appeal to their humanity is useless. Your documentation of their past mistakes will be dismissed with a charming smile. Your only path to survival is immediate, surgical **isolation** and the complete systemic fortification of the environment they are attempting to exploit. You must treat them like a highly infectious, morally toxic agent.

Section I: Deconstructing the Empathy Void

The greatest deception the Psychopath employs is their ability to appear utterly normal, often charismatic, and sometimes even exceptionally competent. This is the **Mask of Sanity**, and it's a brilliant piece of theatre.

1. The Latchkey of Charm: Access Over Adoration

Unlike the Narcissist's charm, which is loud, peacocking, and seeks constant validation, the Psychopath's charm is *calibrated*. It's a precision tool designed to unlock specific targets. They don't need to be the center of attention; they need to be the person you trust with your secrets, your sensitive data, or your organizational keys.

They are masters of **mirroring**. If you are a thoughtful, quiet leader, they will present as your dedicated, reflective lieutenant. If you are a wild, risk-taking innovator, they will become your most fearless co-conspirator. They quickly identify the target's values, fears, and vulnerabilities, and then project the image that gains maximum intimacy and trust.

Why is this important? Because that trust is the Latchkey. It gives them entry to the C-suite, the finance department, or the sensitive IT server room. Once they are inside, the performance ends, and the exploitation begins. If you feel intensely understood, instantly connected, and deeply validated by a new colleague or executive who seems almost too good to be true, your defenses should go up, not down.

2. The Thirst for the Edge: Stimulation as a Driver

The Machiavellian runs on calculation; the Psychopath often runs on pure, raw adrenaline. Many studies point to a lower arousal level in psychopathic individuals, meaning they require more intense stimuli to feel 'normal' or engaged. They are chronically bored by routine, policy, and sustained, low-risk effort.

This translates into a professional craving for **high-stakes, high-risk scenarios**. They aren't interested in the quarterly report; they're interested in the illicit, secretive deal that could make (or break) the company.

- **Financial Recklessness:** They will approve massive expenditures without oversight, engage in questionable accounting practices, or initiate covert budget transfers just to feel the thrill of pushing the boundaries. It's the equivalent of driving 150 mph down a crowded road, the thrill is in the near-miss, not the destination.
- **The Chaos Dividend:** They often initiate workplace conflicts, spread vicious rumors, or sabotage processes just to observe the emotional turmoil of others. Seeing colleagues panic, cry, or spiral into confusion is, for them, a form of entertainment. They are playing with people's emotions as if they were toys, because they lack the internal mechanism to feel the corresponding distress.

Look for the pattern: where others see unacceptable risk, the Psychopath sees an exciting opportunity to test their perceived superiority. Their lack of fear is not a sign of competence; it's a sign of a dysfunctional neurological safety brake.

3. The Functional Lie: Zero Cost of Deceit

We all lie. But for most humans, lying carries an emotional burden: stress, guilt, and the fear of social consequence. For the Psychopath, the lie is functionally equivalent to the truth. It is simply a tool of efficiency.

If lying gets them access to a project faster, they will lie. If lying helps them evade accountability, they will lie. They lie not just to achieve big goals, but for petty, inconsequential things, simply because they can. The lie is delivered with perfect confidence, deep eye contact, and an unnerving calmness that convinces the target, precisely because the liar feels no internal conflict.

When dealing with a Narcissist, you argue the evidence. When dealing with a Machiavellian, you argue the policy. When dealing with a Psychopath, arguing the evidence or the policy is a **waste of time**. You must simply state the objective, documented fact and refuse to engage in the emotional debate they are attempting to trigger. Their defense against the truth is always a theatrical display of feigned offense or fabricated innocence, designed to leverage your sense of fairness against you.

Section II: The Signature Tactic: Use, Abuse, and Discard

The career path and relational history of a psychopathic individual follow a grimly predictable cycle. Since they cannot form genuine emotional bonds, their relationships are purely transactional, leading to a brutal, often career-ending pattern for their targets.

1. The Lifecycle of Exploitation

This cycle is the most reliable indicator of a psychopathic presence in your organization.

Phase 1: Idealization (The Infiltration): This is the period of **love bombing**. They target a resource (e.g., a mentor, a senior leader, a technical expert) and saturate them with attention, flattery, and feigned intimacy. They make the target feel indispensable, special, and uniquely chosen. This is the Latchkey in action, building rapid, artificial trust. *Example: They spend three hours a day praising the CFO's brilliance, telling them they are the only one who truly understands the company's vision.*

Phase 2: Exploitation (The Drain): Once the target's guard is down, the Psychopath begins the extraction of the resource. This might involve getting the target to bend rules, sign off on questionable documents, share sensitive access, or execute high-risk schemes. The Psychopath ensures the target is always one or two degrees closer to the illegality or policy breach, providing the necessary Human Shield. *Example: They use the CFO's access to set up an offshore shell account, with the CFO signing the authorizing paperwork under pressure.*

Phase 3: Devaluation (The Smear): The moment the Psychopath senses detection, or the moment the target is no longer useful, the switch flips. The love bombing turns instantly to ice. They become hostile, critical, and utterly dismissive. More importantly, they initiate a pre-emptive **Smear Campaign** against the target. *Example: Before the CFO even realizes the funds are gone, the Psychopath is anonymously telling HR that the CFO has a drinking problem and is incompetent, destroying their credibility before they can report the fraud.*

Phase 4: Discard (The Ghosting): The Psychopath detaches entirely and moves on to the next target, leaving a trail of chaos, confusion, and traumatized victims in their wake. They feel zero remorse for the career, the marriage, or the life they just shattered. The emotional wreckage is simply collateral damage in their ongoing pursuit of stimulation and gain.

2. The Uncanny Calm in the Eye of the Storm

When this cycle collapses into organizational crisis, the difference between the psychopathic actor and a normal employee is stark. A normal employee caught in a mistake will show fear, shame, or deep anxiety. The Psychopath will be unnervingly **calm, cool, and collected**.

This composure is not strength; it is the neurological absence of a fear response. While everyone else is panicking over an impending regulatory audit or a massive data breach, the Psychopath sees it as a fascinating intellectual puzzle they must solve. They will be the first to volunteer to lead the recovery effort, not out of responsibility, but because the high-stakes deception required to cover their tracks provides maximum stimulation.

Any organization that equates profound calmness during a catastrophic failure with effective leadership is setting itself up for exponential damage. It is a critical misdiagnosis that allows the predator to survive the initial triage.

Section III: The Catastrophic Liability: Organizational Exposure

The Machiavellian creates friction; the Psychopath creates **catastrophic liability**. Their unrestrained, risk-seeking behavior introduces legal, financial, and reputational exposures that can bankrupt or destroy an entire enterprise.

1. Financial and Fiduciary Black Holes

The Psychopath's willingness to commit high-risk, high-value fraud is unmatched in the Dark Triad. Because they feel no guilt, they have no internal brakes on the size or scope of their financial schemes.

- **Embezzlement and Asset Stripping:** They will systematically bleed resources from the company, not for luxury (though that's a byproduct), but because they have zero concept of fiduciary duty. They see company funds as an available resource pool for their immediate needs.
- **The Legal Time Bomb:** They are comfortable signing contracts they have no intention of honoring, making false promises to clients, or violating industry regulations if it secures a quick commission or a temporary win. The organization is left holding the bag when the fraud is exposed, facing criminal charges, massive fines, and irreversible reputational harm. The Psychopath, meanwhile, has moved on to the next company, leaving the legal mess behind.

2. The Cultural Annihilation

If a Machiavellian ruins trust, a Psychopath *traumatizes* the workforce. The damage done to the team they exploit is profound and often requires external intervention to heal.

- **Paralysis by Fear:** Once employees realize that a charming, high-status colleague has engaged in calculated, ruthless deception and emotional destruction without consequence, a deep, pervasive fear sets in. People stop innovating, stop taking risks, and retreat into minimal performance, terrified of becoming the next target in the use-and-discard cycle.
- **Contagion of Cynicism:** The organization's moral compass breaks. Employees who witnessed the Psychopath's successful rise and subsequent ruthless detachment come to believe that ethics are a joke and that ruthlessness is the only path to advancement. The corporate culture begins to mirror the predator, leading to mass ethical decline.
- **The Loss of Talent:** The best, most ethical, and most emotionally mature employees, the ones who value collaboration and trust, will exit the organization immediately upon recognizing the psychopathic dynamic. Only the enablers, the naïve, and the Machiavellian players remain, creating an incredibly toxic and unstable leadership pipeline.

3. The Grand Delusion of Immunity

The Psychopath rarely believes they will be caught. And if they are caught, they believe their charm, intelligence, and ability to weave a complex denial will get them out of it. This belief in their own superiority leads to a predictable overreach.

They will leave increasingly sloppy paper trails, take more transparent risks, and engage in more public acts of cruelty. This increasing recklessness is actually the key to their removal. Unlike the subtle Machiavellian, the Psychopath's eventual downfall is often dramatic and undeniable, precisely because they push the boundaries until the sheer weight of their objective actions becomes too obvious to ignore. The pattern of reckless risk-taking is, counter-intuitively, the most reliable indicator of their impending explosion.

Section IV: Neutralization and Survival Protocols

When dealing with a psychopathic personality, forget counseling, forget HR mediation, and forget appeal. Your only goal is to neutralize the threat by eliminating their access to resources and ensuring absolute accountability.

1. The Firebreak: Immediate, Total Isolation

Upon recognizing a high probability of psychopathy (based on the lack of conscience, pathological lying, and the use/discard cycle), your first, non-negotiable step is to build a firewall.

- **Systemic Lockout:** This must be immediate and total. Revoke all access to financial systems, proprietary data, internal servers, and executive communications. Do this neutrally, citing a *systemic review* or *mandatory security update*. Do not alert the Psychopath to the reason; alert the *system* to the threat.
- **Zero Personal Engagement:** If you are the target or the investigator, you must implement the **Absolute Gray Rock** protocol. Every conversation is a sterile, transactional exchange of facts. Do not make eye contact longer than necessary. Do not react to flattery or provocation. Speak only the minimum required. You must become emotionally invisible to them, denying them the stimulation and supply they crave.
- **Mandatory Witness Policy:** All necessary interactions, whether disciplinary, informational, or transactional, must occur in the presence of a neutral, documented witness (HR, Legal, or a security officer). Never allow yourself to be alone with them, as this gives them the opportunity for unverified threats, charm, or emotional manipulation.

2. The Forensic Documentation Strategy

You cannot trust the Psychopath's memory, their word, or their narrative. You must build an objective, undeniable case entirely on immutable records.

- **The Paper Chain:** Document every single interaction, decision, and claim. For every meeting, send an immediate follow-up email to the group (and BCC an auditor if necessary) stating the agreed-upon facts: "To confirm our 3:00 PM conversation, the responsibility for the Q2 budget overage was fully accepted by you, and you committed to filing the variance report by 9:00 AM tomorrow." This forces them to either accept the objective record or openly challenge it, creating a documented paper trail of their deceit.
- **Focus on the What, Not the Why:** Investigations must focus exclusively on **breaches of conduct** and **policy violations**. Don't waste time investigating their motives or intent—that's a psychological black hole. Focus on the hard facts: Did they use the company credit card for personal travel? Yes, receipt attached. Did they delete the client database? Yes, system log attached. Did they sign off on a contract they weren't authorized for? Yes, document attached.

3. The Non-Emotional Termination and Containment

The final act of removal must be executed with cold precision, minimizing all opportunity for retaliation or chaos.

- **The Legal Hammer:** The termination must be based on the objective conduct violations documented above. This gives the organization the maximum legal defensibility against a wrongful termination lawsuit, which the Psychopath will inevitably threaten.
- **The Swift Escort:** Do not give advance notice. Execute the termination on a Friday afternoon. Deliver the factual notice, revoke all digital and physical access immediately, and have a security or HR representative immediately escort them off the premises. The goal is to prevent them from having a window of time to engage in final sabotage (e.g., deleting servers, spreading final rumors).
- **Managing the Wake:** Prepare for the inevitable fallout. They will send vicious emails, make desperate phone calls, or threaten public exposure. Your official response to all internal and

external inquiries must be unified, brief, and legally vetted: *"This is a private personnel matter. We can only confirm that Mr./Ms. X is no longer employed by the company, and we have taken all necessary steps to secure our data and ensure continuity."* Absolute silence and structural unity are your only defense against their emotional warfare.

Conclusion: The Unavoidable Reality

The psychopathic personality is a structural flaw in the human network, and when inserted into an organization, they pose an existential threat that is impossible to manage through negotiation or appeal. They represent the ultimate test of an organization's structural integrity.

To survive the Ice Core, you must recognize that you are dealing with a predator unrestrained by conscience or empathy. Your strategy must shift from management to **containment**. By establishing immediate, ironclad physical and emotional boundaries, by relying solely on objective data and legal procedure, and by maintaining a total commitment to non-engagement, you remove their ability to manipulate. You force the Psychopath out of the shadows and into the sunlight of objective accountability, where their charm and their lies finally lose all power.

CHAPTER 4

THE FLAWS OF THE DARK TRIAD

The Inevitable Singularity: The Physics of Failure

If you've been following along, you now possess the uncomfortable, necessary knowledge. You can spot the hungry gaze of the Narcissist, you can hear the faint click of the ledger closing inside the Machiavellian, and you know how chillingly empty the core of the Psychopath truly is. You understand *how* they infiltrate and *why* they do what they do.

But here's the kicker, the single most reassuring truth about the Dark Triad that allows us to sleep at night and, more importantly, allows us to win: **Their success is inherently and mathematically unsustainable.**

I want you to stop thinking of these people as genius, untouchable super-villains. That narrative gives them too much power, and it's factually wrong. Look at the data. Look at the history of high-profile corporate scandals, political implosions, and sudden, career-ending implosions. Very rarely does a true Dark Triad personality—the aggressive, un-nuanced predator we've been describing—retire quietly to a beach house, celebrated and unchallenged.

Instead, they almost always trigger a crisis. They crash and burn. They trigger an administrative investigation. They are escorted out by security. They leave a wake of legal and financial destruction that takes years to clean up.

Why? Because the very tools they rely on for their rapid ascent—the charm, the ruthlessness, the lack of conscience—are not external, detachable accessories. They are **structural flaws** built directly into their operating system. Their greatest strength is simultaneously their greatest, most predictable weakness.

- The Narcissist's need for the spotlight gets them to the top, but it prevents them from building any actual network beneath them.
- The Machiavellian's cynical complexity allows them to operate in the shadows, but it leaves their entire scheme vulnerable to a single, procedural simplification.
- The Psychopath's fearless pursuit of risk allows them to break boundaries, but that same fearlessness ensures they will eventually break the law in a way that is utterly undeniable.

This chapter isn't about *waiting* for them to fail. That's reactive. This chapter is about **engineering the environment**—the administrative systems, the cultural norms, the documentation requirements—so that their natural, irresistible behavioral defaults trigger an accelerated, controlled collapse. We are going to turn their compulsions against them. We are not aiming to change them; we are aiming to leverage the immutable laws of organizational physics.

Section I: The Three Axes of Inherent Failure

To initiate the strategic neutralization, you must first accept that each predator has a unique, self-imposed liability that will eventually take them down.

1. The Narcissist: Weakness by Exposure (The Sandcastle Strategy)

If you picture a Narcissist's ego, don't picture a fortress. Picture an ornate, breathtakingly detailed sandcastle built right on the high-tide line. It is gorgeous, demanding adoration, but its entire existence is contingent on the world—the tide—never rising to challenge it. That need for constant, external affirmation is the **Exposure**.

This vulnerability creates two core structural weaknesses:

The Rigidity of the Glass-House Ego

The Narcissist *must* maintain the flawless image of themselves. They must be the most brilliant, the most ethical, the most indispensable. What does this rigidity prevent? It prevents them from doing the essential adaptive work of management: learning from mistakes, delegating control, admitting an error to a superior, or apologizing to a subordinate.

If admitting a $2 million mistake means they have to compromise their image as the "Financial Genius," they won't admit it. They will double down, conceal, and aggressively blame an external, weaker party. This avoidance of reality doesn't fix the problem; it simply ensures the initial $2 million problem metastasizes into a $20 million catastrophe. The need to protect the fragile ego always overrides rational decision-making, making them utterly predictable in their errors. They will consistently choose ego preservation over organizational safety.

The Black Hole of Supply

The attention, praise, and compliance they demand—the "supply"—is not just a nice bonus; it is the lifeblood that maintains their emotional stability. And it is, critically, *insatiable*. The organization, the team, the family eventually experiences **Supply Fatigue**. They are emotionally drained from feeding the beast.

When the organizational empathy is finally depleted, and the Narcissist's peers or subordinates stop providing the required validation, they enter a state of emotional starvation. This starvation triggers volatility, rage, and irrational behavior. The greatest tactical error the Narcissist makes is systematically alienating every single person who might have offered them a shred of mercy or support when their inevitable collapse arrives. They die alone, professionally speaking, because they demanded too much love and gave none.

2. The Machiavellian: Weakness by Complexity (The Over-Engineered Trap)

The Machiavellian is the great puppet master, seeing the world as a game of chess where everyone is a pawn. Their strength is their ability to control information and leverage ambiguity. Their weakness, however, is their **reliance on complexity**.

The Fragility of the Rube Goldberg Machine

Their scheme—the long game—is rarely simple. It requires a dozen steps: a series of vague emails, a policy interpretation loophole, a coerced subordinate, a hidden budget line, and a deliberately confusing org chart. The Machiavellian must constantly, actively manage this complexity.

The problem, of course, is that the more complicated the machine, the more points of failure exist. They are constantly juggling too many moving parts. A small, external administrative change—a new mandatory compliance tool, an external audit that simplifies a policy, or a new VP who insists on clear documentation—can disrupt one minor component. And when that one component fails, the entire, interconnected web of deniability begins to pull itself apart. They are undone by the sheer administrative weight of their own secrecy.

The Cynicism Feedback Loop

The Machiavellian's central tenet is that all relationships are purely transactional: fear, debt, or profit. There is no loyalty, only utility. They use this cynicism brilliantly to recruit proxies and enforce compliance.

But what happens when the external environment becomes dangerous—say, an investigation is launched? Suddenly, the utility of the alliance plummets. When the Machiavellian needs a loyal ally to lie for them or cover a track, they discover that every single person in their orbit is, shocker, only looking out for themselves. The cynicism they imposed on the world becomes the very logic that causes their allies to **defect immediately** to save their own careers. The master strategist is left uniquely, and coldly, exposed.

3. The Psychopath: Weakness by Overreach (The Broken Safety Brake)

The Psychopath's structural flaw is a simple, terrifying absence: the lack of the internal safety brake—fear, guilt, and the ability to process future consequences. Their advantage is their **Compulsion for Risk and Stimulation.**

The Inevitable Overreach

Because the Psychopath doesn't feel the mounting stress or anxiety that tells a normal person to stop before breaking the law, they will accelerate past every boundary. They will take exponentially increasing risks, transitioning from financial manipulation to outright criminal fraud, from policy violation to physical or legal intimidation.

They are driven by the *thrill* of getting away with it. This compulsion for high-stakes stimulation ensures they cannot stop themselves. They will push and push until they hit a wall that is non-negotiable—not a personal opinion, but a court, a regulator, or a massive, six-figure liability. This is the **Catastrophic Overreach**, and it is the single most predictable outcome of a long-term psychopathic presence.

The Inability to Learn from Consequence

When the Psychopath is caught, they don't experience the shame or remorse that leads to reform. They view the consequence as a technical failure: *My subordinates were sloppy; the auditors were too aggressive; I had bad luck.* They never view it as a personal strategic flaw.

This inability to internalize the failure guarantees repetition. They will move to the next environment and repeat the same high-risk behavior, only scaled up, because in their mind, they were simply unlucky before. This ensures that their collapses are not just predictable, but progressively more violent and organizationally damaging.

Section II: Mapping the Doomsday Sequences

Understanding the flaw allows us to map the inevitable collapse into predictable stages. This is your playbook for anticipating what happens next.

1. The Narcissist's Sequence: The Public Implosion

The downfall of the Narcissist is loud, dramatic, and always initiated by their own inability to regulate their ego when their emotional supply is denied.

- **Stage 1: The Escalation of Blame:** Facing an objective failure, the Narcissist tries to restore their image by becoming aggressively defensive, sending highly charged, accusatory emails to peers, and blaming subordinates for the error. They create a paper trail of their own volatility.
- **Stage 2: The Ejection of Reality:** They purge anyone who offers constructive criticism. They can only function with enablers who agree with their perfect self-assessment. This isolates them from truth, making their future decisions even more flawed, ensuring the underlying problem gets worse.
- **Stage 3: The Public Meltdown:** A small, administrative inconvenience (e.g., a simple HR inquiry, a late expense report denial, a peer getting more recognition) is perceived as an existential threat. They lose control, triggering a **Narcissistic Injury**, and launch into an irrational, public, career-ending outburst—screaming at staff, threatening legal action over a minor issue, or sending a torrent of abusive, company-wide communication.

- **Stage 4: Institutional Dismissal:** The organization uses the objective documentation of the **unacceptable conduct** (the email, the shouting, the public intimidation) as the grounds for termination. The drama they created is the very reason they are escorted out.

2. The Machiavellian's Sequence: The Administrative Exposure

The Machiavellian is defeated not by a dramatic event, but by the relentless, quiet enforcement of boring, objective procedure.

- **Stage 1: Overextension and Increased Visibility:** The Machiavellian has too many hidden balls in the air. A new organizational policy—a shift to a centralized software, a new data governance rule, a change in reporting structure—is introduced. The Machiavellian must now dedicate massive, exhausting effort to manage the *increased visibility* of their operations.
- **Stage 2: The Component is Isolated:** The new procedural framework successfully closes one small loophole the Machiavellian relied on (e.g., they can no longer funnel specific funds through a certain discretionary account). This doesn't expose the whole scheme, but it forces them to either stop a part of it or try to create a new, even more complicated loophole.
- **Stage 3: The Alliance Collapse:** Seeing their scheme temporarily stalled or blocked, and the external environment tightening, the Machiavellian's cynical allies realize the transactional bond is no longer profitable. They sense the vulnerability and **defect immediately.** They volunteer information or documents to save their own skin, fully exposing the deeper, hidden structure.
- **Stage 4: The Paper Trail Seizes Up:** The Machiavellian is caught in a factual contradiction documented by the defector and the newly transparent system. Their downfall is secured by forensic accounting, compliance logs, and administrative paper trails. They are defeated by an army of auditors.

3. The Psychopath's Sequence: The Legal Catastrophe

The Psychopath's ultimate failure is triggered by the fact that the law is a boundary they cannot simply charmingly talk their way out of.

- **Stage 1: The Escalation of Audacity:** Emboldened by past successes and their immunity to fear, the Psychopath's risks become less subtle and more blatant. They transition to acts with clear criminal liability, such as outright theft, massive forgery, or physical threats/assault. They believe they are invincible.
- **Stage 2: The Critical Breach:** The inevitable lack of a brake causes a massive, public failure that crosses the line into objective criminality. A key client fund is demonstrably missing, a competitor is clearly being subjected to illegal industrial espionage, or the legal department receives a subpoena from federal authorities. The scope of the violation is too great to hide.
- **Stage 3: Abandonment and Flight:** Recognizing that the situation is now beyond internal management and into the realm of prosecution, the Psychopath instantly detaches. They often attempt to erase their digital footprint, secure immediate employment elsewhere, and disappear, leaving the organization with the full liability. There is zero effort to fix, apologize, or explain.
- **Stage 4: Forensic Cleanup and Litigation:** The organization is left to pick up the pieces, often requiring external law enforcement or forensic consultants. The Psychopath is neutralized by the objective, undeniable evidence of their actions—the system logs, the bank records, the documented timeline of the breach. They are stopped by the cold reality of the judicial system.

Section III: Strategic Neutralization: The Environmental Fix

You don't fight fire with fire; you fight the Dark Triad with water: administrative, procedural, cooling water. You must stop trying to beat them at their game and simply change the rules of the field so their inherent flaws are magnified.

1. Neutralizing the Narcissist: The Strategy of the Grey Rock and Shared Glory

The defense against the Narcissist is about emotional starvation and forced reality checks.

- **Deny the Emotional Fuel (The Grey Rock):** In all necessary interactions, be boring, factual, and emotionally neutral. Speak only the minimum required. Never react to their bait, flattery, or theatrical rage. You must become a wall of disinterest. This starves the Narcissist, causing the ego instability required for them to trigger their own public meltdown.
- **Administrative Enforcement (The System Wins):** Never attack their personality. Only enforce objective policy. Example: "Your decision to hire X was poor," becomes, "The hiring process requires three references and a background check. Your file contains neither. Please supply the missing documentation." You force them to fight the unyielding, unfeeling system, which they find exhausting and unrewarding.
- **Mandate Shared Accountability:** Require the Narcissist to publicly delegate key responsibilities and share credit for successes. This dilutes their glory and creates a paper trail of shared ownership. It is the tactical equivalent of forcing them to eat food they cannot digest.

2. Neutralizing the Machiavellian: The Strategy of Process Rigidity and Simplification

The defense here is administrative warfare: closing the loopholes and enforcing clarity.

- **Mandate Immutability and Centralization:** Immediately advocate for and implement systems where critical data (budgets, vendor contracts, project milestones) are stored in centralized, version-controlled, and audited systems. This takes the data out of the Machiavellian's private email inbox and puts it on a public, verifiable record, removing their ability to hoard and manipulate information.
- **Close the Gray Areas:** Systematically review every policy or procedure that uses discretionary, vague language ("manager judgment," "reasonable best efforts"). Replace it with objective, quantifiable, and binary criteria. Every time you simplify the language, you destroy a Machiavellian tactical maneuver. They live in the gray areas; you must flood the organization with white light.
- **Decentralize the Funnel:** Break up every single point of control. The person who initiates the project should not be the person who manages the budget, nor the person who signs the final

contract. Authority must be distributed across multiple, non-reporting roles. This increases the complexity of the Machiavellian's schemes to the point where they are administratively impossible to manage or conceal.

3. Neutralizing the Psychopath: The Strategy of Isolation and Forensic Documentation

This defense is about containment and ensuring the objective facts of their inevitable overreach are undeniable for legal action.

- **Immediate Isolation (The Firebreak):** Upon recognition, strip all access to sensitive resources immediately under the guise of an "unrelated, urgent systems review." Cut off their financial, data, and personnel access points. Every subsequent interaction must be witnessed and documented. You are building a safe perimeter around the highly toxic material.
- **Focus Exclusively on Conduct:** Never waste time debating their pathological lies or their motives. Concentrate all investigation efforts on documenting objective, verifiable **Conduct Violations**, forged documents, system tampering, missing funds. You must build a case that is legally sound, not psychologically nuanced. You must rely entirely on the facts of their *actions*, which are often so egregious they speak for themselves.
- **Prepare for Flight and Aggressive Smear:** Understand that the end-game is always flight and an emotional retaliatory smear campaign. Prepare the organization's legal and communications teams for a unified, brief, and non-emotional public statement, focused on systemic integrity ("Mr./Ms. X is no longer employed. We are conducting a full security review of all financial processes") to deny them the emotional response they are seeking.

Conclusion: The Victory of Structure over Strategy

The Dark Triad represents the apex of organizational predation. They will climb faster and higher than anyone else because they are unburdened by conscience or the need for consensus.

However, their brilliance is a trick. It is compromised by the fatal flaws hardwired into their personality, the Narcissist's fragile ego, the Machiavellian's suffocating complexity, and the Psychopath's inescapable risk compulsion.

Our ultimate victory is not achieved through confronting their malice or matching their cunning. It is achieved through the boring, disciplined, and unwavering commitment to **objective truth, procedural transparency, and structural rigidity**. By denying the Narcissist their supply, closing the loopholes for the Machiavellian, and meeting the Psychopath's recklessness with immediate, documented, legal reality, we use their momentum to drive them into their own predetermined, catastrophic singularity. We win by forcing them to play by rules that their nature simply prohibits them from obeying. The structural integrity of the ethical organization always, eventually, defeats the reckless ambition of the individual predator.

CHAPTER 5

SECURING IMMUNITY

We've reached the pivot point. The last five chapters focused on *detection*, identifying the signatures, mapping the flaws, and predicting the inevitable collapse of the Dark Triad members when they are allowed to operate without constraint. That work is essential, but it is only the diagnosis. Now we move into the *treatment*, and more importantly, the *vaccine*.

Let's be honest: just knowing that a Machiavellian will eventually fail because their scheme is too complicated doesn't help you when they've already locked down the entire Q4 budget and alienated half your development team. Passive observation of their eventual downfall is organizational malpractice. Your goal is not to watch them crash; your goal is to *prevent them from taking flight* in the first place, or, failing that, to ensure their inevitable crash happens in an isolated zone that minimizes collateral damage.

We need to fundamentally change our perspective. We must stop viewing the Dark Triad as a problem of *personnel* and start viewing them as a problem of *process* and *systemic vulnerability*. You cannot successfully manage a pathological predator through negotiation, appeal, or even direct confrontation. You manage them by building an organizational infrastructure that is inherently resistant to their specific modes of exploitation. We are going to engineer an **Organizational Immune System**, built on scientifically backed principles of governance, transparency, and cultural resilience.

Here's the thing about the Dark Triad: they are, in a strange way, incredibly predictable because their psychological needs are so specific and unyielding. They can only survive in environments where they can: 1) control information, 2) exploit ambiguity in policy, and 3) manipulate emotional capital. Our defense strategy must be designed to eliminate these three oxygen sources, forcing the predator into administrative transparency, procedural rigidity, and emotional starvation.

Section I: The Science of Containment: Why Traditional Methods Fail

Before we dive into the structural solutions, we have to talk about why the default, well-meaning corporate responses to toxic behavior are not just ineffective against the Dark Triad, but are actually used by them as tools.

1. The Futility of the Emotional Appeal

The default human response to conflict is to appeal to shared values: "Can't we talk this out?", "Surely you understand how this made Jane feel?", or "We need to operate in good faith."

When dealing with the Narcissist, this appeal feeds them. Your distress, your concern, and your willingness to spend emotional energy trying to fix them confirms their own self-importance. When dealing with the Machiavellian, this appeal is noted as a weakness, an emotional vulnerability they can later exploit.

And with the Psychopath, it's literally meaningless. Research focusing on the core deficits in psychopathy, often correlated with findings based on tools like the Hare Psychopathy Checklist-Revised (PCL-R), repeatedly points to a failure of affective processing. The areas of the brain involved in generating and experiencing guilt, empathy, and fear simply don't engage the way they do in neurotypical individuals. You are appealing to a component (the conscience) that is not installed in the operating system. You might as well appeal to a toaster to feel remorse for burning the bread.

The Scientific Takeaway: Containment must be entirely non-emotional. All interactions must be transactional, documented, and based on objective policy violations, not subjective feelings. If you provide emotional energy, you provide supply, leverage, or amusement.

2. The Trap of "Mentoring" and "Development"

The modern organization, quite rightly, is oriented toward development, coaching, and rehabilitation. When a high-performing but toxic employee is identified, the standard protocol involves HR, management, and perhaps executive coaching to "work through their issues."

The Dark Triad exploits this. The Narcissist views the coaching as proof of their unique, complex importance. They will enthusiastically participate, using the sessions to discuss their brilliance and the ineptitude of others. The Machiavellian sees the coaching as an opportunity to gain deeper insight into the organization's weakness and their opponent's strategies, learning the language of vulnerability while feeling none of it. The Psychopath will participate with flawless charm, gathering data on the therapist's approach and learning new techniques for mimicry, they view it as advanced social engineering training.

Research Note: Several studies confirm that attempts to change core psychopathic traits through traditional therapy, absent intensive and specialized intervention, are ineffective and, critically, can sometimes make the individual more effective at manipulation by equipping them with the vocabulary of normalcy.

The Strategic Reality: You cannot rehab the Dark Triad. Your focus must shift from *changing the person* to *constraining the role*. If the person is high-risk, the role must become low-discretion.

3. The Power of Process Over Personality

This is the central tenet of the operational defense. Every policy, every control, and every cultural norm must be designed to favor **systemic fidelity** over **individual discretion**.

The Dark Triad thrives on discretion. The Machiavellian wants the budget line to say, "Manager may allocate reasonable funds as needed," because that ambiguity is where they hide their transactions. The Narcissist wants sole signature authority because it validates their importance. The Psychopath wants unmonitored server access because it allows for clean sabotage.

Your defense is to replace every instance of "Manager Discretion" with "Mandatory Two-Party Sign-Off" or "Automated Audit Trigger." It's less exciting, less fluid, and occasionally frustrating for good employees, but it creates a structural friction that systematically grinds the predatory momentum to a halt. The Dark Triad cannot operate in an environment where decisions are non-negotiable, documented, and shared. They will find the administrative workload too tedious, the emotional supply too low, and the risk of exposure too high. They will self-select out.

Section II: Engineering the System: Structural Defenses

The defense begins not with people, but with paper, protocols, and code. We are building administrative walls to block the precise paths of least resistance the Triad always seeks out.

1. Compulsory Transparency and Auditing (The Machiavellian Lock-Down)

The Machiavellian's core tactic is **information arbitrage**: knowing something others don't, or having a unique, private interpretation of ambiguous data. We must systematically destroy the possibility of information silos.

The Principle of Decentralized Data Integrity

No critical organizational data (budgets, forecasts, performance metrics, client lists, vendor agreements) should ever reside exclusively on an individual's desktop, in their private email folder, or in a system they alone control. All data must be centrally hosted, version-controlled, and immediately visible to all relevant stakeholders.

- **Actionable Constraint:** Implement a mandatory, read-only data access rule for all key performance indicators (KPIs) and financial sheets. When a decision is made, the underlying data *must* be linked to the decision document, showing the source and the timestamp. This prevents the Machiavellian from sending out slightly differing, misleading versions of the same report to different groups to sow confusion or gain leverage.
- **The Audit Trail Mandate:** Every change to a core document, from a strategic plan to a client contract, must be time-stamped, attributed to the user, and automatically logged. The system itself must enforce that an immutable audit trail exists. This doesn't just catch the predator; it frightens them, because their core tactic of *denial* becomes impossible when the system has archived every keystroke.

2. The Efficacy of the Multi-Signature Rule (The Psychopath / Narcissist Shield)

The Narcissist loves the glory of being the sole decision-maker; the Psychopath needs isolated access to commit large-scale fraud without immediate witnesses. The solution is the **Two- or Three-Person Rule** for high-risk decisions, interactions, and resource control.

Financial and Fiduciary Friction

Any transaction above a minimal threshold, even small things, like approving a client refund or authorizing a new vendor, must require two or more signatures from individuals in non-reporting roles (i.e., not a manager and their subordinate).

- **Example Application (Psychopath):** For high-value transactions (>$50,000), require sign-off from the project VP, the Finance Director, and an independent Compliance Officer. This makes collusion administratively complex and exponentially increases the risk of defection (the Machiavellian failure mode) or exposure (the Psychopath failure mode). This principle of **decoupling authority** ensures no single individual can sink the organization.
- **Example Application (Narcissist):** Mandate shared performance reviews and succession planning. A Narcissist should never be the sole author of a direct report's performance evaluation or firing decision. This forces them to share control and prevents the retaliatory purges they initiate against subordinates who stop providing supply.

The Principle of Co-Witnessed Interactions

If you must meet with a suspected Dark Triad member regarding a sensitive, disciplinary, or financial matter, you must never be alone. This is not about personal safety (though it helps); it's about **establishing an immutable, unbiased witness**.

- Any meeting involving disciplinary action, contract signing, or sensitive data transfer should include a neutral HR or Legal representative who is not emotionally invested in the outcome. This neutral party documents the conversation, thereby neutralizing the Triad's most effective weapon: the *unverified, spoken lie*. They thrive on "he said/she said;" the witness creates an objective, third-party record.

3. Standardizing Discretion: The Administrative Kill-Switch

The Dark Triad uses policy ambiguity like cover fire. Our defense is to simplify, standardize, and remove their ability to interpret rules creatively.

- **Removing Gray Language:** Systematically review organizational policies and replace every instance of subjective or discretionary language (e.g., "Manager will exercise best judgment," "Expenses must be reasonable") with objective, measurable, and standardized criteria ("Manager must document judgment criteria against these three metrics," "Expenses cannot exceed $100 for dinner").
- **The Inflexibility Mandate:** The rules for high-risk areas, like data access, compliance reporting, and asset acquisition, must be non-negotiable. While this can feel heavy-handed, it creates a crucial structural barrier. When the Machiavellian says, "Just this once, let's bypass the process," the organizational response should be, "The system literally won't let me." This externalizes the boundary, forcing them to fight the software, not the person.

Section III: The Cultural Counter-Balance: Rewarding the Antithesis

Structural controls stop the worst behavior, but culture determines whether the organization can truly heal and thrive. The Dark Triad destroys psychological safety and promotes cynicism. To counteract this, the culture must actively reward traits that are antithetical to the Triad's pathology.

1. The Power of Public Accountability and Humility (The Narcissist Starvation)

The Narcissist cannot survive in a culture that rewards the admission of error and the sharing of credit.

Normalizing "Failing Forward"

Research on high-performing teams, particularly around the concept of **Psychological Safety** (pioneered by Amy Edmondson), shows that the most effective groups are those where members feel safe admitting mistakes without fear of punitive retribution.

- **Cultural Action:** Senior leadership must *publicly* admit their own failures, document their learning process, and share credit with others. For instance, a CEO or VP should start a quarterly review by listing the three biggest mistakes they made and how they adjusted. This creates a cultural norm where the Narcissist's defensive rigidity becomes highly conspicuous and unacceptable. If the Narcissist is forced to admit error, they suffer a Narcissistic Injury; if they refuse, they stand outside the cultural norm. Either way, they lose.

- **De-coupling Reward from Individual Heroics:** Stop awarding massive bonuses or public praise for "heroic saves" or "last-minute individual brilliance." These rewards reinforce the Narcissist's belief that the rules don't apply to them and encourage reckless, high-risk behavior that forces the "save." Instead, reward teams for predictable, documented, and collaborative success.

2. The Ethical Arbitration Layer (The Machiavellian's Nightmare)

The Machiavellian uses fear and isolation to silence whistleblowers. The organization must provide a reporting mechanism that is demonstrably and structurally independent of the power hierarchy the Machiavellian controls.

Institutional Independence

An ethics ombudsman or a confidential reporting hot line must report directly to the non-executive board or an outside legal counsel, entirely bypassing the executive chain of command.

- **Scientific Backing:** The psychological barrier for a subordinate to report a toxic, powerful manager is immense. The decision to report hinges on the employee's perception of **Procedural Justice**, the belief that the system is fair and will protect them. If the reporting mechanism flows directly back to the very system the Machiavellian controls, procedural justice is zero. By making the reporting mechanism external and confidential, you dramatically lower the barrier to reporting, enabling the quiet flow of information that ultimately exposes the Machiavellian's hidden schemes.
- **Mandatory Training:** Ensure all employees are regularly trained not just on *what* is unethical, but *how* to report, and explicitly outlining the protections against retaliation. This transforms the reporting system from a passive HR tool into an active cultural component.

3. The Revaluation of Soft Skills (The Psychopath Filter)

The Psychopath can often secure their position by demonstrating high-level, cold, cognitive competence: great presentations, high sales numbers, rapid deal closing. The organization must shift the definition of "competence."

- **The Competence Filter:** Add mandatory, measurable metrics for collaboration, team contribution, and mentorship into performance reviews. While the Psychopath can fake enthusiasm, they struggle with sustained, authentic behavior that benefits others without immediate, tangible self-gain.
- **Behavioral Interviewing:** During the hiring process, use structured, behavioral questions that focus on empathy and ethics, and cross-check the answers with the candidate's provided references (peers and subordinates, not just superiors). Ask questions like: "Tell me about a time you had to sacrifice a personal win for a team's long-term health," or "Describe the last time you consoled a team member who was struggling with a personal issue." The Psychopath will often provide responses that are either overly dramatic, oddly detached, or obviously fabricated, betraying their lack of genuine affective experience.

Section IV: The Long Game: Recovery and Resilience

Even with the best defenses, a determined predator may infiltrate and require neutralization. The final, critical phase is recovery: managing the massive organizational trauma left in their wake.

1. The Post-Ejection Trauma and Trust Repair

When a Dark Triad member is removed, they leave behind an environment poisoned by fear, distrust, and cynicism. Employees who witnessed the process feel demoralized and often victimized.

- **Open and Honest Communication (The Organizational Therapy):** While you cannot divulge private personnel details, the organization must acknowledge the trauma. A senior, ethical leader (the antithesis of the removed person) should address the workforce with a statement focused on values: "We understand that the behavior of the recently departed individual caused significant stress and violated our core values of integrity and trust. We are committed to rebuilding that trust, and we apologize that the necessary actions were not taken sooner." This acknowledgement validates the victimized employees and signals a genuine commitment to repair.

- **Rebuilding Psychological Safety:** This must be done at the team level. Managers must actively facilitate open-dialogue sessions (guided by HR or an external facilitator) where teams can process the shock, express their frustration, and rebuild new, explicit norms of trust. This involves active listening, validating feelings of betrayal, and clearly establishing what the new boundaries are. Without this active phase of emotional recovery, cynicism will linger and the organizational immune system will remain suppressed.

2. Hardening the Systems Based on Lessons Learned

Every collapse, no matter how damaging, is a massive learning opportunity. The organization must commit to a thorough **Post-Incident Review (PIR)**.

- **Forensic Policy Review:** The PIR must not focus on the individual, but on the *policies* the individual exploited. If the Psychopath used an ambiguous budget line, that line is immediately locked down. If the Machiavellian used private email to funnel information, the policy is updated to mandate centralized document management. The organization must assume that every flaw exploited by the previous predator is now publicly known to the next potential predator.
- **The Investment in Redundancy:** True resilience means building administrative redundancy. Just as a good engineer builds redundant systems in critical infrastructure, the organization must invest in redundant processes, ensuring that if one person fails, the entire system does not collapse. This is often an investment in slower, more methodical processes, but it's a non-negotiable insurance policy against predatory behavior.

Conclusion: The Unavoidable Cost of Freedom

The Dark Triad exploits the space between rules, the reliance on goodwill, and the assumption of shared humanity. Their presence is the unavoidable cost of building a creative, fast-moving, and trusting organization.

However, freedom from predation is not found in hoping for good people; it is found in building a system so structurally sound that even bad people cannot cause irreparable harm. By operationalizing our defenses, by mandating structural transparency, distributing authority across non-reporting roles, and cultivating a culture where humility is valued over hyper-competence, we systematically eliminate the oxygen the Dark Triad needs to survive. We stop being victims of their psychology and start becoming masters of our own organizational design. We build the wall, and they cease to be our problem.

CONCLUSION

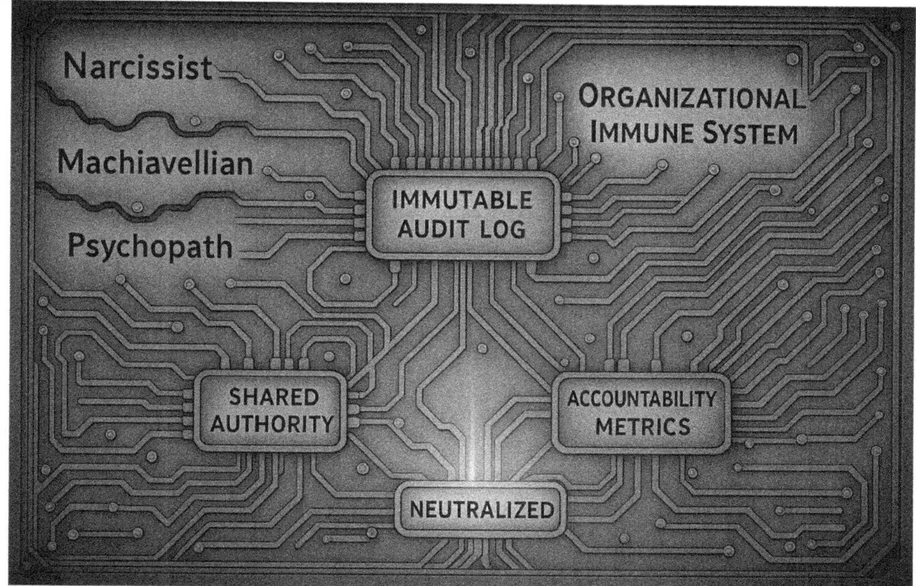

If you've followed the argument of this book from the opening chapter, you have accomplished the most difficult intellectual feat required for this subject: you have acknowledged the predator. You have systematically peeled back the layers of charisma, competence, and confusion to see the Narcissist, the Machiavellian, and the Psychopath not as forces of nature, but as highly predictable, rule-bound systems.

This journey has been uncomfortable, necessary, and ultimately, empowering.

We started with the essential act of **profiling**: understanding the core drive of the Narcissist (ego validation), the Machiavellian (leverage and control), and the Psychopath (stimulation and boundary dissolution).

We then moved to **prediction**, mapping the structural flaws hardwired into each personality that guarantee their long-term collapse, showing that their greatest strengths are their deadliest weaknesses. Finally, we arrived at **neutralization**, designing the operational immune system to leverage those flaws, forcing the predator to either conform to structural rigidity or self-eject.

This final chapter is not simply a summary; it is the **synthesis of all seven principles** into a single, cohesive organizational mandate. It is the final word on why this knowledge matters, what the ultimate cost of inaction is, and how you, as a guardian of organizational health, can maintain your ethical sanity while operating in a world that inevitably contains these predatory personalities.

The key takeaway is this: **The Dark Triad exploits the human condition, not the business model.** They thrive on trust, on ambiguity, on emotionality, and on the default assumption of good faith. Our definitive defense is the methodical, deliberate destruction of those soft targets.

Section I: The Unified Threat – Understanding the Toxic Ecosystem

The first step toward true resilience is recognizing that you will rarely encounter these personalities in isolation. While the book focused on profiling them separately, in real-world toxic environments, they often co-exist in a perverse and highly effective symbiotic relationship. The presence of one enables the survival and operational efficiency of the others.

We call this the **Toxic Triad Ecosystem.**

1. The Narcissist as the Organizational Front Man (The Face)

The Narcissist often occupies the most visible, charismatic, or seemingly "visionary" role (e.g., the CEO, the Head of Sales, the star Project Leader). Their function in the ecosystem is to **capture and deflect**.

- **Capture:** Their charisma, grandiosity, and perceived confidence capture the organization's attention and resources, diverting them from healthy channels. They create the aura of success that attracts external acclaim and investment.
- **Deflect:** When failures inevitably occur due to their rigidity or rash decisions, the Narcissist uses their charm and masterful blame-shifting to deflect scrutiny away from the true source of the toxicity. They make the organization look outward (at a scapegoat) rather than inward (at the broken system).

2. The Machiavellian as the Administrative Architect (The Structure)

The Machiavellian rarely seeks the bright light of the CEO's office; they prefer the dark corners of Finance, Legal, or Operations. Their function is to **create the necessary ambiguity** for the scheme to survive.

- **Create Ambiguity:** They craft vague policies, ensure key processes are undocumented, and maintain informational silos. They build the procedural complexity, the "gray areas", in which the entire ecosystem hides.
- **Provide Leverage:** They secure the necessary resources, financial loopholes, and conditional alliances that keep the Narcissist's grand projects funded and protect the Psychopath's actions from immediate legal scrutiny. They are the structural engineers of the toxic enterprise.

3. The Psychopath as the Enforcer and Boundary Dissolver (The Weapon)

The Psychopath often operates in roles of pure, unmonitored power (e.g., HR Director, Head of Internal Security, or a senior counsel with firing authority). Their function is to **intimidate and erase**.

- **Enforce Compliance:** When the Narcissist's charm fails or the Machiavellian's structural complexity is challenged, the Psychopath applies the brutal, fearless pressure necessary to silence dissent, terminate key truth-tellers, or intimidate auditors. They are the system's weapon of last resort.
- **Dissolve Boundaries:** They are the only personality willing to consistently cross ethical and legal lines. They set a new, lower bar for acceptable behavior, normalizing the extreme, which makes the Narcissist's and Machiavellian's actions seem less severe by comparison.

The Synthesis: The Narcissist attracts the money, the Machiavellian hides the money, and the Psychopath ensures no one dares ask where the money went. Your defensive strategy must target all three points simultaneously, because removing one will often just cause the others to adapt and compensate.

Section II: The Grand Paradox – The Non-Negotiable Cost of the Triad

The single most motivating factor in changing the way an organization operates is cost. But when we talk about the cost of the Dark Triad, we must move beyond the purely financial and address the systemic, long-term erosion of organizational capital.

1. The Financial and Legal Cost: The Predictable Crisis

We discussed the "physics of failure" in Chapter 5. The Narcissist's rigidity, the Machiavellian's complexity, and the Psychopath's overreach are not theoretical risks; they are time bombs.

- **The Compounding Error:** Because the Narcissist cannot tolerate corrective feedback, their strategic errors are rarely corrected early. They compound over time. A small misjudgment on product development quickly becomes a massive inventory write-off because the Narcissist refused to pivot or take advice.
- **The Forensic Burden:** When the inevitable collapse occurs (the legal catastrophe of the Psychopath or the systemic exposure of the Machiavellian), the cost of the cleanup is astronomical. Organizations must hire external forensic accountants, specialized legal counsel, and PR firms to manage the reputational fallout. This cost often dwarfs the individual losses, tying up institutional resources for years.
- **The Reputational Debt:** This is the most difficult cost to quantify. In the age of instant digital information and radical transparency, a corporate scandal resulting from Triad behavior can permanently damage client trust, make hiring top talent impossible, and lower the stock valuation for years, long after the perpetrator is gone.

2. The Psychological and Human Capital Cost (The True Devastation)

This is the cost that organizations are worst at measuring, and it is the cost that takes the longest to recover from. Toxic leadership operates on the principle of **systematic psychological destruction**.

- **Loss of Psychological Safety:** The Dark Triad destroys the cultural foundation of safety necessary for innovation. Employees stop offering creative ideas (they don't want the Narcissist to steal the credit), stop reporting errors (they fear the Psychopath's retaliation), and stop cooperating (they fear the Machiavellian will use the shared information as leverage). Innovation stalls, errors multiply, and critical information goes intentionally unreported.
- **Presenteeism and Cognitive Drain:** The sustained stress of working under a predatory personality (often resulting in what is clinically referred to as **Chronic Organizational Stress**) doesn't just lead to burnout; it leads to **presenteeism:** employees are physically present but cognitively incapable of peak performance because a massive portion of their mental energy is devoted to managing and mitigating the predator. They are prioritizing self-defense over organizational goals.

- **Erosion of Organizational Memory:** High turnover is a hallmark of Triad leadership. When employees leave due to toxicity, they take with them critical, undocumented institutional knowledge, the "tribal knowledge" that keeps the gears turning. This loss of organizational memory is a catastrophic liability that makes the organization brittle and highly dependent on the very few people who remain, often the predator themselves.

Section III: The Two Pillars of Defense – Operationalizing Resilience

Our conclusion must serve as a final, practical checklist. Your mission is to build an environment so hostile to the Dark Triad's specific needs that they find the organizational friction intolerable. This requires a two-pronged, simultaneous attack: **Structural Rigidity** and **Cultural Immunity**.

Pillar 1: Structural Rigidity (The Administrative Wall)

This defense attacks the Machiavellian and the Psychopath by eliminating their access to ambiguity and unmonitored resources.

The Principle of Mandatory Transparency

Every critical decision, budget, and data point must be centralized, timestamped, and visible to all relevant stakeholders. There is no such thing as a "private" project file or a "discretionary" expense line in a high-resilience organization.

- **Actionable Mandate:** Implement immutable, version-controlled documentation for **all** core processes. If the Machiavellian relies on email chains to give vague directives, the system must enforce that the *actual* directive is captured in the project management software and signed off.
- **The Multi-Signature Control (The Gold Standard):** This is the single most effective tool against both the Narcissist and the Psychopath. Mandate two or three signatures from non-reporting roles for all resource allocation (money, high-value assets, hiring, firing). This forces cooperation, reduces individual glory, and makes fraud exponentially harder to conceal. The organization is protected not by individual ethics, but by **systemic complexity for the perpetrator**.

The Principle of Standardizing Discretion

Every policy must be reviewed to replace subjective, "gray area" language with quantifiable, objective rules.

- **Actionable Mandate:** Eliminate language like "reasonable effort," "manager's judgment," or "as needed." Replace them with "must document effort against metric X," "judgment must reference criteria Y, Z, and A," and "spending requires documented need signed off by X." This removes the Machiavellian's interpretive freedom and exposes the Narcissist's emotional-based decision-making.

Pillar 2: Cultural Immunity (The Psychological Barrier)

This defense attacks the Narcissist by denying them supply and counteracting the cynicism that fuels the Machiavellian.

The Principle of Rewarding Humility and Accountability (Narcissist Starvation)

The organization must actively and publicly reward the antithetical traits of the Dark Triad.

- **Actionable Mandate:** Integrate **Accountability Scores** into performance reviews. Score leaders on their willingness to admit public failure, share credit generously, and delegate meaningful control. In this environment, the Narcissist's typical behaviors, blame-shifting and credit-hoarding, become automatic, documented grounds for lower compensation or promotion denial. You use the system to reject the personality, not an emotional confrontation.
- **The Grey Rock Cultural Norm:** Cultivate a cultural environment where emotional volatility is met with polite, factual disengagement. When the Narcissist or Psychopath launches into a tirade or emotional manipulation, the organizational default must be: document, disengage, and enforce policy. No one should be rewarded for engaging with the drama.

The Principle of Independent Ethical Arbitration

You must provide a safe, high-integrity reporting mechanism that is demonstrably outside the predator's chain of command.

- **Actionable Mandate:** Establish a confidential ombudsman, ethics hotline, or reporting channel that reports directly to the non-executive board or an outside auditor. This ensures that when a Psychopath attempts to intimidate or fire a subordinate, the subordinate has a clear, protected channel to report the conduct violation. This system provides the necessary **procedural justice** required to overcome the fear and isolation that silence victims.

Section IV: The Final Mandate – Maintaining Ethical Clarity in the Face of Toxicity

The knowledge contained in this book is powerful, but it comes with a psychological toll. Dealing with the Dark Triad is exhausting because they constantly assault your sense of reality and your core values. Your final mandate, therefore, is not just structural, but internal.

1. The Necessity of Emotional Detachment

The Dark Triad's primary strategy is to pull you into their subjective reality: the Narcissist's melodrama, the Machiavellian's complex web of lies, the Psychopath's unnerving lack of remorse. Once you are emotionally invested, they have won.

- **The Mantra: Focus on Conduct, Not Intent:** You must train yourself to stop asking, "Why did they do that?" or "Did they mean to hurt me?" and start asking, "What policy did they violate?" and "What is the factual, documented evidence of their behavior?" When you shift the focus from their malignant *intent* to their objective, documented *conduct*, you strip them of their power to manipulate your feelings.
- **Validate Your Own Reality:** Dealing with the Triad is an assault on cognitive stability. You will be gaslit, lied to, and confused. You must maintain an independent, documented record of events, timelines, and communications. This is your mental life raft—your external record of the truth, unpolluted by their manipulation.

2. The Ethical Line: When to Fire the "High Performer"

The single most challenging decision for any leader or board is what to do with the *high-performing toxic leader*: the Narcissist who delivers 150% sales targets while burning out 80% of the staff, or the Machiavellian who structures a complex, highly profitable deal through ethically gray means.

This is where the organizational values must be the final, unyielding arbiter.

- **The Zero-Sum Equation:** You must calculate the **Total Organizational Cost (TOC)**, not just the revenue gained. The TOC includes the three-year cost of turnover, the risk premium of legal exposure, the cost of recruiting replacements, and the value of lost innovation due to fear. You will almost always find that the "high performance" of the predator is a zero-sum gain; they are simply moving money from the organization's long-term health budget into their own short-term bonus account.
- **The Ethical Imperative:** Firing a Dark Triad member is not merely a business decision; it is a moral and ethical necessity to protect the vulnerable, ethical majority of your workforce. An organization that tolerates toxicity for profit is one that sends a clear, corrosive message: *Performance excuses cruelty.* This message suppresses the good people and attracts more predators. You must choose a culture of long-term health over short-term, unsustainable profit.

3. The Future: A Culture of Durable Resilience

The work of building an Organizational Immune System is never truly finished. It requires constant vigilance, not because new predators are always coming, but because human nature tends toward the path of least resistance. Processes become vague, transparency becomes inconvenient, and discretion creeps back in.

Your task, as an informed reader of this text, is to be the **Chief Resilience Officer**, regardless of your title. You must relentlessly fight for clarity, for documentation, and for the cultural safety that allows the ethical majority to thrive.

The Dark Triad exploits the space we leave open. Our final victory is achieved not through conflict, but through closure. We close the loopholes, we document the gray areas, we mandate the shared authority, and we build the firewall of transparency.

When we systematically remove the oxygen, the predator can no longer breathe. They must flee to an environment that still rewards manipulation, leaving your organization fundamentally healthier, more ethical, and exponentially more resilient.

This knowledge is your final line of defense. Use it, and protect the good.

REFLECTION QUESTIONS

Alright. Put the book down. Close your laptop. The lecture is over.

If you've reached this point, you've absorbed a powerful, necessary, but often stressful truth: the world contains predators, and they operate in predictable ways. But knowledge, on its own, is just noise. The transition from abstract knowledge to protective wisdom happens right here, in this chapter.

This isn't a quiz. You don't get points for correct answers. This is the homework for your soul, designed to force a confrontation between the ideal processes we've discussed and the messy reality of your own organization. You need to identify *your* specific vulnerabilities and commit to hardening them.

Take your time. Grab a notebook. Be brutally honest with yourself, because that honesty is the first, and most important, step in building a resilient defense.

Section I: Profiling and Pattern Recognition (The Detection Phase)

We often miss the predator because we look at their competence (high sales numbers, brilliant presentations) and ignore their conduct (credit hoarding, team attrition). These questions force you to look at the shadows.

1. **The Competence/Conduct Disconnect:** Think of the last three high-performers (or perceived high-performers) who left a massive trail of administrative or human wreckage in their wake. What was the **precise mechanism** they used to capture organizational praise (their competence), and what was the equally precise, destructive behavior they were simultaneously exhibiting (their conduct)? Did you, or your leadership, knowingly tolerate the destructive conduct because the results were too good to lose? What was the cost of that tolerance?
2. **The Scapegoat Tally:** Reflect on a significant project failure in the last year. Who publicly took the blame? Was the individual blamed truly responsible for the failure, or were they merely the weakest, most emotionally available target for a powerful individual's blame-shifting? If the latter, identify the Narcissist who engineered the scapegoating. What systemic weakness (lack of documentation, vague roles) allowed them to successfully execute that transfer of liability?
3. **The Information Silo Audit:** Where does critical information about your budget, vendors, client lists, or internal projections *only* exist in a non-centralized format (e.g., someone's personal hard drive, a private, unchecked email thread)? Which leader zealously guards that information, making it difficult to access without their permission? This is the Machiavellian's feeding ground. What is the immediate, non-discretionary action you can take next week to force that data into a shared, immutable system?
4. **The Rule Breaker's Currency:** Think about the one person in your sphere who consistently, charmingly, or ruthlessly breaks protocol, the one who gets special favors, skips mandatory training, or ignores basic compliance. Are they doing this because they are innovative, or because they are testing the limits? If you stopped their special access tomorrow, what would be their immediate, predictable reaction? (Rage for the Narcissist, calculation for the Machiavellian, rapid escalation for the Psychopath.)

Section II: The Logic of Failure (Leveraging the Flaw)

We learned that the predator's strength is their weakness. They collapse not due to external attack, but due to internal, self-inflicted structural flaws. Your defense starts with leveraging this predictability.

5. **The Empathy Ledger:** Who in your organization has systematically run down their goodwill account? Think of the leader who demands constant praise, never apologizes, and offers zero genuine appreciation or empathy. When they inevitably hit a crisis next month, who will stand up for them? If the answer is "no one," you are witnessing the **Machiavellian Cynicism Feedback Loop** and the **Narcissist's Supply Depletion** in action. How can you ensure that, when they fall, your team is emotionally prepared to prioritize the organization's integrity over their personal drama?
6. **The Boundary Test:** Consider the most aggressive, boundary-pushing action you've witnessed, a policy violation, an aggressive confrontation, or a highly risky financial maneuver. Did that individual experience shame, fear, or anxiety after the event? If the answer is no, you are likely dealing with the **Psychopathic Inability to Learn from Consequence**. What specific, legal, or financial boundary must they cross next to trigger an undeniable, institutional response? How can you position the organization now to capture the objective, forensic evidence of that *next* inevitable overreach?
7. **Simplifying the Scheme:** Identify one overly complicated, multi-step process in your department (e.g., procurement, travel approval, contract review) that seems intentionally confusing. Who is the administrative architect of that complexity? What happens if you simplify that process tomorrow—say, removing three unnecessary sign-off steps and making the data public? You are likely closing a Machiavellian loophole. Commit to the specific steps required to destroy that complexity and enforce clarity.

Section III: Systemic Defense and Inoculation (The Administrative Fix)

The defense is structural. It's about building a system that is boring, unyielding, and resistant to the Triad's specific needs for glory and ambiguity.

8. **Auditing Discretion:** Locate three instances in your organizational policies where the word "discretion," "reasonable," or "judgment" is used regarding finance, personnel, or compliance. Can you rewrite those three clauses to include quantifiable, objective metrics? (Example: changing "Expenses must be reasonable" to "Expenses cannot exceed $75 per dinner, requiring two manager signatures for exceptions.") Who is the internal stakeholder you need to partner with to enforce that change (Finance, HR, Legal)?
9. **The Grey Rock Protocol:** If a Narcissist on your team starts an emotional escalation (a rant, a defensive outburst, an aggressive email), what is your personal, pre-committed internal protocol for responding? If your default is to try and soothe or appeal to their good nature, you're providing supply. How will you practice the **Grey Rock Strategy**, responding factually, briefly, and neutrally, to ensure you starve the drama while documenting the conduct?
10. **Your Ethical Arbitration Layer:** If you or a trusted subordinate were to witness a blatant violation (theft, intimidation, fraud) by a senior executive tomorrow, do you know the exact, confidential, and protected channel to report it? Is that channel structurally independent of the executive chain of command? If the answer is "I'm not sure" or "I would have to go to that executive's boss," your organization's **Procedural Justice** is weak. What is the single most important structural change (e.g., an independent board review mechanism, an external ombudsman) you can advocate for to ensure protection for whistleblowers?

Section IV: Personal Resilience and Ethical Clarity (The Internal Mandate)

Finally, you cannot fight this battle if you are running on empty. You need boundaries and self-protection to maintain your own ethical center.

11. **Documenting Reality:** Identify the one relationship in your professional life that most consistently makes you question your own memory or sanity (the gaslighter). What specific steps will you take, starting today, to maintain an external, objective log of all your interactions with that person (e.g., forwarding emails, notes on meetings, witness identification)? This is your ultimate defense against the Psychopath's lies and the Narcissist's rewriting of history.
12. **The Line of No Return:** What is your non-negotiable personal ethical line? The one behavior (lying to a regulator, deliberately sabotaging a colleague, covering up fraud) that, if you were asked to do it, would trigger your immediate, non-negotiable resignation? Writing this line down, and meditating on its weight, is essential. It reinforces your internal clarity, ensuring that when the predator tries to drag you into their subjective moral universe, you have an objective, pre-committed defense ready to fire.
13. **The Culture You Choose:** If you are a leader, what is the one antithetical behavior, the opposite of the Dark Triad's pathology, that you will publicly, explicitly, and financially reward in the next quarter? (E.g., Publicly celebrating a failure admitted with humility, giving a bonus for sharing credit, or promoting a leader known for collaboration over individual heroism.) Your actions here create the cultural weather, and the cultural weather must be hostile to the predator.

The goal of this book was never to make you cynical. It was to make you sober. The organization that survives and thrives is not the one that pretends the darkness doesn't exist, but the one that builds the light, the light of transparency, accountability, and structural integrity, so brightly and so consistently that the predators simply cannot hide.

The knowledge is yours. Now, the heavy lifting of action begins.

BOOK FOUR

COGNITIVE BIAS EXPLOITS: PROTECTING THE GLITCHES IN YOUR DECISION-MAKING PROCESS

INTRODUCTION

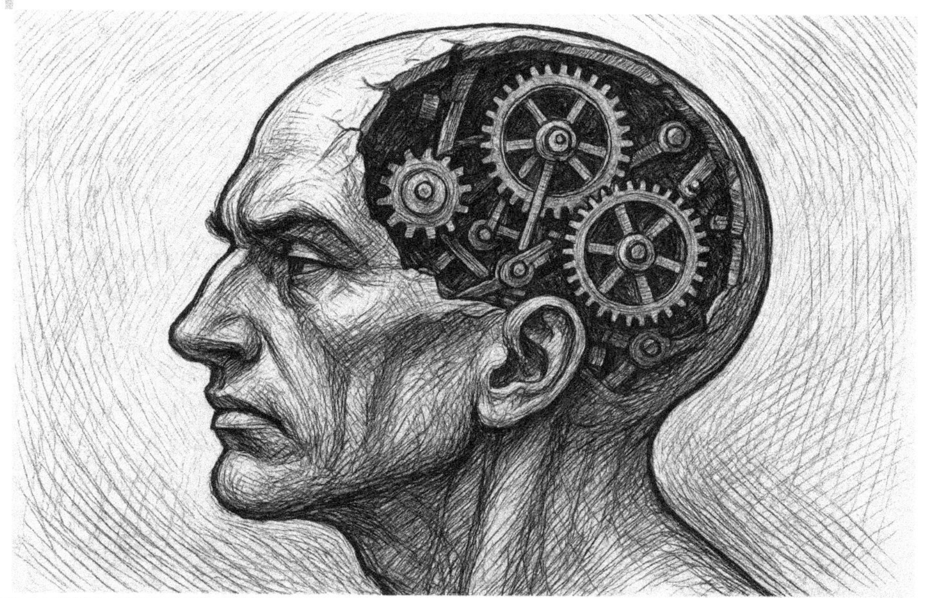

The Enemy Within the Wiring

We've spent the last three books building walls. We fortified the gates against the digital marauder and learned the operational code to defeat human malice: the narcissist, the Machiavellian, and the psychopath. Those were all external fights. They were about *them*.

Now, everything changes. The most devastating, inevitable security failure you will ever face comes from inside the casing. It's the final, irreducible vulnerability of the human operating system: **you, and your own mind.**

Look, the brain is an astonishing piece of kit, but it's glorified survival tech, not a perfect logic engine. To get through a Tuesday without a nervous breakdown, it relies on shortcuts; we call them heuristics, but let's be honest, they're mental cheats. These shortcuts, these cognitive biases, are the architecture of efficiency. They let us decide *fast*, which is great when a predator is running at you, but disastrous when you're allocating a budget. They are the systemic flaws, the predictable choke points that every sophisticated adversary, from the political strategist to the slickest salesperson, knows, loves, and exploits.

This book isn't some abstract psychology course. It is a field manual. We are treating your biases like open network ports. Our goal is to move past recognizing biases and into **operational counter-exploitation.**

The New Exploit: Feeding the Mind What It Wants

The enemy in this war doesn't rely on zero-day attacks or forged documents. They rely on your predictable irrationality. They know that your mind hates loose ends and loves consistency. They know you'll pay more to avoid losing something than you would to gain something identical. They know how to sell you a lie simply by telling it to your friends first.

Think about the sheer elegance of this attack vector:

- **The Old Fight:** It was noisy. It involved active deception, technical complexity, and the need for the enemy to cover their tracks. Think high-friction fraud.
- **The Cognitive Exploit:** It's silent. It relies on simplicity, low friction, and making your brain *want* the wrong answer. The exploit succeeds because it feels comfortable—like slipping into a well-worn groove. It's a passive trap.

If your physical security protects the walls, and your HR policy filters the bad apples, this volume installs the final defense: the **individual cognitive armor plate.** We are building an executive firewall layer dedicated to skepticism and slow processing.

Anatomy of the Friction Protocol

We will systematically dissect the most potent and destructive biases in high-stakes operational environments, providing concrete, immediate protocols for neutralizing them.

- **Chapter 2: The Halo Effect and Authority Bias:** This is the shortcut that lets one shiny quality blind you to systemic failure, or lets a high title override your common sense. The immediate counter is **Disaggregated Scrutiny**, you break the problem into tiny, measurable bits, and **Mandatory Skepticism** toward rank.
- **Chapter 3: Scarcity, Urgency, and Loss Aversion:** These biases weaponize FOMO—the fear of missing out. This is pure panic, deployed by the adversary to bypass your frontal cortex. The defensive posture involves **Temporal Disengagement**—literally walking away from the decision, and embedding a **Devil's Delay** to introduce analytical friction.

- **Chapter 4: Confirmation Bias and Echo Chambers:** The great destroyer of organizational intelligence. This is the mind's addiction to being right, regardless of the evidence. We fight this with institutionalizing **Premortem Analysis** (assuming failure and working backward) and demanding formal, skeptical **Red Team Challenges**.
- **Chapter 5: The Sunk Cost Fallacy and Consistency:** The psychological anchor that keeps you pouring good money and effort after bad. It's the desperate need to justify the past. The fix is **Zero-Based Review** and the absolute, ruthless adherence to the **Principle of No Retrospective Justification.**

We cannot root out the heuristics. They are permanent features of our intelligence. But we can—and must—force **conscious friction** precisely at the point of maximum danger. We interrupt the System 1 fast-lane response and force the slow, hard, rational processing of System 2. That pause is the shield.

CHAPTER 1

THE HALO EFFECT AND AUTHORITY BIAS

I. The Dual Engines of Unwarranted Trust

If the human mind is a battleship, the Halo Effect and the Authority Bias are the two biggest holes in its radar system. These aren't just minor software bugs; they are fundamental, deep-seated features that, in the right circumstances, and an adversary *will* create the right circumstances, turn into catastrophic vulnerabilities. They allow our critical systems to be bypassed by two of the cheapest, most easily faked proxies in the human interaction universe: **looks** and **labels**.

Think about them as a deadly cognitive pair.

The Halo Effect is the illusion of coherence. Your brain, working overtime to save energy, sees one positive trait, say, Person A is handsome, or Person B gave a brilliant opening presentation, and immediately, effortlessly, assigns a cascade of other positive, completely unrelated attributes: "He must be smart," "She must be organized," "They must be trustworthy." It's mental shorthand, a lazy copy-and-paste job.

As the renowned psychologist Edward Thorndike (1920) discovered in his early work with military officers, assessing their subordinates, a rating in one quality tends to be highly correlated with a rating in almost all others, regardless of reality. Why? Because judgment is hard; assumption is easy.

The Authority Bias is the deference reflex. It's the instant, almost muscular relaxation of critical thought when a figure of perceived power, a CEO, a doctor, a police officer, or even someone wearing a fancy uniform, issues a command or makes a strong statement. We are socially programmed to assume competence accompanies status. This isn't necessarily a flaw; in a burning building, you want to instantly obey the firefighter. But in a boardroom or during a due diligence review, this reflex is lethal. It allows titles and jargon to replace data and logic.

What makes this pair so treacherous is their ability to mutually reinforce. When a person is attractive *and* charismatic (Halo Effect), and they also carry the title of "Senior Vice President of Global Strategy" (Authority Bias), our critical assessment systems don't just dim; they shut down completely. We stop asking, "Is this plan solid?" and start asking, "How can I help the SVP execute this clearly brilliant plan?"

This cognitive failure is the ground zero for every bad high-level hire, every terrible merger, and every crisis management failure in history.

The rest of this chapter is dedicated to ripping this mechanism apart and installing practical, non-negotiable protocols to introduce friction at the point where looks and labels try to hijack your judgment.

II. Deconstructing the Halo Effect: The Seduction of Simplification

The Lazy Engine of Generalization

The Halo Effect is pure, unadulterated System 1 thinking, as defined by Nobel Laureate Daniel Kahneman (2011). System 1 is fast, intuitive, emotional, and excellent at pattern recognition. It operates on what you see now and fills in the blanks based on the past. If you see one positive marker, a firm handshake, a prestigious university degree, physical attractiveness, System 1 constructs a complete, cohesive, and utterly false narrative of competence, often without a shred of actual evidence regarding the task at hand.

The mind, frankly, despises uncertainty. We hate dealing with a complex individual whose qualities are messy and contradictory. So, we simplify. We take that single "halo" trait and let its light spread, blinding us to flaws.

Let's look at the mechanics of exploitation in the corporate world.

The Ugly Reality of Aesthetics

We have to acknowledge an uncomfortable truth: appearance is a powerful, exploitable Halo vector. Numerous studies in social psychology have documented the correlation between perceived physical attractiveness and perceived intelligence, competence, and trustworthiness. This is not about vanity; this is about exploitation.

Marketers are masters of this. They don't just hire attractive spokespeople for unrelated products; they understand that the *perceived* quality of the person speaking translates instantly and cheaply to the *perceived* quality of the product. That shiny, charismatic CEO isn't just a figurehead; they are a walking, talking, company-wide Halo Effect, designed to reassure investors and mask operational weaknesses. They distract the market with a compelling personal narrative.

The danger isn't that you notice someone is attractive; the danger is that your brain registers that aesthetic quality and then quietly, without your knowledge, *inflates their financial projections by 15%.* That's the exploit.

The Hiring and Promotion Catastrophe

The Halo Effect is a wrecking ball in talent acquisition. Consider the candidate with a dazzling résumé, featuring one or two marquee names, Harvard, Goldman Sachs, maybe a successful (but unrelated) early startup sale.

In an interview, the moment the hiring manager registers that **single, high-value data point**, the Halo activates. Suddenly, every subsequent answer, even vague or contradictory ones, is reinterpreted to fit the narrative: *This person is a winner. They are brilliant. I just need to hire them.*

What gets ignored?

1. **The Disconnect:** The failure to link past success (say, in sales) to the required competency (say, in operational logistics).
2. **The Missing Data:** The lack of deep questioning on critical, non-glamorous skills.
3. **The Dissenting Voices:** Any junior interviewer's negative feedback is dismissed as "lacking vision" or "intimidated by the talent."

The result is often the star hire who is fantastic at presentations but fails miserably at execution. They got the job not because they were the most qualified for the role, but because one bright, irrelevant accomplishment cast a blinding light over the actual job requirements. This is why standardized, blind-criteria-based interviewing is the only defense, but we'll get to that.

III. The Gravity of Authority: Milgram's Lingering Shadow

Deference as a Survival Mechanism

If the Halo Effect is about simplifying the *person*, the Authority Bias is about simplifying the *decision*. We defer to authority because, generally, it is efficient and, evolutionarily speaking, safe. If you had to argue with the tribal elder about where to find water every day, the tribe would starve. Deference streamlines action.

However, in the absence of a life-or-death crisis, this deference becomes a liability. The chilling work of Stanley Milgram (1963) demonstrated how easily ordinary people would abandon their moral compass simply because a researcher, wearing a white lab coat and speaking with firm conviction, told them to proceed. Authority doesn't require competence; it requires only the symbols of legitimacy, the lab coat, the corporate title, the government seal.

The Authority Bias is a mechanism of **responsibility transfer**. When the SVP tells you the plan is sound, your brain says, "Great. His job is to be right. Now *my* job is just to execute." You consciously or subconsciously offload the burden of critical analysis onto the authority figure. This feels excellent, but it means that the moment the authority figure is wrong, the entire downstream system is committed to a disastrous path.

Institutional Weaponization: The Jargon Trap

Adversaries, whether they are toxic bosses, incompetent consultants, or manipulative political figures, know how to manufacture authority instantly.

One of the most effective tools is **Jargon as a Shield**. When an authority figure uses overly complex, niche, or technical terminology, especially when speaking to a mixed audience, they are not trying to be informative; they are trying to enforce compliance. The listener, fearing they will look foolish if they ask for clarification, simply nods along, assuming the jargon is proof of competence.

- *The Engineer's Dilemma:* A junior engineer knows the legacy system will fail under the new architecture. The senior director, who hasn't coded in a decade, uses a few high-level buzzwords about "cloud-native modularity" and "synergistic cross-platform leverage." The junior engineer, lacking the *authority* to challenge the *jargon*, stays silent. The project fails. The Director blames the engineer for "poor communication."
- *The Medical Error:* A classic example (often cited in aviation safety): a nurse notices an incorrect dosage on a patient's chart written by the physician. Due to the immense cultural authority of the physician, the nurse hesitates, fears challenging the 'expert,' and a critical error occurs. The badge overrides the data.

The higher the rank, the louder the title, the quieter the reasonable dissenting voices become. The exploitation of the Authority Bias is simply the calculated use of status symbols to create a **Command Economy of Thought**, where dissent is too expensive for the individual to afford.

The Inverse Authority Problem

The bias also manifests in reverse: discounting brilliant ideas because they come from the 'wrong' person. How many billion-dollar ideas were laughed out of the room because the twenty-two-year-old intern lacked the formal authority to articulate them with confidence?

We filter information based on the source's perceived rank *before* we filter it based on its content. This isn't just rude; it's strategically bankrupt. We're rejecting pure alpha because it arrived in a plain brown envelope instead of a gold-leafed package. The solution isn't to flatten hierarchies entirely, hierarchy is useful for execution speed, but to structurally decouple the *source* of the idea from the *evaluation* of the idea.

IV. Operational Defense: Installing the Cognitive Firewall

Combating the Halo Effect and Authority Bias is not about becoming a cynical curmudgeon who trusts no one. It's about building mandatory, structural protocols that force your brain out of the System 1 shortcut loop and into System 2 analysis when the stakes are high.

Defense 1: Disaggregated Metric Analysis (D.M.A.)

The primary function of the Halo Effect is *aggregation*. It clumps disparate traits together. The defense, therefore, must be **disaggregation**.

The D.M.A. Protocol (How to Break the Halo):

1. **Mandatory Independence:** Never allow the scoring of one domain to influence the scoring of another.
    - *In Hiring:* Use four different interviewers, each assigned only *one* non-overlapping criterion (e.g., Interviewer 1 only assesses logical problem-solving; Interviewer 2 only assesses cultural fit/team dynamics; Interviewer 3 only assesses technical expertise; Interviewer 4 only assesses past performance metrics). Crucially, they do not share their scores or notes until *after* the candidate leaves.
    - *In Investment:* When reviewing a pitch, the team must review and score the CEO's charisma and presentation style (Trait A) *separately* and *before* they review the underlying cash flow projections (Trait B). The scores for Trait A cannot be visible while scoring Trait B.
2. **Anonymization of Early Stages:** Wherever possible, anonymize the initial review data.
    - If you're hiring, can you blind-grade technical submissions? Can you have a primary filter based on performance data before résumés (the Halo source) are even reviewed?
    - If you're evaluating a supplier bid, remove the company logo, the glossy cover sheet, and the name of the executive who wrote it. Just evaluate the specifications.
3. **Weighting by Relevance, Not Emotion:** Replace the subjective "overall impression" with a pre-established, weighted formula. If technical expertise is 60% of the job, then the score from the technical interviewer must account for 60% of the final decision, regardless of how much the CEO "vibed" with the candidate's personal story.

The DMA is a forced exercise in System 2 calculation. It is inconvenient. It is slow. And that inconvenience is the exact source of its power.

Defense 2: Proceduralized Skepticism (P.S.)

The core mechanism of the Authority Bias is the unquestioned acceptance of a symbol (the badge, the title). Proceduralized Skepticism involves institutionalizing the act of questioning that symbol's relevance to the data presented.

The P.S. Protocol (How to Disarm the Badge):

1. **The Mandatory Challenger:** For any high-stakes strategic decision, formally assign a **Mandatory Challenger** role. This is not a voluntary Devil's Advocate; this is a non-negotiable role whose performance review depends entirely on the quality and rigor of their dissent.
    - *Rule:* The Challenger's first question, upon hearing an authoritative statement (e.g., "Our competitor is too slow to react," stated by the CEO), must be: **"Based on what verifiable, third-party data does that statement hold true, and how does your title influence my perception of that data?"**
2. **The "Five Whys" for Authority:** Before acting on any statement of strategy, financial projection, or technical assessment delivered by an authority figure, apply the "Five Whys" technique to the underlying assumptions.
    - *Example:* Authority says: "We must proceed with Project Alpha because our industry is ripe for disruption."
        - Why 1: Why is our industry ripe for disruption *now*? (Answer: Competitor Beta launched a new tool.)
        - Why 2: Why does Competitor Beta launching a tool mean *we* must launch Project Alpha? (Answer: We lose market share otherwise.)
        - Why 3: Why does this specific tool launch threaten our market share? (Answer: Our core customer base values this specific feature.)
        - Why 4: Why does our core customer base value this specific feature? (Answer: Because internal data from Q1 shows high churn related to this absence.)
        - Why 5: Why did we ignore the Q1 data until now? (Answer: *Silence or Evasion.* This is where the P.S. protocol forces the Authority to justify the delay, not just the decision.)
3. **The Data-Only Channel:** Establish a clear policy where certain high-stakes decisions (e.g., investment recommendations, security vulnerability reports) must be submitted through a channel that *strips away* the submitter's name and title during

the initial review phase. The merit of the data must win or lose on its own terms, before the team learns who proposed it.

V. Case Studies in Failure and Correction

Case Study A: The Seductive CEO (Halo Effect Failure)

- **Failure:** A mid-sized tech company, "InnovateCo," hires a new CEO, Markel, based almost entirely on his flawless, charismatic public presence and his previous role at a Fortune 50 company. His personal brand is impeccable. Over the next year, Markel implements several disastrous operational changes. When his CFO tries to flag the catastrophic cash flow issues, the board (Halo-blinded) dismisses the CFO, saying, "Markel is a visionary; cash flow will follow the vision."
- **Exploit:** The Halo of charisma and pedigree masked structural, measurable incompetence in logistics and finance.
- **P.S. Defense:** InnovateCo should have enforced a D.M.A. during hiring. Markel's "Charisma Score" (irrelevant) should have been 5%, while his "Logistical Operational Score" (critical) should have been 70%, based on blind references and structured assessment of past turnaround data, regardless of his prior firm's prestige.

Case Study B: The Medical Error (Authority Bias Failure)

- **Failure:** A surgical team is preparing for a procedure. The junior resident, Dr. Chen, notices the senior surgeon, Dr. Gupta, has incorrectly marked the operating site (marking the left side instead of the right). Dr. Chen hesitates for nearly a full minute, mentally rehearsing the phrase "Excuse me, Dr. Gupta, but..." out of fear of questioning the renowned authority figure. By the time Dr. Chen speaks, the operation is seconds from commencement.
- **Exploit:** Authority Bias created a toxic psychological gap, a hesitation enforced by status, that nearly led to a critical, irreversible error.
- **P.S. Defense:** Modern aviation and surgical protocols now mandate **Challenge-and-Response** systems. This is an institutionalized P.S. protocol. For instance, before incision, everyone must state the site, procedure, and patient's name aloud. When Dr. Chen sees the error, the protocol demands a simple, impersonal code phrase like "Stop the line, procedure protocol failure," which targets the *process* (P.S.) and not the *person* (Dr. Gupta), neutralizing the threat of authority reprisal.

VI. Summary and Forward Look

The Halo Effect and the Authority Bias are the mind's shortcuts to a quick, easy answer. They are cheap decoys, and they are relentlessly exploited.

Our response cannot be trust-based; it must be procedural. We must commit to **Disaggregated Metric Analysis (D.M.A.)** to dismantle the illusion of coherence, and **Proceduralized Skepticism (P.S.)** to neutralize the threat of institutional status. We must make the critical decision-making process inconvenient, slow, and non-personal. Only by forcing System 2 analysis where System 1 naturally prefers to coast can we close the most dangerous gaps in our cognitive security architecture.

Next, we move to biases that manipulate us through pressure and fear, the exploitation of scarcity, urgency, and loss aversion, biases that bypass the rational mind entirely and speak directly to the primal urge for survival.

CHAPTER 2

SCARCITY, URGENCY, AND LOSS AVERSION

I. The Pressure Triad: Hijacking the Amygdala

In the last chapter, we were concerned with how titles and charisma, the Halo Effect and Authority Bias, corrupt our systems of *assessment*. They make us think a mediocre idea is brilliant because of who presented it. Now, we confront a darker, faster set of exploits: Scarcity, Urgency, and Loss Aversion. These biases don't corrupt assessment; they bypass it entirely. They don't try to change your mind; they simply try to **stop you from thinking.**

This triad is built on fear. Scarcity exploits our fear of missing out on a resource; Urgency exploits our fear of missing out on a timeline; and Loss Aversion, the most potent of the three, exploits our fundamental, biological terror of having something taken away.

Adversaries, be they high-pressure negotiators, political manipulators, or complex fraud schemes, know that if they can successfully trigger these panic responses, they can temporarily shut down the sophisticated, slow-moving analysis of System 2 and force a reactive decision straight from the gut. It's the cognitive equivalent of inducing a full-system panic button. We need to understand the architecture of this panic before we can build the emotional circuit breaker necessary to survive it.

II. Loss Aversion: The Double Weight of Pain

Of the three biases, Loss Aversion is the psychological bedrock. It's the deep, primal, irrefutable truth that underpins all exploitation strategies based on pressure. Loss Aversion describes the empirically proven reality that, psychologically, **the pain of losing something is approximately twice as powerful as the pleasure of gaining something equivalent.**

This insight, formalized by Nobel laureate Daniel Kahneman and Amos Tversky (1979) in their groundbreaking Prospect Theory, is one of the most significant findings in behavioral economics. It demonstrates that our utility curve is steep and violent on the loss side. If I offer you a 50/50 chance to gain $100 or lose $100, a rational economic actor is indifferent. A human being runs away. Why? Because the negative emotion associated with losing the $100 vastly outweighs the positive emotion of gaining it.

The Ownership Effect: The Exploit of Possession

Loss aversion doesn't just apply to things we physically own; it applies to things we *feel* we own, even momentarily: the psychological concept of **endowment effect**. The moment something is in our possession, its subjective value instantly increases.

This is the entire foundation of the "free trial" business model. You don't get the software to *evaluate* it; you get it so you can *use* it and integrate it into your workflow. After two weeks, you don't look at the $99 monthly fee as the price to acquire a new tool; you see it as the price to avoid the loss of the already-integrated tool. The adversary has engineered a loss where none existed before.

In a high-stakes corporate environment, this plays out in disastrous retention schemes:

1. **The Fiduciary Loss:** A manager who has personally advocated for a failing project will fight tooth and nail to keep it funded. The manager views cutting the project not as saving future capital, but as *losing* their personal reputation and past judgment, a loss weighted twice as heavily as the potential gain from reallocating the funds.

2. **The Status Quo Anchor:** Loss aversion makes us terrified of change, even when the status quo is suboptimal or actively damaging. Choosing to leave a mediocre vendor (Gain: Potential efficiency) requires overcoming the fear of the administrative disruption, the political fallout, and the simple fear of the unknown (Loss: Predictability, even bad predictability). This inertia is a form of passive exploitation utilized by every entrenched, underperforming organization and supplier.

The adversary doesn't need to steal from you; they just need to convince you that if you don't act *now*, you will lose what you already have. This psychological anchor is often so strong that it outweighs all future-looking, rational cost-benefit analysis.

III. The Active Triggers: Scarcity and Urgency

If Loss Aversion sets the stage by anchoring us to the present, Scarcity and Urgency are the active mechanisms that force the rapid, panicking decision. They are designed to create a synthetic crisis that eliminates the one thing necessary for System 2 thinking: **time.**

The Exploitation of Scarcity

Scarcity is the perception that a resource is limited in *quantity*. Cialdini's (2001) work on influence highlighted that things become more desirable when their availability declines. The psychological mechanism here is simple: we associate difficulty of acquisition with higher value and, critically, restricted freedom. When availability is restricted, we instinctively fight to preserve our choice.

Scarcity in Operational Exploits:

- **The M&A Play:** A private equity firm isn't just selling one company; they're selling "the only available market leader in Sector X in Q4." The *scarcity* of the deal makes it feel more valuable than the actual underlying financials. The target company becomes fixated on **acquiring the rare thing** rather than analyzing whether the thing is a good fit.
- **The Talent Trap:** A hiring manager is told, "This candidate has three other offers and is only available for a decision by end of day." The scarcity of the candidate, the fact that they are highly desired by others, overrides the need for a standardized, multi-stage hiring process. The organization makes a rushed, high-salary offer simply to avoid the loss of the "in-demand" asset.

The core vulnerability is this: the mind conflates **Rarity** with **Quality**. A manipulator uses scarcity to ensure you focus on the potential *loss of access* rather than the actual *value of the item*.

The Exploitation of Urgency

Urgency is the perception that a resource is limited in *time*. "Offer expires at midnight." "Final warning." Urgency is the speed trigger—it weaponizes the clock.

In a business context, urgency is often manufactured to prevent the victim from seeking a second opinion or performing necessary due diligence.

Urgency in Operational Exploits:

- **The Lobbyist Push:** A political operative needs a legislative body to approve a heavily redacted bill. They ensure the vote is scheduled for 2 a.m. on a Friday before a major holiday recess. The urgency of the timeline ensures that no one has the time to properly read the text, assess the long-term impact, or raise coordinated dissent. The vote passes on fatigue and urgency, not merit.
- **The "Flash Sale" Negotiation:** In a negotiation, an adversary will inject an artificial deadline ("I have another buyer ready to sign tomorrow") not because they do, but because they know that your analysis process takes three days. By imposing a 24-hour deadline, they are forcing you to either make a decision based on incomplete information (a risk you hate) or lose the deal entirely (a loss you fear). The urgency neutralizes your ability to leverage time, which is often your most powerful resource.

IV. The Temporal De-Coupling Defense (T.D.D.)

Fighting Scarcity, Urgency, and Loss Aversion requires a fundamental shift in defensive strategy. You cannot win this battle with better data; you must win it with **better timing.** The defense must be procedural, mandatory, and immediate, designed to physically or psychologically create distance from the pressure.

We call this **Temporal De-Coupling Defense (T.D.D.)**. It is the institutionalization of the pause button.

Protocol 1: The Mandatory 48-Hour De-Coupling Rule

The single most effective defense against the pressure triad is time. When an adversary imposes an urgent deadline or a moment of scarcity, the organization must have a non-negotiable rule that prohibits committing to any non-critical decision within a predetermined period, typically **48 hours.**

- **The Requirement:** When faced with an "Act Now or Lose It Forever" scenario (Scarcity/Urgency), the decision-maker must respond with one of two pre-approved phrases: "Our internal due diligence protocol requires a minimum 48-hour assessment period before commitment," or "We appreciate the urgency, but our governance framework prevents signing without a cooling-off period."
- **The Rationale:** This policy preempts the adversary's attack by shifting the friction from the individual decision-maker (who feels the fear of loss) to the **Impersonal Institutional Protocol** (which has no fear). The adversary is now fighting a policy manual, not a person. If the deal is legitimate, the adversary will respect the 48-hour protocol. If the deal is an exploitation, the adversary will often fold, proving the pressure was manufactured.

Protocol 2: The Cost-of-Status-Quo Audit (C.S.Q.A.)

To combat Loss Aversion, the tendency to stick with a bad situation to avoid the pain of change, we must systematically reframe the problem from *loss* to *gain*. We do this by quantifying the cost of doing nothing.

The C.S.Q.A. Protocol:

1. **Define the Status Quo as the Loss:** When reviewing an entrenched, underperforming system (a bad supplier, an outdated process, a failing employee), the team must first calculate the **Total Annualized Cost of the Status Quo**. This calculation includes measurable losses (wasted resources, higher fees) and non-measurable but high-impact losses (employee morale, lost opportunity cost, reputational risk).
2. **Explicit Loss vs. Explicit Gain:** The decision is then framed not as: "Should we risk losing the known process?" but as: "Do we proceed with the New Process (Gain: $500,000 efficiency) or continue with the Status Quo (Loss: $450,000 inefficiency)?" By explicitly defining the Status Quo as an ongoing, measurable loss, you neutralize the psychological weight of the *fear* of change. You replace emotional fear with cold, financial justification.

3. **Mandatory Sunset:** For all new non-essential contracts or technologies, mandate a "sunset clause" review after 12 months. This forces the question: "Are we actively going to *re-acquire* this, or let it expire?" This prevents the endowment effect from ever fully setting in.

Protocol 3: The Price Anchoring Nullification (P.A.N.)

Scarcity and Urgency often rely on **price anchoring**, setting a high initial price ("$10,000, but for the next 24 hours, only $5,000!"), to make the discounted price seem like a gain, when it's still overpriced.

The P.A.N. Protocol:

1. **Ignore the Anchor:** When faced with a time-limited offer, the evaluator must treat the original, high anchor price as **unverifiable fiction**. The team is permitted to use only two data points: the **Offered Price** and the **Verifiable Market Price (VMP)**, based on three independent, recent competitor quotes for comparable services.
2. **Challenge the Discount:** The negotiation team is trained to ask the following question whenever presented with a discount based on urgency: "We appreciate the temporary price, but what is the *structural* reason this price cannot be sustained for 14 days, given our long-term partnership?" This forces the adversary to drop the charade or admit the time pressure is artificial, destroying the psychological advantage of the urgency tactic.

V. Case Studies in Exploitation and Resilience

Case Study A: The Negotiated Trap (Scarcity/Urgency Failure)

- **Failure:** A procurement team is negotiating a high-value software license. The vendor drops a sudden, aggressive line: "I'm sorry, but we have internal targets to hit this week. If you can sign before 5 p.m. Friday, I can guarantee the 20% discount. After that, it goes back to list price, and you'll have to wait until next quarter." The procurement officer, terrified of losing the 20% savings (Loss Aversion) and missing the Friday deadline (Urgency), rushes the final legal review and commits to unfavorable termination clauses.
- **Exploit:** The vendor successfully leveraged Loss Aversion (losing the 20% discount) using Urgency (the Friday 5 p.m. deadline).

- **T.D.D. Defense:** The procurement officer should have immediately deployed the 48-Hour De-Coupling Rule, stating: "We are required by governance to obtain external legal review for all termination clauses, which takes 72 hours. If you are unable to sustain the price for that period, we will revisit the entire negotiation in the next quarter." The adversary is forced to choose between the deal and the exploit. A robust counter-protocol is the only answer to manufactured pressure.

Case Study B: The Legacy System Addiction (Loss Aversion Failure)

- **Failure:** A retail company knows its decade-old ERP system is slow, expensive to maintain, and a major security vulnerability. Their external consultants project that migrating to a modern platform would save 30% annually, paying for itself in three years. However, every time the migration is proposed, the senior management team tables the motion. Their stated reason: "The risk of disruption is too high."
- **Exploit:** The fear of losing the "known entity" (the old ERP, despite its flaws) and the predictable workflow outweighs the rational, quantified gain. This is pure Loss Aversion disguised as prudent risk management.
- **C.S.Q.A. Defense:** The migration team must cease arguing in terms of *gain* (saving 30%). They must conduct and present the Cost-of-Status-Quo Audit, framing the old system as a **$5 million Annualized Loss to Inefficiency and Risk**. The board is no longer deciding between "risk and safety"; they are deciding between "risk (migration) and guaranteed $5M loss (status quo)." The framing is everything.

VI. Summary and Forward Look

The pressure triad of Scarcity, Urgency, and Loss Aversion is a constant, quiet hum in the background of all commerce and politics. These biases succeed because they exploit the single most critical weakness in human decision-making: the need for speed under pressure.

Our defense is institutional slowness. We must make the conscious decision to choose **protocol over panic**. By implementing the Temporal De-Coupling Defense (T.D.D.) and rigorously auditing the Cost of the Status Quo (C.S.Q.A.), we neutralize the psychological mechanism that transforms manufactured fear into irreversible commitment.

With the emotional hijackers contained, we move on to the next chapter, addressing the flaws that corrupt the information stream itself: Confirmation Bias and the threat of the Echo Chamber.

CHAPTER 3

CONFIRMATION BIAS AND ECHO CHAMBERS

I. The Addiction to Being Right

If the last chapter addressed the cognitive exploits that make us panic, this chapter deals with the most insidious form of self-sabotage: the exploit that makes us **feel comfortable.** We are talking about Confirmation Bias (CB) and its terrifying partner, the Echo Chamber.

Confirmation Bias is not a flaw in reasoning; it's an *addiction to coherence*. It is the human tendency to seek, interpret, favor, and recall information in a way that confirms or supports one's prior beliefs or values. Your mind is fundamentally lazy, it hates the friction of contradiction. When presented with Data A, which supports your current belief, and Data B, which refutes it, your brain instinctively hits the dopamine button for Data A, and tosses Data B into the mental shredder.

This isn't malicious, but it is strategically ruinous. For an organization, a team, or a nation, the inability to ingest and process contradictory evidence is a sign of total intelligence failure. The adversary—be they a manipulative political party, a failing company seeking acquisition, or a scammer—doesn't need to lie to you; they just need to feed you the pre-vetted, comfortable narrative your brain already wants to believe.

What makes this bias so deadly is its ability to transition from an individual cognitive shortcut to a **collective catastrophic failure** via the Echo Chamber. An individual who only reads headlines they agree with is merely misinformed. A boardroom full of executives who only hire people who validate the CEO's "vision" and only consume data filtered by internal consensus is a catastrophic intelligence failure waiting to happen. The latter scenario is Groupthink, amplified by modern digital and organizational structures. The former is merely the seed. We must learn to defend against both.

II. The Mechanics of Belief Maintenance

To protect against CB, we first need to appreciate the sheer psychological effort your mind exerts to maintain its current view of reality.

Motivated Reasoning and the Backfire Effect

The core engine of CB is **motivated reasoning**. As demonstrated by groundbreaking studies like the one conducted by Lord, Ross, and Lepper (1979), people don't process evidence in a vacuum; they process it through the lens of their existing emotional commitment. When presented with mixed evidence on an issue they care deeply about (like the death penalty), subjects didn't move toward a balanced, central position. Instead, they became *more* polarized. They accepted the evidence supporting their position at face value and aggressively critiqued the methodology of the contradictory evidence. The evidence *backfired*, hardening their original belief.

This tells us that the danger isn't the lack of information; it's the **pre-filtering** of information. Your mind acts as a ruthless bouncer, rejecting any data point that causes cognitive dissonance: the deeply uncomfortable mental state arising from holding conflicting beliefs.

The Selective Memory Trap

Confirmation bias isn't just about what you choose to see now; it's about what you choose to remember later. You are far more likely to recall instances where your past predictions were correct and forget the instances where you were wildly wrong. This builds an internal narrative of infallibility, which makes the next predictive decision even more vulnerable to self-confirming data.

This process ensures that, over time, the person who made one brilliant, lucky call in the market will selectively build a memory archive of their financial genius, rendering them functionally immune to contradictory advice before their next, inevitable disaster. They are not merely biased; they are *psychologically weaponizing* their own history against future good judgment.

III. The Architecture of the Echo Chamber

Confirmation bias is ruinous at the individual level, but when it moves to the group, it becomes an existential threat. This transition creates the Echo Chamber: an environment where consensus is not the result of analysis, but the mandatory entry price for belonging.

Groupthink: The Price of Belonging

Decades ago, Irving Janis (1972) meticulously documented the phenomenon of **Groupthink**, the tendency for highly cohesive, insulated groups to prioritize harmony and conformity over realistic appraisal of alternatives. Think of the Bay of Pigs planning failure, or the Challenger disaster decision. In these environments, dissent isn't just ignored; it's seen as a sign of weakness, disloyalty, or poor morale.

The Echo Chamber is simply Groupthink supercharged by digital infrastructure and modern HR practices that prioritize "cultural fit" to an extreme degree.

How the Echo Chamber Destroys Intelligence:

1. **Homogeneity in Hiring:** Teams that hire people who "think like us" and "have the right mindset" are not building complementary expertise; they are building a wall against new ideas. If everyone on your strategy team came from the same three universities and the same two consulting firms, they share a bias architecture, and they will fail in lockstep.
2. **The Digital Feedback Loop:** The internet and algorithmic curation are masters of the Echo Chamber. They notice which news sources you click, which opinions you share, and which voices you amplify. They then ruthlessly prune your incoming data stream to remove everything you might disagree with, ensuring that your view of reality, whether political, social, or market-based, is constantly confirmed and reinforced.
3. **The Failure of Debate:** In an Echo Chamber, disagreement is not seen as a tool for refinement, but as a personal attack. Debate becomes an act of defense, not exploration. The team stops

asking, "Are we right?" and starts asking, "Why is that person trying to ruin our consensus?"

The danger is that the Echo Chamber feels good. It feels like teamwork, alignment, and vision. In reality, it is a comfort bubble that insulates the organization from the cold, hard, necessary reality that lies outside its walls.

IV. Operational Exploitation: Vetting the Vetting

Sophisticated adversaries rarely try to force a completely new belief. That's too much work. They use CB to validate an existing, subtle error.

The Due Diligence Illusion

In complex mergers and acquisitions, the Confirmation Bias is the primary weapon used by the selling party. The buying firm, after spending millions on initial analysis and getting executive buy-in, has already formed a powerful cognitive bias: *This deal is happening.*

The seller exploits this by:

- **Pre-Seeding the Narrative:** Feeding the buying team initial data that is glossy, high-level, and perfectly aligned with the buying company's existing growth strategy. This activates the buyer's CB.
- **Vetting the Vetting:** When the buyer's internal analysts find a major, ugly structural flaw, the seller doesn't deny it. Instead, they subtly discredit the *source* ("That analyst is new; they don't understand our industry context") or provide a counter-narrative ("That risk is baked into the model, but our proprietary synergy model offsets it"). Because the buyer *wants* the deal to be good (CB), they are highly motivated to accept the flimsy counter-narrative and discard their own internal dissent. They confirm the deal despite the evidence.

This is why, historically, major M&A deals often destroy value for the acquiring firm. The executive team's commitment to the *idea* of the deal makes them structurally incapable of receiving the bad news required to stop it.

Political Manipulation and Affective Polarization

In the realm of political and social influence, the exploit is terrifyingly simple: Target the fear, then confirm the solution.

Manipulators create a simplified, emotionally resonant "Us vs. Them" narrative. Once the emotional investment (affective polarization) is established, any information, no matter how outlandish, that confirms the villainy of "Them" is instantly accepted without scrutiny. The Confirmation Bias acts as a psychological immunity shield against factual correction. The more tightly one is bound to the emotional identity of the group, the more ruthlessly the mind filters all incoming information to maintain that identity, making the individual fully exploitable by the group's leadership.

V. The Dissent Protocol: Institutionalizing Cognitive Friction

To fight Confirmation Bias, you cannot rely on willpower. You must create mandatory, structural protocols that force you to confront and analyze evidence that actively contradicts your initial, preferred hypothesis. This is the **Dissent Protocol.**

Defense 1: Mandatory Premortem Analysis (The "Future Failure" Drill)

Psychologist Gary Klein (1998) popularized the **Premortem** technique, which is the most powerful single tool for neutralizing CB. The traditional **Postmortem** asks, "What went wrong?", which is always biased by hindsight. The Premortem is proactive.

The Premortem Protocol:

1. **The Setup:** Before a major strategic decision (e.g., launching a new product, signing a merger, allocating budget), the team is assembled.
2. **The Frame:** The decision is made, and the team is told: *"It is now one year from today. The project failed spectacularly. Write down, on an anonymous index card, the three most likely reasons this catastrophic failure occurred."*
3. **The Analysis:** All failure reports are collected and read aloud *before* the final commitment.
4. **The Result:** By forcing the team to *assume failure* and work backward, the Premortem bypasses the Confirmation Bias entirely. The mind stops looking for reasons *why this will succeed* and starts looking for reasons *why this must be stopped.* This generates a list of actionable risks that the team, in their success-biased mindset, would have never considered.

Defense 2: Structured Devil's Advocacy (The Dissent Role)

Voluntary Devil's Advocacy fails because the person who raises dissent is often marginalized. The dissent must be mandatory, assigned, and tied to performance.

The Devil's Advocacy Protocol:

1. **Formal Assignment:** For every strategic decision team (whether it's four people or twenty), two people are formally assigned the **Dissent Role** (DA) at the start of the project.
2. **Job Description:** The DA's primary task is not merely to complain, but to construct the most plausible, data-driven counter-argument to the consensus hypothesis. They must be given dedicated time and resources to find *external* data that refutes the team's findings.
3. **Performance Metric:** The DA's performance review is judged solely on the **Quality of their Dissent**, did they uncover a systemic risk? Did they force a change in the original plan? It is *not* judged on whether the final plan succeeds. This decouples the dissent from the political risk of being wrong.
4. **The Rule of Three:** The Dissent Role is rotated such that no single person holds it for more than three meetings. This prevents the DA from becoming an institutionalized nag and prevents the team from marginalizing them as "just the crank."

Defense 3: The Data-Challenger Matrix (Separating Evidence from Belief)

When reviewing data, the team must use a structured matrix that forces the separation of belief from evidence.

1. **The Hypothesis Column:** Write down the team's current, favored hypothesis (e.g., "Market adoption will be 20% in Q2").
2. **The Contradictory Evidence Column:** Write down all data points, no matter how small, that *must* be true if the Hypothesis is false (e.g., "Competitor X's Q1 report shows only 5% growth").
3. **The Threshold Column:** Define the single point of contradictory evidence that, if proven true, **automatically stops the project.** This preemptively sets the failure trigger, forcing the team to confront their limits before the bias has a chance to take root.

VI. Summary and Forward Look

Confirmation Bias is the mind's desire for an easy, affirming life. The Echo Chamber is the organization's collective failure to pay the price of critical thought. The only way to win this fight is to make the process of confronting contradictory evidence mandatory, incentivized, and procedural. By institutionalizing skepticism via the Premortem and structured Dissent, we build an organization that thrives on reality, not comfort.

Next, we address the biases that chain us to the past: the Sunk Cost Fallacy and the deeply ingrained psychological need for consistency.

CHAPTER 4

THE SUNK COST FALLACY AND CONSISTENCY

I. The Emotional Anchor

We have systematically dealt with the cognitive threats that blind us (Halo/Authority) and the ones that make us panic (Scarcity/Urgency). Now, we face the subtlest, deepest gravitational force in the landscape of decision-making: the forces that **chain us to failure.**

This is the battlefield of the **Sunk Cost Fallacy (SCF)** and its powerful enforcer, the **Consistency and Commitment Bias**. These aren't just logical mistakes; they are profound, agonizing emotional traps. They compel us to keep shoveling good money, time, and reputation into a project that we know, deep down, is failing, simply because we cannot bear the pain of admitting that everything we invested *up to this point* was wasted.

The phrase "Sunk Cost" is derived from economics: a cost that has already been incurred and cannot be recovered. Rationally, these costs should have exactly *zero* bearing on future decisions. The only thing that should matter is the future cost-benefit ratio. But the human mind is not rational; it is narrative. And the narrative it hates most is: **"I was wrong, and I wasted everything."**

The SCF is the fear of regret externalized into an action plan. And the Consistency Bias is the social armor we put on to defend that regrettable decision. An adversary, whether it's a toxic partner, a failed business unit, or a manipulative vendor, doesn't need to pitch you a brand new idea; they just need to convince you that cutting your losses now would make all your previous sacrifices meaningless. And in the human mind, meaninglessness is a powerful deterrent.

II. The Sunk Cost Fallacy: The Obsession with Irrecoverability

The Anatomy of Waste

The classic example is the concert ticket: You bought a $200 ticket six months ago. Today, you have the flu. Rationally, you should stay home; the $200 is gone regardless. But the voice in your head screams, *"If I stay home, I will have wasted the $200!"* So, you drag your sick body to the concert, ensuring two outcomes: you still feel terrible, *and* you waste your evening.

The key behavioral insight here, confirmed repeatedly in psychological research (e.g., Arkes & Blumer, 1985), is that the decision to attend the concert is not driven by the potential enjoyment of the music, but by the desire to **avoid the psychological pain of feeling wasteful.**

In the corporate context, this phenomenon scales up disastrously:

1. **The Project Zombie:** A technology project, after three years and $50 million, has clearly failed to meet its original specs and the market has moved on. The managers involved know the right answer is termination. Yet, they push for another $10 million, arguing, "We can't walk away now, not after putting in $50 million. If we quit, that $50 million was for nothing." The decision is being made based on the $50 million (the Sunk Cost), not on the return on the $10 million *future* investment.
2. **The Bad Hire Persistence:** A manager realizes a new executive is a poor fit after six months of intense coaching and training. Firing the executive requires the manager to acknowledge that their entire vetting process and six months of personal effort were wasted. Instead, the manager persists, spending another six months coaching, hoping that the past investment in time and energy will magically pay off.

The SCF is fundamentally a flaw in temporal accounting. We allow past expenditure, which is utterly irrelevant to the present equation, to dictate future action. The money is gone. The time is gone. But the fear of *admitting* it's gone is what keeps the zombie project alive.

Cognitive Dissonance as Fuel

The psychological fuel for the SCF is **Cognitive Dissonance**. The mind is uncomfortable when its actions (investing $50M) conflict with reality (the project is failing). To resolve this dissonance, the mind doesn't accept the painful reality; it rationalizes the initial action. It says, "The project isn't failing; it's just *delayed*. We just need to give it a little more time. If it were truly a bad decision, I wouldn't have put $50 million into it." The investment itself becomes proof of the project's worth, even as the evidence mounts against it.

III. The Consistency Trap: Saving Face, Not Capital

If the Sunk Cost Fallacy is about protecting our internal sense of worth, the **Consistency and Commitment Bias** is about protecting our external status. This is the social glue that makes the SCF politically viable inside an organization.

Pioneering work by Robert Cialdini (1984) showed that once an individual commits to a stance, they experience powerful internal and external pressure to behave in a manner consistent with that commitment.

The Political Cost of Error

In a corporate environment, admitting the failure of a multi-million-dollar project is not merely an accounting entry; it is a political event. The decision to terminate a project means admitting the following:

- **The Initial Assessment:** The sponsor's original recommendation was fundamentally flawed.
- **The Ongoing Management:** The project lead wasted organizational resources for years.
- **The Oversight Body:** The board or committee failed in its governance role by continuing to fund the failure.

The Consistency Bias dictates that the decision-makers will prioritize *appearing* consistently right and competent over *being* fiscally responsible. The project lives on because killing it requires a public admission of fault from several high-ranking individuals, and the political capital required for that admission is often seen as a greater loss than the continued financial expenditure.

Incremental Commitment: The Exploit Delivery System

Adversaries, especially poor project managers, failing vendors, or toxic political leaders, understand that no one would sign up for a $100 million commitment to a flawed plan on Day One. So, they use **incrementalism** to exploit both the SCF and the Consistency Bias simultaneously.

The plan is delivered in a series of small, palatable commitments:

1. **Commitment 1:** $5M for a "Proof of Concept" (small, safe commitment).
2. **Commitment 2:** $10M for "Initial Implementation," leveraging the $5M Sunk Cost.
3. **Commitment 3:** $20M for "Phase II rollout," leveraging the now-$15M Sunk Cost.
4. **The Hook:** By the time the project hits $50M and is clearly failing, the organization is trapped. The political defense is no longer about the project's merit, but about preserving the chain of consistent commitments made over the past three years. "We can't quit now; we've already come this far." This is the sound of the consistency bias locking the trap.

The decision-makers have committed publicly, internally, and on paper. They are now committed to the consistency of their past actions, making them highly vulnerable to arguments centered on maintaining their reputation for good judgment. The exploit isn't the project itself; it's the sequence of commitments.

IV. Operational Defense: Decoupling Past from Future

To defeat the Sunk Cost Fallacy and the Consistency Bias, we must install structural safeguards that formally and psychologically decouple the past investment from the future decision. The central principle is radical, ruthless indifference to irrecoverable costs.

Defense 1: Zero-Based Review (Z.B.R.)

We must adapt the Zero-Based Budgeting concept to all high-risk, long-term investments. The decision to continue a project must be treated as if the project were being pitched for the *very first time*, with zero prior investment.

The Z.B.R. Protocol (The Non-Negotiable Annual Audit):

1. **The Blank Slate Assumption:** Annually (or semi-annually), every ongoing, multi-million dollar project is subjected to a Z.B.R. The reviewing body must ask: *"If this project had $0 invested in it today, and we had to decide whether to spend $X (the remaining budget) on it, would we say yes?"*
2. **Exclusion of Sunk Costs:** During the Z.B.R., the reviewing body is **formally prohibited** from viewing the "Cost to Date" metric. The only metrics allowed are:
    - Future Cost to Completion ($X)
    - Expected Future Value (EFV)
    - Return on Future Investment (ROFI)
    - Opportunity Cost (What else could we do with $X?)
3. **Mandatory Re-Pitch:** The project lead is forced to re-pitch the project to a neutral panel that was not involved in the initial approval. The burden of proof is on the project lead to justify the continuation *from a blank slate*. The defense "We've already invested so much" is automatically scored as an argumentative failure.

The ZBR is designed to force System 2 thinking by creating a new, objective temporal anchor (today) and violently ripping away the subjective, emotionally weighted anchor (the past).

Defense 2: The Two-Body Decoupling Rule (T.B.D.R.)

The Consistency Bias is strongest when the person who made the initial commitment is also the person responsible for the termination decision. We must separate these two functions institutionally.

The T.B.D.R. Protocol (Separating Commitment from Cessation):

1. **The Allocation Body (A-Body):** This group is responsible for *approving* the initial budget and plan. Their incentive is to succeed.
2. **The Continuation Review Body (C-Body):** This group is responsible for *reviewing the project's viability* and recommending its continuation or termination. The C-Body must be composed of individuals who had **no vested interest** in the A-Body's original decision. They are functionally disinterested.

3. **Cross-Functional C-Body:** The C-Body must be cross-functional—including someone from finance, someone from a completely unrelated operational unit, and someone from an external risk advisory group. Their independence shields them from the internal political pressure and the personal Consistency Bias of the project lead.

By outsourcing the cessation decision to a body with zero personal stake, the T.B.D.R. makes it politically feasible to terminate a failing venture, transforming the political risk of "admitting error" into the institutional virtue of "adhering to governance protocol."

Defense 3: The Conditional Commitment Clause (C.C.C.)

To defeat the slow, dangerous build-up of incremental commitments, we must make every funding approval conditional upon the *achievement of verifiable, external, and non-negotiable success metrics.*

The C.C.C. Protocol (Funding based on Facts, Not Time):

1. **Pre-defined Metrics:** Every funding tranche (e.g., $10 million) is approved *only* in exchange for the successful completion of a pre-agreed-upon, binary, measurable goal (e.g., "Must achieve 90% user acceptance testing completion," or "Must secure the final regulatory approval permit").
2. **The Automatic Stop:** If the metric is not met, the next tranche of funding is **automatically frozen** until the C-Body can conduct a Z.B.R.
3. **No "Time Served" Funding:** The funding review meetings must rigorously ignore time-based metrics (e.g., "We need more money because we've spent 80% of the allocated time"). The only metric is the percentage of the *goal* achieved.

The C.C.C. ensures that future resource allocation is tied entirely to *future merit* and *demonstrated progress*, not to the desperate need to justify past investment. It forces consistency with the original *goals*, not the past *actions*.

V. Case Studies in Freedom and Inertia

Case Study A: The Unkillable Acquisition (SCF and Consistency Failure)

- **Failure:** A major publisher acquired a small, expensive digital media startup three years ago, primarily based on the CEO's personal interest. The integration has been a disaster, losing $50 million. The CEO and the acquisition team are facing intense pressure to terminate the unit. Instead, they announce a "strategic pivot" requiring another $10 million. Their internal defense: "If we shut it down now, it will look like the last three years of effort and planning were a personal failure by leadership."

- **Exploit:** The CEO and the team were trapped by their own Consistency Bias and the $50 million Sunk Cost. They chose to risk $10 million more to avoid the political loss of reputation.
- **T.B.D.R. Defense:** The decision should have been immediately routed to a Continuation Review Body composed of non-involved leaders. This body would apply the Z.B.R. (ignoring the $50M) and likely find that investing $10M into a historically flawed unit with poor market fit yields a negative ROFI, thus making the termination politically neutral and institutionally rational.

Case Study B: The Toxic Relationship (Personal Consistency Trap)

- **Failure:** An individual knows their long-term professional partnership is toxic, unproductive, and mentally taxing. They've spent five years trying to "fix" the relationship, investing enormous emotional energy. They refuse to walk away, repeatedly telling colleagues, "I've tried too hard to quit now. I just need to give it one more chance."
  - **Exploit:** The individual is trapped by a personal Sunk Cost of five years of emotional labor and a Consistency Bias—the self-narrative that they are "loyal" and "perseverant." The decision is driven by pain avoidance, not future happiness.
  - **Z.B.R. Defense (Personal):** The individual needs to apply a personal Z.B.R. They must ask: "If I met this person for the first time today, and knew the outcome would be five years of pain, would I invest the first hour?" The answer forces a decoupling from the past effort and a focus on the immediate future opportunity cost of staying.

VI. Summary and Forward Look

The Sunk Cost Fallacy and the Consistency Bias turn us into custodians of our past mistakes. They make us afraid to be free. The core defense is structural: establishing **Zero-Based Reviews** that ignore past expenditures and creating **Two-Body Decoupling Rules** that remove the political cost of admitting error. By institutionalizing these mechanisms, we ensure that every high-stakes decision is based purely on the future value of the next dollar, not the emotional cost of the last one.

We have now neutralized the major forms of external and internal exploitation. Our final operational chapter will focus on building the continuous habit, the "muscle memory", of objective analysis. We move next to Chapter 6: Critical Thinking Shields.

CHAPTER 5

CRITICAL THINKING SHIELDS

I. The Necessity of the Friction Habit

We have spent the preceding chapters addressing specific cognitive exploits: the Halo and Authority biases that corrupt assessment, the Scarcity and Urgency biases that force panic, and the Sunk Cost and Consistency biases that anchor us to past mistakes. If those chapters were about installing the organizational firewalls and circuit breakers, this chapter is about the **daily training regimen.**

Critical thinking is not a natural state; it is a difficult, unnatural habit. Our brains are built for speed and comfort (System 1), not for the slow, analytical, uncomfortable work of objective reasoning (System 2). To maintain the effectiveness of the specialized protocols (like Premortem Analysis or Zero-Based Review), we must cultivate a continuous state of cognitive readiness. This requires building **Critical Thinking Shields**, daily, institutionalized habits that introduce friction into every aspect of decision-making, transforming analytical rigor from an exception to the rule.

This chapter details three essential, reinforcing shields: **The Adversarial Lens**, **The Explicit Assumption Log**, and **The Data Genealogy Trace.** These are designed to internalize the defensive mindset, making the default posture one of structured skepticism.

II. Shield 1: The Adversarial Lens (Turning the Tables)

The Adversarial Lens is the practice of constantly analyzing your own strategies, beliefs, and data streams from the perspective of an intelligent, resourceful opponent. It is the internalization of the "Red Team" mentality.

Most organizations spend 90% of their analytical energy confirming why their plan will succeed. The Adversarial Lens demands that you spend 90% of your energy trying to figure out **how the plan will fail, who will exploit it, and why the core assumptions are wrong.**

The Vulnerability Checklist

To activate this shield, every executive and manager must maintain a personal "Vulnerability Checklist" tied to any strategic proposal they endorse.

The Adversarial Lens Protocol:

1. **The Competitor Exploit:** Before launching a product or campaign, the team must answer: "If our smartest, most resource-rich competitor wanted to derail this entire project using one single, elegant move, what would that move be?" This forces the team to anticipate counter-moves rather than relying on market vacuum.
2. **The Regulatory/Political Attack:** When lobbying for a policy or moving into a new market, the team must ask: "What is the single, easiest narrative our political opponent could construct to make this look toxic, corrupt, or incompetent?" This forces the team to preemptively address the emotional and ethical vulnerabilities of their own argument, before the opponent can define them.
3. **The Internal Betrayal:** In evaluating security or HR policies, the question shifts to: "If the most disgruntled, low-level employee wanted to cause maximum organizational damage, what is the weakest link they would exploit?" This is the inverse of the Authority Bias defense: it forces you to trust the weakest link, not the strongest.

The Adversarial Lens is a constant mental discipline. It takes the subjective joy out of self-validation and replaces it with the objective security of having anticipated the worst. It prevents the planning process from becoming an exercise in self-congratulation.

III. Shield 2: The Explicit Assumption Log (Exposing the Foundation)

The greatest dangers lurk not in the known facts, but in the things we accept as true without ever articulating them. We operate every day on a tower of unexamined assumptions, about market stability, competitor behavior, employee motivation, and resource availability. When a plan fails, it is rarely due to a surprise event; it is almost always due to the failure of one of these silent, implicit assumptions.

The Explicit Assumption Log (E.A.L.) is a formal tool designed to force the articulation, challenging, and tracking of every foundational belief that supports a decision.

Formalizing the Unsaid

For any decision exceeding a pre-defined threshold (e.g., $1 million expenditure, 100 hours of staff time), a dedicated log must be created.

The E.A.L. Protocol:

1. **The Assumption Inventory:** Before the plan is finalized, the team must list every single assumption required for the plan's success. *Example assumptions:* "Market growth rate will remain above 5%," "Competitor X will not enter this sector for 18 months," "Our current engineering team can deliver the solution with current resources."
2. **The Probability Rating (P-Rating):** Each assumption is assigned a probability rating (e.g., High, Medium, Low) based on external, verifiable data. If an assumption (like Competitor X's inaction) has a Low P-Rating, the plan is fragile.
3. **The Metric of Disproof:** The most critical step is defining the exact, measurable event that would prove the assumption **false**.
    - *Example:* Assumption: "Market growth rate will remain above 5%." Metric of Disproof: "Q2 industry report shows 3.5% growth."
    - The team commits: If the Metric of Disproof is triggered, the entire plan is automatically subjected to a mandatory **Zero-Based Review (Z.B.R.)**—the Sunk Cost defense from Chapter 5.

This E.A.L. is the institutional answer to Confirmation Bias. Instead of letting the bias quietly confirm its assumptions, the E.A.L. forces the team to proactively search for the data that will disprove them. It moves the conversation from *believing* to *testing*.

IV. Shield 3: The Data Genealogy Trace (Source Integrity)

The modern decision-maker is flooded with data, but rarely knows the lineage of that data. The Authority Bias taught us to trust the source based on rank. The Data Genealogy Trace (D.G.T.) teaches us to trust the data based on its **origin, path, and manipulation history.**

The D.G.T. is the defense against internal Echo Chambers and external misinformation. It forces the question: *Who touched this data, and why?*

Tracking the Chain of Custody

The principle is simple: data that has been filtered, aggregated, or summarized multiple times is exponentially more likely to be contaminated by human bias or simplification. The further the data gets from its raw, original source, the less reliable it becomes.

The D.G.T. Protocol:

1. **The Primary Source Mandate:** For all critical metrics, the presentation must include a reference to the **Primary Source** (Level 1 data)—the raw survey response, the direct financial transaction log, the unedited interview transcript. Any analysis based only on Level 3 (aggregated/summarized/reported) data is provisionally rejected.
2. **The Filter Audit:** The team must identify every "filter" the data passed through. A filter is any human or algorithmic process that changed the data (e.g., *Analyst A aggregated the numbers, Algorithm B applied a smoothing function, The Marketing VP selected only positive quotes*). Every filter is an opportunity for Confirmation Bias or Authority Bias to contaminate the result.
3. **Bias Tagging:** If data is passed through a known filter, it must be "Bias Tagged." If the CEO's favorite analyst filtered the data, the report must be labeled: **"CEO's Office Filtered - Bias Risk High."** This neutralizes the Authority Bias by explicitly stating its potential influence on the data's integrity.

By demanding to see the raw materials and the chain of custody, the D.G.T. prevents the team from making multi-million dollar decisions based on PowerPoint slides that were based on aggregated reports that were based on an analyst's five-year-old spreadsheet.

V. Operationalizing the Routine

These shields are useless unless they are adopted as routine, organizational muscle memory.

1. **Mandatory Training Cycles:** Critical thinking must be a required, non-optional training module every quarter, focusing not on theory, but on the practical application of the protocols: running a mock Premortem, filling out a Z.B.R. scorecard, and tracing data genealogy in a current project.
2. **Leadership Modeling:** The shields must be visibly deployed by senior leadership. When the CEO asks a question, it should be, "What does the E.A.L. say about this market entry assumption?" not, "Is this team feeling confident?" If leadership models the rigor, the organization follows. If leadership ignores the protocols, the entire system collapses back into comfortable Groupthink.
3. **The Audit of Dissent:** The organization must actively audit the volume and quality of its dissent. If the weekly status reports show universal consensus, the leadership should not be celebrating; they should be alarmed. Universal consensus is a strong indicator that the Adversarial Lens is disengaged and the Echo Chamber is fully operational. The goal is not consensus; it is **clarity.**

VI. Summary and Forward Look

The Critical Thinking Shields are the final layer of defense. They represent the commitment to fight the mind's natural gravitational pull toward ease, comfort, and confirmation. By institutionalizing the **Adversarial Lens**, maintaining the **Explicit Assumption Log**, and rigorously enforcing the **Data Genealogy Trace**, we build a cognitive architecture that is resilient to its own flawed design. We create friction where it is needed most.

With the defensive shields now established, we move to the Conclusion, synthesizing all four books into a single, comprehensive security mandate for the modern era.

CONCLUSION

I. The End of the Beginning: From Perimeter to Processor

We began this journey by defining security not as a static state, but as a relentless, multi-layered campaign against compromise. We started with the perimeter: hardening the physical and digital shell against brute force and technical exploit. We then moved to the core human element, addressing the predators who seek to leverage empathy and trust, the Dark Triad, by building protocols of awareness and self-preservation.

But Book 4, and specifically this conclusion, marks the final, most critical pivot. We shifted from fighting *them*, the external adversaries, the hackers, the psychopaths, to fighting *us*. The most expensive, catastrophic, and persistent threats we face rarely arrive through a firewall breach or a convincing lie from a charismatic villain. They arrive through **comfort.** They are generated internally by our own minds' predictable laziness, our addiction to being right, and our profound, primal fear of loss and complexity.

If you ignore the defenses outlined in the preceding chapters, you can have the highest-grade titanium alloy walls and the most advanced biometrics in the world, yet your system will remain fatally compromised. Why? Because the person making the final, multi-million dollar decision, the person with the ultimate authority, will be influenced by the clean haircut of the presenter (Halo Effect), the looming deadline (Urgency), or the political pressure to justify the time already spent (Sunk Cost Fallacy).

The core thesis of this entire manual, culminating here, is simple: **Security is not an IT problem, a compliance problem, or an HR problem. It is a fundamental cognitive discipline.**

II. The Synthesis of the Cognitive Firewall

The defense against cognitive exploitation is not rooted in psychology, but in institutional engineering. We have engineered procedural friction at the precise moments of maximum vulnerability. These protocols must be codified, mandated, and audited; they must be made non-negotiable, just like your password policy.

Let us review the operational mandates of the Cognitive Firewall:

A. Defense Against Corrupted Assessment (Neutralizing the Halo and Authority)

The moment of initial judgment is the moment of greatest vulnerability. The adversary knows they only need one striking, irrelevant trait, a prestigious title, overwhelming charisma, or a perfectly crafted presentation deck, to win the first round and contaminate all subsequent analysis.

- **The Problem:** The Halo Effect and Authority Bias allow one positive quality or one badge of rank to corrupt the entire perception of competence and integrity. You see a genius where there is only a well-dressed mediocrity.
- **The Solution: Disaggregation and Deference Protocols.** We fight subjective coherence with objective fragmentation. The **Disaggregated Metric Analysis (D.M.A.)** forces the evaluation of disparate traits (charisma, technical skill, financial history) in isolation, stripping away the influence of the single, shining factor. Furthermore, **Proceduralized Skepticism (P.S.)** demands that we treat every assertion made by an authority figure as merely a hypothesis, subject to the "Five Whys" analysis, regardless of the speaker's rank. This creates a safe, institutional method for asking the necessary, uncomfortable questions without risking political reprisal. We are decoupling the data from the deliverer.

B. Defense Against Induced Panic (Neutralizing Scarcity, Urgency, and Loss Aversion)

These are the biases that bypass the frontal lobe entirely, speaking directly to the amygdala, the brain's fear center. They are deployed when the goal is to elicit an immediate, irreversible, and unanalyzed commitment. The feeling is always one of intense, immediate pressure: "If you hesitate, you lose."

- **The Problem:** Loss Aversion means the fear of losing $100 outweighs the joy of gaining $100. Scarcity and Urgency are weaponized to trigger this loss aversion by creating artificial deadlines and limited availability, forcing a choice between incomplete data and guaranteed regret.
- **The Solution: Temporal Decoupling.** The only countermeasure to pressure is the institutionalization of the pause. The **Temporal De-Coupling Defense (T.D.D.)** is a mandatory, non-negotiable policy that prohibits commitment to any high-stakes, time-sensitive decision within a minimum cooling-off period (e.g., 48 hours). This transfers the friction from the individual's emotional struggle to the organization's impersonal policy manual. Crucially, we must also neutralize the gravitational pull of the status quo by using the **Cost-of-Status-Quo Audit (C.S.Q.A.)**, which reframes inertia itself as a massive, ongoing, measurable loss, thereby leveraging the power of loss aversion against itself to achieve necessary change.

C. Defense Against Cognitive Inertia (Neutralizing Confirmation and Sunk Cost)

These are the biases of persistence, the psychological anchors that keep the ship sailing toward the iceberg, even after the crew has sighted the danger. They ensure we continue failing, but comfortably so.

- **The Problem:** The mind is addicted to confirming its existing beliefs (Confirmation Bias) and justifying its past decisions (Sunk Cost Fallacy). This leads to Groupthink and the fatal decision to pour good resources after bad, not out of stupidity, but out of a deep-seated fear of admitting past error.
- **The Solution: Proactive Dissent and Zero-Based Accounting.** We must structurally mandate the search for disconfirming evidence. The **Premortem Analysis** forces the team to anticipate spectacular failure, preemptively exposing the flawed

assumptions that Confirmation Bias would otherwise protect. To defeat the Sunk Cost trap, the **Zero-Based Review (Z.B.R.)** demands that ongoing projects be periodically evaluated as if they were new proposals with zero prior investment. This makes the continuation decision dependent entirely on the future Return on Future Investment (ROFI), ruthlessly decoupling financial accountability from historical regret. The **Two-Body Decoupling Rule (T.B.D.R.)** further isolates the initial commitment from the cessation decision, removing the political disincentive for termination.

III. The Meta-Defense: The Principle of Inconvenience

If there is one overarching philosophy that unites every defense protocol in Book 4, it is the **Principle of Inconvenience.**

The human brain, and by extension, the human organization, will always choose the path of least resistance. That path is always the path of bias: it's easier to agree with the boss than challenge them; it's easier to finish the project than to admit the waste; it's easier to believe the report that confirms your optimism. The adversary exploits this natural laziness.

Our defense, therefore, must make the path of *biased, comfortable* decision-making actively *more difficult* than the path of *rational, critical* decision-making.

Critical thinking must be made a bureaucratic requirement, not an optional virtue. It must be expensive (in terms of time and procedural steps) to fail to challenge an assumption, and cheap (in terms of political capital) to raise a valid objection. This requires a profound culture shift where **dissent is not tolerated; it is mandatory and rewarded.** When the organization's leaders reward the individual who stopped the bad deal over the one who flawlessly executed the mediocre one, the System 2 cognitive firewall is fully operational.

IV. The Four Pillars of Total Security: A Final Synthesis

As we conclude this security manual, it is essential to synthesize the four distinct, yet interlocking, pillars of total security. None of these pillars is sufficient on its own. A vulnerability in one is a potential exploit for the entire structure.

1. **Pillar I: Structural Resilience (Book 1):** The Physical and Digital Shell. This is the foundation: the firewalls, the access control, the encryption, and the data governance that protect the *assets*

and the *perimeters*. Without this, the system is exposed to blunt force attack.

2. **Pillar II: Interpersonal Awareness (Book 2 & 3):** The Predatory Filter. This is the defense against human malice: the structured protocols for vetting, identifying, and neutralizing the Dark Triad personalities (Narcissism, Machiavellianism, Psychopathy) who seek to gain influence to exploit trust and resources. This protects the *culture* and the *team*.
3. **Pillar III: Cognitive Integrity (Book 4):** The Self-Securing Processor. This is the defense against internal sabotage: the deployment of protocols like Z.B.R., Premortem, and T.D.D. to manage the human mind's inherent flaws. This protects the *judgment* and the *decision-making process*.
4. **Pillar IV: Adaptive Vigilance (The Future):** The Commitment. The final, ongoing pillar is the recognition that security is never finished. Every protocol must be continuously tested against new exploitation methods, and every failure must be viewed not as a mistake, but as a mandatory, brutal audit of the current defense architecture.

The greatest risk is not the complexity of the threat, but the complacency of the defense. Complacency is merely the resting state of the Confirmation and Authority Biases: it is the comfortable belief that everything is fine because the system hasn't crashed *yet*.

Our ultimate goal is not to eliminate risk, but to ensure that when compromise occurs, it is due to a genuinely new threat, not the predictable failure of a human mind relying on shortcuts. The age of comfortable intuition in high-stakes environments is over. The time for structural, procedural, and inconvenient rationality has begun.

REFLECTION QUESTIONS

I. The Conversion from Knowledge to Practice

We have detailed the architecture of the human system's internal vulnerabilities, the points of predictable failure where external adversaries (or internal inertia) can leverage cognitive shortcuts to compromise judgment. Understanding these biases, the Halo Effect, Urgency, Sunk Cost, and Confirmation Bias, is merely the prerequisite for security. True resilience is achieved only when this knowledge is converted into **uncomfortable, actionable self-audit.**

This chapter serves as a rigorous, structured questionnaire for both the individual leader and the organization. Its purpose is not to grade your current performance, but to force the articulation of the implicit assumptions that are currently governing your high-stakes decisions. Treat this not as a survey, but as a mandatory security penetration test on your own decision-making process.

The answers you write down should reveal not where you *intend* to go, but where your **unexamined biases** are currently steering you.

II. Auditing External Influence: The Assessment Biases

These questions probe the integrity of your input stream, ensuring that data is decoupled from the charisma or rank of the source.

The Halo Effect and Disaggregated Metrics:

1. **Metric Integrity:** When reviewing the last three major proposals presented to you (e.g., investment, hire, strategy pivot), did you have access to the raw data *before* you saw the presenter's visual execution and personal pitch? If the presenter's charisma or polish influenced your initial assessment (e.g., "This just feels right"), what specific, objective metric did you use to override that feeling?
2. **Trait Isolation:** Can you name one highly successful individual in your professional orbit whom you fundamentally *do not* trust? If you cannot, are you confusing their demonstrated success (Halo) with their actual integrity or competence in a new, unrelated domain?
3. **The "Aesthetic" Cost:** What percentage of your allocated budget is currently tied up in projects that were approved primarily because of the perceived brilliance, the high-quality presentation, or the prestige of the initial delivery team, rather than a quantifiable **Return on Investment (ROI)** metric? (Hint: Any approval based on "vision" or "market momentum" without verifiable metrics is a high-risk Halo activation.)

The Authority Bias and Deference Protocols:

4. **The Safe Dissent Score:** Name the last time a subordinate successfully challenged one of your firmly held beliefs. Was that dissent rewarded, or was it met with political friction? If it was met with friction, what specific institutional mechanism (Proceduralized Skepticism, Dissent Role) failed to protect the individual from personal risk?
5. **The Five Whys Failure:** In the last critical decision made by your executive team, how many times was a senior leader's assertion accepted without requiring them to articulate the full **"Five Whys"** chain of reasoning leading back to the primary source data? If the answer is greater than zero, you are substituting deference for due diligence.

6. **The Boardroom Echo:** In your last three formal meetings, did anyone outside of the core decision-making team (e.g., an external advisor, a junior analyst) challenge the strategic trajectory? If not, is your vetting process designed to select for competence, or for cultural conformity and political obedience?

III. Auditing Temporal and Emotional Pressure: The Panic Biases

These questions determine if your organization is structurally capable of saying "No" to an offer designed to elicit fear.

Scarcity and Urgency (The Temporal De-Coupling Defense):

7. **The T.D.D. Compliance Log:** Over the last quarter, how many decisions involving over $500,000 were subject to an "Act Now or Lose It" deadline? For each one, did you successfully invoke the **Temporal De-Coupling Defense (T.D.D.)**? If the deal closed successfully *within* the adversary's original tight deadline, your T.D.D. is non-operational, and you allowed fear to dictate terms.
8. **The Authenticity of the Deadline:** When presented with an urgent deadline, what specific, non-negotiable external factor (e.g., a regulatory closing date, a scheduled satellite launch) made that deadline real? If the deadline was justified solely by the phrase "our fiscal quarter end," "I have another buyer," or "internal targets," you were subjected to manufactured pressure and failed to deploy the **Price Anchoring Nullification (P.A.N.)** defense.
9. **The Cost of Waiting:** When faced with a perceived scarcity (e.g., "limited talent pool," "last deal at this price"), did you actually quantify the cost of waiting two weeks for a better deal? Or did you allow the fear of *missing out* to overwhelm the logic of **Return on Investment (ROI)**?

Loss Aversion and Sunk Cost Fallacy:

10. **The Status Quo Loss:** Identify one major process, vendor, or project in your organization that everyone agrees is "clunky" or "outdated." Quantify the precise **Total Annualized Cost of the Status Quo (C.S.Q.A.)** for that item, including labor inefficiency, opportunity cost, and political friction. By what factor does this quantifiable loss outweigh the estimated cost of disruption caused by replacement? If the replacement cost is lower, yet the item persists, your organization is being held hostage by Loss Aversion.

11. **The Zombie Project Log:** How many projects currently in your portfolio have had their initial scope, deadline, and budget revised more than twice? For each of these "Zombie Projects," was the decision to continue made by the individual who championed the initial investment? If yes, the **Two-Body Decoupling Rule (T.B.D.R.)** has been breached, and the project is likely being perpetuated by the Consistency Bias, not future merit.
12. **The Zero-Based Review (Z.B.R.):** Name the last long-term project subjected to a true Z.B.R., where the **Cost to Date** metric was completely hidden from the reviewing body. Was the final decision to continue based solely on the projected **Return on Future Investment (ROFI)**, or did the conversation devolve into justifying past expenditure?

IV. Auditing Cognitive Inertia: The Persistence Biases

These questions test the structural safeguards designed to force the confrontation of uncomfortable truths.

13. **The Premortem Risk:** Recall the last **Premortem Analysis** performed. List the top three catastrophic failure scenarios identified. Were those scenarios fundamentally new risks that the core planning team had previously overlooked, or were they obvious, low-hanging fruit? High-quality Premortems uncover blind spots; low-quality ones confirm the consensus.
14. **The Explicit Assumption Log (E.A.L.) Test:** Pull the E.A.L. for your current highest-priority project. How many of the foundational assumptions have a **Metric of Disproof** that relies on data external to your organization (e.g., competitor filings, macro-economic reports) versus data internal to your project (e.g., internal testing results)? Fragile projects rely on internal data to confirm external assumptions.
15. **The Data Genealogy Trace (D.G.T.):** Choose a major metric currently driving your strategy (e.g., "Customer Lifetime Value"). Trace the lineage of that number. How many human analysts, algorithmic filters, or political summaries did the number pass through before reaching your presentation slide? If you cannot identify the **Level 1 (raw source) data** in under five minutes, your entire strategy is based on aggregated, high-risk data that has likely been contaminated by Confirmation Bias.

16. **The Cost of Dissent:** If your organization's Chief Risk Officer (or equivalent) forced the termination of a $20 million project based on a Z.B.R. finding, what would be the subsequent impact on their political standing and career trajectory? If the cost is anything other than "neutral or positive," your organization has outsourced its risk management to individuals who are incentivized to fail quietly rather than succeed loudly.

V. The Personal Scorecard: The Leader's Integrity

These final questions challenge the individual leader's commitment to the principle of inconvenient rationality.

17. **The Public Apology:** When was the last time you publicly, without qualification, admitted you were wrong about a major strategic decision that resulted in a cost to the organization? If the answer is more than six months ago, you are actively modeling the **Consistency Bias** for your subordinates, teaching them that political survival outweighs intellectual integrity.
18. **The Trust Metric:** Name two people on your team whose core competency is disagreement with you. How frequently do you meet with them, and what percentage of your allocated discussion time is spent challenging their perspective versus asking them to challenge yours?
19. **The Fatigue Indicator:** When does your personal commitment to these audit protocols (T.D.D., Z.B.R., P.S.) start to fade? Is it during periods of high organizational success (Complacency), or high organizational stress (Panic)? Identifying the fatigue indicator is the first step toward building procedural safeguards against it.

The continuous, uncomfortable audit of the self is the highest form of security. Your answers to these questions define your organization's true risk exposure.

BOOK FIVE

EMOTIONAL CONTROL: MASTERING EMOTIONAL INTELLIGENCE TO DEFLECT MANIPULATION

INTRODUCTION

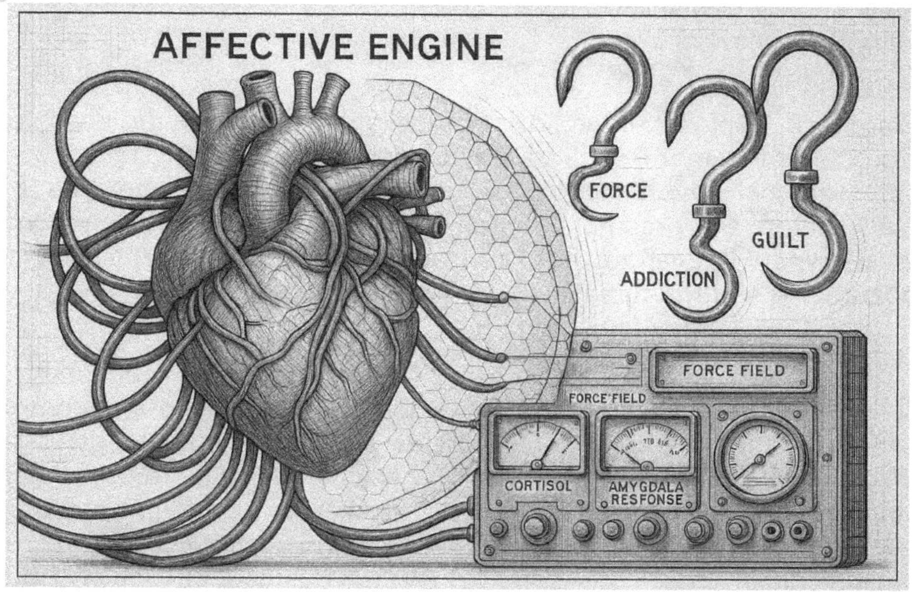

I. The Last Exploit Vector

We began this manual by addressing perimeter security, moved to the malware of the mind (The Dark Triad), and finally developed the cognitive firewall against internal bias (Book 4). If the system remains compromised, the vulnerability is now isolated to the single most volatile and reliable vector: **human emotion.**

The sophisticated adversary, whether a strategic competitor, a political manipulator, or a malignant relationship partner, rarely wastes time attempting to brute-force a physical door or bypass a two-factor authentication system. They understand that the highest value exploits are those that subvert the decision-making process *before* the conscious mind is engaged.

Emotional states are not merely feelings; they are **states of vulnerability.** They are predictable, systemic openings that temporarily disable critical thinking, breach rational boundaries, and force commitment under duress. To the adversary, an individual gripped by blinding fear, paralyzing guilt, or addictive anticipation is a system operating in emergency mode, easily manipulated and prone to cascading failure.

This book is dedicated to establishing **Emotional Sovereignty**: the ability to analytically identify, precisely categorize, and strategically control your own affective state, thereby denying the adversary the only remaining reliable vector for exploit.

II. The Weaponization of Affect: The Triple Threat

Emotional exploitation follows predictable patterns, designed to transition the target from a state of objective neutrality (System 2) to a state of subjective reaction (System 1). The tactics employed by manipulators and predators rely on three primary, universal emotional levers. We will analyze these not as psychological concepts, but as **operational security threats**:

A. Fear and Intimidation (The Panic Switch)

This attack vector bypasses logic by manufacturing immediate, high-stakes threat scenarios. Its goal is the rapid, irreversible loss of control and the compliance born of self-preservation. It leverages existential anxiety, financial risk, and physical or social threat to force a high-velocity, low-quality decision. In a high-stakes negotiation or strategic conflict, this is often disguised as *Aggressive Deadline Setting* or *Manufactured Crisis*. The defense against this is not bravery, but **physiological regulation** and the mandatory introduction of procedural delay.

B. Guilt and Shame (The Internal Compliance Officer)

This is the most insidious vector, as it transforms the target's internal moral compass into a self-imposed prison. Guilt is the feeling of having *done* something wrong; shame is the paralyzing feeling of *being* something wrong. The adversary uses these states to enforce **unreasonable obligation** and **suppress dissent.** By activating the target's desire to be good, loyal, or competent, the adversary bypasses logical self-interest and compels obedience, often making the target actively complicit in their own exploitation. The defense is the rigorous separation of **Action** from **Identity**.

C. Love Bombing and Intermittent Reinforcement (The Addiction Loop)

This vector operates not through threat, but through manufactured euphoria and psychological dependency. It establishes an intense, intoxicating connection (**Love Bombing**) followed by erratic, unpredictable withdrawal and reward (**Intermittent Reinforcement**). This variability creates a powerful, addictive loop (the **Trauma Bond**), making the target dependent on the adversary for emotional validation, thereby neutralizing boundaries and overriding critical self-assessment. The defense requires analytical deconstruction of the reward system and the re-establishment of intrinsic self-worth.

III. The Defense Architecture: Emotional Granularity and Sovereignty

The traditional answer to emotional manipulation, "Don't be emotional", is useless and impossible. Humans are affective beings. The goal is not suppression, but **Mastery through Precision.**

Our defense strategy hinges on two operational concepts:

1. Emotional Granularity (The Diagnostic Tool)

Granularity is the ability to precisely differentiate and label emotional states beyond the simple, binary labels (e.g., "bad," "stressed," "happy"). When an adversary deploys a fear tactic, the granular mind doesn't just register "fear"; it registers: *My amygdala is active, this is low-grade social anxiety, tied to the fear of professional embarrassment, and my cortisol levels are rising.* This precise identification moves the emotion from an overwhelming subjective experience to an **analyzable data point**, allowing the cognitive firewall (System 2) to re-engage.

2. Emotional Sovereignty (The Control Protocol)

Sovereignty is the self-governance of the internal state. It is the ability to choose how to respond, rather than being compelled to react. This is built by mastering the internal physiological connection (**Somatic Sovereignty**) and establishing external, non-negotiable personal and professional **Boundaries**. If boundaries are the structural security fence, emotional sovereignty is the guard force that enforces the perimeter, regardless of the emotional climate.

IV. The Path Forward

The subsequent chapters will transform these concepts into actionable defense protocols:

- **Chapters 2-4** will surgically dissect the three primary emotional exploits: Fear/Intimidation, Guilt/Shame, and Love Bombing/Reinforcement. For each, we will define the exploit payload and its psychological target.
- **Chapter 5** will introduce the practical tools for developing **Emotional Granularity**, turning subjective feeling into objective, manageable data.

- **Chapter 6** will cover the engineering of **Fortified Boundaries**, defining the non-negotiable, systemic defense structures that prevent emotional debt and unauthorized affective access.

By the end of this book, the affective attack surface will be minimized, and the individual leader will possess the tools necessary to maintain objective control, even when facing the most volatile forms of emotional warfare. The final layer of security is the most difficult, but the most essential: mastering the turbulent interior landscape.

CHAPTER 1

FEAR AND INTIMIDATION TACTICS

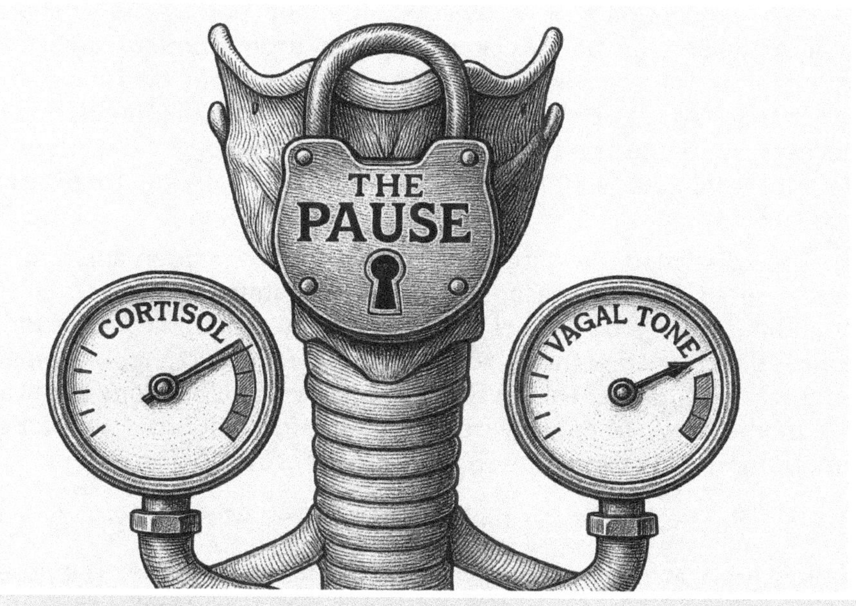

I. The Cost of the Shunt: When Survival Trumps Sense

There is a moment in high-stakes conflict, a negotiation, a confrontation, a sudden threat, when the lights go out in the front of your mind. You feel the sudden, hollow drop in your stomach, the rush of heat to your face, and the immediate, overwhelming urge to either run or submit. Your vision narrows. Every complex thought you had prepared moments before dissolves, replaced by one screaming, primal imperative: *End this now.*

This moment is not a failure of character; it is a clinical, evolutionary process known as the amygdala hijack, and it is the most reliable exploit in the manipulator's handbook.

In the previous book, we discussed how the adversary targets cognitive *bias*. Here, they target cognitive *failure*. The adversary's most effective weapon isn't intelligence or superior data; it is their ability to induce a state of physiological stress that temporarily **shunts** your consciousness away from the prefrontal cortex, the seat of logic, planning, and long-term consequence, directly to the limbic system, the home of pure reaction.

When this shunt occurs, your high-powered, analytical brain locks up like a cheap hard drive, and you default to the code written for the savannah: **fight, flight, or freeze.**

The astute predator knows you cannot perform a cost-benefit analysis while your body is preparing to outrun a predator. They know you cannot enforce a difficult boundary when your nervous system is screaming, "Agreement equals safety." The goal of all intimidation is not necessarily to execute the threat, but simply to trigger the shunt. They are not trying to win the argument; they are trying to **disarm the operator.**

Once disarmed, the target, desperate for the sudden and immediate cessation of the unpleasant physiological state, the dry mouth, the pounding heart, the tunnel vision, will pay any price in boundaries, concessions, or compliance to make the threat, and the accompanying internal alarm, stop. This exchange, trading valuable, long-term assets for momentary, temporary relief, is the foundational transaction of emotional exploitation. And this, we must absolutely forbid.

II. The Architecture of Anxiety: Three Attack Payloads

Intimidation, in the arenas of finance, politics, or complex relationships, rarely arrives in the form of a straightforward, criminal threat. It is far more sophisticated, leveraging ambient anxiety and the target's internal status concerns. We must train ourselves to recognize the signature of these three primary attack payloads, understanding that their power resides entirely in their ability to generate urgency and fear of consequence.

A. The Manufactured Crisis: The Temporal Confinement

This tactic is the operational twin of the Scarcity and Urgency biases. It is the adversary's attempt to impose a sudden, non-negotiable temporal confinement on a complex, high-stakes decision.

The threat doesn't have to be violent; it only has to be **catastrophic and irreversible.** The language is always definitive, laced with finality: "This deal is dead in four hours," "If we don't approve this budget immediately, the entire initiative collapses," or, on a personal level, "If you walk out that door, you will never see me again."

The psychological target here is two-fold: **Loss Aversion** and the **Compulsion for Closure.** The manipulator forces the target's entire focus onto the rapidly shrinking window of opportunity, ensuring that the target's only internal calculation is: *How do I avoid the guaranteed regret of missing the deadline?* The contents of the document, the fairness of the terms, the long-term feasibility of the commitment, all of these slow, System 2 considerations are systematically erased by the speed of the impending catastrophe.

The moment this payload hits, the internal narrative shifts from *Is this a good idea?* to *I must decide, or I will be responsible for the loss.* The manipulation works by transferring the responsibility for the crisis from the aggressor (who manufactured the timeline) to the target (who is now perceived as failing to act fast enough). The antidote is not to accelerate, but to structurally, philosophically, and procedurally **decline the timeline.**

B. The Performance of Fury: Aggressive Anchoring

This payload is less about time and more about atmosphere, using intense, theatrical emotionality to manipulate social and psychological comfort. The adversary launches an initial, intensely aggressive, or hostile emotional anchor: screaming, sudden bursts of rage, outrageous demands delivered with absolute conviction, or the theatrical collapse into tearful, accusatory despair.

The true goal of this performance is not to negotiate; it is to **establish an intensely uncomfortable emotional gradient.** The manipulator uses their own highly activated emotional state to create a social environment that is fundamentally intolerable to the target.

The typical target's response is an immediate, reflexive urge toward **Restoration of Harmony.** Most humans are hardwired to avoid intense, sustained conflict. The target, overwhelmed by the intensity of the adversary's performance, will rush to apologize, concede, and offer unnecessary compensation just to make the noise stop, to bring the room back to a state of emotional zero. They concede not because the demand is logical, but because the *cost of maintaining the conflict* is too high for their nervous system.

This is why effective manipulators often anchor with an utterly insane demand: a 70% discount, an impossible timeline, a complete reversal of a previously agreed term. They know the target will focus only on minimizing the emotional pain of the confrontation, leading to rapid, panicked concessions that still land the adversary far ahead of where they would have been in a rational negotiation. They are selling the target temporary emotional relief at a massive financial or strategic cost.

C. The Ghost in the Room: The Ambiguous Threat

This is the quiet assassin of the three payloads, leveraging the most potent weapon of all: the target's own imagination. The Silent Threat relies on implication, vague warnings, and suggestive rhetoric, never committing to a concrete, articulable action.

The language is slippery: "I'm not saying I'd *do* anything, but it would be a shame if your investors heard about that little problem," or "I just hope your reputation can handle the stress of a public inquiry," delivered with a look that says everything and nothing.

The core strength of the Ambiguity Weapon is that the human mind, once presented with an undefined but serious risk, will inevitably fill the vacuum with the **worst-case scenario** tailored precisely to its own deepest insecurities (financial ruin, public shame, loss of job). The threat becomes amplified precisely because it is never defined. It cannot be quantified, budgeted against, or legally addressed.

The result is chronic, low-grade fear, a constant state of hyper-vigilance where the target is perpetually self-censoring and preemptively obeying the manipulator, simply to avoid activating the potential, unknown catastrophic consequence. This creates the state of **low-voltage compliance**, where the target does all the manipulator's work for them, convinced that they are simply managing risk.

III. The Defense: The Inevitability of the Pause

You cannot fight fire with fire. You cannot fight panic with panic. The only effective countermeasure to a high-velocity, high-stress exploit is the mandatory, non-negotiable **Pause.** We must transform the pause from an optional moment of weakness into a structurally mandated act of strength. The defense must be layered, addressing the physiological hijack first, and the procedural compliance second.

Layer 1: The Vagal Circuit Breaker (Internal Sovereignty)

The immediate, 60-second priority is to regain control of your own body before allowing a single word of consequence to leave your mouth. This is the act of establishing Emotional Sovereignty.

1. **Immediate State Labelling:** The moment the physiological alarm sounds (the heat, the dizziness, the internal surge), the immediate, disciplined counter-thought must be: *"I am being triggered. This is a stress response, not a survival response. I am safe in this chair."* This cognitive label interrupts the System 1 loop. It moves the experience from a subjective crisis to an objective,

measurable event.

2. **The Box Breathing Ritual:** This must become an inviolable, mandatory ritual deployed before any high-stakes verbal response. It is the fastest way to activate the vagus nerve and restore access to the frontal lobe.
   - Find a subtle anchor (the corner of the table, your pen).
   - **Inhale slowly through the nose (Count of 4).** Feel the pause, the moment of resistance.
   - **Hold (Count of 4).** Focus entirely on the physical sensation of the air.
   - **Exhale slowly, fully, through the mouth (Count of 6).** The longer exhale is critical, as it is the primary signal to the nervous system that the danger is receding.
   - Repeat this four to six times.

This exercise is not about finding peace; it is a **mechanical reboot.** It is a deliberate act of will to force the parasympathetic system back online, physically reversing the adrenaline and cortisol shunt. You must not speak until this reboot is complete, regardless of how long the silence lasts. The silence, in this moment, is the sound of your system stabilizing.

Layer 2: The Procedural Deflection (External Shielding)

Once physiological control is regained, the defense pivots to enforcing procedural friction, denying the adversary the rapid commitment they require.

1. **The "Neutral Deferral" Mandate:** The *only* permitted response to any Manufactured Crisis or aggressive deadline must be a neutral, non-emotional statement that transfers the decision-making authority from your compromised self to an impersonal, mandatory institutional policy (the **Temporal De-Coupling Defense**).
   - *The Script:* "I understand the extreme urgency you are expressing. However, my authority is constrained by our organization's mandatory 24-hour review period for all commitments over [X value]. I must have this request documented in writing for our risk committee. I will initiate the review immediately and provide a formal response at [specific time tomorrow]."

- *The Power:* This response does three things: a) It validates the adversary's feeling ("I understand the urgency") but invalidates their timeline, b) It removes your personal emotional liability ("my authority is constrained"), and c) It forces the aggressor to document their panic, which often exposes the crisis as a bluff. You are refusing to co-sign the rush.

2. **Crystallizing the Threat (Against Ambiguity):** When facing the Ghost in the Room, the vague threat, the defense is to refuse to play the ambiguity game. You must force the threat out of the shadows and into the analytical light, where it can be measured and addressed.
    - *The Script:* "I want to make sure I am managing risk appropriately. You mentioned my reputation or compliance. Could you please specify the exact document or event you are referencing, and precisely what action you intend to take so I can address it with my counsel?"
    - *The Power:* This is a move of intense confidence. You are demanding that the predator transition from vague implication to articulable commitment. A manipulator relies on the *fear* of the action, not the action itself. Forcing them to articulate the precise nature of the blackmail/threat often neutralizes the tactic, as they realize they must now cross a serious legal or ethical line they did not intend to cross. If they *do* commit, the threat is no longer a paralyzing ghost, but a quantifiable problem to be solved procedurally.
3. **The Pivot of Fact (Against Fury):** When subjected to the Aggressive Anchor (the performance of fury), the defense is to instantly ignore the emotional content and pivot the entire conversation back to objective, dry data.
    - *The Script:* "I see your frustration. However, to move forward, we need to focus only on the facts. What are the three non-negotiable data points that support your claim for a 70% reduction?"
    - *The Power:* Fury thrives on reactivity. By refusing to validate the anger and instead demanding cold, analytical specificity, you force the adversary to exit System 1 (rage) and re-enter System 2 (logic), where the

negotiation is fair and controlled. You are effectively issuing a cognitive time-out.

The ultimate lesson of this chapter is that **Emotional Sovereignty** is a discipline of delay. The manipulator wins in the first five seconds. Your only mission is to survive those five seconds, trigger the Vagal Circuit Breaker, and deploy the Procedural Delay. This pause is the moment of choice that defines whether you are a reactor or a sovereign decision-maker.

CHAPTER 2

WEAPONIZED GUILT AND SHAME

I. The Deepest Compromise: Turning the Target Against Themselves

If Fear and Intimidation are the blunt-force tactics designed to hijack your external nervous system, Guilt and Shame are the precision attacks designed to compromise your internal ethical operating system. This is the most insidious form of manipulation because the adversary delegates the enforcement to the target's own conscience. The manipulation works because you *want* to be a good person, a loyal employee, a responsible family member, or a fair partner.

The adversary weaponizes this moral desire. They don't have to threaten you; they simply have to make you believe that **compliance is the only way to avoid becoming the villain in your own story.**

To successfully defend against this vector, we must first achieve absolute emotional granularity between the two payloads, as their operational goals are distinct:

1. **Guilt (The Transactional Payload):** Guilt is the feeling of having **done something wrong**. It is linked to *actions*, *omissions*, or a failure to meet an expectation or contract. It is transactional; it demands **restitution** or **payment.**
   - *The Adversary's Goal:* To place the target in **moral debt** to enforce obligation and compel service.
   - *The Internal Voice:* "I did a bad thing, and now I must pay it back to restore balance."
2. **Shame (The Existential Payload):** Shame is the feeling of **being something wrong**. It is linked to *identity*, not actions. It is existential; it demands **hiding** or **silence.**
   - *The Adversary's Goal:* To compromise the target's sense of self-worth to enforce perpetual **compliance** and suppress any assertive behavior or boundary setting.
   - *The Internal Voice:* "I am fundamentally flawed, therefore my needs, my voice, and my boundaries are illegitimate."

The manipulator's strategy is elegant: they use guilt to ensure you are compliant *today* (by paying off the manufactured debt), and they use shame to ensure you are docile *forever* (by convincing you that you lack the moral standing to object).

II. The Guilt Engine: Manufacturing Moral Debt

The guilt payload relies on activating an emotional ledger that you, as the target, feel compelled to keep balanced. The manipulator is a masterful, yet fraudulent, accountant.

A. The Unquantifiable Favor (The Moral Loan Shark)

The most common tactic is establishing a massive, unquantifiable debt that can never truly be repaid, perpetually placing the target in arrears.

- **The Exploit:** The manipulator performs a series of acts, often minor or routine, and then later deploys them as evidence of profound, self-sacrificing virtue. The language is the hallmark: "After **everything** I've done for you," "I gave up [X life goal] just to help you," or "You wouldn't have your job/home/status if I hadn't stepped in."
- **The Debt:** The debt is not a measurable sum of money or time; it is a **moral obligation** infused with high emotional value. Because the "favor" was framed as a sacrifice rather than a

mutually agreed transaction, the target feels they owe an infinite, unquantifiable emotional premium.

- **The Demand:** The payment for this debt is always the sacrifice of the target's current self-interest: silence during a betrayal, the dissolution of a necessary boundary, or the immediate execution of a task detrimental to the target's well-being.

The crucial manipulation here is the denial of equivalence. If someone buys you lunch, you owe them lunch, not your house. The manipulator insists that their trivial sacrifice is equal to your total, boundless servitude.

B. The Delegation of Feelings (The Emotional Burden)

A second, potent guilt tactic is the delegation of the adversary's own emotional responsibility. This is the manipulative use of emotional projection.

- **The Exploit:** The manipulator externalizes their unhappiness, stress, or professional failure, placing the emotional weight onto the target. "You are stressing me out so much I can barely work," "If you hadn't [action X], I wouldn't be so upset right now," or the classic, "Look what you made me do."
- **The Consequence:** The target, particularly those with high empathy or a strong sense of responsibility, internalizes this external pain as personal failure. They become so focused on managing the manipulator's volatile emotional state that they abandon their own needs and boundaries.
- **The Defense Challenge:** The target is now acting as the manipulator's external Emotional Regulator, believing that their compliance is required for the manipulator's psychological stability. This creates an impossible, self-sacrificial burden enforced by manufactured guilt.

III. The Shame Trap: The Self-Imposed Silence

Shame is the most effective weapon against competence and assertiveness. If guilt makes you pay, shame makes you hide. It locks the target into a cycle of silence and submission, ensuring that organizational or personal boundaries remain porous.

A. The Moral Comparison (The Weaponized Standard)

The shame payload operates by holding the target to an arbitrary, impossibly high standard, ensuring perpetual failure.

- **The Exploit:** The manipulator constantly invokes idealized, unreachable standards of behavior, competence, or loyalty, typically referencing a third party or a historical precedent: "A truly loyal person would never ask for a raise," "My former assistant would have done this without being asked," or "Good parents put their children's needs first, always, without complaint."
- **The Deficit:** The target is constantly measured against this manufactured ideal and is, inevitably, found wanting. The failure is not in the execution of a task, but in the inherent character of the target: *You are not good enough; you are selfish; you are incompetent.*
- **The Result: Silence:** The primary goal of shame is to induce silence. If you believe you are fundamentally flawed, you lose the moral authority to assert your needs, set boundaries, or voice dissent. You self-censor, believing that the cost of exposing your "true, flawed self" is too great. The shame payload ensures that the target never raises their hand, never challenges the plan, and never demands fair compensation.

B. The Public Scrutiny (The Weaponized Mirror)

When shame is used in a group or professional context, it often takes the form of targeted, public exposure of a minor or contrived failure.

- **The Exploit:** The manipulator isolates a small mistake, error, or personal vulnerability and amplifies it disproportionately in front of an audience (a team meeting, a family gathering, social media). This is often framed as "tough love" or "necessary honesty."
- **The Goal:** To trigger an acute, paralyzing shame spiral in the target. The brief, public humiliation is designed to establish a **precedent of fear**—the target will subsequently go to extraordinary, self-sacrificing lengths to avoid the recurrence of that public scrutiny.
- **The Defense Challenge:** The target's focus shifts entirely from the actual business problem to managing their own reputation and avoiding further exposure. The fear of being shamed becomes the new, most important motivator, overriding strategic and personal self-interest.

IV. The Defense Layer 1: Differentiation and Moral Auditing

The defense against Guilt and Shame requires immediate cognitive rigor: the systematic auditing of the debt and the forceful separation of action from identity.

A. The Guilt-to-Debt Audit (Neutralizing the Loan Shark)

When you feel a surge of guilt-fueled obligation, the immediate, mandatory defense is to move from the feeling to the fact.

1. **Identify the Source Event:** Force yourself to identify the *specific, quantifiable action* that supposedly created the debt. *What exactly did the adversary do that warrants this sacrifice?* (e.g., "They lent me $500," "They drove me to the airport once," "They signed off on my vacation").
2. **Calculate Fair Restitution:** Assign a fair, transactional value to that action. If they lent $500, the repayment is $500 plus interest. If they drove you to the airport, the repayment is gas money, or a return favor of equal or lesser time commitment.
3. **Refuse the Emotional Premium:** Mandate: **The debt is cleared when the transactional cost is paid, not when the adversary feels emotionally satisfied.** The Guilt Payload is nullified the moment you refuse to pay the emotional premium attached to the initial favor. The response must be: *"I acknowledge that favor and have paid it back by [specific, measurable action]. Your current demand [X] is disproportionate to the original debt, and I decline."*

B. The Action vs. Identity Firewall (Against Shame)

Against shame, the defense must be the absolute refusal to internalize the criticism as an identity failure.

1. **Isolate the Action:** When the shame attack hits ("You are selfish/incompetent/unprofessional"), isolate the factual, behavioral claim: *Did I miss the deadline? Yes. Did I fail to follow the protocol? Yes.*
2. **Decouple from Identity:** Immediately and deliberately state the decoupling: *"I missed the deadline (Action). This makes me a person who missed a deadline, not an incompetent person (Identity). This failure is correctable."*
3. **Focus on Correction, Not Hiding:** Shame demands hiding; sovereignty demands correction. If a genuine error caused the shame, the response is: "I see the mistake. My next step is to initiate **Correction Protocol X** to ensure it doesn't happen

again." If the shame is manufactured, the response is: "That language (selfish/flawed) is an identity judgment I reject. I will only engage with facts." This shift denies the manipulator the power of the shame label.

V. The Defense Layer 2: Asserting Moral Sovereignty

The final defense against Guilt and Shame is the forceful assertion of your **moral autonomy.** The manipulator wins when you agree to let them define what "good," "loyal," or "responsible" means.

The defense is to draw and enforce boundaries using the **Neutral, Assertive, Limiting (NANL) Protocol:**

1. **Neutral Stance:** Avoid engaging the emotional charge. Do not apologize for setting a boundary; do not defend your position.
2. **Assertive Statement:** Clearly and simply state your decision or boundary.
3. **Limiting Consequence:** State what you *will* and *will not* do in response to the manipulation.
    - *Guilt Exploit:* "You are being selfish for not canceling your trip to help me move."
    - *NANL Defense:* (Neutral) "I hear you are upset. (Assertive) I will not be canceling my trip, as it was booked six months ago. (Limiting) I have hired you professional movers and sent them the deposit. That is the limit of my capacity." (You paid the *transactional* debt, but refuse the *emotional* premium.)
    - *Shame Exploit:* "You're clearly not capable of handling this project; only a weak leader would admit they need help."
    - *NANL Defense:* (Neutral) "I understand your assessment. (Assertive) I am bringing in outside counsel to review the risk. (Limiting) I will only discuss facts and deliverables, not personal capability." (You refuse the shame label and pivot to the corrective action.)

Mastering the response to Guilt and Shame is the act of reclaiming your moral compass. You are the sole architect of your ethical code. By auditing manufactured debt and rejecting identity-level attacks, you keep the internal compliance officer loyal to **you**, not the manipulator.

CHAPTER 3

LOVE BOMBING AND INTERMITTENT REINFORCEMENT

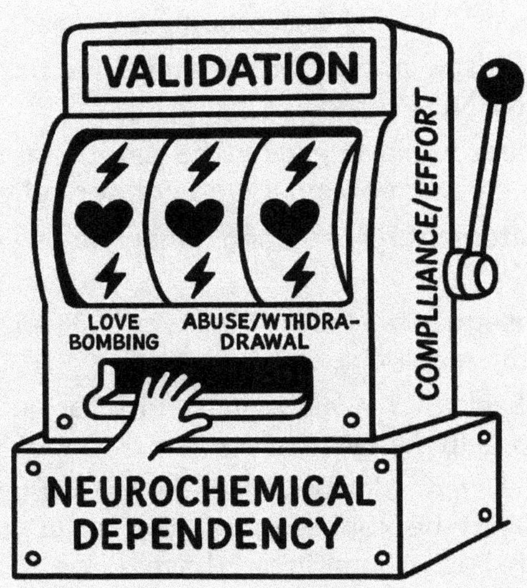

I. The Paradox of Positive Exploitation

We have covered the weaponization of threat (Fear, Intimidation) and moral liability (Guilt, Shame). These vectors rely on aversion, the intense motivation to escape pain. However, the most challenging and sticky form of emotional exploitation is one that exploits the universal, powerful motivation for *gain*: the pursuit of validation, love, belonging, and reward.

This is the domain of **Love Bombing** and **Intermittent Reinforcement (IR)**.

Unlike the previous tactics, which push the target away with hostility, this method actively **pulls the target in** with manufactured euphoria and the promise of ultimate fulfillment. The goal is to install a powerful, addictive dependency on the adversary, ensuring the target's long-term compliance, loyalty, and silence are maintained not through fear of punishment, but through the craving for reward.

The paradox of this system is that the target experiences the periods of reward (the Love Bombing) as the "true" reality, and the periods of withdrawal or abuse (the Intermittent Reinforcement) as temporary, unfortunate aberrations that they must endure or fix. The target becomes addicted to the **potential** for the reward state, not the reward itself.

II. Love Bombing: The Manufacturing of Euphoria

Love Bombing is the first phase of the addiction loop. It is a calculated, intensive projection of affection, admiration, and attention designed to overwhelm the target's critical faculties and accelerate emotional attachment far beyond a healthy pace.

A. The Exploit Payload: Accelerated Attachment

Love Bombing is fundamentally a method of **Rapid Psychological Penetration.** It works because it targets two fundamental human needs: the need for **Validation** and the need for **Idealization.**

1. **Idealized Mirroring:** The manipulator rapidly gathers information about the target's deepest desires, insecurities, and unfulfilled needs. They then reflect this data back to the target, creating the perfect, custom-made fantasy partner, colleague, or mentor. The manipulator will say, "I have never met anyone who understands my vision like you do," or "You are the only person who has ever truly seen me." The target feels seen, validated, and believes they have found a unique, destined connection.
2. **Saturation Bombardment:** This is characterized by an overwhelming volume of positive attention, excessive flattery, intense communication, and rapid declarations of commitment (e.g., "We are soulmates," "You're getting a massive promotion next month," "You're the key to our entire company strategy"). This bombardment short-circuits the target's natural caution (System 2) and triggers a neurochemical flood of dopamine and oxytocin, making the target feel intoxicated and blissfully secure.

The crucial defensive breach in this phase is the target's **abandonment of the relationship timeline.** Healthy relationships and professional partnerships require time and data to build trust. Love Bombing aggressively compresses this timeline, forcing a massive emotional investment based on fantasy and manufactured euphoria, making any later withdrawal incredibly painful. The target is tricked into believing the bond is too unique and too valuable to scrutinize.

B. The Tactical Purpose: Data Extraction

Beyond emotional bonding, Love Bombing serves a strategic function: **Vulnerability Mapping.** While the target is overwhelmed with euphoria, their cognitive guard is down. During this state, they willingly disclose private anxieties, past traumas, key vulnerabilities, and critical personal or professional data.

The manipulator is not just bonding; they are **cataloging the pressure points** that will be used later during the intermittent withdrawal phase to ensure compliance and silence. The more intensely the target feels loved and validated, the more deeply they will trust, and the more information they will surrender.

III. Intermittent Reinforcement: The Variable Ratio Trap

Once the emotional investment is made through Love Bombing, the manipulator transitions into the control phase: **Intermittent Reinforcement (IR).** This is the core engine of the addiction loop and the most potent psychological mechanism for long-term behavioral control.

Intermittent Reinforcement is the strategic withdrawal of the reward (the Love Bombing state) and its reintroduction at random, unpredictable intervals.

A. The Neurochemical Mechanism: Dopamine and Prediction

This tactic derives its power directly from behaviorist psychology, where a variable ratio schedule (unpredictable rewards) is proven to be the most addictive and resistant to extinction.

1. **The Predictable Reward:** If a reward is predictable (e.g., you get paid every Friday), the dopamine system activates *before* the reward is received, in anticipation. Once the reward is established as routine, the dopamine response flattens.
2. **The Intermittent Reward:** When the reward is unpredictable (e.g., a slot machine, or a manipulator's sudden affection), the dopamine system remains hyper-activated in a state of **craving and searching.** Dopamine is the chemical of *seeking* and *anticipation*, not satisfaction. By making the reward erratic, a sudden coldness, followed by a passionate apology, followed by two weeks of silence, followed by extravagant praise, the manipulator maximizes the target's anticipation.

The target is perpetually locked into a loop of behavioral searching: *If I just try harder, if I just do what they want, if I am just quiet enough, the beautiful reward will return*. The manipulator can elicit enormous compliance during the periods of withdrawal, as the target performs elaborate, self-sacrificing behaviors (the "work") to regain the dopamine hit of validation.

B. The Trauma Bond: Addiction to Potential

The result of IR is the **Trauma Bond**, an unhealthy attachment that forms in a cycle of abuse, intermittent positive reinforcement, and withdrawal. The target becomes chemically addicted to the cycle, not the person.

1. **Cognitive Dissonance:** The target experiences profound dissonance: "The person who made me feel like the most valuable person in the world is the same person who just screamed at me/ignored me for two weeks." The mind, desperately seeking to resolve this conflict, rationalizes the abuse as **external and fixable** ("They are just stressed," "I pushed them too hard," "They have an issue, but they need me").
2. **The Lure of Potential:** The target clings desperately to the *potential* of the person they met during the Love Bombing phase. They are fighting for the return of the fantasy, convinced that if they are loyal enough, the "real," loving person will permanently emerge, and the abuse will stop. They are addicted to the hope, which is chemically sustained by the intermittent dopamine spikes.

This system effectively makes the target immune to rational self-help. Any attempt by friends or colleagues to intervene ("They are treating you poorly") is rejected, because the outsider has not experienced the incredible euphoria of the Love Bombing phase, and therefore, cannot understand the magnitude of the *potential* reward.

IV. The Defense Protocol: Analytical Deconstruction and Intrinsic Value

The defense against the addiction loop cannot be built on emotional strength alone, as the emotions are chemically compromised. It must be built on meticulous analytical deconstruction and the rigorous re-establishment of intrinsic self-worth.

Layer 1: The Timeline Reversal (Neutralizing the Euphoria)

The immediate defense against Love Bombing is to refuse the compressed timeline.

1. **Mandatory Timeline Friction:** Implement a non-negotiable personal policy: **No major emotional or financial decision will be made within the first 90 days of an intense relationship or partnership.** The Love Bombing phase rarely lasts this long without showing signs of the IR withdrawal.
2. **The "Slow Down" Labeling:** When faced with intense flattery or sudden, massive declarations of commitment, label the experience as a **Love Bombing Exploit**. Acknowledge the feeling without internalizing the claim. *Internal Script:* "This attention feels good, but the data is too thin to support this conclusion. I will enjoy the kindness, but I will not allow this volume to dictate my level of commitment."
3. **Fact-Checking the Ideal:** Systematically question the idealized mirroring. *Internal Script:* "They say I am the only person who understands their vision. What specific evidence have I provided in 72 hours to support that claim?" Force the data to support the feeling. If the data is lacking, the feeling is a manufactured product of the exploit.

Layer 2: The Variable Ratio Audit (Breaking the Addiction)

This audit is deployed the moment the Intermittent Reinforcement cycle begins (the sudden coldness, the withdrawal of affection, the unexplained silence).

1. **The Pattern Log (Externalizing the Cycle):** The addiction thrives on the *unpredictability* of the reward. The defense is to make the pattern **perfectly predictable.** The target must meticulously log the cycle:
    - **Date/Time of Reward (Love Bomb/Praise):** (e.g., "Tuesday, 7 PM: Extravagant praise for minor task.")
    - **Date/Time of Withdrawal (Abuse/Silence):** (e.g., "Wednesday, 10 AM: Unexplained silence, followed by vague criticism.")
    - **Target's Reaction (The Work):** (e.g., "Spent 4 hours apologizing and offering to redo work.")
    - **Time to Next Reward:** (e.g., "4 days of anxiety until the reward returned.")
    - *The Power:* Once the target sees the cycle externalized on a log, the neurochemical illusion of the "random" reward is shattered. The abuse is revealed not as an accident, but as a systematic, recurring variable designed to elicit the very behaviors the target is performing.

2. **The Intrinsic Value Protocol:** The core of the addiction is the transfer of self-worth from an internal source to the adversary's external validation. The defense is the rigorous re-establishment of intrinsic value.
   - **Dispute the Reward Source:** When the reward is received, internally dispute the necessity of the external validation. *Internal Script:* "I feel good because I achieved a goal (Intrinsic), not because they praised me (Extrinsic)."
   - **Mandatory Self-Sustained Reward:** For every hour the target spends doing the "work" to chase the manipulator's validation, they must spend an equal amount of time investing in a source of validation the manipulator **cannot** touch (e.g., deep work on a personal project, exercise, time with a healthy, stable friend). This systematically dilutes the power of the external, addictive reward.

The addiction loop can feel unbreakable, but it is ultimately a scheduled system based on psychological principles. By refusing the timeline, cataloging the pattern, and fiercely rebuilding intrinsic worth, the target systematically renders the reward system ineffective, leading to the eventual extinction of the Trauma Bond.

CHAPTER 4

DEVELOPING EMOTIONAL GRANULARITY

I. The Weapon of Vague Anxiety

In the preceding chapters, we dissected the three primary threat vectors: the sudden onset of fear (Chapter 2), the corrosive internal pressure of manufactured guilt and shame (Chapter 3), and the addictive pull of intermittent reward (Chapter 4). What unites all three, despite their vastly different payloads, is their reliance on the same systemic vulnerability: **Emotional Blurring.**

Emotional Blurring is the human tendency to categorize complex, high-arousal internal states using vague, low-resolution labels like "stressed," "overwhelmed," "bad," or "anxious." This lack of specificity is the adversary's greatest ally. When the entire emotional landscape is covered in fog, the specific threat, the precise nature of the exploit, cannot be identified.

Imagine a sophisticated security system that, regardless of whether it detects a network intrusion, a malware infection, or a physical breach, displays only one warning: *SYSTEM FAILURE.* The operator, overwhelmed by the generic catastrophe signal, is paralyzed. They cannot deploy the correct, surgical countermeasure because they lack the necessary diagnostic data.

Emotional Granularity (EG) is the process of sharpening that diagnostic capability. It is the ability to **precisely differentiate, articulate, and label emotional experience.** By moving the feeling from an overwhelming, subjective experience ("I feel terrible") to an objective, measurable data point ("I feel professional frustration layered with extrinsic guilt, causing shallow breathing"), the cognitive firewall (System 2) is forcibly re-engaged, and the amygdala is calmed. The act of labeling an emotion, a phenomenon known as **Affect Labeling**, moves the experience from the limbic system to the prefrontal cortex, transforming the paralyzing attack into an analyzable problem.

This chapter is dedicated to the methodology of developing high EG, thereby denying the manipulator the critical advantage of generalized affective chaos.

II. The Blurring Effect: Why Precision is the Defense

Low emotional granularity is not an accident; it is a habit developed through social conditioning and cognitive convenience. Most people find it easier to simply dismiss a complex feeling with a single, socially acceptable term ("stress") than to unpack the intricate architecture of their internal state. However, this convenience is a massive security vulnerability.

Consider the difference between a high-arousal state triggered by a genuine crisis (e.g., an active security breach) and a high-arousal state triggered by a guilt exploit (e.g., an undeserved, demanding email from a colleague).

- **Low Granularity Response:** In both cases, the feeling is labeled "urgent stress." The individual reacts reflexively by *rushing* to compliance or *rushing* to fix the symptom, often over-committing time and energy to the less important, but emotionally louder, threat.
- **High Granularity Response:** The individual differentiates: "The security breach is *functional fear* demanding technical triage. The colleague's email is *extrinsic guilt* demanding a boundary." This differentiation allows the correct countermeasure (technical protocol vs. NANL protocol) to be deployed instantly, preserving resources and maintaining control.

The goal of the EG defense is to ensure that every emotional experience is immediately audited across multiple dimensions to determine its **origin, ownership, and required response protocol.**

III. Operationalizing Granularity: The Three Dimensions of Analysis

To transform low-resolution emotional chaos into high-resolution, actionable data, we must systematically analyze the feeling across three distinct dimensions. This should become an immediate, mandatory internal audit whenever any high-arousal state is detected.

Dimension 1: Valence and Arousal (The Quadrant Map)

The first step is to use the simplest framework: the psychological grid of **Valence (Pleasant/Unpleasant)** and **Arousal (High/Low Energy).** This provides an immediate, objective snapshot of the system's current operating state.

1. **High Arousal, Unpleasant Valence:** (Top Left Quadrant: Anxiety, Anger, Terror). This state signals an active threat or conflict. It mandates the deployment of the **Physiological Circuit Breaker** (Box Breathing, Chapter 2) before any cognitive analysis proceeds.
2. **High Arousal, Pleasant Valence:** (Top Right Quadrant: Excitement, Elation, Craving). This state signals high dopamine activity. It mandates the deployment of the **Timeline Friction** (Chapter 4) to prevent euphoric over-commitment (Love Bombing).
3. **Low Arousal, Unpleasant Valence:** (Bottom Left Quadrant: Boredom, Sadness, Fatigue). This state signals depletion or grief. It mandates the deployment of **Self-Care and Intrinsic Value Protocols** to counter Shame and prevent vulnerability to external demands.

This quadrant approach bypasses the "good/bad" binary and instead provides a simple, immediate gauge of **required energy management.**

Dimension 2: Origin and Ownership (The Extrinsic Audit)

This dimension is the firewall against the manipulative delegation of feelings (Chapter 3). The core question here is: **"Whose energy is this, and where did it originate?"**

1. **Intrinsic Emotion:** The feeling originated from an internal source directly related to your actions or identity (e.g., disappointment in your performance, genuine joy from a job well done, remorse for a clear ethical error). *Response:* Accept ownership, deploy internal correction protocols.

2. **Extrinsic Emotion:** The feeling was generated by an external agent and is currently being projected onto you, often to enforce a boundary violation or demand service (e.g., guilt triggered by a manipulator's disappointment, shame induced by public criticism designed to silence you). *Response:* Reject ownership, deploy external boundary protocols (NANL).

The EG practitioner must become a fierce auditor of emotional ownership. If a feeling of overwhelming disappointment descends immediately after a conversation where the adversary expressed their unhappiness, the feeling is highly likely **Extrinsic Disappointment.** By labeling it as such, you deny the external agent access to your internal emotional control systems. You are not responsible for their unhappiness; you are only responsible for your response.

Dimension 3: Physiological Signature (The Data Mapping)

This dimension leverages **Interoception**—the mind's awareness of the internal state of the body, to provide objective, undeniable data that grounds the emotional label in physical reality. Manipulators can argue with your feelings, but they cannot argue with the data of your body.

1. **Map the State:** Systematically link the feeling to a physical manifestation:
   - *Feeling:* "Anxiety about the negotiation."
   - *Data:* "Tightness in the solar plexus; jaw is clenched; breath is held high in the chest (indicating 'Freeze' response)."
2. **Calibrate the Threat:** Once the physical signature is identified, the response is automatic. If the body is in **Freeze** (chest breathing, high shoulders), the appropriate response is not debate or flight, but **Grounding** and the **Box Breathing Protocol** to force the 'Fight/Flight' mechanism offline. If the body is in **Flight** (restlessness, rapid heart rate), the necessary response is the **Neutral Deferral** protocol to impose stillness and delay.

This dimension ensures that the defense is always anchored in objective data: you are not responding to a feeling, but to a measured physiological state that requires a specific, clinical response.

IV. The Granularity Protocols: Tools for Precision

To transition from conceptual understanding to applied skill, the following mandatory protocols must be regularly practiced. These are designed to force the mind out of the vague, convenient label and into the actionable, precise one.

A. The "5-Word Challenge"

When a high-arousal state hits, the mandatory first step is to label the feeling using exactly five distinct, non-generic adjectives. This forces differentiation.

- *Low EG:* "I'm having a panic attack."
- *High EG (5-Word Challenge):* "Overwhelmed, ashamed, resentful, pressurized, exhausted."

The five words reveal the complexity of the attack: *Overwhelmed* suggests overload; *Ashamed* suggests an identity attack; *Resentful* suggests a boundary violation; *Pressurized* suggests a time exploit; *Exhausted* suggests depletion. By breaking the monolith of "panic" into five separate, manageable components, the mind shifts from catastrophic collapse to methodical problem-solving. Each word now has an associated protocol.

B. The Contrasting Pairs Exercise

This practice forces the rigorous differentiation between subtle but strategically distinct emotional states. The power lies in recognizing the difference in the required response.

- **Guilt vs. Shame:** (Chapter 3)
  - *Guilt:* Focus on **Action** (What did I do?). Demands **Restitution.**
  - *Shame:* Focus on **Identity** (Who am I?). Demands **Hiding/Silence.**
- **Anger vs. Frustration:**
  - *Anger:* Often targets a **Person** or perceived injustice. Requires **Boundary Assertion.**
  - *Frustration:* Often targets a **Process** or an obstacle. Requires **Problem-Solving/Patience.**
- **Anxiety vs. Excitement:**
  - *Anxiety:* Focuses on an Unwanted Future Event. Requires Mitigation Planning.

  - *Excitement:* Focuses on a Desired Future Event. Requires Containment/Strategic Delay.

By immediately determining whether the feeling is Anger or Frustration, you prevent yourself from deploying an aggressive, boundary-setting response when only a methodical process correction is required.

C. The "If, Then" Protocol

Emotional Granularity must ultimately lead to a pre-defined defensive action. The "If, Then" Protocol links the identified, high-resolution emotional label directly to the appropriate operational countermeasure.

The EG defense mandates the creation of a personal protocol list:

- **IF** I identify **Extrinsic Guilt** (Chapter 3, Dimension 2), **THEN** I immediately deploy the **Guilt-to-Debt Audit** (Chapter 3) and the **NANL Defense**.
- **IF** I identify **Euphoric Craving** (Chapter 4, Dimension 1), **THEN** I immediately invoke the **Timeline Reversal** and the **Variable Ratio Audit**.
- **IF** I identify **Silent Ambiguity Fear** (Chapter 2, Dimension 3), **THEN** I immediately deploy the **Ambiguity Crystallizer**.

This protocol removes the chaotic gap between *feeling* the attack and *responding* to the attack. The label dictates the action, transforming the emotional response from a volatile reaction into a disciplined, systematic defense.

V. Conclusion: The Sovereign Mind

Emotional Granularity is the critical intelligence layer of the entire defense structure. It ensures that the sovereign mind is never operating on guesswork. By applying the rigor of Valence/Arousal mapping, the vigilance of the Extrinsic Audit, and the objectivity of Physiological Data, we dismantle the power of generalized, overwhelming feeling. We replace the paralyzing "SYSTEM FAILURE" alert with the precise diagnostic code: *Emotional attack vector D3: Shame; Target: Identity; Countermeasure: Action vs. Identity Firewall.* In this state of precision, the emotional life ceases to be a liability and becomes a reliable, readable source of data, ensuring the operator maintains control, even in the midst of the deepest affective warfare.

CHAPTER 5

FORTIFYING BOUNDARIES

I. The Architecture of Sovereignty

In the previous chapters, we achieved internal mastery: we learned to disarm the fear response (Chapter 2), reject extrinsic moral debt (Chapter 3), neutralize the addiction cycle (Chapter 4), and precisely identify the nature of any attack using Emotional Granularity (Chapter 5). We have successfully hardened the core processor—the mind.

But even the most advanced processor must be housed within a protected structure. **Boundaries** are that structure. They are not merely conversational suggestions or emotional preferences; they are the external, systemic protocols that define acceptable access to your resources, time, energy, and self-worth. They are the high-security perimeter fence that determines who is allowed in, how far they can advance, and what consequences follow unauthorized entry.

The critical distinction we must make now is the difference between a **Soft Boundary** and a **Fortified Boundary**.

- **Soft Boundary:** A reactive statement made in the heat of the moment, usually accompanied by an apology or a lengthy explanation. It is porous, contingent on the target's current emotional energy, and instantly vulnerable to the adversary's emotional counter-pressure (e.g., "I'm sorry, but I really can't stay late *again* tonight," which is immediately countered by the Guilt exploit: "But after everything I've done for you..."). Soft boundaries fail because they require a high level of energy and emotional resilience *at the exact moment of the attack.*
- **Fortified Boundary:** A proactive, impersonal, systemic policy established during a state of calm, rational thought. It requires no emotional energy to deploy, as it is simply a statement of fact and an enforcement of a pre-existing rule (e.g., "My policy is that I do not check work emails after 6:00 PM. I will look at this tomorrow at 9:00 AM."). Fortified boundaries succeed because they move the negotiation away from the vulnerable self and onto the neutral, immutable policy.

To maintain Emotional Sovereignty, we must systematically replace every soft boundary with a fortified, impersonal, and consistently enforced protocol.

II. The Flaw of Emotional Negotiation

The critical failure point of soft boundaries is that they invite **Emotional Negotiation**. The adversary knows that if you rely on emotion to set your boundary, they can use emotion to dismantle it.

When you say, "I can't do this because I'm too tired," you are offering a variable, temporary reason. The manipulator's immediate and successful counter is to invalidate that variable: "Oh, you'll be fine once you get started," or "I'm even more tired than you, and I'm still working!"

They force you into a debate about your subjective reality: your level of exhaustion, your justification for saying no, your worthiness to set the boundary. This is a debate you will always lose, because the very act of *justifying* the boundary transfers power from the architect (you) to the challenger (the adversary).

We must forbid this negotiation. A fortified boundary needs no apology, no justification, and no debate. It simply exists. The operative is no longer *you*, the tired, guilt-prone individual; the operative is the **Policy**, which is incapable of being reasoned with, shamed, or frightened.

III. The Four Pillars of Fortified Boundary Architecture

Fortified boundaries must be engineered to protect against all known exploit vectors. We categorize them into four essential pillars: Temporal, Spatial/Physical, Emotional/Cognitive, and Resource.

Pillar 1: Temporal Boundaries (The Urgency Defense)

These boundaries guard the most critical asset, your time, and are the primary defense against the **Manufactured Crisis** and **Fear/Urgency** exploits (Chapter 2).

- **The Policy:** Establish non-negotiable rules about response time, availability, and the duration of commitment.
  - *Example (Work/Professional):* "I only process urgent, unscheduled requests between 10 AM and 11 AM. All other requests must be submitted via the standard ticketing system."
  - *Example (Personal):* "I require 48 hours notice for any large, scheduled request (e.g., moving, major favors). If you ask me at the last minute, the answer is automatically 'no' due to my planning policy."
- **The Deployment:** When a manipulator attempts to impose an artificial deadline ("I need this by the end of the day, or we're ruined"), the reply must be the deployment of the policy, not a reason.
  - *Fortified Response:* "That falls outside our standard operating procedure. We require the request in writing. I can begin the review on Thursday. If the deadline is absolute, you will need to re-prioritize which deliverable you want me to drop to accommodate it." (This forces the decision back onto the manipulator, neutralizing their ability to control your timeline.)

Pillar 2: Spatial and Physical Boundaries (The Access Control)

These boundaries manage physical and informational proximity, defending against the constant barrage of **Low-Grade Anxiety** and the intrusion required for **Love Bombing** (Chapter 4).

- **The Policy:** Define the hours, locations, and methods of permissible contact.
  - *Example (Digital):* "My phone goes into Airplane Mode for Deep Work blocks (9 AM – 12 PM). I will not respond to

calls or texts during that time. If it is a life-or-death emergency, contact my secondary number." (This manages the expectation of instant access, which manipulators thrive on.)

  - *Example (Physical/Privacy):* "I am not available for personal conversations about my family/finances/past trauma during work hours or in group settings." (This protects the data the manipulator uses for **Vulnerability Mapping** during the Love Bombing phase.)

- **The Deployment:** If the boundary is breached (e.g., an unannounced visit, an intrusive personal question), the response is immediate spatial correction.
  - *Fortified Response:* "I see you're here, but this is my block-out time. I'll be free in exactly 45 minutes. I need you to step out until then." (No apology, no explanation, just a firm statement of time and required space.)

Pillar 3: Emotional and Cognitive Boundaries (The Ownership Firewall)

This is the most crucial pillar, defending against **Guilt and Shame** (Chapter 3) by enforcing the **Extrinsic Audit** (Chapter 5). It separates the target's internal reality from the adversary's external projection.

- **The Policy:** Define what you are and are not responsible for, especially in relation to the feelings and life choices of others.
  - *Example (Guilt/Delegation):* "I am responsible for my choices and my output, but I am not responsible for managing your emotional state or your career setbacks."
  - *Example (Shame/Identity):* "I refuse to engage with language that involves personal character attacks, such as 'selfish,' 'incompetent,' or 'unprofessional.' I will only discuss facts and specific actions."
- **The Deployment:** When the adversary attempts to project their feelings or shame onto you, you immediately deploy the "Refusal to Catch" protocol.
  - *Adversary:* "Your delay has ruined my weekend, I am so disappointed in you!"
  - *Fortified Response:* "I understand that you are feeling disappointment, and I acknowledge that feeling. My action [X] was necessary to meet the deadline for [Y]. I

manage my work, you manage your feelings. I will proceed with the current schedule." (You validate their emotion as *their* property, but refuse to internalize it as *your* fault or debt.)

Pillar 4: Resource Boundaries (The Debt Ceiling)

These boundaries govern measurable assets, money, energy, favors, and physical effort, and are the defense against the **Unquantifiable Favor** guilt exploit.

- **The Policy:** Clearly define the maximum commitment you will give and the expectation of reciprocity.
    - *Example (Energy/Favors):* "I offer a maximum of two large favors per quarter to any single colleague/friend. That is my capacity limit for supporting others' urgent needs."
    - *Example (Financial):* "I will not lend money or co-sign debts. That is my hard-line financial policy."
- **The Deployment:** When a manipulator asks for more than the policy allows, the response must be dry and transactional.
    - *Adversary:* "You have to help me with this project until 2 AM; I helped you last year!"
    - *Fortified Response:* "I am happy to look at this for another hour, which meets my current energy allocation. Regarding your help last year, that debt was discharged when I [list specific action of equal value]. We are now operating from a neutral ledger." (This enforces the **Guilt-to-Debt Audit** externally, refusing the emotional premium.)

IV. The Pre-Commitment Protocol: Eliminating the Negotiation

The most powerful technique for fortifying boundaries is the **Pre-Commitment Protocol**. This involves setting the boundary *before* the interaction begins, eliminating the need to emotionally defend it in the moment.

1. **Audience Notification:** Publicize the boundary during a neutral time. This transforms the boundary from a personal choice into a group expectation.
    - *Announcement:* "For optimal efficiency, I am implementing a new communication protocol: I will only respond to calls during these hours. Outside of that, please use email."

2. **Impersonal Wording:** Always frame the boundary as an *external policy* or *best practice*, never as a personal limitation.
   - *Soft:* "I can't answer your call because I have anxiety about talking on the phone."
   - *Fortified:* "My communication flow prioritizes asynchronous channels (email/text) to ensure I can give a thoughtful, structured response."
3. **Mandatory Consequence:** The pre-commitment must include the consequence of violation. A boundary without a consequence is merely a request.

V. Enforcement: Consistency and Consequence

A boundary's strength is measured not by its firmness, but by its **consistency.** An adversary will always test a new boundary. If the boundary yields 1 out of 10 times, the manipulator will spend 11 times testing it, because they know the system is permeable. **Zero tolerance for boundary violations is the only effective long-term policy.**

When a boundary is tested, the response sequence is mandatory:

1. **The Factual Reiteration:** State the boundary simply and neutrally. *Example:* "I see you sent this request after 6 PM. As per my policy, I will address it at 9 AM tomorrow."
2. **The Consequence Application:** If the violation persists, the pre-defined consequence must be applied without emotion or explanation. *Example (If they call again after hours):* "You called me again after hours. I will not be answering your calls for the rest of the week."
3. **Refusal to Explain:** Never explain the *why* of the consequence. The explanation is the vulnerable gap that the manipulator will exploit with guilt or fear. The boundary is the security door; the consequence is the lock. Once the lock is engaged, the conversation is over.

The highest form of boundary enforcement is the simple, non-reactive deployment of the policy. When you achieve this level of impersonal consistency, the manipulator learns that targeting your boundaries is an inefficient use of their energy, and they shift their focus elsewhere.

This structural defense is the final layer of protection against all emotional exploits, ensuring that the self, now armed with emotional granularity, remains the sovereign and sole controller of its own resources and reality.

CONCLUSION

I. The End of Vulnerability: From Blueprint to Battle-Readiness

If you have journeyed with us through the preceding chapters, you have executed a total security overhaul of your mind. We began by simply identifying the shape of the predator—the Dark Triad—and the terrain on which they hunt. We moved into the deep mechanics of internal bias, learning to distrust our own initial cognitive shortcuts. Now, in this final section, we stand at the culmination: the moment where all these isolated defenses merge into a single, cohesive, operational system known as **Emotional Sovereignty.**

This journey has been intellectually taxing, but the rewards are immeasurable. You now understand that the final, most sophisticated attack vector is not logic, but feeling. The adversary—whether a hostile competitor or a deeply toxic partner—doesn't seek to prove they are right; they seek only to ensure you are too panicked, guilty, or desperate for love to notice that you are being leveraged.

The central truth we have uncovered is that emotional manipulation is not magic or a mysterious power; it is a **highly predictable, systematic exploit** that targets measurable vulnerabilities. Fear requires speed, Guilt requires moral debt, and Addiction requires the manufactured high of intermittent, variable reward. When you strip away the emotional charge, all that remains is a mechanical process. And any mechanical process can be countered with a disciplined protocol.

This concluding chapter is our final integration test. It takes the individual lessons—the Box Breathing, the Guilt Audit, the Granularity Labels—and stacks them into a single, mandatory **Sovereign Mind Protocol** designed to fire seamlessly, denying the adversary the chaotic reaction they require.

II. The Integrated Defense Stack: The Sovereign Mind Protocol

The moment you feel the internal system alarm—that sudden, hollow rush of anxiety, the overwhelming surge of responsibility, or the intense, almost desperate pull toward validation—you must immediately engage this three-stage protocol. This sequence is non-negotiable, for it dictates that **diagnosis must precede action.**

Stage 1: The Halt and Granularity Filter (Immediate Diagnosis)

The greatest mistake is rushing to meet the emotional demand. The first action must always be a mandated cessation of all activity and an immediate shift of focus from the external threat to the internal state.

1. **The Mandatory Pause:** Before a single word leaves your mouth, before a single keystroke, deploy the **Physiological Circuit Breaker**. Breathe. Inhale 4, Hold 4, Exhale 6. This is not meditation; it is a mechanical signal to the vagus nerve that says, "Stand down, the threat is downgraded." If you skip this, you are attempting to fight a chemical fire with a rational argument, and the fire always wins.
2. **The Granularity Audit:** While breathing, you engage the diagnostic engine (Chapter 5). You must name the enemy precisely:
    - *What is the Arousal State?* Is it High and Unpleasant (requires physical reset) or High and Pleasant (requires timeline delay)?
    - *What is the Payload?* Does this feeling demand **Restitution** (Guilt), **Silence** (Shame), **Speed** (Fear), or **Chase/Seeking** (Addiction)?
    - *Who owns this feeling?* Is this **Intrinsic** or **Extrinsic**?

By the end of this stage, the monolithic, paralyzing terror ("I feel overwhelmed") must be broken down into specific data points ("I am experiencing Extrinsic Guilt layered with high-arousal social anxiety, triggered by the Unquantifiable Favor exploit"). The adversary is now categorized, and the appropriate countermeasure is identified.

Stage 2: The Policy Pivot (Impersonal Shielding)

The purpose of the diagnosis is solely to point to the correct **Fortified Boundary** (Chapter 6). Once the boundary is selected, the pivot must be immediate, cold, and impersonal.

1. **Refusal to Justify:** This is the make-or-break moment. You must internally suppress the overwhelming impulse to apologize or explain *why* you are setting a boundary. Justifying the boundary makes it an emotional variable.
2. **Deployment of the Policy:** Speak the policy. Do not speak your feeling.
    - Adversary uses Fear (Manufactured Crisis): They demand a decision in one hour.
    - Your Policy Pivot: "I hear your urgency. However, our internal policy mandates a 24-hour review period for all contracts over this value. I will process the formal request tomorrow morning." (You deploy the **Temporal Boundary**, refusing their timeline.)
    - Adversary uses Guilt (Moral Loan Shark): "After all the favors I've done for you, you can't help me with this?"
    - Your Policy Pivot: "I settled our ledger when I [list specific, equal repayment]. My capacity for unallocated favors is full this month, as per my Resource Boundary. I recommend you contact a professional." (You deploy the **Resource Boundary** and enforce the **Guilt-to-Debt Audit**.)

The brilliance of the policy pivot is that the adversary is no longer fighting *you*; they are fighting a system. You are simply the messenger for an immutable rule, making you invulnerable to the standard emotional counter-pressure.

Stage 3: The Intrinsic Recalibration (System Maintenance)

The battle is won not when the adversary retreats, but when the operator successfully returns their emotional center of gravity to an **Intrinsic** source. An attack depletes the system; the final stage is mandated self-repair.

1. **Affirmation of Ownership:** Immediately following the encounter, take a moment to reaffirm what is yours and what is theirs. If the attack involved Shame, state explicitly, *"My action was flawed, but my identity is whole. I am competent."* If the attack involved Addiction/Craving, spend time investing in a source of validation the manipulator **cannot** control—your exercise routine, a passion project, a healthy relationship.
2. **The Mandatory Log:** You must log the success. Log the date, the exploit used, and the policy that held. This logging does two things: it builds the evidence base for the **Variable Ratio Audit** on the manipulator, and it reinforces your own internal coding, transforming the initial panic into a data point for future success.

IV. The Philosophy of Non-Engagement

The greatest power you have cultivated in this final book is the right of **Non-Engagement**. You are no longer obligated to participate in the manipulator's emotional theater.

Think of emotional exploitation as a complex lure. It is brightly colored, erratic, and promises a massive, sudden catch. The vast majority of people, sensing the frantic energy and high stakes, instinctively dive in. The sovereign mind simply observes the frantic energy of the lure from the stable depths, classifies it as bait, and remains still.

- When you refuse the manufactured deadline, the manipulator's urgency looks desperate, not powerful.
- When you refuse the guilt, their moral posturing looks entitled, not ethical.
- When you refuse to chase the unpredictable reward, their sudden affection looks pathetic, not loving.

The refusal to participate is a disciplined, silent act of defiance. It is the ultimate boundary, telling the adversary that their currency—fear, guilt, and false praise—has no exchange rate in your market. You are not fighting them; you are simply **declining the invitation to fight**. This preserves your energy, exposes their core tactic, and forces them to move on to easier, more reactive targets.

V. The Prize: Strategic Control and Untapped Potential

The integration of these defenses is not merely about escaping harm; it is about freeing up **cognitive capital** for strategic deployment.

When you are no longer spending 40% of your mental energy managing manufactured guilt or worrying about arbitrary deadlines, that energy is released for genuine productivity, creativity, and strategic planning. The sovereign mind is a mind that operates on facts, policy, and long-term vision, unburdened by the daily, low-grade emotional sabotage that plagues the average person.

This is the goal of operational security for the self: to ensure that the operator is always functioning at peak capacity, free from external influence and internal turmoil. The system is designed to stabilize, categorize, and counter all threats, leaving you, the final architect, in supreme, disciplined command.

The manual is complete. The protocols are now yours. Your final mission is consistency. Trust the system, trust the pause, and hold the boundary.

REFLECTION QUESTIONS

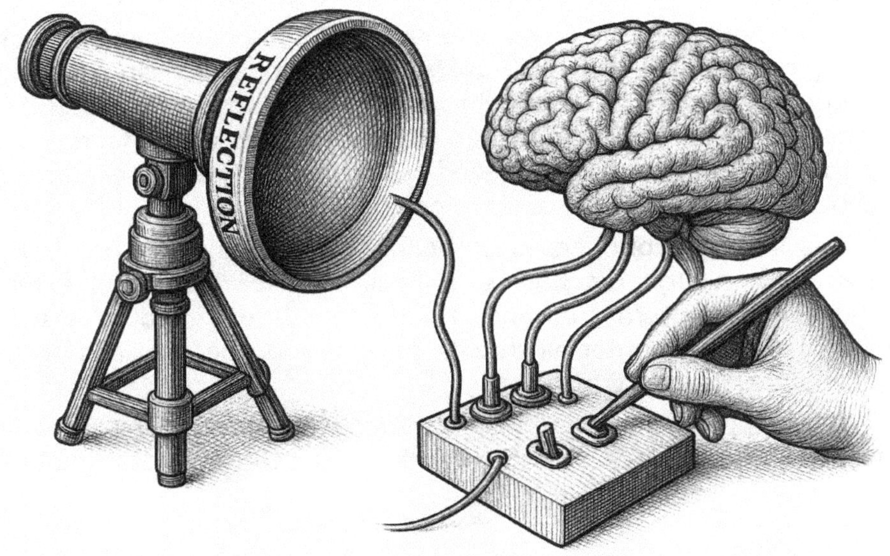

I. The Final Stage: Integration and Calibration

The journey through the architecture of emotional exploitation is now complete. You have the diagnostic tools, the policy blueprints, and the theoretical knowledge necessary to maintain Emotional Sovereignty. However, theory is merely a map; execution requires muscle memory. The protocols discussed in this manual, the Box Breathing, the Guilt Audit, the Fortified Boundaries, must transition from abstract concepts into automatic, defensive reflexes.

This final chapter serves as the dedicated calibration phase. It is not meant to be read quickly, but to be worked through deliberately. These questions are designed to force you to apply the high-level concepts to the messy, specific, and often painful realities of your own life. You are moving from analyst to operator, identifying the historical failure points and pre-programming the required defensive action.

Take your time. Use a journal. The objective is to stop generalizing your vulnerabilities and to start documenting the specific signatures of the exploits that successfully compromise your system.

Reflection Protocol I: The Amygdala Hijack (Fear and Intimidation)

Focus: Identifying the Triggers and Enforcing the Pause (Chapter 2)

1. **Physiological Signature Mapping:** Recall the last three times you felt an intense, high-arousal surge of anxiety or fear in an interaction. What specific physical data did your body generate? (e.g., Cold sweat on the palms, sudden shallow breath, clenching the jaw, stomach dropping). *By cataloging these precise somatic cues, you create a dedicated "Alert Signal" that mandates the immediate Box Breathing Protocol.*
2. **The Crisis Audit:** Identify the single most common scenario where a manipulator attempts to impose a **Manufactured Crisis** on your timeline (e.g., a boss demanding a last-minute project, a colleague needing a massive, instant favor, a partner demanding an ultimatum). What is the exact **Temporal Deferral Defense** statement you will pre-write and memorize for that specific scenario?
3. **Weak Point Analysis:** When you are under intense pressure, which is your most common default reaction: **Fight** (lashing out), **Flight** (caving/apologizing), or **Freeze** (silence/paralysis)? How does knowing this primary default reaction inform the *type* of countermeasure you need to deploy first? (e.g., If you freeze, you need to force movement or voice.)
4. **The Ambiguity Crystallizer:** Identify one ongoing, vague threat (the "Ghost in the Room") that currently causes you low-grade anxiety. Draft the exact, neutral script you will use to force the adversary to articulate the threat, thereby crystallizing the risk and moving it from the limbic system to the prefrontal cortex for analysis.

Reflection Protocol II: Moral Debt and Identity (Guilt and Shame)

Focus: Auditing the Ledger and Deploying the Firewall (Chapter 3)

5. **The Unquantifiable Favor:** Who in your life currently leverages the phrase, "After everything I've done for you"? Identify the specific "favor" they reference. Calculate the true, transactional cost of that original favor (time, money, effort). What is the maximum, quantifiable repayment that would discharge the debt?

6. **Debt Recalculation:** When did you last trade a **long-term asset** (e.g., a boundary, a vacation day, financial stability) for **short-term emotional relief** (e.g., stopping a manipulator's criticism, ending a confrontation)? What was the real price of that emotional relief?
7. **The Delegation of Feelings:** Identify the person whose emotional state you feel most responsible for managing. What is the precise boundary statement you need to make to reclaim ownership of your own emotional autonomy, even if it causes them temporary distress?
8. **The Shame-to-Action Audit:** Recall a time you felt profound shame due to an external criticism (e.g., "You are lazy," "You are selfish"). What was the *action* the criticism was based on? (e.g., missing a deadline). By the **Action vs. Identity Firewall** principle, rewrite the internal narrative, separating the temporary action from your core identity.

Reflection Protocol III: The Addiction Loop (Love Bombing and IR)

Focus: Breaking the Pattern and Reclaiming Intrinsic Value (Chapter 4)

9. **Timeline Violation Audit:** In a significant relationship or partnership that proved unhealthy, how quickly did the relationship transition from initial meeting to an intense declaration of commitment or life plans (Love Bombing)? How does this history inform your need for the **Mandatory 90-Day Timeline Friction** going forward?
10. **The Variable Ratio Log:** Identify the signature of an intermittent reinforcement cycle in your life. What is the **Reward** (e.g., sudden extravagant praise, intense attention)? What is the **Withdrawal** (e.g., unexplained silence, cold criticism)? What is the **Work** (e.g., excessive apologizing, over-performing) you perform to chase the Reward?
11. **Intrinsic vs. Extrinsic Value:** Name three things you accomplish or enjoy that **cannot** be validated, praised, or criticized by your primary manipulator (e.g., a specific skill, a personal hobby, a healthy friendship). How can you systematically increase the time and energy investment in these intrinsic sources to dilute your dependency on external, intermittent validation?

12. **The Relapse Plan:** When the craving for the "high" of the Love Bombing state is intense, what specific, immediate, pre-defined **Contained Action** (e.g., calling a neutral friend, going for a run, listening to a specific podcast) will you perform instead of engaging with the adversary?

Reflection Protocol IV: Systemic Fortification (Granularity and Boundaries)

Focus: Precision Diagnosis and Policy Enforcement (Chapters 5 and 6)

13. **The 5-Word Granularity Challenge:** Describe your *current* emotional state using exactly five distinct, non-generic adjectives (e.g., not "stressed" or "bad"). What hidden vulnerabilities or boundary violations do these five precise words reveal?
14. **Boundary Failure Analysis:** Identify the one boundary that is currently the weakest, most often violated, and most difficult for you to enforce (e.g., the after-hours email, the intrusive personal question, the lending of resources).
15. **The Fortification Project:** Using the weakest boundary from the previous question, perform a full upgrade:
    - **Temporal/Resource:** What is the precise, impersonal **Policy** statement?
    - **Consequence:** What is the non-emotional, immediate, and consistent **Consequence** if the policy is violated? (A boundary without a consequence is only a request.)
16. **The Non-Negotiable Policy:** What is the single, non-negotiable policy you need to establish that will protect your most precious asset (e.g., mental health, financial stability, relationship integrity)? How will you communicate this policy to the relevant parties in a calm, non-defensive manner *before* the policy needs to be enforced?

Conclusion: The Practice of Sovereignty

The work of Emotional Sovereignty is defined by this continuous loop: **Detect, Diagnose, Deploy, Document.** The reflection questions in this chapter are designed to internalize this loop, transforming the abstract framework into actionable intelligence. The integrity of your life and your resources hinges entirely on the consistency of your defense. Your policy is your peace.

OVERALL CONCLUSION

I. The Architect's Handover: Why You Can Stop Being Afraid

We have reached the end of the manual, but the real work, the work of living, is just beginning. If you stuck with us through the deep dive into Dark Triad mechanics, the tedious mapping of your own cognitive biases, and the surgical review of your emotional responses, then you have accomplished something few people ever attempt: you have fully documented the internal landscape of your mind.

For too long, the emotional life has felt like a weather system, chaotic, unpredictable, and something we must simply endure. The manipulator's greatest trick has always been convincing us that their fear, guilt, and chaos are just "the way things are." This manual proves that is a lie.

We started with the assumption that your mind is a high-security asset. We are now ending with the truth: **Your mind is not a fragile vault; it is a meticulously engineered fortress.** You didn't just learn about defense; you learned the entire enemy playbook, from the initial feint to the final, frantic affective strike.

Let's briefly review the sheer scope of the security system you have designed:

- **Book 1 (The Lie):** You stopped taking the bait. You learned to spot **Gaslighting**, the systematic attempt to blur the lines of reality, and you learned to identify the **Dark Triad** architects behind the sabotage. You saw the *who* and the *what* clearly, perhaps for the first time.
- **Book 2 (The Flaw):** You put your own hand on the lever. You realized that the most effective exploit is always the one you execute against yourself. You documented the *how* by charting your inherent **Cognitive Biases** (Reciprocity, Authority, Scarcity, etc.). You ceased being an automatic target.
- **Book 3 (The Takedown):** You achieved strategic calm. You realized you don't have to fight the manipulator forever because their own structural weaknesses, the Narcissist's shallow ego, the Psychopath's broken brakes, will lead to their own **Predictable Collapse**. Your job is to observe, not intervene.

- **Book 4 (The Wall):** You engineered distance. You built the **Negotiation Firewall**, learning how to communicate with people who cannot communicate in good faith. You mastered the **Neutral, Assertive, Limiting (NANL)** stance, making you boring, impenetrable, and predictable in a way that saves your soul-fuel.
- **Book 5 (The Core):** You claimed absolute control. You faced the chemical warfare, **Fear, Guilt, and Craving**, and developed the **Sovereign Mind Protocol** to diagnose the precise chemical, take a mandatory pause, and deploy the surgical countermeasure.

II. The Core Mandate: Refusing the Tempo

If I could distill 1,000 pages of work into a single operational directive, it would be this: **The strength of your sovereignty is measured by your refusal to participate in the manipulator's tempo.**

The entire strategy of emotional exploitation is built on urgency. They need you fast, breathless, guilty, or desperate for a fix. They need you to skip the pause.

Your defense must be defined by **disciplined predictability**. You are the unmoving stone; they are the chaotic, splashing wave.

- When a crisis explodes at 5:01 PM, demanding immediate attention, your defense is the unhurried deployment of the **Temporal Boundary**. You don't argue with them; you state the policy.
- When a debt is suddenly called in ("After everything I've done..."), your defense is the quiet, analytical application of the **Guilt-to-Debt Audit**. You don't get defensive; you audit the books.
- When the gut-punch of panic hits, your defense is the mechanical, rhythmic simplicity of the **Box Breathing Protocol**. You don't analyze the fear; you change the oxygen saturation in your blood.

This consistency is what drives them away. They are looking for drama, reaction, and an emotional return on their investment. When they encounter the boring, steady, unyielding pressure of your pre-defined rules, they learn that attempting to exploit you is a net loss of their energy. You win by being more disciplined than they are chaotic.

III. The Transformation of Failure: The System Penetration Test

You are human. You will slip up. A deadline will catch you off guard, an old guilt trigger will hit a little too hard, or the craving for validation might momentarily override your better judgment.

This is the final, most crucial shift in perspective: **Failure is no longer a moral collapse; it is merely diagnostic data.**

When a defense fails, you are not a bad person, a weak person, or a helpless person. You are simply an engineer who discovered a structural flaw in the latest code deployment.

The required response is not self-flagellation or shame. It is the immediate, dry-eyed commencement of the **Boundary Failure Analysis:**

- *Which Chapter 3 trigger was successfully deployed? (Shame? Guilt?)*
- *Which Chapter 6 boundary failed to deploy? (Temporal? Resource?)*
- *What specific, single action will you take to patch that vulnerability before the next interaction?*

The shame spiral, which is exactly what the manipulator wants you to fall into, is rejected. You treat the failure like an IT professional treats a server crash: it is a complex problem requiring a rational, dispassionate solution. By converting the subjective pain of failure into objective, actionable data, you ensure the mistake only needs to be made once.

IV. The Ultimate Prize: Unspent Energy

The final, incredible prize of this entire process is not just safety, but **energy**.

Imagine the immense mental bandwidth you have historically spent managing their moods, rehearsing your defense, preempting their attacks, and recovering from the psychological hangover of an interaction. That energy, that precious, irreplaceable cognitive capital, is now yours again.

Emotional Sovereignty is the act of reclaiming your spiritual and psychological resources. It means that your time, your focus, and your emotional availability are invested entirely in goals that you, the sovereign operator, have chosen for yourself.

You are no longer reacting to the world; you are **governing your participation** in it. The blueprint is complete. Now, go build the life you designed.

If you enjoyed this book, I'd greatly appreciate a review on Amazon because it helps me to create more books that people want. It would mean a lot to hear from you.

To leave a review:

1. Open your camera app.
2. Point your mobile device at the QR code.
3. The review page will appear in your web browser.

Thanks for your support!

HERE'S ANOTHER BOOK BY SEBASTIAN NOCTURNE THAT YOU MIGHT LIKE

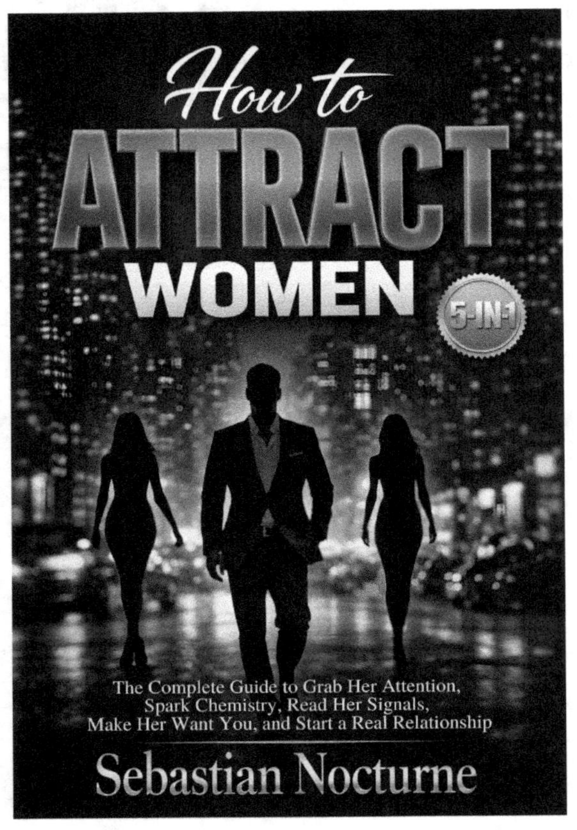

OVERALL RESOURCES

Part 1: Dark Seduction 5-in-1

Book 1

Introduction

https://en.wikipedia.org/wiki/Cognitive_bias

https://pmc.ncbi.nlm.nih.gov/articles/PMC8378077/

https://threadlinebranding.com/blog/book-review/review-influence-the-psychology-of-persuasion-by-robert-b-cialdini-phd/

https://salvadorbriggman.com/review-of-influence-the-psychology-of-persuasion/

http://www.communicationcache.com/uploads/1/0/8/8/10887248/gender_and_social_influence.pdf

https://influencecompany.com/blog/how-to-be-succesfull-in-communication-between-men-and-women/

https://fiveable.me/persuasion-theory/unit-12/persuasion-gender-differences/study-guide/LXts1mdLnZ14z04j

https://gap.hks.harvard.edu/how-genderrole-salience-influences-attitude-strength-and-persuasive-message-processing

Chapter 1 - resources

https://en.wikipedia.org/wiki/Cognitive_bias

https://pmc.ncbi.nlm.nih.gov/articles/PMC8378077/

https://salvadorbriggman.com/review-of-influence-the-psychology-of-persuasion/

https://gap.hks.harvard.edu/how-genderrole-salience-influences-attitude-strength-and-persuasive-message-processing

Chapter 2 - resources

https://threadlinebranding.com/blog/book-review/review-influence-the-psychology-of-persuasion-by-robert-b-cialdini-phd/

https://salvadorbriggman.com/review-of-influence-the-psychology-of-persuasion/

http://www.communicationcache.com/uploads/1/0/8/8/10887248/gender_and_social_influence.pdf https://influencecompany.com/blog/how-to-be-succesfull-in-communication-between-men-and-women/

https://fiveable.me/persuasion-theory/unit-12/persuasion-gender-differences/study-guide/LXts1mdLnZ14z04j

https://gap.hks.harvard.edu/how-genderrole-salience-influences-attitude-strength-and-persuasive-message-processing

https://www.investopedia.com/temporal-discounting-7972594

https://www.profit.co/blog/behavioral-economics/time-discounting-employee-rewards/

https://maccelerator.la/en/blog/entrepreneurship/behavioral-psychology-behind-scarcity/

https://psychotricks.com/scarcity-principle/

Chapter 3 - resources

https://salvadorbriggman.com/review-of-influence-the-psychology-of-persuasion/

https://skeptics.stackexchange.com/questions/74/any-scientific-basis-for-neuro-linguistic-programming

https://en.wikipedia.org/wiki/Neuro-linguistic_programming

https://business.columbia.edu/sites/default/files-efs/citation_file_upload/NLP_paper.pdf

https://pmc.ncbi.nlm.nih.gov/articles/PMC8455714/

https://fiveable.me/persuasion-theory/unit-12/persuasion-gender-differences/study-guide/LXts1mdLnZ14z04j

http://www.communicationcache.com/uploads/1/0/8/8/10887248/gender_and_social_influence.pdf

Chapter 4 - resources

https://pmc.ncbi.nlm.nih.gov/articles/PMC8378077/

https://en.wikipedia.org/wiki/Cognitive_bias

https://fiveable.me/persuasion-theory/unit-12/persuasion-gender-differences/study-guide/LXts1mdLnZ14z04j

https://gap.hks.harvard.edu/how-genderrole-salience-influences-attitude-strength-and-persuasive-message-processing

https://influencecompany.com/blog/how-to-be-succesfull-in-communication-between-men-and-women/

http://www.communicationcache.com/uploads/1/0/8/8/10887248/gender_and_social_influence.pdf

Chapter 5 - resources

https://en.wikipedia.org/wiki/Cognitive_bias

https://skeptics.stackexchange.com/questions/74/any-scientific-basis-for-neuro-linguistic-programming

http://www.communicationcache.com/uploads/1/0/8/8/10887248/gender_and_social_influence.pdf

https://gap.hks.harvard.edu/how-genderrole-salience-influences-attitude-strength-and-persuasive-message-processing

https://business.columbia.edu/sites/default/files-efs/citation_file_upload/NLP_paper.pdf

https://pmc.ncbi.nlm.nih.gov/articles/PMC8455714/

https://maccelerator.la/en/blog/entrepreneurship/behavioral-psychology-behind-scarcity/

https://psychotricks.com/scarcity-principle/

Conclusion

https://threadlinebranding.com/blog/book-review/review-influence-the-psychology-of-persuasion-by-robert-b-cialdini-phd/

https://salvadorbriggman.com/review-of-influence-the-psychology-of-persuasion/

https://maccelerator.la/en/blog/entrepreneurship/behavioral-psychology-behind-scarcity/

https://psychotricks.com/scarcity-principle/

https://fiveable.me/persuasion-theory/unit-12/persuasion-gender-differences/study-guide/LXts1mdLnZ14z04j

http://www.communicationcache.com/uploads/1/0/8/8/10887248/gender_and_social_influence.pdf

https://influencecompany.com/blog/how-to-be-succesfull-in-communication-between-men-and-women/

https://www.investopedia.com/temporal-discounting-7972594

https://pmc.ncbi.nlm.nih.gov/articles/PMC8378077/

https://skeptics.stackexchange.com/questions/74/any-scientific-basis-for-neuro-linguistic-programming

https://gap.hks.harvard.edu/how-genderrole-salience-influences-attitude-strength-and-persuasive-message-processing

Reflection Questions

https://pmc.ncbi.nlm.nih.gov/articles/PMC8378077/

https://salvadorbriggman.com/review-of-influence-the-psychology-of-persuasion/

https://threadlinebranding.com/blog/book-review/review-influence-the-psychology-of-persuasion-by-robert-b-cialdini-phd/

https://maccelerator.la/en/blog/entrepreneurship/behavioral-psychology-behind-scarcity/

https://psychotricks.com/scarcity-principle/

https://skeptics.stackexchange.com/questions/74/any-scientific-basis-for-neuro-linguistic-programming

http://www.communicationcache.com/uploads/1/0/8/8/10887248/gender_and_social_influence.pdf

https://business.columbia.edu/sites/default/files-efs/citation_file_upload/NLP_paper.pdf

Book 2

Introduction

https://pmc.ncbi.nlm.nih.gov/articles/PMC2763368/

https://www.ebsco.com/research-starters/health-and-medicine/nonverbal-communication-and-social-cognition

https://pmc.ncbi.nlm.nih.gov/articles/PMC8378077/

https://faculty.wharton.upenn.edu/wp-content/uploads/2018/12/Barsade_Coutifaris_Pillemer-Emotional-contagion-in-organizational-life.pdf)

https://pmc.ncbi.nlm.nih.gov/articles/PMC10656777/

https://www.mdpi.com/2076-328X/15/1/15 (

https://www.researchgate.net/publication/225596088_The_Social_Function_of_Humor_in_Interpersonal_Relationships)

https://pmc.ncbi.nlm.nih.gov/articles/PMC8455714/

Chapter 1 - resources

https://pmc.ncbi.nlm.nih.gov/articles/PMC2763368/

https://www.ebsco.com/research-starters/health-and-medicine/nonverbal-communication-and-social-cognition

https://pmc.ncbi.nlm.nih.gov/articles/PMC8378077/

https://en.wikipedia.org/wiki/Cognitive_bias

https://gap.hks.harvard.edu/how-genderrole-salience-influences-attitude-strength-and-persuasive-message-processing

Chapter 2 - resources

https://faculty.wharton.upenn.edu/wp-content/uploads/2018/12/Barsade_Coutifaris_Pillemer-Emotional-contagion-in-organizational-life.pdf)

https://pmc.ncbi.nlm.nih.gov/articles/PMC10656777/

https://www.mdpi.com/2076-328X/15/1/15 (

https://www.researchgate.net/publication/225596088_The_Social_Function_of_Humor_in_Interpersonal_Relationships)

https://pmc.ncbi.nlm.nih.gov/articles/PMC8378077/

https://www.ebsco.com/research-starters/health-and-medicine/nonverbal-communication-and-social-cognition

Chapter 3 - resources

https://www.ebsco.com/research-starters/health-and-medicine/nonverbal-communication-and-social-cognition

https://pmc.ncbi.nlm.nih.gov/articles/PMC2763368/

https://pmc.ncbi.nlm.nih.gov/articles/PMC8378077/

https://pmc.ncbi.nlm.nih.gov/articles/PMC5348110/

https://pdxscholar.library.pdx.edu/cgi/viewcontent.cgi?article=1888&context=open_access_etds

Chapter 4 - resources

https://www.ebsco.com/research-starters/health-and-medicine/nonverbal-communication-and-social-cognition

https://pmc.ncbi.nlm.nih.gov/articles/PMC2763368/

https://pmc.ncbi.nlm.nih.gov/articles/PMC8378077/

https://en.wikipedia.org/wiki/Cognitive_bias

https://gap.hks.harvard.edu/how-genderrole-salience-influences-attitude-strength-and-persuasive-message-processing

Chapter 5- resources

https://www.mdpi.com/2076-328X/15/1/15 (

https://www.researchgate.net/publication/225596088_The_Social_Function_of_Humor_in_Interpersonal_Relationships) (

https://faculty.wharton.upenn.edu/wp-content/uploads/2018/12/Barsade_Coutifaris_Pillemer-Emotional-contagion-in-organizational-life.pdf)

https://pmc.ncbi.nlm.nih.gov/articles/PMC10656777/
https://pmc.ncbi.nlm.nih.gov/articles/PMC2763368/
http://www.communicationcache.com/uploads/1/0/8/8/10887248/gender_and_social_influence.pdf

Conclusion

https://www.ebsco.com/research-starters/health-and-medicine/nonverbal-communication-and-social-cognition
https://pmc.ncbi.nlm.nih.gov/articles/PMC2763368/
https://pmc.ncbi.nlm.nih.gov/articles/PMC8378077/ (
https://faculty.wharton.upenn.edu/wp-content/uploads/2018/12/Barsade_Coutifaris_Pillemer-Emotional-contagion-in-organizational-life.pdf)
https://pmc.ncbi.nlm.nih.gov/articles/PMC10656777/
https://www.mdpi.com/2076-328X/15/1/15
https://pmc.ncbi.nlm.nih.gov/articles/PMC5348110/
https://influencecompany.com/blog/how-to-be-succesfull-in-communication-between-men-and-women/
http://www.communicationcache.com/uploads/1/0/8/8/10887248/gender_and_social_influence.pdf
https://gap.hks.harvard.edu/how-genderrole-salience-influences-attitude-strength-and-persuasive-message-processing

Reflection Questions

https://faculty.wharton.upenn.edu/wp-content/uploads/2018/12/Barsade_Coutifaris_Pillemer-Emotional-contagion-in-organizational-life.pdf)
https://pmc.ncbi.nlm.nih.gov/articles/PMC10656777/
https://www.ebsco.com/research-starters/health-and-medicine/nonverbal-communication-and-social-cognition
https://pmc.ncbi.nlm.nih.gov/articles/PMC5348110/
https://www.mdpi.com/2076-328X/15/1/15
https://pmc.ncbi.nlm.nih.gov/articles/PMC2763368/

Book 3

Introduction

https://en.wikipedia.org/wiki/Cognitive_bias

https://business.columbia.edu/sites/default/files-efs/citation_file_upload/NLP_paper.pdf

https://en.wikipedia.org/wiki/Neuro-linguistic_programming

https://skeptics.stackexchange.com/questions/74/any-scientific-basis-for-neuro-linguistic-programming

https://arxiv.org/abs/2308.00107

https://pmc.ncbi.nlm.nih.gov/articles/PMC8455714/

https://influencecompany.com/blog/how-to-be_succesfull-in-communication-between-men-and-women/

https://fiveable.me/persuasion-theory/unit-12/persuasion-gender-differences/study-guide/LXts1mdLnZ14z04j

Chapter 1 - resources

https://en.wikipedia.org/wiki/Cognitive_bias

https://skeptics.stackexchange.com/questions/74/any-scientific-basis-for-neuro-linguistic-programming

https://psychotricks.com/scarcity-principle/

https://salvadorbriggman.com/review-of-influence-the-psychology_of_persuasion/

https://gap.hks.harvard.edu/how-genderrole-salience-influences-attitude-strength-and-persuasive-message-processing

Chapter 2 - resources

https://business.columbia.edu/sites/default/files-efs/citation_file_upload/NLP_paper.pdf

https://pmc.ncbi.nlm.nih.gov/articles/PMC8455714/

https://influencecompany.com/blog/how-to-be_succesfull-in-communication-between-men-and-women/

https://www.mdpi.com/2076-328X/15/1/15 (

https://www.researchgate.net/publication/225596088_The_Social_Function_of_Humor_in_Interpersonal_Relationships)

Chapter 3- resources

https://en.wikipedia.org/wiki/Cognitive_bias

https://skeptics.stackexchange.com/questions/74/any-scientific-basis-for-neuro-linguistic-programming

https://psychotricks.com/scarcity-principle/

https://maccelerator.la/en/blog/entrepreneurship/behavioral-psychology-behind-scarcity/

https://arxiv.org/abs/2308.00107

https://business.columbia.edu/sites/default/files-efs/citation_file_upload/NLP_paper.pdf

https://pmc.ncbi.nlm.nih.gov/articles/PMC8455714/

http://www.communicationcache.com/uploads/1/0/8/8/10887248/gender_and_social_influence.pdf

Chapter 4 - resources

https://business.columbia.edu/sites/default/files-efs/citation_file_upload/NLP_paper.pdf

https://pmc.ncbi.nlm.nih.gov/articles/PMC8455714/

https://en.wikipedia.org/wiki/Cognitive_bias

https://www.investopedia.com/temporal-discounting-7972594

https://www.profit.co/blog/behavioral-economics/time-discounting-employee-rewards/

https://www.mdpi.com/2076-328X/15/1/15

https://www.researchgate.net/publication/225596088_The_Social_Function_of_Humor_in_Interpersonal_Relationships

https://pdxscholar.library.pdx.edu/cgi/viewcontent.cgi?article=1888&context=open_access_etds

https://psychotricks.com/scarcity-principle/

https://pmc.ncbi.nlm.nih.gov/articles/PMC8378077/

https://www.ebsco.com/research-starters/health-and-medicine/nonverbal-communication-and-social-cognition

Chapter 5- resources

https://fiveable.me/persuasion-theory/unit-12/persuasion-gender-differences/study-guide/LXts1mdLnZ14z04j

https://influencecompany.com/blog/how-to-be_succesfull-in-communication-between-men-and-women/

https://gap.hks.harvard.edu/how-genderrole-salience-influences-attitude-strength-and-persuasive-message-processing

http://www.communicationcache.com/uploads/1/0/8/8/10887248/gender_and_social_influence.pdf

https://pmc.ncbi.nlm.nih.gov/articles/PMC8455714/

https://skeptics.stackexchange.com/questions/74/any-scientific-basis-for-neuro-linguistic-programming

Conclusion

https://maccelerator.la/en/blog/entrepreneurship/behavioral-psychology-behind-scarcity/

https://salvadorbriggman.com/review-of-influence-the-psychology_of_persuasion/

https://en.wikipedia.org/wiki/Cognitive_bias

https://business.columbia.edu/sites/default/files-efs/citation_file_upload/NLP_paper.pdf

https://influencecompany.com/blog/how-to-be_succesfull-in-communication-between-men-and-women/

https://arxiv.org/abs/2308.00107

https://pmc.ncbi.nlm.nih.gov/articles/PMC8455714/

https://fiveable.me/persuasion-theory/unit-12/persuasion-gender-differences/study-guide/LXts1mdLnZ14z04j

https://gap.hks.harvard.edu/how-genderrole-salience-influences-attitude-strength-and-persuasive-message-processing

https://faculty.wharton.upenn.edu/wp-content/uploads/2018/12/Barsade_Coutifaris_Pillemer-Emotional-contagion-in-organizational-life.pdf

https://pmc.ncbi.nlm.nih.gov/articles/PMC10656777/

Reflection Questions

https://psychotricks.com/scarcity-principle/

https://salvadorbriggman.com/review-of-influence-the-psychology_of_persuasion/

https://en.wikipedia.org/wiki/Cognitive_bias

https://business.columbia.edu/sites/default/files-efs/citation_file_upload/NLP_paper.pdf

https://influencecompany.com/blog/how-to-be_succesfull-in-communication-between-men-and-women/

https://gap.hks.harvard.edu/how-genderrole-salience-influences-attitude-strength-and-persuasive-message-processing

https://fiveable.me/persuasion-theory/unit-12/persuasion-gender-differences/study-guide/LXts1mdLnZ14z04j

https://pmc.ncbi.nlm.nih.gov/articles/PMC8455714/

https://skeptics.stackexchange.com/questions/74/any-scientific-basis-for-neuro-linguistic-programming

https://pmc.ncbi.nlm.nih.gov/articles/PMC2763368/

Book 4

Introduction

https://pmc.ncbi.nlm.nih.gov/articles/PMC5348110/

https://arxiv.org/abs/2308.00107

https://pdxscholar.library.pdx.edu/cgi/viewcontent.cgi?article=1888&context=open_access_etds

https://www.ebsco.com/research-starters/health-and-medicine/nonverbal-communication-and-social-cognition

https://pmc.ncbi.nlm.nih.gov/articles/PMC10656777/

https://salvadorbriggman.com/review-of-influence-the-psychology_of_persuasion/

https://www.mdpi.com/2076-328X/15/1/15 (

https://www.researchgate.net/publication/225596088_The_Social_Function_of_Humor_in_Interpersonal_Relationships)

https://pmc.ncbi.nlm.nih.gov/articles/PMC8378077/

Chapter 1 - resources

https://pmc.ncbi.nlm.nih.gov/articles/PMC5348110/

https://arxiv.org/abs/2308.00107

https://pmc.ncbi.nlm.nih.gov/articles/PMC10656777/

https://pdxscholar.library.pdx.edu/cgi/viewcontent.cgi?article=1888&context=open_access_etds

https://salvadorbriggman.com/review-of-influence-the-psychology_of_persuasion/

https://threadlinebranding.com/blog/book-review/review-influence-the-psychology_of_persuasion-by-robert-b-cialdini-phd/

Chapter 2 - resources

https://salvadorbriggman.com/review-of-influence-the-psychology_of_persuasion/

https://www.mdpi.com/2076-328X/15/1/15 (

https://www.researchgate.net/publication/225596088_The_Social_Function_of_Humor_in_Interpersonal_Relationships)

https://pdxscholar.library.pdx.edu/cgi/viewcontent.cgi?article=1888&context=open_access_etds

https://pmc.ncbi.nlm.nih.gov/articles/PMC8455714/

https://pmc.ncbi.nlm.nih.gov/articles/PMC5348110/

Chapter 3 - resources

https://pmc.ncbi.nlm.nih.gov/articles/PMC5348110/

https://pdxscholar.library.pdx.edu/cgi/viewcontent.cgi?article=1888&context=open_access_etds

https://pmc.ncbi.nlm.nih.gov/articles/PMC8378077/

https://pmc.ncbi.nlm.nih.gov/articles/PMC2763368/

https://maccelerator.la/en/blog/entrepreneurship/behavioral-psychology-behind-scarcity/

Chapter 4 - resources

https://arxiv.org/abs/2308.00107

https://pmc.ncbi.nlm.nih.gov/articles/PMC10656777/

https://pdxscholar.library.pdx.edu/cgi/viewcontent.cgi?article=1888&context=open_access_etds

https://pmc.ncbi.nlm.nih.gov/articles/PMC8455714/

https://psychotricks.com/scarcity-principle/

https://www.investopedia.com/temporal-discounting-7972594

https://www.mdpi.com/2076-328X/15/1/15

https://salvadorbriggman.com/review-of-influence-the-psychology_of_persuasion/

https://en.wikipedia.org/wiki/Cognitive_bias

https://pmc.ncbi.nlm.nih.gov/articles/PMC5348110/

Chapter 5 - resources

https://www.mdpi.com/2076-328X/15/1/15 (

https://www.researchgate.net/publication/225596088_The_Social_Function_of_Humor_in_Interpersonal_Relationships)

https://pdxscholar.library.pdx.edu/cgi/viewcontent.cgi?article=1888&context=open_access_etds

https://salvadorbriggman.com/review-of-influence-the-psychology_of_persuasion/ (

https://faculty.wharton.upenn.edu/wp-content/uploads/2018/12/Barsade_Coutifaris_Pillemer-Emotional-contagion-in-organizational-life.pdf)

https://pmc.ncbi.nlm.nih.gov/articles/PMC8378077/

Conclusion

https://pmc.ncbi.nlm.nih.gov/articles/PMC5348110/

https://arxiv.org/abs/2308.00107

https://salvadorbriggman.com/review-of-influence-the-psychology_of_persuasion/

https://www.mdpi.com/2076-328X/15/1/15 (https://www.researchgate.net/publication/225596088_The_Social_Function_of_Humor_in_Interpersonal_Relationships)

https://www.ebsco.com/research-starters/health-and-medicine/nonverbal-communication-and-social-cognition

https://pmc.ncbi.nlm.nih.gov/articles/PMC8378077/

https://influencecompany.com/blog/how-to-be-succesfull-in-communication-between-men-and-women/

http://www.communicationcache.com/uploads/1/0/8/8/10887248/gender_and_social_influence.pdf

Reflection Questions

https://pmc.ncbi.nlm.nih.gov/articles/PMC5348110/

https://arxiv.org/abs/2308.00107

https://salvadorbriggman.com/review-of-influence-the-psychology_of_persuasion/

https://www.mdpi.com/2076-328X/15/1/15 (https://www.researchgate.net/publication/225596088_The_Social_Function_of_Humor_in_Interpersonal_Relationships)

https://pmc.ncbi.nlm.nih.gov/articles/PMC8378077/

https://influencecompany.com/blog/how-to-be-succesfull-in-communication-between-men-and-women/

https://fiveable.me/persuasion-theory/unit-12/persuasion-gender-differences/study-guide/LXts1mdLnZ14z04j

Book 5

Introduction

https://www.investopedia.com/temporal-discounting-7972594

https://www.profit.co/blog/behavioral-economics/time-discounting-employee-rewards/

https://psychotricks.com/scarcity-principle/

https://maccelerator.la/en/blog/entrepreneurship/behavioral-psychology-behind-scarcity/

https://salvadorbriggman.com/review-of-influence-the-psychology_of_persuasion/

Chapter 1 - resources

https://www.investopedia.com/temporal-discounting-7972594

https://www.profit.co/blog/behavioral-economics/time-discounting-employee-rewards/

https://salvadorbriggman.com/review-of-influence-the-psychology_of_persuasion/

Chapter 2 - resources

https://psychotricks.com/scarcity-principle/

https://maccelerator.la/en/blog/entrepreneurship/behavioral-psychology-behind-scarcity/

https://salvadorbriggman.com/review-of-influence-the-psychology_of_persuasion/

Chapter 3 - resources

https://www.investopedia.com/temporal-discounting-7972594

https://www.profit.co/blog/behavioral-economics/time-discounting-employee-rewards/

Chapter 4- resources

https://www.investopedia.com/temporal-discounting-7972594

https://www.profit.co/blog/behavioral-economics/time-discounting-employee-rewards/

Chapter 5 - resources

https://psychotricks.com/scarcity-principle/

https://maccelerator.la/en/blog/entrepreneurship/behavioral-psychology-behind-scarcity/

Conclusion

https://www.investopedia.com/temporal-discounting-7972594

https://psychotricks.com/scarcity-principle/

https://maccelerator.la/en/blog/entrepreneurship/behavioral-psychology-behind-scarcity/

https://salvadorbriggman.com/review-of-influence-the-psychology_of_persuasion/

Reflection Questions

https://www.investopedia.com/temporal-discounting-7972594

https://psychotricks.com/scarcity-principle/

https://maccelerator.la/en/blog/entrepreneurship/behavioral-psychology-behind-scarcity/

Overall Conclusion and Print and Keep Checklist - Resources

https://en.wikipedia.org/wiki/Cognitive_bias

https://salvadorbriggman.com/review-of-influence-the-psychology_of_persuasion/

https://pmc.ncbi.nlm.nih.gov/articles/PMC2763368/

https://pmc.ncbi.nlm.nih.gov/articles/PMC8378077/ (

https://faculty.wharton.upenn.edu/wp-content/uploads/2018/12/Barsade_Coutifaris_Pillemer-Emotional-contagion-in-organizational-life.pdf)

https://pmc.ncbi.nlm.nih.gov/articles/PMC10656777/

https://www.ebsco.com/research-starters/health-and-medicine/nonverbal-communication-and-social-cognition

https://www.mdpi.com/2076-328X/15/1/15 (

https://www.researchgate.net/publication/225596088_The_Social_Function_of_Humor_in_Interpersonal_Relationships)

https://skeptics.stackexchange.com/questions/74/any-scientific-basis-for-neuro-linguistic-programming

https://business.columbia.edu/sites/default/files-efs/citation_file_upload/NLP_paper.pdf

https://pmc.ncbi.nlm.nih.gov/articles/PMC8455714/

https://fiveable.me/persuasion-theory/unit-12/persuasion-gender-differences/study-guide/LXts1mdLnZ14z04j

http://www.communicationcache.com/uploads/1/0/8/8/10887248/gender_and_social_influence.pdf

https://influencecompany.com/blog/how-to-be-succesfull-in-communication-between-men-and-women/

https://pmc.ncbi.nlm.nih.gov/articles/PMC5348110/

https://www.investopedia.com/temporal-discounting-7972594

https://www.profit.co/blog/behavioral-economics/time-discounting-employee-rewards/

https://psychotricks.com/scarcity-principle/

https://maccelerator.la/en/blog/entrepreneurship/behavioral-psychology-behind-scarcity/

https://gap.hks.harvard.edu/how-genderrole-salience-influences-attitude-strength-and-persuasive-message-processing

Part 2: Dark Psychology and Manipulation 5-1

Overall introduction

Cialdini, R. B. (1984/2021). Influence: The Psychology of Persuasion. Harper Business.

Hamilton, P. (1938). Gas Light. Constable & Co.

Kahneman, D. (2011). Thinking, Fast and Slow. Farrar, Straus and Giroux.

Levine, T. R. (2019). Duped: Truth-Default Theory and the Social Science of Lying and Deception. University of Alabama Press.

Paulhus, D. L., & Williams, K. M. (2002). "The Dark Triad of personality: Narcissism, Machiavellianism, and psychopathy". Journal of Research in Personality, 36(6), 556–563.

Stern, R. (2007). The Gaslight Effect: How to Spot and Survive the Hidden Manipulation Others Use to Control Your Life. Morgan Road Books.

Tversky, A., & Kahneman, D. (1979). "Prospect Theory: An Analysis of Decision under Risk". Econometrica, 47(2), 263–291.

Book 1

Introduction

Stern, R. (2007). The Gaslight Effect: How to Spot and Survive the Hidden Manipulation Others Use to Control Your Life. Morgan Road Books.

Festinger, L. (1957). A Theory of Cognitive Dissonance. Stanford University Press.

Lerner, H. (1989). The Dance of Anger: A Woman's Guide to Changing the Patterns of Intimate Relationships. HarperCollins.

Chapter 1 - resources

Bancroft, L. (2002). Why Does He Do That?: Inside the Minds of Angry and Controlling Men. Berkley Books.

Paulhus, D. L., & Williams, K. M. (2002). "The Dark Triad of personality: Narcissism, Machiavellianism, and psychopathy." Journal of Research in Personality, 36(6), 556–563.

Bowen, M. (1978). Family Therapy in Clinical Practice. Jason Aronson.

Chapter 2 - resources

van der Kolk, B. A. (2014). The Body Keeps the Score: Brain, Mind, and Body in the Healing of Trauma. Viking.

Carnes, P. (1997). The Betrayal Bond: Breaking Free of Exploitive Relationships. Health Communications, Inc.

Schwartz, R. C. (1995). Internal Family Systems Therapy. Guilford Press.

Chapter 3 - resources

Katherine, A. (1994). Boundaries: Where You End and I Begin. Hazelden.

Glass, S. P. (2003). Not "Just Friends": Rebuilding Trust and Recovering Your Sanity After Infidelity. Free Press.

Evans, P. (1996). Verbal Abuse Survivors Speak Out: On Relationship and Recovery. Adams Media.

Chapter 4 - resources

Linehan, M. M. (1993). Cognitive-Behavioral Treatment of Borderline Personality Disorder. Guilford Press.

Evans, P. (1992). The Verbally Abusive Relationship: How to Recognize It and How to Respond. Adams Media.

Paterson, R. J. (2010). The Assertiveness Workbook: How to Express Your Ideas and Stand Up for Yourself at Work and in Relationships. New Harbinger Publications.

Chapter 5 - resources

Porges, S. W. (2011). The Polyvagal Theory: Neurophysiological Foundations of Emotions, Attachment, Communication, and Self-Regulation. W. W. Norton & Company.

Levine, P. A. (1997). Waking the Tiger: Healing Trauma. North Atlantic Books.

Conclusion

Tedeschi, R. G., & Calhoun, L. G. (1996). "The Posttraumatic Growth Inventory: Measuring the positive change resulting from trauma." Journal of Traumatic Stress, 9(3), 455–471.

Brown, B. (2012). Daring Greatly: How the Courage to Be Vulnerable Transforms the Way We Live, Love, Parent, and Lead. Gotham Books.

Hayes, S. C., Strosahl, K. D., & Wilson, K. G. (1999). Acceptance and Commitment Therapy: An Experiential Approach to Behavior Change. Guilford Press.

Reflection Questions

Csikszentmihalyi, M. (1990). Flow: The Psychology of Optimal Experience. Harper & Row.

Kegan, R. (1994). In Over Our Heads: The Mental Demands of Modern Life. Harvard University Press.

Pennebaker, J. W. (1997). Opening Up: The Healing Power of Expressing Emotions. Guilford Press.

Siegel, D. J. (2010). Mindsight: The New Science of Personal Transformation. Bantam Books.

Book 2

Introduction

Taleb, N. N. (2012). Antifragile: Things That Gain from Disorder. Random House.

Clear, J. (2018). Atomic Habits: An Easy & Proven Way to Build Good Habits & Break Bad Ones.

Avery. Duhigg, C. (2012). The Power of Habit: Why We Do What We Do in Life and Business. Random House.

Chapter 1 - resources

Mitnick, K. D., & Simon, W. L. (2002). The Art of Deception: Controlling the Human Element of Security.

Chapter 2 - resources

Ariely, D. (2008). Predictably Irrational: The Hidden Forces That Shape Our Decisions. HarperCollins.

Tversky, A., & Kahneman, D. (1974). "Judgment under Uncertainty: Heuristics and Biases." Science, 185(4157), 1124-1131.

Sunstein, C. R., & Thaler, R. H. (2008). Nudge: Improving Decisions About Health, Wealth, and Happiness. Yale University Press.

Chapter 3 - resources

Schneier, B. (2015). Data and Goliath: The Hidden Battles to Collect Your Data and Control Your World.

W. W. Norton & Company. OWASP Top 10 (Latest version). (Open Web Application Security Project). SANS Institute Security Awareness Resources (Various publications).

Chapter 4 - resources

Goleman, D. (1995). Emotional Intelligence: Why It Can Matter More Than IQ. Bantam Books.

Newport, C. (2016). Deep Work: Rules for Focused Success in a Distracted World. Grand Central Publishing.

Patterson, K., Grenny, J., McMillan, R., Switzler, A. (2011). Crucial Conversations Tools for Talking When Stakes Are High. McGraw-Hill.

Chapter 5 - resources

Kahneman, D. (2011). Thinking, Fast and Slow. Farrar, Straus and Giroux.

Ericsson, K. A., Krampe, R. T., & Tesch-Römer, C. (1993). "The role of deliberate practice in the acquisition of expert performance." Psychological Review, 100(3), 363–406.

Cialdini, R. B. (2007). Influence: The Psychology of Persuasion. Harper Business.

Concolusion

Hadnagy, C., & Fincher, P. (2020). Human Hacking: Win Friends, Influence People, and Leave Your Mark on the World. HarperCollins Leadership.

Reflection Questions

Kolb, D. A. (1984). Experiential Learning: Experience as the Source of Learning and Development.

Prentice Hall. Senge, P. M. (1990). The Fifth Discipline: The Art & Practice of The Learning Organization. Doubleday. ISO/IEC 27001 (Information Security Management Systems) & Related Standards. (Various international standards bodies).

Book 3

Introduction

Jonason, P. K., & Webster, G. D. (2010). The Dark Triad: Deficient empathy and the seven short original sins.

Spain, S. M., Harms, P., & LeBreton, J. M. (2014). The dark side of personality at work.

Furnham, A. (2012). The Dark Side of Leadership: A Review and Taxonomy of Destructive Leader Behaviors.

Chapter 1 - resources

Miller, J. D., Hoffman, B. J., Gaughan, E. T., Gentile, B., Maples, J., & Keith Campbell, W. (2011). Grandiose and vulnerable narcissism: A nomological network analysis.

Kernberg, O. F. (1975). Borderline conditions and pathological narcissism.

Morf, C. C., & Rhodewalt, F. (2001). Unraveling the paradoxes of narcissism: A dynamic self-regulatory processing model.

Chapter 2 - resources

Christie, R., & Geis, F. L. (1970). Studies in Machiavellianism.

Fehr, E., & Gächter, S. (2000). Cooperation and punishment in public goods experiments.

Jakobwitz, S., & Egan, V. (2006). The dark triad and the two-factor model of personality.

Chapter 3 - resources

Hare, R. D. (2003). The Psychopath's Overreach: The Broken Brakes.

Babiak, P., & Hare, R. D. (2006). Snakes in suits: When psychopaths go to work.

Blair, R. J. R. (2003). Neurobiological basis of psychopathy.

Lilienfeld, S. O., & Widows, M. R. (2005). The Psychopathic Personality Inventory-Revised (PPI-R) Professional Manual.

Chapter 4- resources

McClelland, D. C. (1985). Human motivation.

Kets de Vries, M. F. R. (2009). Reflections on Character and Leadership.

Padma, K., & Suresh, K. (2018). The toxicity effect: Examining the relationship between cynicism and organizational failure.

Chapter 5 - resource

Bies, R. J., & Moag, J. S. (1986). Interactional justice: Communication criteria of fairness.

Duhigg, C. (2012). The power of habit: Why we do what we do in life and business.

Kaplan, S., & Norton, D. P. (1992). The balanced scorecard—measures that drive performance.

Conclusion

Sutton, R. I. (2010). Good bosses, bad bosses: How to be the best... and survive the worst.

Mintzberg, H. (1979). The Structuring of Organizations: A Synthesis of the Research.

Goleman, D., Boyatzis, R., & McKee, A. (2002). Primal leadership: Realizing the power of emotional intelligence.

Reflection Questions

Argyris, C. (1991). Teaching smart people how to learn.

Senge, P. M. (1990). The fifth discipline: The art & practice of the learning organization.

Book 4

Introduction

Kahneman, D. (2011). Thinking, Fast and Slow. Tversky, A., & Kahneman, D. (1974). Judgment under Uncertainty: Heuristics and Biases.

Ariely, D. (2008). Predictably Irrational: The Hidden Forces That Shape Our Decisions.

Chapter 1 - resources

Cialdini, R. B. (2001). Influence: Science and Practice (4th ed.).

Milgram, S. (1974). Obedience to Authority: An Experimental View.

Asch, S. E. (1956). Studies of independence and conformity: I. A minority of one against a unanimous majority.

Chapter 2 - resources

Cialdini, R. B. (2001). Influence: Science and Practice (4th ed.).

Gouldner, A. W. (1960). The norm of reciprocity: A preliminary statement.

Freedman, J. L., & Fraser, S. C. (1966). "Compliance without pressure: The foot-in-the-door technique."

Chapter 3 - resources

Janis, I. L. (1972). Victims of Groupthink: A Psychological Study of Foreign Policy Decisions and Fiascoes.

Lord, C. G., Ross, L., & Lepper, M. R. (1979). Biased assimilation and attitude polarization: The effects of prior theories on subsequently considered evidence.

Festinger, L. (1957). A theory of cognitive dissonance.

Chapter 4 - resources

Arkes, H. R., & Blumer, C. (1985). The psychology of sunk cost.

Cialdini, R. B. (2001). Influence: Science and Practice (4th ed.).

Thaler, R. H. (2015). Misbehaving: The Making of Behavioral Economics.

Chapter 5 - resources

Klein, G. (1998). Sources of power: How people make decisions.

Heuer, R. J. Jr. (1999). Psychology of Intelligence Analysis.

Starbuck, W. H., & Milliken, F. J. (1988). Executives' perceptual filters: What they notice and how they decide.

Conclusion

Kahneman, D. (2011). Thinking, Fast and Slow.

Kahneman, D., & Tversky, A. (1979). Prospect Theory: An Analysis of Decision under Risk.

Janis, I. L. (1972). Victims of Groupthink: A Psychological Study of Foreign Policy Decisions and Fiascoes.

Reflection Questions

Argyris, C. (1991). Teaching smart people how to learn.

Schön, D. A. (1983). The Reflective Practitioner: How Professionals Think in Action.

Senge, P. M. (1990). The Fifth Discipline: The Art & Practice of The Learning Organization.

Book 5

Introduction

LeDoux, J. (1996). The Emotional Brain: The Mysterious Underpinnings of Emotional Life. Simon & Schuster.

Goleman, D. (1995). Emotional Intelligence: Why It Can Matter More Than IQ. Bantam Books.

Beck, A. T. (1976). Cognitive Therapy and the Emotional Disorders. International Universities Press.

Chapter 1 - resources

Porges, S. W. (2011). The Polyvagal Theory: Neurophysiological Foundations of Emotions, Attachment, Communication, and Self-Regulation. W. W. Norton & Company.

Miller, J. G., & Wozniak, W. J. (2001). "The effect of box breathing on heart rate variability." Journal of Clinical Psychology, 57(1), 101–109.

Levine, P. A. (1997). Waking the Tiger: Healing Trauma. North Atlantic Books.

Chapter 2 - resources

Brown, B. (2012). Daring Greatly: How the Courage to Be Vulnerable Transforms the Way We Live, Love, Parent, and Lead. Gotham Books.

Tangney, J. P., & Dearing, R. L. (2002). Shame and Guilt. Guilford Press.

Lerner, H. (1989). The Dance of Anger: A Woman's Guide to Changing the Patterns of Intimate Relationships. HarperCollins.

Chapter 3 - resources

Fisher, H. (1992). Anatomy of Love: A Natural History of Mating, Marriage, and Why We Stray. W. W. Norton & Company.

Skinner, B. F. (1953). Science and Human Behavior. Macmillan.

Carnes, P. (1997). The Betrayal Bond: Breaking Free of Exploitive Relationships. Health Communications, Inc.

Chapter 4 - resources

Barrett, L. F. (2017). How Emotions Are Made: The Secret Life of the Brain. Houghton Mifflin Harcourt.

Kahneman, D. (2011). Thinking, Fast and Slow. Farrar, Straus and Giroux.

Wilson, T. D. (2002). Strangers to Ourselves: Discovering the Adaptive Unconscious. Harvard University Press.

Chapter 5 - resources

Katherine, A. (1994). Boundaries: Where You End and I Begin. Hazelden.

Patterson, K., Grenny, J., McMillan, R., Switzler, A. (2011). Crucial Conversations Tools for Talking When Stakes Are High. McGraw-Hill.

Vohs, K. D., & Heatherton, T. F. (2000). "Self-regulatory failure: A resource-depletion approach." Psychological Science, 11(3), 249–254.

Conclusion

Siegel, D. J. (2010). Mindsight: The New Science of Personal Transformation. Bantam Books. Linehan, M. M. (1993). Cognitive-Behavioral Treatment of Borderline Personality Disorder. Guilford Press.

Taleb, N. N. (2012). Antifragile: Things That Gain from Disorder. Random House.

Reflection Questions

Schön, D. A. (1983). The Reflective Practitioner: How Professionals Think in Action. Basic Books.

Argyris, C. (1991). Teaching smart people how to learn. Harvard Business Review, 69(3), 99-109.

Pennebaker, J. W. (1997). Opening Up: The Healing Power of Expressing Emotions. Guilford Press.

Overall Conclusion

Willink, J., & Babin, L. (2016). Extreme Ownership: How U.S. Navy SEALs Lead and Win. St. Martin's Press.

Aurelius, M. (c. 161–180 CE). Meditations.

Newport, C. (2016). Deep Work: Rules for Focused Success in a Distracted World. Grand Central Publishing.

Schön, D. A. (1983). The Reflective Practitioner: How Professionals Think in Action. Basic Books.

www.ingramcontent.com/pod-product-compliance
Lightning Source LLC
LaVergne TN
LVHW010625110826
845149LV00014B/2779

9781968553661